Contents at a Glance

1
2
3
4
5
6
7
8
9
10

Contents

8

9

10

Introduction

QuickSteps books are recipe books for computer users. They answer the question "How do I…" by providing a quick set of steps to accomplish the most common tasks with a particular operating system or application.

The sets of steps are the central focus of the book. QuickSteps sidebars show how to quickly perform many small functions or tasks that support the primary functions. QuickFacts sidebars supply information that you need to know about a subject. Notes, Tips, and Cautions augment the steps; they are presented in a separate column to not interrupt the flow of the steps. The introductions are minimal rather than narrative, and numerous illustrations and figures, many with callouts, support the steps.

QuickSteps books are organized by function and the tasks needed to perform that function. Each function is a chapter. Each task, or "How To," contains the steps needed for accomplishing the function along with the relevant Notes, Tips, Cautions, and screenshots. You can easily find the tasks you need through:

- The Table of Contents, which lists the functional areas (chapters) and tasks in the order they are presented
- A How To list of tasks on the opening page of each chapter
- The index, which provides an alphabetical list of the terms that are used to describe the functions and tasks
- Color-coded tabs for each chapter, or functional area, with an index to the tabs in the Contents at a Glance (just before the Table of Contents)

Conventions Used in this Book

Microsoft Office Word 2003 QuickSteps uses several conventions designed to make the book easier for you to follow:

- A in the table of contents and in the How To list in each chapter references a QuickSteps sidebar in a chapter, and a references a QuickFacts sidebar.
- **Bold type** is used for words or objects on the screen that you are to do something with—for example, "click the **Start** menu, and then click **My Computer**."
- *Italic type* is used for a word or phrase that is being defined or otherwise deserves special emphasis.
- Underlined type is used for text that you are to type from the keyboard.
- SMALL CAPITAL LETTERS are used for keys on the keyboard such as **ENTER** and **SHIFT**.
- When you are expected to enter a command, you are told to press the key(s). If you are to enter text or numbers, you are told to type them.

How to...

- Starting Word in Different Ways
  - Use the Start Menu to Start Word
  - Leave Word
  - Explore the Word Window
- Using Word Toolbars
  - Use the Mouse
- Using Menus
  - Use the Task Pane
- Using Help
  - Access Help
  - Do Research
  - Work with the Office Assistant
- Setting Preferences
  - Customize Word Toolbars
  - Customize Word Menus
  - Update Word

Chapter 1
Stepping into Word

Microsoft Word is the most widely used word processing program. Most personal computers (PCs) have some version of Word installed, and most people with PCs probably have Word available to them as well as some experience in its use. Word is both simple to use and highly sophisticated, offering many features that commonly go unused. It is a "sleeper" product: it delivers a high degree of functionality even when only a small percentage of its capabilities are used. The purpose of this book is to acquaint you with many of those additional features that can enhance your experience of using of Word.

In this chapter you will familiarize yourself with Word; see how to start and leave it; use Word's windows, panes, toolbars, and menus; learn how to get help; and find out how to customize Word.

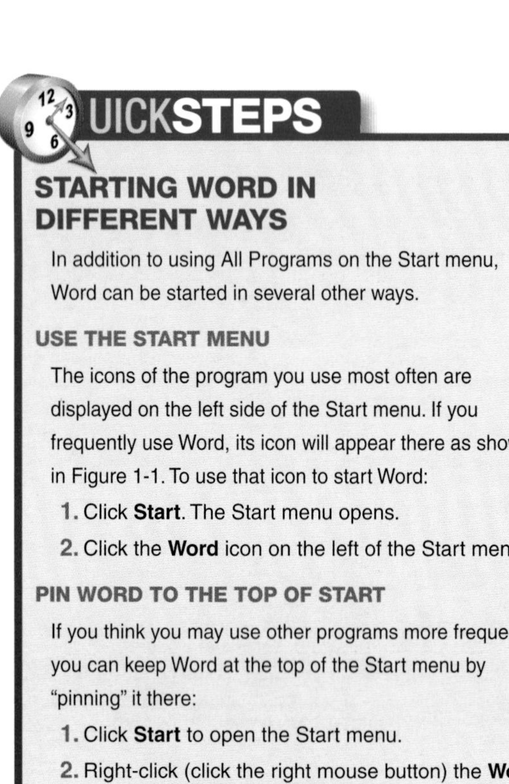

QUICKSTEPS

STARTING WORD IN DIFFERENT WAYS

In addition to using All Programs on the Start menu, Word can be started in several other ways.

USE THE START MENU

The icons of the program you use most often are displayed on the left side of the Start menu. If you frequently use Word, its icon will appear there as shown in Figure 1-1. To use that icon to start Word:

1. Click **Start**. The Start menu opens.
2. Click the **Word** icon on the left of the Start menu.

PIN WORD TO THE TOP OF START

If you think you may use other programs more frequently, you can keep Word at the top of the Start menu by "pinning" it there:

1. Click **Start** to open the Start menu.
2. Right-click (click the right mouse button) the **Word** icon and click **Pin To Start Menu**.

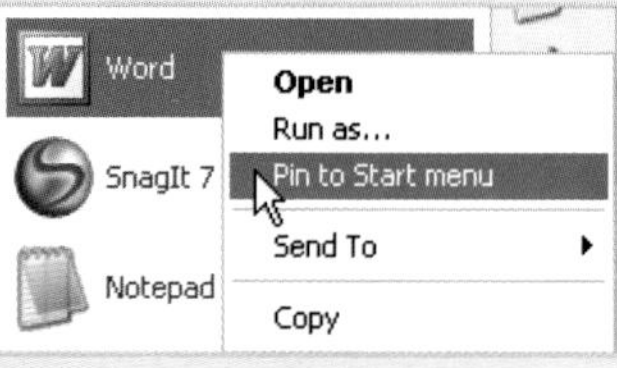

CREATE A DESKTOP SHORTCUT

An easy way to start Word is to create a shortcut icon on the desktop and use it to start the program.

1. Click **Start**, select **All Programs**, and choose **Microsoft Office**.
2. Right-click **Microsoft Office Word 2003**, choose **Send To**, and click **Desktop (Create Shortcut)**.

Continued...

Start and Leave Word

Starting Word depends on how Word was installed and what has happened to it since its installation. In this section you'll see a surefire way to start Word and some alternatives. You'll also see how to leave Word.

Figure 1-1: The foolproof way to start Word is via the Start menu.

STARTING WORD IN DIFFERENT WAYS *(Continued)*

USE THE QUICK LAUNCH TOOLBAR

The Quick Launch toolbar is a small area on the taskbar next to the Start button. You can put a Word icon on the Quick Launch toolbar and use it to start Word. If your Quick Launch toolbar is not visible, open it and put a Word icon there.

1. Right-click a blank area of the taskbar, select **Toolbars**, and click **Quick Launch**. The Quick Launch toolbar is displayed.
2. Open **Start**, select **All Programs**, choose **Microsoft Office**, and drag **Microsoft Office Word 2003** to where you want it on the Quick Launch toolbar.

Use the Start Menu to Start Word

If no other icons for or shortcuts to Word are available on your desktop, you can always start Word using the Start menu:

1. Start your computer if it is not already running, and log on to Windows if necessary.
2. Click **Start**. The Start menu opens.
3. Select **All Programs**, choose **Microsoft Office**, and click **Microsoft Office Word 2003**, as shown in Figure 1-1.

Leave Word

To leave Word when you are done using it:

- Click the **File** menu and click **Exit**.

  –Or–

- Click **Close** on the right of the title bar. 

Explore Word

Word uses a wide assortment of windows, toolbars, menus, and special features to accomplish its functions. Much of this book explores how to find and use all of those items. In this section you'll learn to use the most common features of the default Word window, including the parts of the window, the buttons on the principal toolbars, the major menus, and the task pane.

Explore the Word Window

The Word window has many features to aid you in creating and editing documents. The view presented to you when you first start Word is shown in Figure 1-2. The principal features of the Word window are introduced in Table 1-1 and will be described further in this and other chapters of this book.

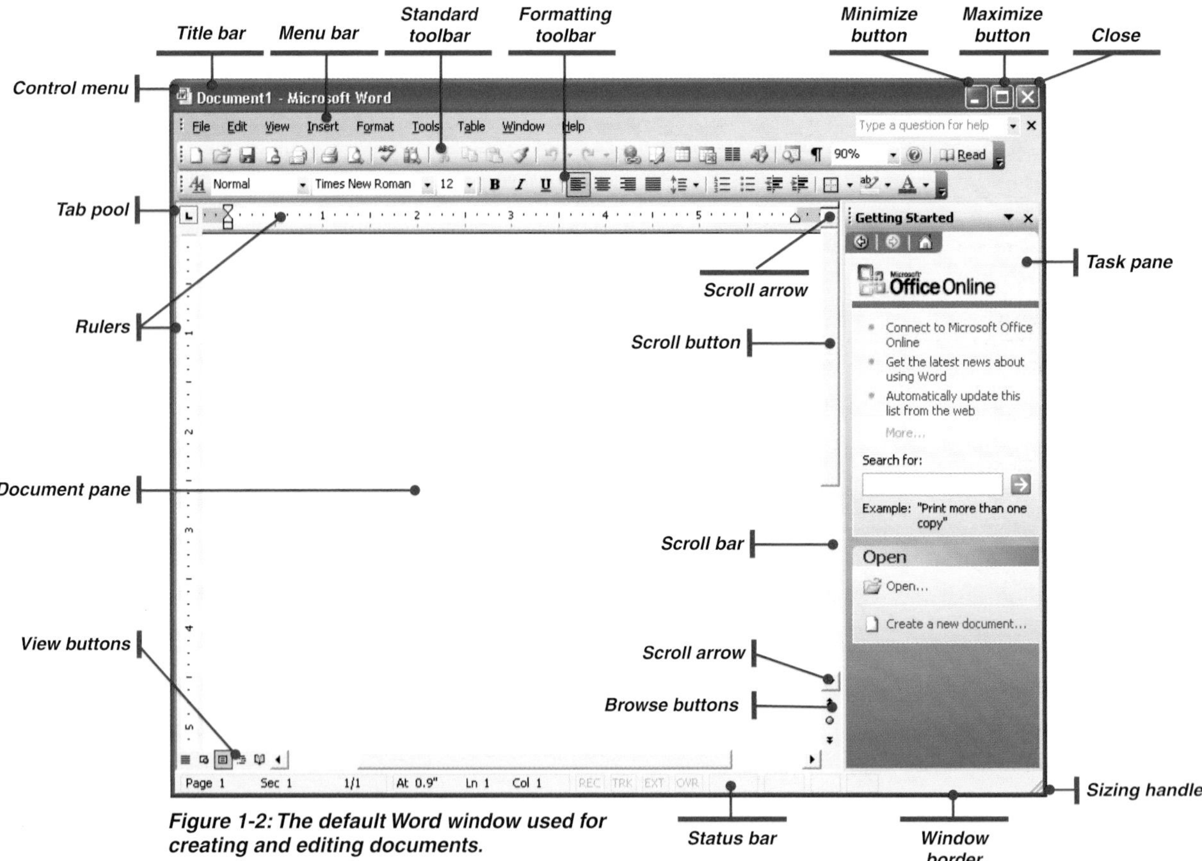

Figure 1-2: The default Word window used for creating and editing documents.

TABLE 1-1: PRINCIPAL FEATURES OF THE WORD WINDOW

WORD FEATURES	DESCRIPTION
Title bar	Contains the name of the open document and the controls for the window
Menu bar	Contains the primary controls for Word, divided into categories
Standard toolbar	Allows direct access to many of the basic functions for Word
Formatting toolbar	Allows direct access to many of the formatting features in Word
Minimize button	Minimizes the window to an icon on the taskbar
Maximize button	Maximizes the window to fill the screen
Close	Exits Word and closes the window
Task pane	Displays options for your current task, such as getting started
Scroll arrow	Moves the contents of the pane in the direction of the arrow
Scroll button	Moves the contents of the pane in the direction it is dragged
Scroll bar	Moves the contents of the pane in the direction it is clicked
Browse buttons	Enables you to specify an object to use for navigation (for example, pages, tables, or headings) and navigate quickly to the previous or next instance of that object
Sizing handle	Sizes the window in the direction it is diagonally dragged
Document pane	Displays the contents of the document being created or edited
Status bar	Displays information about the open document
Window border	Sizes the window by being dragged
View buttons	Controls the current view of the document being displayed
Rulers	Enables you to see the precise position of text and other objects in a document
Tab pool	Allows you to select the type of tab stop you want to place
Control menu	Contains the controls for resizing, moving, and closing the window itself

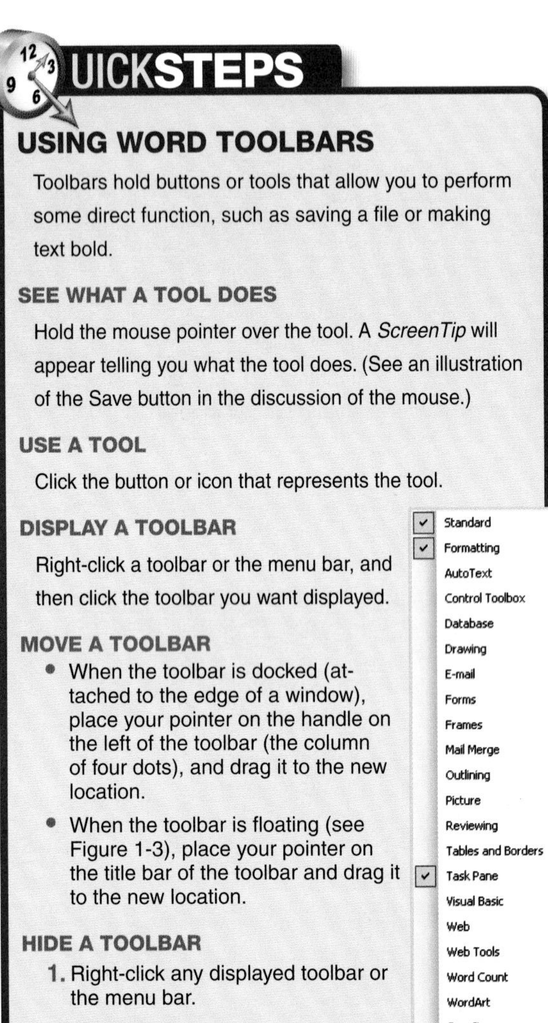

USING WORD TOOLBARS

Toolbars hold buttons or tools that allow you to perform some direct function, such as saving a file or making text bold.

SEE WHAT A TOOL DOES

Hold the mouse pointer over the tool. A *ScreenTip* will appear telling you what the tool does. (See an illustration of the Save button in the discussion of the mouse.)

USE A TOOL

Click the button or icon that represents the tool.

DISPLAY A TOOLBAR

Right-click a toolbar or the menu bar, and then click the toolbar you want displayed.

MOVE A TOOLBAR

- When the toolbar is docked (attached to the edge of a window), place your pointer on the handle on the left of the toolbar (the column of four dots), and drag it to the new location.
- When the toolbar is floating (see Figure 1-3), place your pointer on the title bar of the toolbar and drag it to the new location.

HIDE A TOOLBAR

1. Right-click any displayed toolbar or the menu bar.
2. In the context menu, click the toolbar to remove the check mark.

TIP

When you drag a toolbar next to the edge of the window, the toolbar automatically attaches itself to the window and becomes docked.

Use the Mouse

A *mouse* is any pointing device—including trackballs, pointing sticks, and graphic tablets—with two or more buttons. This book assumes you are using a two-button mouse. Moving the mouse moves the pointer on the screen. You *select* an object on the screen by moving the pointer so that it is on top of the object and then pressing the left button on the mouse.

You may control the mouse with either your left or right hand; therefore, the buttons may be switched. (See *Windows XP QuickSteps*, published by McGraw-Hill/Osborne, for how to switch the buttons.) This book assumes the right hand controls the mouse and the left mouse button is "*the* mouse button." The right button is always called the "right mouse button." If you switch the buttons, you must change your interpretation of these phrases.

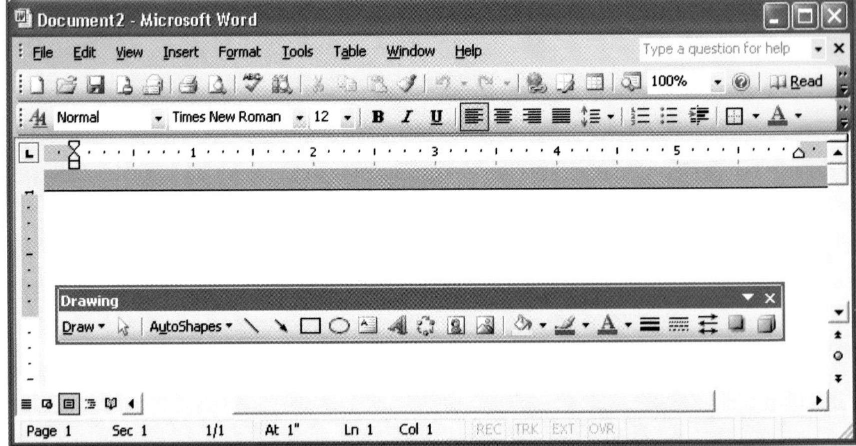

Figure 1-3: A toolbar can be attached to any edge of the Word window, or it can be floating in or out of the window.

USING MENUS

Menus are the primary means of control in Word. Many menu options are also on toolbars or some other control. When you can't find a control, look at the menus.

OPEN A MENU WITH THE MOUSE

Click the menu.

OPEN A MENU WITH THE KEYBOARD

Press **ALT+** the underlined letter in the menu name. For example, press **ALT+F** to open the File menu.

EXPAND A MENU

By default, when you open a menu, only the most common options are displayed. To see the full menu:

- Click the downward-pointing arrowheads at the bottom of the menu.

  –Or–

- Wait a few seconds, and the menu will automatically expand.

FORCE THE DISPLAY OF FULL MENUS

You can force menus to fully open every time:

1. Click the **Tools** menu and click **Customize**.
2. Click the **Options** tab and click **Always Show Full Menus**.

OPEN A SUBMENU

A number of menu options have a right-pointing arrow on their right to indicate that a submenu is associated with that option. To open the submenu:

Move the mouse pointer to the menu option with a submenu, and the submenu will open.

SELECT A MENU OPTION

To select a menu option:

Click the menu to open it, then click the option.

Five actions can be accomplished with the mouse:

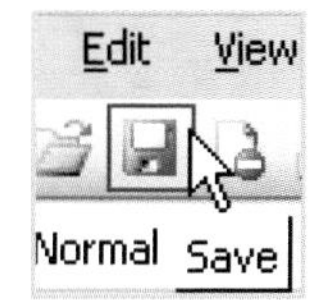

- **Point** at an *object* on the screen (a button, an icon, a menu or one of its options, or a border) to highlight it. To *point* means to move the mouse so that the tip of the pointer is on top of the object.
- **Click** an object on the screen to *select* it, making that object the item that your next actions will affect. Clicking will also open a menu, select a menu option, or activate a button or "tool" on a toolbar. *Click* means to point at an object you want to select and quickly press and release the left mouse button.
- **Double-click** an object to open or activate it. *Double-click* means to point at an object you want to select, then press and release the left mouse button twice in rapid succession.
- **Right-click** an object to open a context menu containing commands used to manipulate that object. *Right-click* means to point at an object you want to select, then quickly press and release the right mouse button. For example, right-clicking selected text opens the context menu on the right:

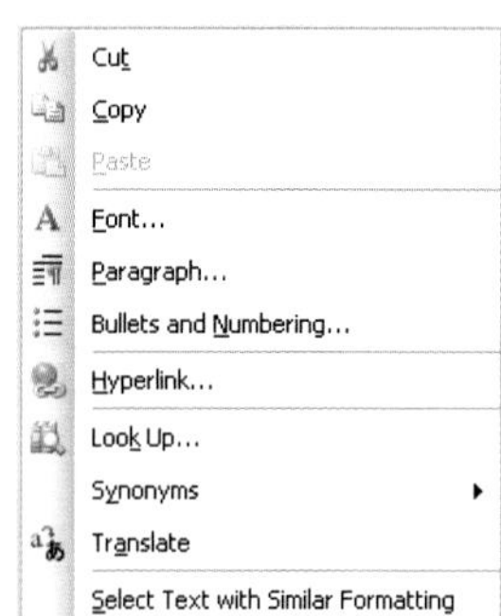

- **Drag** an object to move it on the screen to where you want it moved within the document. *Drag* means to point at an object you want to move and then press and hold the left mouse button while moving the mouse. The object is dragged as you move the mouse. When the object is where you want it, release the mouse button.

NOTE

What is displayed when you first open a menu and what is displayed on a shortened toolbar will change to reflect which menu options and which toolbar tools you use.

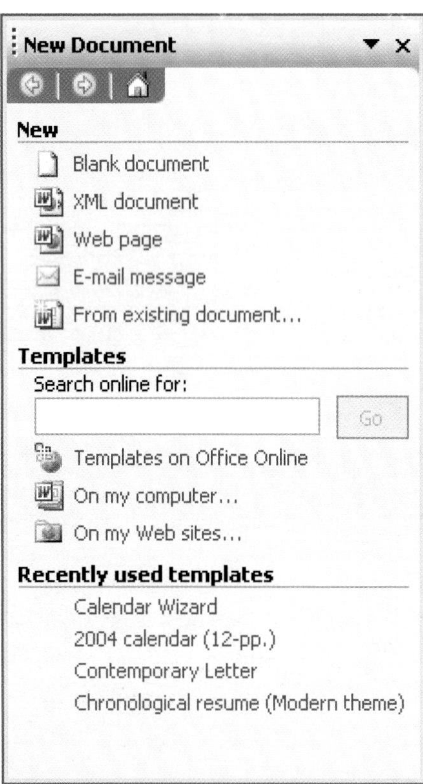

Figure 1-4: The New Document task pane allows you to create one of several types of documents using one of several templates.

Use the Task Pane

The task pane on the right of the Word window displays options for your current task. When you first start Word, the Getting Started task pane is displayed, as you saw in Figure 1-2. There are 13 other task panes, some that appear automatically as you start a task, such as New Document, shown in Figure 1-4, and others that you can make appear.

OPEN ANOTHER TASK PANE

With a task pane already open, click **Other Task Panes** (the down arrow on the current task pane title bar), and then select the name of the task pane you want.

DISPLAY THE TASK PANE

If the task pane is not currently open, you can open it by pressing **CTRL+F1** (hold down **CTRL** while pressing **F1**) or by opening the **View** menu and clicking **Task Pane**.

CLOSE THE TASK PANE

To close the task pane, click the **Close** icon on the task pane title bar, or press **CTRL+F1**. ☒

SCROLL THROUGH TASK PANES BEING USED

To move back and forth through the task panes you have been working with, click the **Back** and **Forward** arrows on the task pane toolbar.

GO TO THE GETTING STARTED TASK PANE

Click **Home** on the task pane toolbar.

MOVE A TASK PANE

Task panes appear *docked* on the right side of the Word window, but they can be moved to become *floating*. To move a task pane:

UICKSTEPS

USING HELP

PRINT A HELP TOPIC

Click the **Print** icon in the Help topic dialog box toolbar.

SHOW/HIDE THE OFFICE ASSISTANT

Click the **Help** menu, and then click **Show The Office Assistant** or **Hide The Office Assistant**, depending on whether you want to show or hide it (you may have to expand the menu).

NOTE

When you turn off the Office Assistant or the Type A Question For Help box, you are not deleting it—you are just hiding it.

NOTE

When you are working offline, only reference tools provided with Word, such as a thesaurus, are available.

Point to the stacked-dots *handle* on the left end of the task pane title bar. The pointer becomes a four-sided arrow. Do one of the following:

- To dock the task pane on one of the other edges of the window, drag the task pane to one of the four edges.

  –Or–

- To float the task pane, drag the task pane to any convenient non-edge location on the screen.

Get Help

Microsoft provides substantial assistance, tailored to whether you are working online or offline, to Word users. If you are offline, you will get quick, but more limited, help. If you are or can be online, help will be slower but more comprehensive.

Access Help

Access Help using one of these techniques:

DISPLAY THE WORD HELP TASK PANE

The Word Help task pane, shown in Figure 1-5, provides links to several assistance tools and forums, including a table of contents, access to downloads, contact information, and late-breaking news on Word. To display the Word Help task pane:

Figure 1-5: The Word Help task pane provides links to several avenues of online and offline assistance.

- Click the **Help** menu to open it, and select **Microsoft Office Word Help**.

  –Or–

- Click the **Microsoft Office Word Help** icon on the Standard toolbar.

  –Or–

- Press **F1**.

> **NOTE**
>
> The Office Assistant may not be installed in Word. If you want to use the Assistant, turn it on as described in this chapter, and confirm that you want to install it.

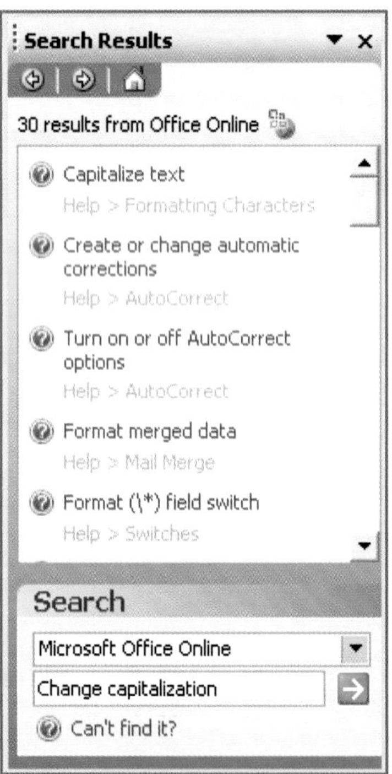

Figure 1-6: From the Search Results pane, you can search both online and offline Help as well as other sources.

ASK A QUESTION

Quickly ask a question about Word directly from the menu bar without using the Word Help task pane:

1. Type your question in the Type A Question For Help text box on the right of the menu bar.
2. Press **ENTER**. The Search Results pane will open, as you can see in Figure 1-6. Click one of the search results, and the Microsoft Office Word Help will open and display the requested information.

HIDE THE TYPE A QUESTION FOR HELP BOX

To remove the display of the Type A Question For Help box (it is available in both the Help and Search Results task panes and from the Office Assistant—see "Work with the Office Assistant," later in this chapter):

1. Click the **Tools** menu and click **Customize**. The Customize dialog box will open.
2. Right-click the **Type A Question For Help** box on the menu bar.
3. Click the check mark beside the **Show Ask A Question** box, removing the check mark.
4. Click **Close** on the Customize dialog box. When the dialog box is closed, the text box is removed from the menu bar.

Do Research

Doing research on the Internet using Word's Research command, which displays the Research task pane (see Figure 1-7), allows you to enter your search criteria and specify references.

1. Open **Help** in one of the ways described earlier in this chapter.

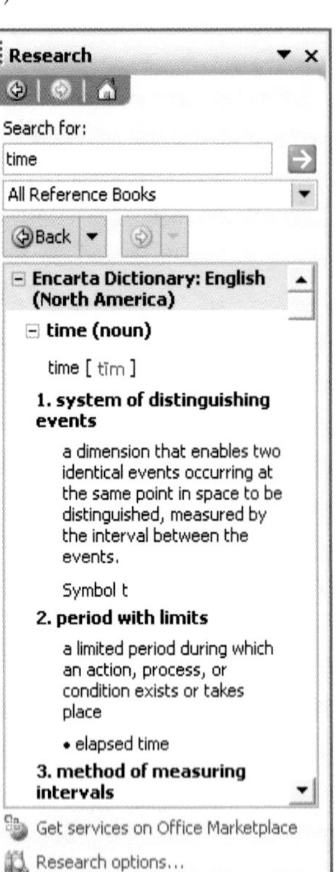

Figure 1-7: In the Research pane, you can search a dictionary, a thesaurus, an encyclopedia, and several other sources.

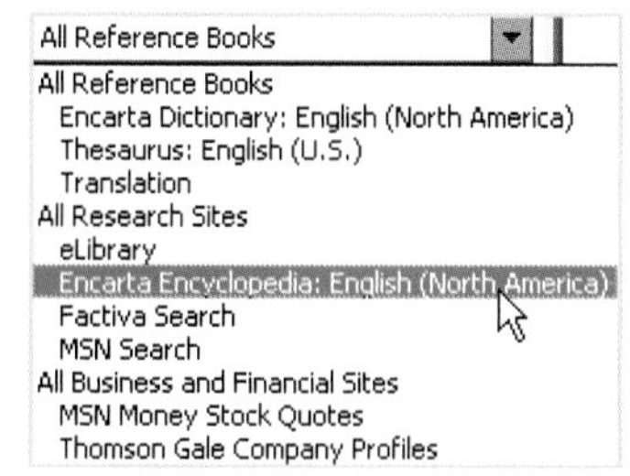

2. In the Word Help pane title bar, open the drop-down list and click **Research**. The Research pane will open.
3. Enter your search criteria in the Search For text box.
4. Beneath the text box, a reference source is selected. To change the reference source, open the list box and click a reference to be searched.
5. Click the **Go** arrow.

Work with the Office Assistant

The Office Assistant is an animated character that provides tips and messages that may be helpful, as well as providing a way to search and access Help.

TURN THE OFFICE ASSISTANT ON OR OFF

Click the **Help** menu and click **Show The Office Assistant** or **Hide The Office Assistant**.

USE THE OFFICE ASSISTANT

The Office Assistant will observe what you are doing and offer tips and alerts as you go along. In addition, you can click the **Office Assistant**, type a question, and click **Search** to search online and offline Help. The Search Results pane will automatically open with the results.

CHANGE THE OFFICE ASSISTANT

The Office Assistant has several characters you can choose to use in place of the paper clip (called "Clippit"). It also has several options that can be activated.

1. Click the **Office Assistant** and click **Options**. The Office Assistant dialog box will open.
2. Click the **Gallery** tab, and then click **Next** and **Back** to scroll through the various available characters.
3. Click the **Options** tab and select how you want to use the Office Assistant, as shown in Figure 1-8. Click **OK**.

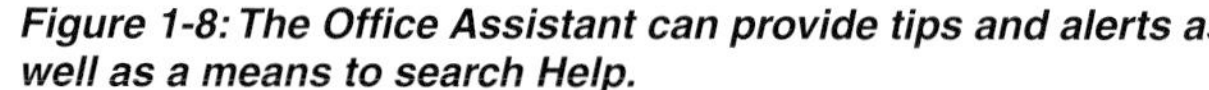

Figure 1-8: The Office Assistant can provide tips and alerts as well as a means to search Help.

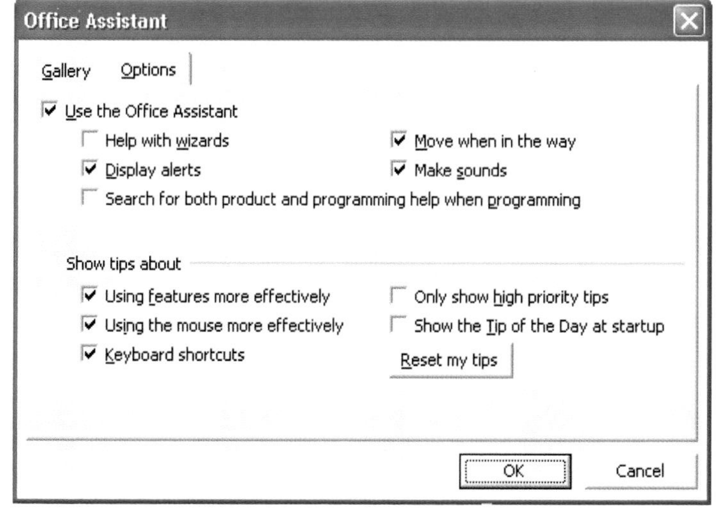

QUICKSTEPS

SETTING PREFERENCES

Setting preferences allows you to adapt Word to meet your needs. The Options dialog box provides access to these settings.

1. Click the **Tools** menu, and then click **Options** to open the Options dialog box.
2. Click the **View** tab if it is not already open, as shown in Figure 1-9.

SELECT SCREEN ELEMENTS TO SHOW

Select the parts of the screen that you want to display.

SELECT FORMATTING MARKS TO DISPLAY

Select the formatting marks you want to see—**All** is a good choice.

SET GENERAL AND OTHER OPTIONS

1. Click the **General** tab (see Figure 1-10**)**.
2. Review and select (check mark) the General Options that are correct for your situation. If you are unsure about an option, keep the default and see how well that setting works for you.
3. When you have set the General Options as you want, click each of the other tabs, review the settings and making the changes you want.
4. When you have finished selecting your preferences, click **OK** to close the Options dialog box.

NOTE

As you drag the command from the dialog box to the toolbar, you will initially drag a small rectangle containing an "X," signifying the command can't be placed where it is. The rectangle will change into a plus sign, signifying a copy, when the pointer is over the toolbars, and then into an I-beam icon over the individual icons. This I-beam icon marks the insertion point where the command icon will be inserted between the adjoining icons in the toolbar.

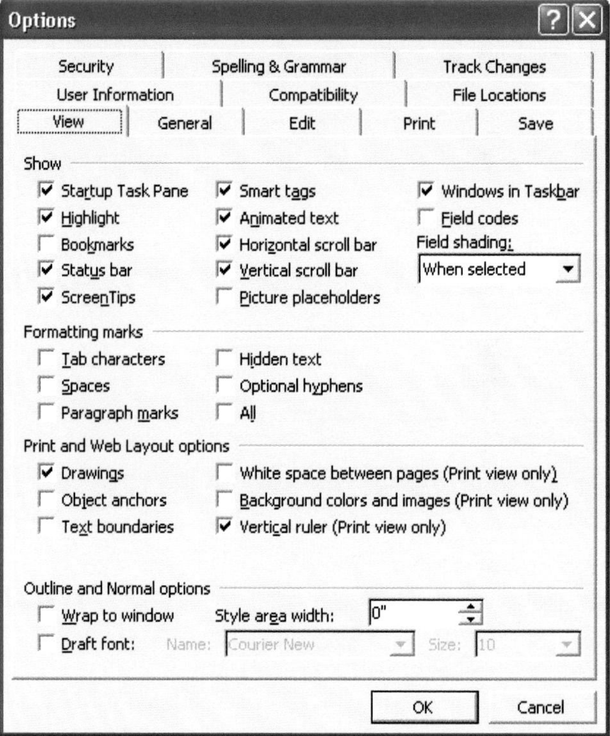

Figure 1-9: The Tools Options View tab provides a number of preference settings.

TIP

Don't worry about messing things up. To reset a toolbar, click **Customize** on the Tools menu, select the toolbar in the Toolbars tab, click **Reset**, choose the template you are using, and click **OK**. To reset a menu, also in the Customize dialog box, right-click the menu in the menu bar (not in the dialog box), and choose **Reset** from the context menu.

TIP

You can move an icon on a toolbar by pressing and holding **ALT** while dragging the icon, and you can copy an icon on a toolbar by pressing and holding **CTRL+ALT** while dragging the icon.

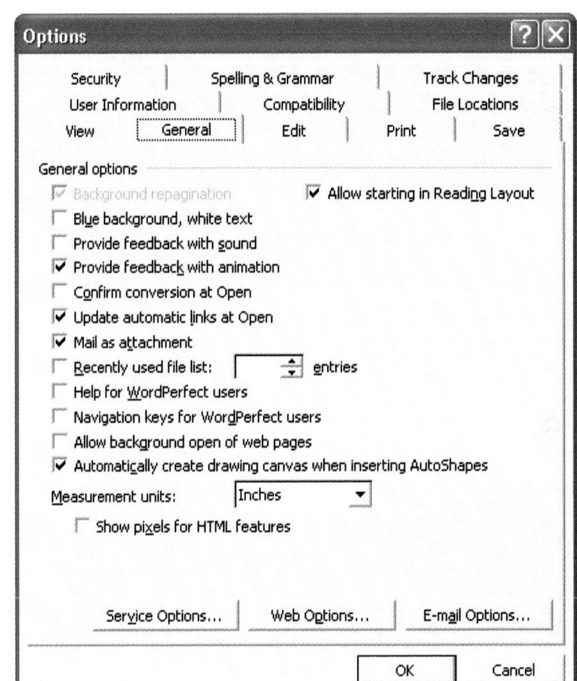

Figure 1-10: Many basic preferences used in Word are set in the General Options dialog box.

Customize Word

Word provides a number of ways to customize both how it looks and how it operates. Some of these customization options have already been discussed in this chapter, and others will be discussed in later chapters. Here you'll see how to set some of the preference options, how to customize the toolbars and menus, how to create a user profile, and how to update Word.

Customize Word Toolbars

You can customize a toolbar by adding commands or menus to an existing toolbar. You can also create a new toolbar and add commands or menus to that.

Figure 1-11: You can drag commands from a number of categories to existing and to newly created toolbars.

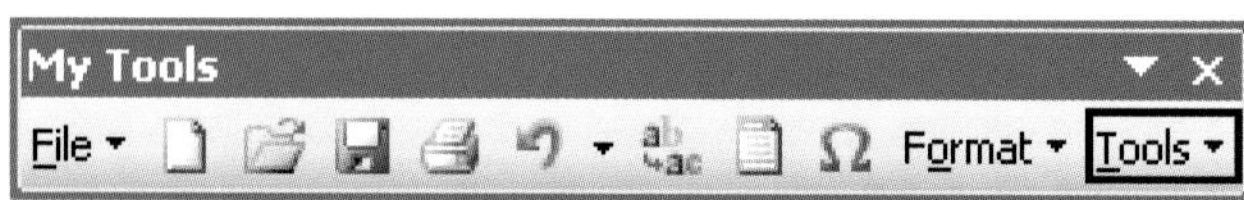

Figure 1-12: You can create a custom toolbar that is a mixture of menus and tools, possibly replacing existing menus and toolbars.

ADD COMMANDS TO A TOOLBAR

If you find some toolbar buttons are not as convenient as you would like, or if you frequently use a feature that is not on one of the toolbars, you can rearrange the buttons or add commands to a toolbar.

1. Click the **Tools** menu, click **Customize**, and click the **Commands** tab.
2. Under Categories, select the category in which the command is found.
3. Under Commands, find the command and drag it from the dialog box to where you want it on the toolbar (see Figure 1-11).
4. Click **Close** when you are finished.

CREATE A CUSTOM TOOLBAR

You can create a custom toolbar, such as the one shown in Figure 1-12, with the commands you most frequently use, avoid displaying several toolbars, and make more open space for the documents you will create.

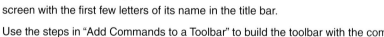

1. Click the **Tools** menu, click **Customize**, and click the **Toolbars** tab.
2. Click **New**. The New Toolbar dialog box will be displayed.
3. Enter the name of the new toolbar, keep it available to the Normal.dot template (see Chapter 4), and click **OK**. A small toolbar will appear on the screen with the first few letters of its name in the title bar.
4. Use the steps in "Add Commands to a Toolbar" to build the toolbar with the commands you want.

DRAG A MENU TO A TOOLBAR

Word provides several menus you can add to a custom or existing toolbar.

1. Click the **Tools** menu, click **Customize**, and click the **Commands** tab.
2. Select **Built-in Menus** from the Categories list.
3. Drag the menu you want to the destination toolbar. See "Add Commands to the Toolbar," earlier in this chapter, for steps on how to move commands.

DELETE A TOOLBAR

You can delete only custom toolbars that you have created:

1. Click the **Tools** menu, click **Customize**, and click the **Toolbars** tab.
2. Click the toolbar you want to delete.
3. Click **Delete**. You will be asked if you really want to delete the toolbar.
4. Click **OK** and click **Close**.

Customize Word Menus

Customizing a menu is similar to customizing a toolbar. It can be done by adding commands to an existing menu or by creating a new menu and adding commands to it.

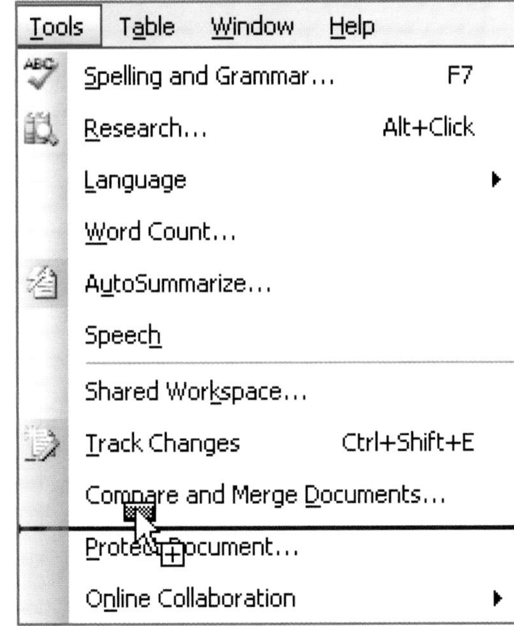

Figure 1-13: You can drag new menu options from the Customize dialog box opened from the Tools menu.

ADD COMMANDS TO A MENU

If you find the options on a menu are not as convenient as you would like, or if you frequently use a feature that is not on one of the menus, you can rearrange the options or add commands as new options on a menu:

1. Click the **Tools** menu, click **Customize**, and click the **Commands** tab.
2. Under Categories, select the category where the command is found.
3. Under Commands, find the command and drag it from the dialog box to where you want it on the menu, as shown in Figure 1-13.
4. Click **Close** when you are finished.

TIP

When typing the name of a menu, type an ampersand (&) just before the character in the name that you want to be able to use with **ALT** to open the menu.

Name
Reset
Delete
Name: &Name

NOTE

Word may prompt you to save changes to the Normal template when you exit Word. If you want to save the menu and toolbar changes you have made, you must click **Yes** to save the changes to the Normal template.

DELETE COMMANDS FROM A MENU

You can delete both existing commands and commands that you add to menus:

1. Click the **Tools** menu, click **Customize**, and click the **Commands** tab.
2. Drag the command off the menu.
3. Click **Close**.

–Or–

1. Press **CTRL+ALT+MINUS** (hyphen).
2. Click the menu with the command you wish to delete.
3. Click on the command.

CREATE A CUSTOM MENU

You can create a custom menu that holds the options you most frequently use:

1. Click the **Tools** menu, click **Customize**, and click the **Commands** tab.
2. Under Categories, click **New Menu**. Under Commands, drag **New Menu** to where you want the new menu on the menu bar.

New Menu

3. Right-click the new menu, enter the name of the new menu in the Name text box, and press **ENTER**.
4. Use the steps "Add Commands to the Menu" to build the menu with the commands you want.

DELETE A MENU

You can delete only custom menus that you have created:

1. Click the **Tools** menu, click **Customize**, and click the **Commands** tab.
2. Drag the menu off the menu bar and out of the window.
3. Click **Close**.

Update Word

Microsoft periodically releases updates for Office and Word (these are almost always problem fixes and not enhancements). You can check on available updates, download them, and install them from Word.

1. Click **Help** and click **Check For Updates**. This will open your Internet browser and connect to the Microsoft Office Online web site, as shown in Figure 1-14.

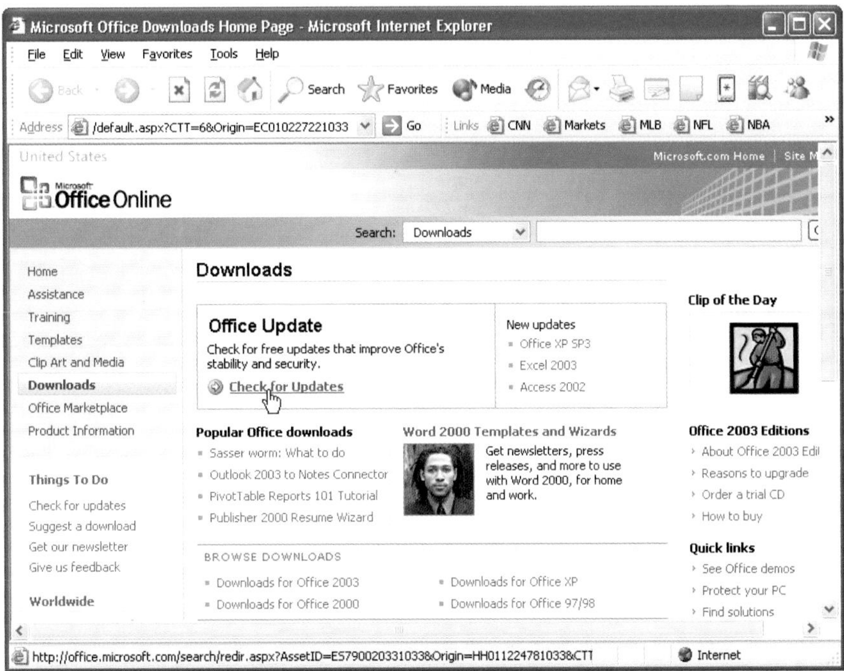

Figure 1-14: One of the primary reasons to check for and download Office and Word updates is to get needed security patches.

2. Click **Check For Updates** under the Office Update heading, and follow the instructions. Your system will be checked for any necessary updates, and you will be given the opportunity to download and install them if you choose, as you can see in Figure 1-15.
3. When you have downloaded the updates you want, close your web browser.

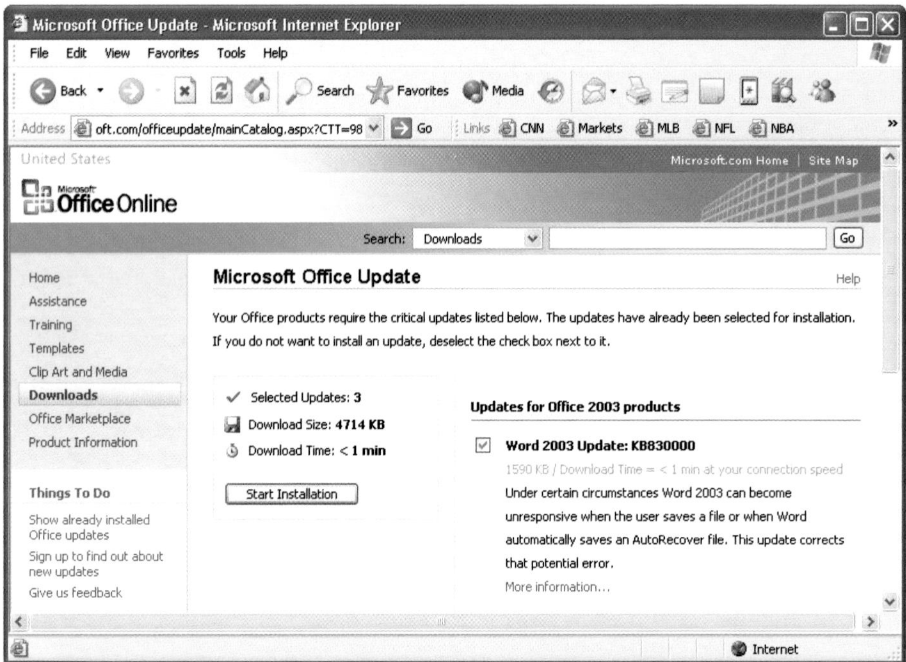

Figure 1-15: Although you have gone into the Office Update web site from Word, you will be given the opportunity to download the updates for all the Office products you have.

How to...

- *Start a New Document*
- *Use a Unique Template*
- *Use a Wizard*
- *Locate an Existing Document*
- *Search for an Existing Document*
- *Import a Document*
- *Entering Special Characters*
- *Enter Text*
- *Determine Where Text Will Appear*
- *Choose Insert or Overtype Text*
- *Start a New Line*
- *Select Text*
- *Copy and Move Text*
- *Delete Text*
- *Move around in a Document*
- *Go to a Particular Location*
- *Find and Replace Text*
- *Using Wildcards*
- *Check Spelling and Grammar*
- *Save a Document for the First Time*
- *Saving a Document*
- *Save a Document Automatically*

Chapter 2
Working with Documents

Microsoft Office Word 2003 allows you to create and edit *documents*, such as letters, reports, invoices, plays, and books. The book you are reading now was written in Word. Documents are printed on one or more pages and are probably bound by anything from a paper clip to stitch binding. In the computer, a document is a called a *file*, an object that has been given a name and is stored on a disk drive. For example, the name given to the file for this chapter is Chap02.doc. "Chap02" is the file name, and ".doc" is the file extension. Most files produced by Word use the ".doc" extension.

In this chapter you'll see how to create new documents and edit existing ones. This includes ways to enter, change, and delete text, as well as to find, select, copy, and move text.

Create a New Document

NOTE

The remainder of this chapter assumes that Word has been started and is open on your screen.

In the days before computers, creating a new document was termed "starting with a clean sheet of paper." Today, it is "starting with a blank screen"—actually, a blank area within a window on the screen, as shown in Figure 2-1. You can create a new document in three ways: using the default or "normal" document, using a unique template on which to base the document, and using a wizard to help create the document.

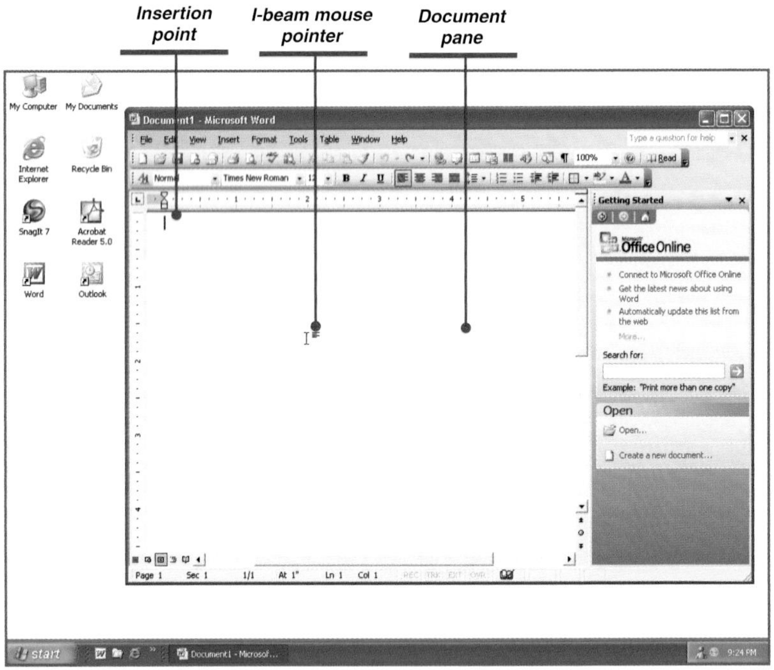

Figure 2-1: When you first start Word, the blank document pane is ready for you to create a document immediately.

Start a New Document

Starting Word opens up a blank document pane into which you can start typing a new document immediately. The blinking bar in the upper-left of the document pane, called the *insertion point*, indicates where the text you type will appear.

To start Word, use one of the ways described at the beginning of Chapter 1.

Use a Unique Template

A template is a special kind of document that is used as the basis for other documents you create. The template is said to be "attached" to the document, and every Word document must have a template attached to it. The template acts as the framework around which you create your document. The document that is opened automatically when you start Word uses a default template called Normal.dot (referred to as "the Normal template") that contains standard formatting settings. Other templates can contain boilerplate text, formatting for the types of document they create, and even automated procedures. Word is installed on your computer with a number of templates that you can use, and you can access other templates through Office Online.

TIP

Just as Word documents normally use a .doc extension, Word templates normally use a .dot extension.

NOTE

You can also create and use your own templates, as described in Chapter 4 under "Creating and Modifying Templates."

USE A TEMPLATE ON YOUR COMPUTER

With Word open on your computer:

1. Click the **File** menu, and then click **New**. The New Document task pane will open, as shown in Figure 2-2.
2. In the Templates section, click **On My Computer**. The Templates dialog box will open.
3. Click the **Letters & Faxes** tab, and then click the **Contemporary Letter** template, as you can see in Figure 2-3.
4. Click **OK** to open a new document based on the Contemporary Letter template. Follow the instructions in the template to complete the letter.

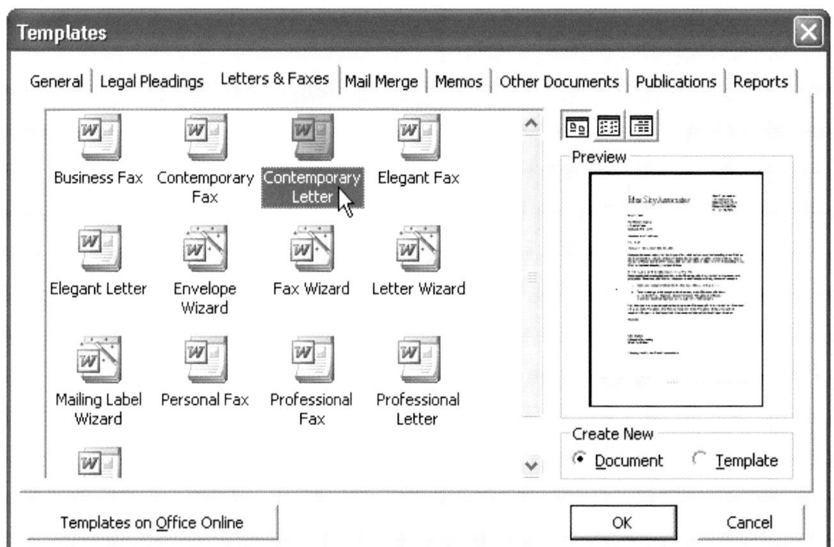

Figure 2-3: Word automatically installs a number of templates on your computer.

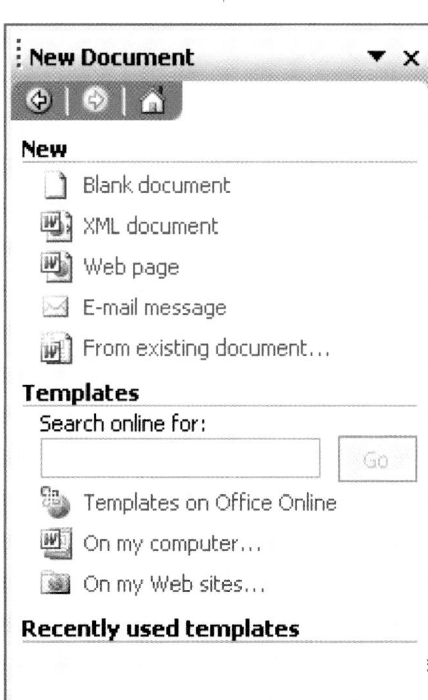

Figure 2-2: The New Document task pane gives you choices for how to start a document.

Figure 2-4: Microsoft offers many templates online for Word and its other products.

USE AN OFFICE ONLINE TEMPLATE

With Word open on your computer:

1. Click the **File** menu, and then click **New**. The New Document task pane will open.
2. In the Templates section of the task pane, click **Templates On Office Online**. The Internet Explorer will start and open the Office Online template.
3. Click on a link and follow it by clicking successive links until you see Download Now. Click that and a new document is opened with the template in Word, as shown in Figure 2-4.

Use a Wizard

A *wizard* is a template that includes an automated setup procedure to help you make required choices and enter necessary information. Wizards are stored with the templates. To use the Calendar Wizard:

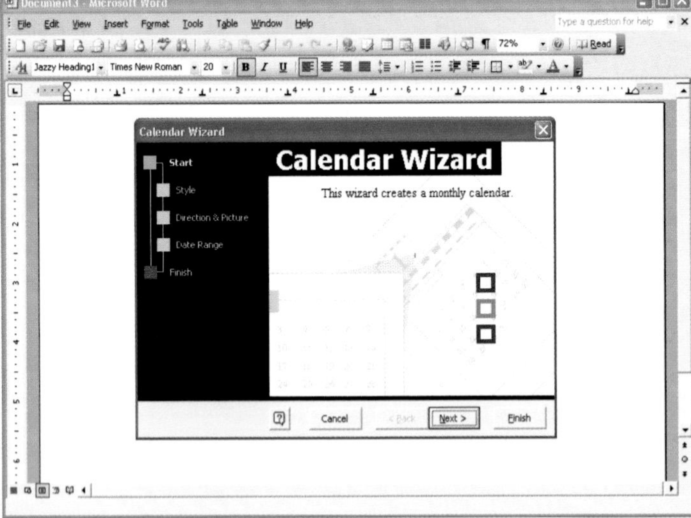

Figure 2-5: Wizards ask you questions in order to customize a template to fit your needs.

1. Click the **File** menu, and then click **New**. In the Templates section, click **On My Computer**.
2. In the Templates dialog, click the **Other Documents** tab, and then double-click the **Calendar Wizard**. If you are using this template for the first time, it will first be installed. Then, a new window and document will open, and the Calendar Wizard dialog box will appear within it, as you can see in Figure 2-5.
3. Click **Next** to start the wizard. Select the style you want to use, and click **Next** again. Continue to answer the questions as they are presented, clicking **Next** as needed.

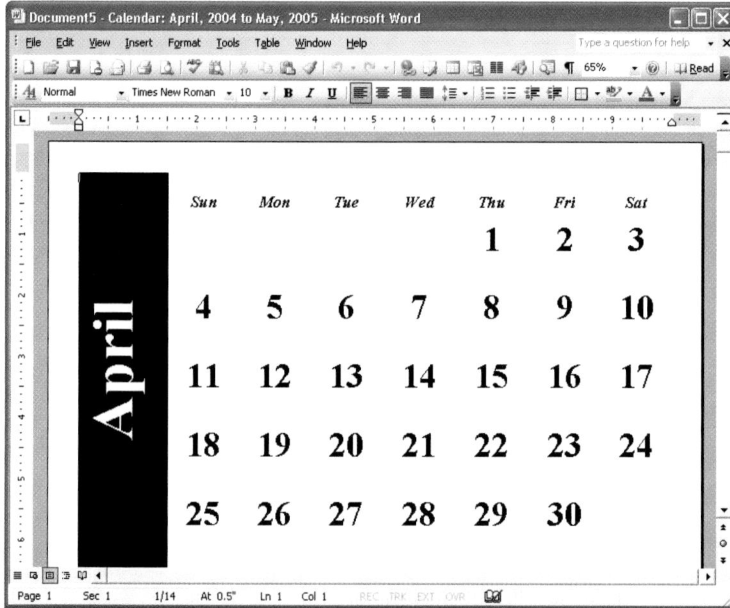

Figure 2-6: Wizards can do a lot of custom formatting for you, saving you both time and the necessity for learning how to do it.

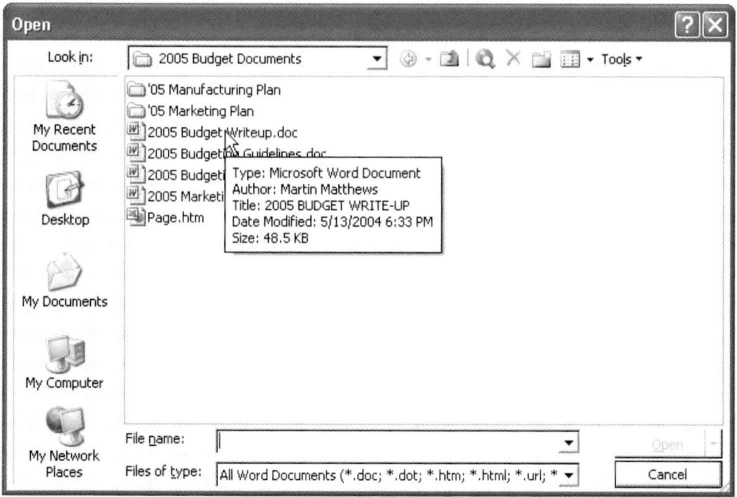

Figure 2-7: When you hold the mouse pointer over a document name, you get additional information about the document.

4. When you have answered all the wizard's questions, click **Finish**. You can see what my answers to the wizard's questions produced in Figure 2-6.

Open an Existing Document

After creating and saving a document, you may want to come back and work on it later. You may also want to open and work on a Word or other document created by someone else. To do this, you must first locate the document and then open it in Word. You can locate the document either directly from Word or search for it in either Word or My Computer.

Locate an Existing Document

With Word open on your screen:

1. Click the **File** menu, and click **Open**. The Open dialog box will appear.
2. Double-click the folder or sequence of folders you need to open in order to find the document.
3. When you have found the document you want to open (see Figure 2-7), double-click it. It will appear in Word, ready for you to begin your work.

Search for an Existing Document

If you have a hard time finding a document using the direct approach described immediately above, you can search for it either in Word or in My Computer.

> **TIP**
>
> Accessing File Search from the File Open dialog box is handy when you are trying to open a file and realize you don't know where the file is.

SEARCH FOR A DOCUMENT IN WORD

A document search performed in Word looks for a piece of text that is contained in the document or some property of the document such as the name of the author, the creation date, or the name of the file. The Basic search is for text in the document.

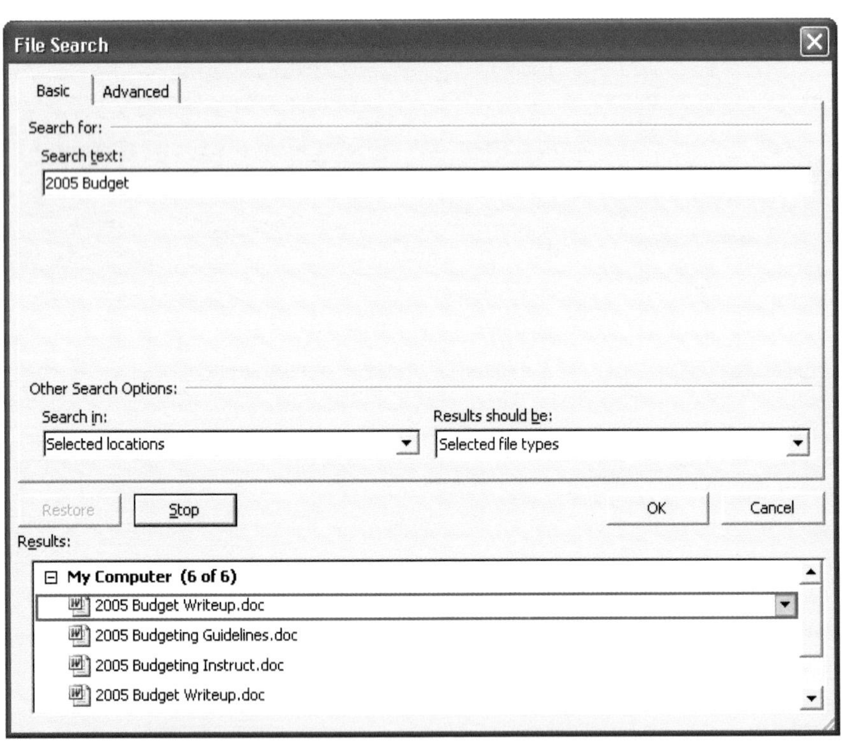

Figure 2-8: Searching for text within a document is relatively slow because of the need to go through the contents of all the documents in the locations being searched.

1. Click the **File** menu and click **Open**. Click **Tools** on the right of the toolbar, and then click **Search**. The File Search dialog box will open with the Basic tab available.

   –Or–

   Click the **File** menu and click **File Search**. The File Search task pane will open. The task pane has the same fields at the File Search dialog box.
2. Enter the text you want to search for (see Figure 2-8), select the locations to search (probably My Computer) and the types of files to search (probably just Word files).
3. Click **Go**. This search is relatively slow and can take several minutes. The Results list will contain the files that meet your search criteria, as you can see in Figure 2-8.
4. Double-click the file you want and then click **Open** to open it in Word.

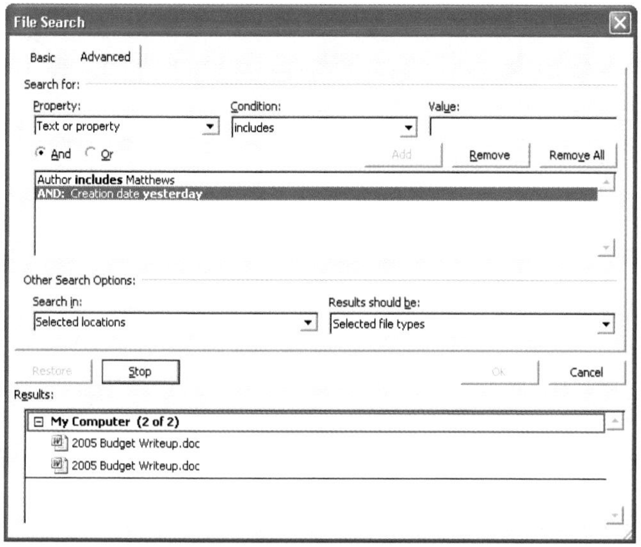

Figure 2-9: *If you get a lot of files when you do a Basic search, use the Advanced search to narrow down the results.*

The Advanced search is for one or more properties of the document. With the File Search dialog box open (see the preceding set of steps):

1. Select a property on which to search (such as the Author), a condition to apply to that property (such as Includes), and a value that condition has to satisfy (for example, the last name of the author). Click **Add**.
2. If you want to search on an additional property, determine if both properties must be met, and, if so, click **And**. If the presence of either property is adequate, click **Or**.
3. Select the property, condition, and value of the second property, and then click **Add**.
4. Repeat Steps 2 and 3 until you have added all the properties on which you want to search.
5. Select the locations to search and the type of files you want, and then click **Go**. Depending on the properties you are using, this search may go faster and, if done properly, should get fewer results (see Figure 2-9).
6. Double-click the file you want, and then click **Open** to open it in Word.

Figure 2-10: My Computer allows you to search for a document and, once it is found, use it to start Word.

SEARCH FOR A DOCUMENT IN MY COMPUTER

My Computer allows you to search for any kind of file, including Word documents. With Windows running on your computer:

1. Click **Start** to open the Start menu, and then click **My Computer** to open it.
2. Click **Search** in the toolbar to open the Search companion, and then click **Documents**.
3. Select the time period in which the document was last modified, enter part or all of the document's file name, and click **Search**. The search will take place and display the files it finds in the right pane, as shown in Figure 2-10.
4. Double-click the file or document to start Word (if it is not already open) and open the document within it.

Import a Document

If you have a word processing document created in a program other than Word, you can most likely open it and edit it in Word.

1. Click the **File** menu, and click **Open**. The Open dialog box will appear.
2. Double-click the folder or sequence of folders you need to open in order to find the document.
3. Click the **down arrow** on the right of the File Of Type drop-down list box to display the list of files that you can directly open in Word, as shown next (see Table 2-1 for a complete list).

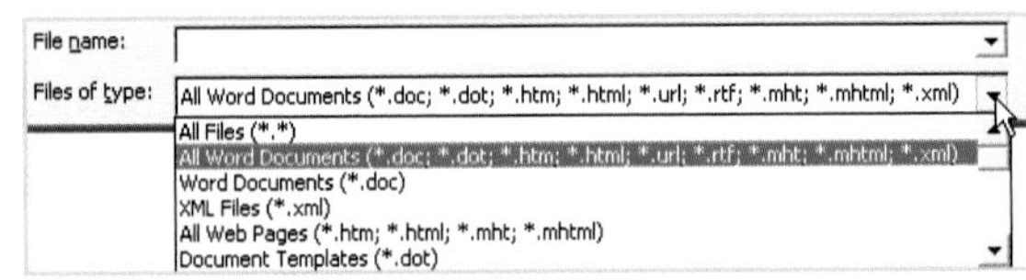

4. Click the file type you want to open. The Open dialog box will list only files of that type.
5. Double-click the file that you want to open. Depending on the file, you may get one of several messages. A common message indicates that the file need a converter and asks if you want to install it. Click **Yes**.

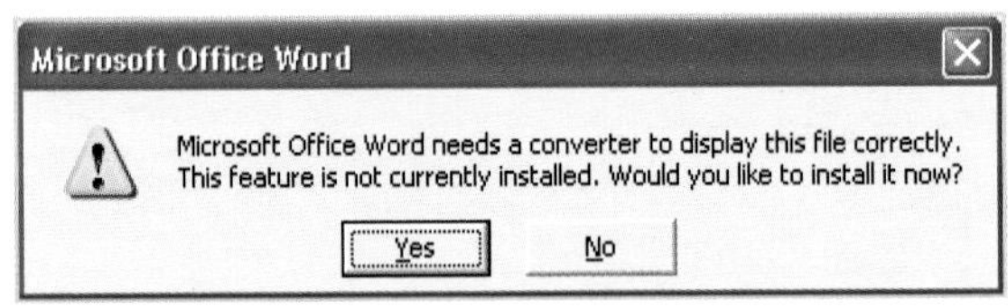

TABLE 2-1: FILE TYPES THAT WORD CAN OPEN DIRECTLY

FILE TYPE	EXTENSION
InkWriter/Note Taker files	.pwi
InkWriter/Note Taker templates	.pdt
Outlook address book files	.olk
Personal address book files	.pab
Plain text files	.txt
Pocket Word document files	.psw, .pwd
Pocket Word template files	.pwt
Rich Text Format file	.rtf
Schedule+ Contacts files	.scd
Web page files	.htm, .html, .mht, .mhtml
Windows Write files	.wri
Word 6.0/95 for Windows and Mac files	.doc
Word 97 files	.doc
Word document files	.doc
Word document template files	.dot
WordPerfect 5.x and 6.x files	.doc, .wpd
Works 6.0 and 7.0 files	.wps
XML files	.xml

QUICKSTEPS

ENTERING SPECIAL CHARACTERS

Entering a character that is on the keyboard takes only a keystroke, but many other characters and symbols exist beyond those that appear on the keyboard. For example: ©, £, Ã, ≤, ¶, and •. You can enter these characters using either the Symbol dialog box or a sequence of keys.

SELECT SPECIAL CHARACTERS FROM THE SYMBOL DIALOG BOX

1. Move the insertion point to where you want to insert the special character(s).
2. Click **Insert** in the menu bar, and then click **Symbol**. The Symbol dialog box will open.
3. Scroll through the characters until you find the one you want, and then double-click that character, as shown in Figure 2-11.
4. Click **Close**. You should see the special character or symbol where the insertion point was.

ENTER SPECIAL CHARACTERS FROM THE KEYBOARD

If you look at the bottom-middle of Figure 2-11, you'll see a shortcut key of ALT+0149 can be used to enter a bullet character. This numeric shortcut key must be entered on the numeric keypad.

1. Move the insertion point to where you want to insert the special characters.
2. Press **NUM LOCK** to put the numeric keypad into numeric mode.
3. Press and hold **ALT** while pressing all four digits (including the leading zero) on the numeric keypad.
4. Release **ALT**. The special character will appear where the insertion point was.

The shortcut keys for some of the more common special characters are shown in Table 2-2.

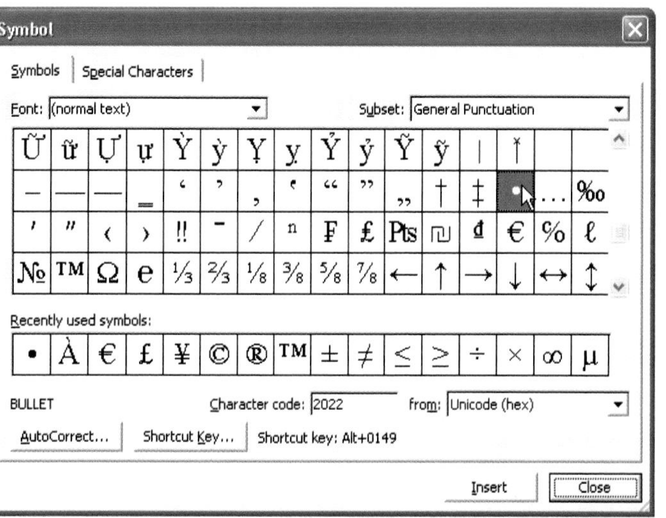

Figure 2-11: The Symbol dialog box contains several complete alphabets as well as many special characters and symbols.

TABLE 2-2: SHORTCUT KEYS FOR COMMON CHARACTERS

CHARACTER	NAME	SHORTCUT KEYS
•	Bullet	ALT+0149
©	Copyright	ALT+CTRL+C
™	Trade Mark	ALT+CTRL+T
®	Registered	ALT+CTRL+R
¢	Cent	CTRL+/ , C
£	Pound	ALT+0163
€	Euro	ALT+CTRL+E
–	En dash	CTRL+NUM-
—	Em dash	ALT+CTRL+NUM-

NOTE

In Table 2-2, the "," means to release the previous keys and then press the following key(s). For example, for a ¢, press and hold **CTRL** while pressing **/**, then release **CTRL** and press **C**. In addition, "NUM" means to press the following key on the numeric keypad. So, "NUM-" means to press "-" in the top-right of the numeric keypad.

1 2 3 4 5 6 7 8 9 10

Write a Document

Whether you create a new document or open an existing one, you will likely want to enter and edit text. Editing, in this case, includes adding and deleting text as well as selecting, moving, and copying it.

Enter Text

To enter text in a document that you have newly created or opened, simply start typing. The characters you type will appear in the document pane at the insertion point and in the order that you type them.

Determine Where Text Will Appear

The *insertion point*, the blinking vertical bar shown earlier in Figure 2-1, determines where text that you type will appear. In a new document, the insertion point is obviously in the upper-leftmost corner of the document pane. It is also placed there by default when you open an existing document. You can move the insertion within or to the end of existing text using either the keyboard or the mouse.

MOVE THE INSERTION POINT WITH THE KEYBOARD

When Word is open and active, the insertion point moves every time you press a character or directional key on the keyboard (unless a menu or dialog box is open or the task pane is active). The directional keys include TAB, BACKSPACE, and ENTER as well as the four arrow keys, and HOME, END, PAGE UP, and PAGE DOWN.

MOVE THE INSERTION POINT WITH THE MOUSE

When the mouse pointer is in the document pane, it appears as an I-beam, as you saw in Figure 2-1. The reason for the I-beam is that it fits between characters on the screen. You can move the insertion point by moving the I-beam mouse pointer to where you want the insertion point and clicking.

NOTE

The Special Characters tab of the Symbol dialog box contains the most widely used special characters as well as their shortcut keys.

TIP

You can insert multiple special characters in sequence by selecting one after the other in the Symbol dialog box.

TIP

The AutoCorrect as you type feature, which is discussed in Chapter 4, also provides a quick way of entering commonly used special characters such as Copyright, Trademark, Registered, and en and em dashes.

Choose Insert or Overtype Text

When you press a letter or a number key with Word in its default mode (as it is when you first start it), the insertion point and any existing text to the right of the insertion point is pushed to the right and down on a page. This is also true when you press the TAB or ENTER keys. This is called *insert* mode: new text pushes existing text to the right.

If you press the INSERT (or INS) key, Word is switched to *overtype* mode, and the OVR indicator is enabled in the status bar.

OVR

In overtype mode, any character key you press types over (replaces) the existing character to the right of the insertion point. Overtype mode does not affect the TAB and ENTER keys, which continue to push existing characters to the right of the insertion point to the right and down.

NOTE

In both insert and overtype modes, the directional keys move the insertion point without regard to which mode is enabled.

Start a New Line

If you are used to typing on a typewriter, you have learned to press Return at the end of each line to go to the next line. In Word, as in all word processing programs, you simply keep typing and the text will automatically wrap around to the next line. Only when you want to break a line before it would otherwise end must you manually intervene. There are four instances where manual line breaks are required:

- At the **end of a paragraph**—to start a new paragraph, press **ENTER**.
- At the **end of a short line** within a paragraph—to start a new line, press **SHIFT+ENTER**.
- At the **end of a page**—to force the start of a new page, press **CTRL+ENTER**.
- At the **end of a section**—to start a new section, press **CTRL+SHIFT+ENTER**.

You can also enter breaks using the mouse:

1. With the insertion point where you want the break, click the **Insert** menu and click **Break**. The Break dialog box will open.
2. Select the type of break you want to insert, and click **OK**.

NOTE

Section breaks are used to define columns within a page and to define different types of pages, as you might have with differently formatted left and right pages. The use of section breaks, columns, and different types of pages are described in Chapter 4.

Select Text

In order to copy, move, or delete text, you first need to select it. *Selecting text* means to identify it as a separate block from the remaining text in a document. You can select any amount of text, from a single character up to an entire document. As text is selected, it is highlighted, changed to white characters on a black background, as you can see in Figure 2-12. You can select text with both the mouse and the keyboard.

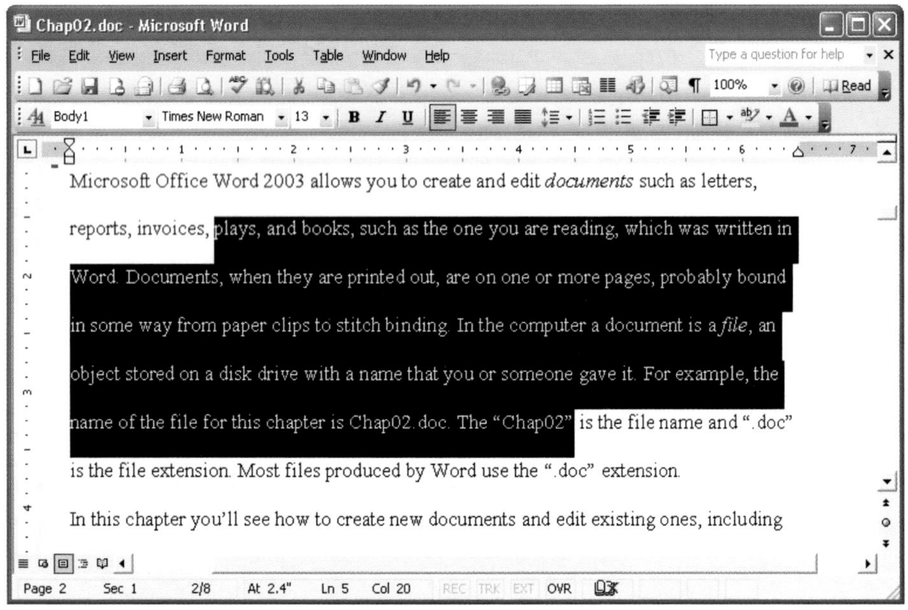

Figure 2-12: You will always know what you moving, copying, or deleting because it is highlighted on the screen.

SELECT TEXT WITH THE MOUSE

You can select varying amounts of text with the mouse.

- **Select a single word** by double-clicking that word.
- **Select a single line** by clicking on the far left of the line when the I-beam mouse pointer becomes an arrow (this area on the left is call the *selection bar*).
- **Select a single sentence** by pressing and holding **CTRL** while clicking in the sentence.
- **Select a single paragraph** by double-clicking in the selection bar opposite the paragraph.
- **Select an entire document** by pressing and holding **CTRL** while clicking in the selection bar anywhere in the document.
- **Select one or more characters** in a word, or select two or more words by clicking:
  1. Click to place the insertion point to the left of the first character.
  2. Press and hold **SHIFT** while clicking to the right of the last character.
  3. Release **SHIFT** and the selected text will be highlighted.

- **Select one or more characters** in a word or to select two or more words by dragging:
  1. Move the mouse pointer to the left of the first character.
  2. Press and hold the mouse button while dragging the mouse pointer to the right of the last character.
  3. Release the mouse button and the selected text will be highlighted.

NOTE

You can select the entire document from the keyboard by pressing **CTRL+A**.

SELECT TEXT WITH THE KEYBOARD

1. Use the arrow keys to move the insertion point the left of the first character you want to select.
2. Press and hold **SHIFT** while again using the arrow keys to move the insertion point to the right of the last character you want to select.
3. Release **SHIFT** and the selected text will be highlighted.

TIP

After selecting one area using the keyboard, the mouse, or the two together, you can select further independent areas by pressing and holding **CTRL** while using any of the mouse selection techniques.

Copy and Move Text

Copying and moving text are very similar. Think of copying text as moving it and leaving a copy behind. Both copying and moving are done in two steps:

1. Selected text is copied or cut from its current location to the Clipboard.
2. The contents of the Clipboard are pasted to a new location identified by the insertion point.

USE THE CLIPBOARD

The *Clipboard* is a location in the computer's memory that is used to store information temporarily. There are actually two clipboards that can be used:

- The **Windows Clipboard** can store one object, either text or a picture, and pass that object within or among Windows programs. Once an object is cut or copied to the Windows Clipboard, it stays there until another object is cut or copied to the Clipboard or until the computer is turned off. The Windows Clipboard is used by default.
- The **Office Clipboard** can store up to 24 objects, both text and pictures, and pass those objects within or among Office programs. Once the Office Clipboard is enabled, all objects that are cut or copied are kept on the Office Clipboard until the 25th object is cut or copied, which will replace the first object. All objects on the Office Clipboard are lost from the Clipboard when the computer is turned off.

CUT TEXT

When you *cut text*, you place it on the Clipboard and delete it from its current location. When the Clipboard contents are pasted to the new location, the text has been *moved* and no longer exists in its original location. To cut and place text on the Clipboard, select it and then:

- Press **CTRL+X**.

  –Or–

- Click the **Edit** menu, and then click **Cut**.

  –Or–

- Click **Cut** in the Standard toolbar. 

COPY TEXT

When you *copy* text to the Clipboard, you also leave it in its original location. Once the Clipboard contents are pasted to the new location, you have the same text in two places in the document. To copy text to the Clipboard, select it and then:

- Press **CTRL+C**.

  –Or–

- Click the **Edit** menu, and then click **Copy**.

  –Or–

- Click **Copy** in the Standard toolbar. 

PASTE TEXT

To complete a copy or a move you must *paste* the text from the Clipboard onto either the same or another document where the insertion point is located. A copy of the text stays on the Clipboard and can be pasted again. To paste the contents of the Clipboard:

- Press **CTRL+V**.

  –Or–

- Click the **Edit** menu, and then click **Paste**.

  –Or–

- Click **Paste** in the Standard toolbar. 

USE THE PASTE OPTIONS SMART TAG

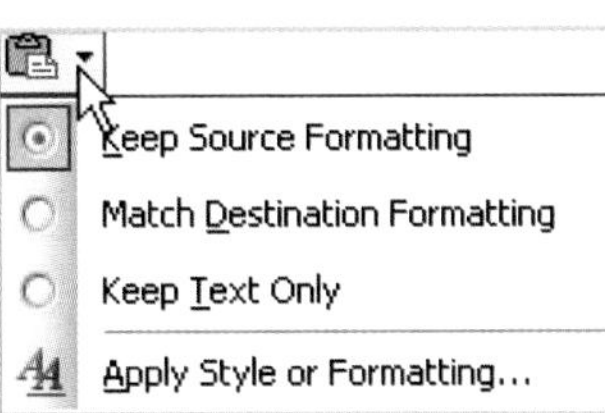

The Paste Options smart tag appears when you paste text. It asks you if you want to Keep Source Formatting (the original formatting of the text), Match Destination Formatting (change the formatting to that of the surrounding text), or Keep Text Only (remove all formatting from the text). The Paste Options smart tag is most valuable when you can see the paste operation has resulted in formatting you don't want.

CUT AND COPY TO THE OFFICE CLIPBOARD

If you cut, copy, and paste with Word in its default start-up configuration, you will be utilizing the Windows Clipboard. To use the Office Clipboard, you must first enable it. Then, all cutting, copying, and pasting, as described earlier, is done using the Office Clipboard. To enable the Office Clipboard, select the text you want to cut or copy, and then:

- Press **CTRL+C** twice.

  –Or–

- Click the **Edit** menu, and then click **Office Clipboard**.

  –Or–

- Click **Copy** twice in the Standard toolbar.

When the Office Clipboard is enabled, the default calls for the Clipboard task pane to open and display its contents (see Figure 2-13). As long as the Office Clipboard remains open, you can then continue to cut and copy normally and the next 23 items will go on the Clipboard. There is also a way to copy, cut, and paste with the Office Clipboard when it is closed. See "Control the Office Clipboard" later in this chapter.

NOTE

Only pressing or clicking the **Copy** commands twice opens the Office Clipboard. Pressing or clicking the **Cut** commands twice doesn't do it. Once the Office Clipboard is open, using **Cut** will put the selected text or object on it.

PASTE FROM THE OFFICE CLIPBOARD

With the Office Clipboard enabled, pressing CTRL+V or either of the other paste command variants will paste the last item you cut or copied (as with the Windows Clipboard). If you want to paste one of the other entries on the Office Clipboard, you need to select it first, and then use any of the regular

NOTE

To close the Office Clipboard and revert to the Windows Clipboard, click **Close** at the top of the task pane. The items you placed on the Office Clipboard while it was open will stay there until you shut down Word, but only the last item you cut or copied after closing the Office Clipboard down will be displayed.

paste commands. Office also gives you several unique ways to paste from its clipboard (assuming that you have already placed the insertion point where you want the results to go):

- Click the entry in the Office Clipboard.

  –Or–

- Click the down arrow on the right of the entry, and click **Paste**.

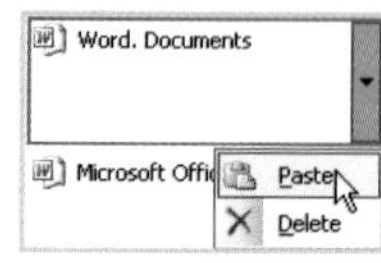

  –Or–

- Click **Paste All** above the list of items in the Office Clipboard to paste all of the Clipboard's contents at the insertion point.

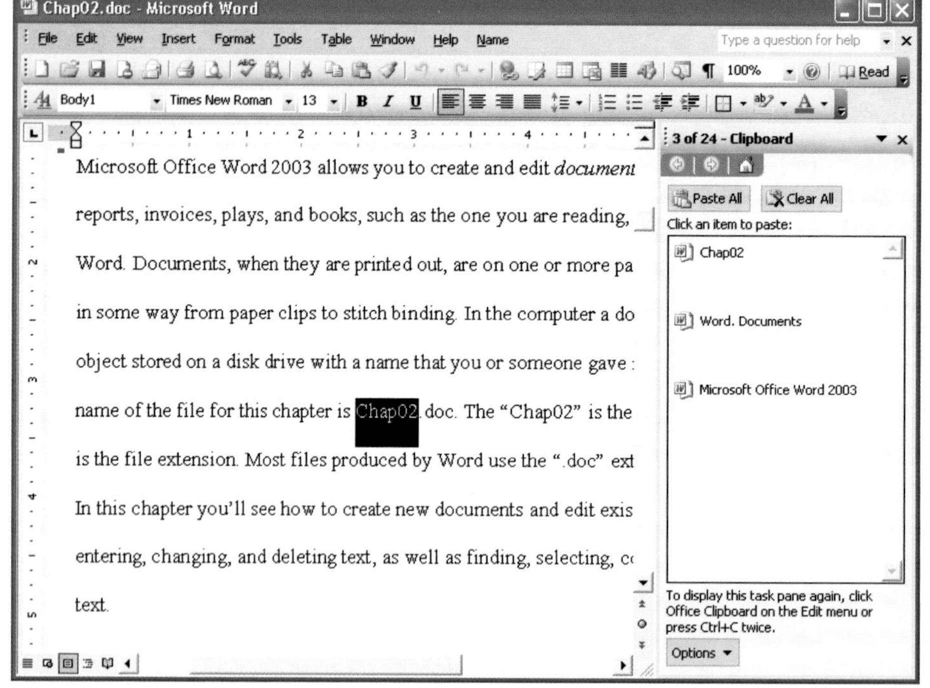

Figure 2-13: The Office Clipboard lets you keep several things on the Clipboard that you want to paste.

CONTROL THE OFFICE CLIPBOARD

The Office Clipboard provides several means to control its function and contents:

- **Clear All** (at the top, next to Paste All)—to delete everything from the Office Clipboard
- **Delete** (in the context menu opened from the right of each item, beside Paste)—to remove just that item from the Office Clipboard
- **Options** button (at the bottom)—to open the Options menu:

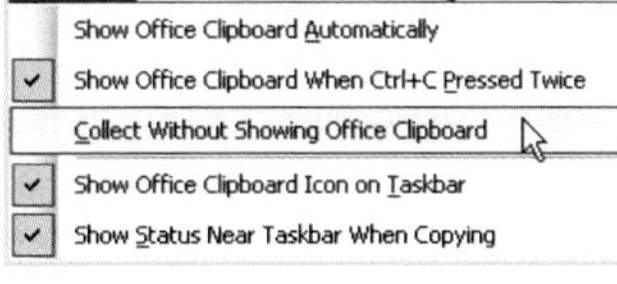

  - **Show Office Clipboard Automatically** turns on Office Clipboard when you start Word (or other Office programs) and appears the second time you cut or copy an item.
  - **Show Office Clipboard When CTRL+C Pressed Twice** is the default mode for turning on the Office Clipboard.
  - **Collect Without Showing Office Clipboard** turns on Office Clipboard when you start an Office program but doesn't automatically display it.
  - **Show Office Clipboard Icon On Taskbar** places an in icon on the right of the taskbar that can be used to control Office Clipboard when the task pane is not displayed.
  - **Show Status Near Taskbar When Copying** tells you which of the 24 items you are currently cutting or copying.
- **Context menu** (opened by right-clicking the Office Clipboard icon in the tray on the right of the taskbar)—to show the Office Clipboard, clear all of its contents, stop collecting items on the Clipboard, and open the Options menu discussed immediately above

TIP

Passing (or, *hovering*) the mouse pointer over the taskbar icon for Office Clipboard tells you the number of items on the Office Clipboard. Double-clicking the taskbar icon for Office Clipboard opens it.

1

2

3

4

5

6

7

8

9

10

TIP

You can generally undo the last several operations by repeatedly issuing one of the Undo commands.

NOTE

Under certain circumstances, especially while formatting, the Redo Edit menu option becomes Repeat. This will be discussed further in Chapter 3.

NOTE

You can recover deleted text using Undo in the same way you can reverse a cut or a paste.

NOTE

You select a picture by clicking it. Once selected, a picture can be copied, moved, and deleted from a document in the same ways as text, using either the Windows or Office Clipboards. See Chapter 7 for further discussion about working with pictures.

UNDO A MOVE OR PASTE

To undo a move or paste:

- Press **CTRL+Z**.

  –Or–

- Click the **Edit** menu and then click **Undo**.

  –Or–

- Click **Undo** on the Standard toolbar. 

REDO AN UNDO

To redo many undos:

- Press **CTRL+Y**.

  –Or–

- Click the **Edit** menu and then click **Redo**.

  –Or–

- Click **Redo** in the Standard toolbar. 

Delete Text

Deleting text removes it from its current location *without* putting in the Clipboard. To delete a selected piece of text:

- Press **DELETE,** or **DEL**.

  –Or–

- Click the **Edit** menu, click **Clear**, and then click **Contents**.

Edit a Document

After entering all the text into a document, most people want to edit it and, possibly, revise it at a later date. You'll want to be able to move around the document, quickly moving from location to location.

> **NOTE**
>
> Some of the ways used to move around a document move the insertion point as you go, and some only change what you are looking at within the document, moving your view to a new location. In the latter case, if you find that you want the insertion point where you are looking, click there or use one of the arrow keys to move the insertion point. The insertion point will appear.

Move around in a Document

Word provides a number of ways to move around a document using the mouse and the keyboard.

MOVE WITH THE MOUSE

You can easily move the insertion point by clicking in your text anywhere on the screen, but how do you move to some place you cannot see? You have to change what you are looking at, and Word provides two sets of tools to use with the mouse to do just that: the scroll bars and the browse buttons, as shown in Figure 2-14.

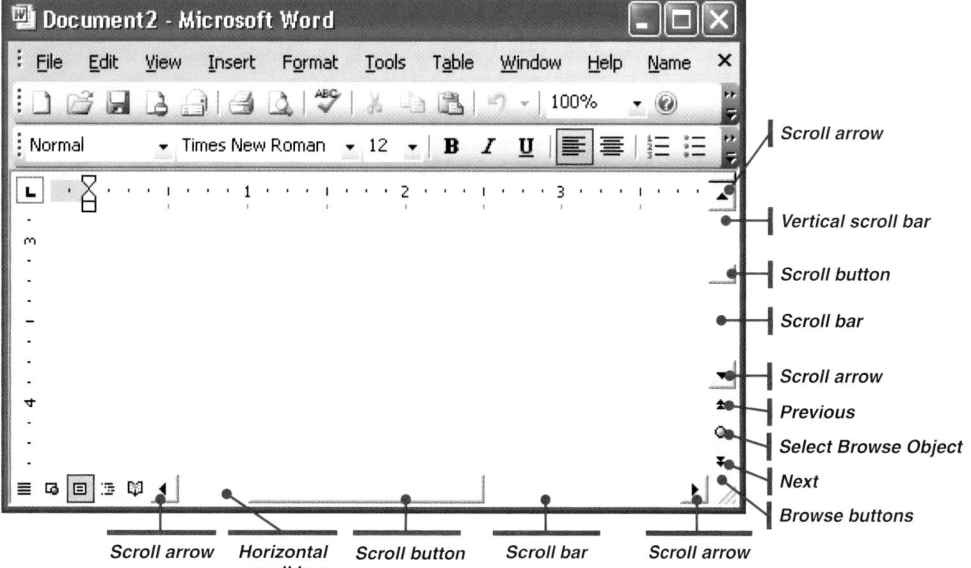

Figure 2-14: The scroll bars and browse buttons allow you to move easily to different locations within your document.

> **NOTE**
>
> The "view buttons" in the lower left of the Word window change the way the document is displayed, not the location in the document.

USE THE SCROLL BARS

There are two scroll bars, one for moving vertically within the document, and one for moving horizontally. Each scroll bar contains four controls for getting you where you want to go. Using the vertical scroll bar, you may:

- **Move upward by one line** by clicking the upward pointing scroll arrow.
- **Move upward or downward** by dragging the scroll button in the corresponding direction.
- **Move by one screen's height** by clicking in the scroll bar above the scroll button to move towards the beginning of the document, or by clicking below the scroll bar to move towards the end of the document.
- **Move downward by one line** by clicking the downward pointing scroll arrow.

The horizontal scroll bar has similar controls, only these are used for moving in a horizontal plane.

USE THE BROWSE BUTTONS

The browse buttons allow you to specify the type of object by which you want to browse through the document. The most obvious browse object, and the default, is a page. With that as the object, you can browse through a document going forward or back a page at a time.

Clicking the center **Select Browse Object** opens a menu of objects from which to select. By selecting one of these objects—such as a page, a heading, a comment, or an edit—you can move through the document going from one chosen object to the next. Often overlooked, this feature can be very handy.

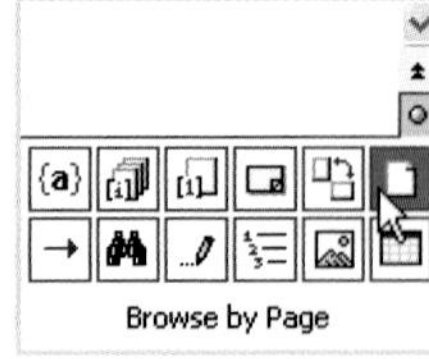

MOVE WITH THE KEYBOARD

These keyboard commands, used for moving around your document, also move the insertion point:

- **One character left or right** using the LEFT or RIGHT ARROW
- **One line up or down** using the UP or DOWN ARROW
- **One word left or right** using CTRL+LEFT ARROW or CTRL+RIGHT ARROW
- **One paragraph up or down** using CTRL+UP ARROW or CTRL+DOWN ARROW
- **To the beginning or end of a line** using HOME or END
- **To the beginning or end of a document** using CTRL+HOME or CTRL+END
- **One screen up or down** using PAGE UP or PAGE DOWN
- **To the previous or next instance of the current browse object** using CTRL+PAGE UP or CTRL+PAGE DOWN
- **To the top or bottom of the window** using CTRL+ALT+PAGE UP or CTRL+ ALT+PAGE DOWN

NOTE

You can also move a number of items relative to your current position by entering a + or a – and a number. For example, if Page is selected and you enter -3, you will be moved backwards three pages.

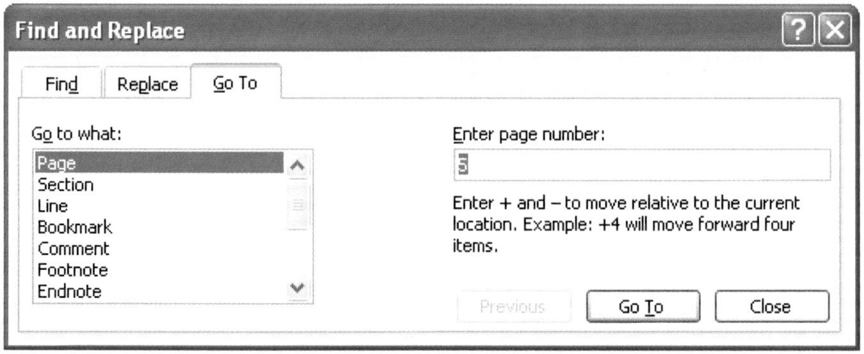

Go to a Particular Location

The Go To command opens the dialog box, shown in Figure 2-15, that allows you to go immediately to the location of some object, such as a page, a footnote, or a table. You can open the dialog box by:

- Pressing the F5 function key
- Pressing CTRL+G
- Clicking the **Edit** menu, and then clicking **Go To**
- Double-clicking the left end of the status bar

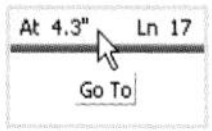

After opening the dialog box, select the object you want to go to from the list on the left, and then enter the number or name of the object in the text box on the right. For example, select **Page** on the left and enter 5 on the right to go to page 5.

Figure 2-15: The Go To command allows you to go to a particular page as well as to other particular items within a document.

TIP

If you want your search to find just the word "ton" and not things like "Washington" or "tonic." you can either put a space at both the beginning and end of the word in Find What ("ton"), or click **More** in the Find And Replace dialog box and then click **Find Whole Words Only**. The latter is the preferred way to do this because putting a space after the word would not find the word followed by a comma or a period.

TIP

If you find that the Find and Replace dialog box is getting in the way after finding the first occurrence of a word or phrase, you can close the dialog box and use **SHIFT+F4** to find the remaining occurrences. Also, once you have used Find, you can close the Find and Replace dialog box and use the Find Next or Previous Browse buttons to browse by Find, or you can press **CTRL+PAGE DOWN** or **CTRL+PAGE UP** to move quickly from one instance of the search term to the next.

Find and Replace Text

Often, you'll want to find something that you know is in the document, but you are not sure where, or even how many times, that item occurs. This is especially true when you want to locate names or words that are sprinkled throughout a document. For example, if you had repeatedly referred to a table on page 4 and, for some reason or another, the table had moved to page 5, you would need to search for all occurrences of "page 4" and change them to "page 5." In this example, you not only want to *find* "page 4," but you also want to *replace* it with "page 5."

Word allows you to do a simple search for a word or phrase as well as to conduct an advanced search for parts of words, particular capitalization, and words that sound alike.

FIND TEXT—SIMPLE CASE

In the simple case where you just want to search for a word or phrase:

1. Click the **Edit** menu and click **Find**. The Find And Replace dialog box will open.
2. Enter the word or phrase for which you want to search in the Find What text box.
3. Click **Find Next**. The first occurrence in the document below the current insertion point will be highlighted, as you can see in Figure 2-16.
4. To find additional occurrences, continue to click **Find Next** or press **SHIFT+F4**. When you are done (you will be told when the entire document has been searched), click **Close**.

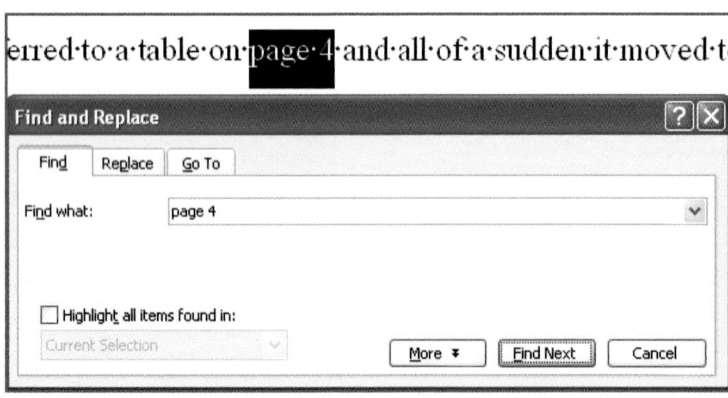

Figure 2-16: When you search for a word or phrase, the Find command can highlight individual occurrences or all occurrences at once.

> **NOTE**
>
> Instead of repeatedly clicking **Find Next** to highlight each occurrence of an item, you can click **Highlight All Items Found In**, select **Main Document**, and click **Find All**. This will highlight all occurrences of what you are searching for and allow you to observe them, but as soon as you click anywhere in the document, the highlights will all go away. If you press **SHIFT+F4**, **CTRL+PAGE UP**, **CTRL+PAGE DOWN**, or one of the browse buttons, you will highlight only the next occurrence.

> **TIP**
>
> Depending on how Office (and therefore Word) 2003 was installed on your computer, you may or may not have **CTRL+F** identified as shortcut keys for Edit Find. If your Edit menu does not show **CTRL+F** opposite Find (click the Edit menu to see), you can identify and use these keys by clicking the **Tools** menu and clicking **Customize**. Then, in the Commands tab, click **Keyboard**, select **Edit** as the category and **EditFind** as the command. Click in the **Press New Shortcut Key** text box, press **CTRL+F**, click **Assign**, and click **Close** twice. **CTRL+F** will appear opposite Find on the Edit menu and will be usable immediately.

FIND TEXT—ADVANCED CASE

By clicking **More** in the Find And Replace dialog box, you will find that Word provides a number of features to make your search more sophisticated (see Figure 2-17). These include specifying the direction of the search as well as finding:

- Only specific capitalization of a word or phrase
- Only whole words, so when searching for "equip" you don't get "equipment"
- Words or phrases that contain a set of characters by using wildcards to represent the unknown part of the word or phrase (see the "Using Wildcards" QuickSteps)
- Words that sound alike but are spelled differently (homonyms)
- A word in all its forms—noun, adjective, verb, or adverb (for example, ski, skier, and skiing)
- Specific types of formatting, such as a particular word formatted in bold and/or in a particular font
- Specific special characters, such as paragraph marks, em dashes (—), or nonbreaking spaces (can't be the first or last character in a line)

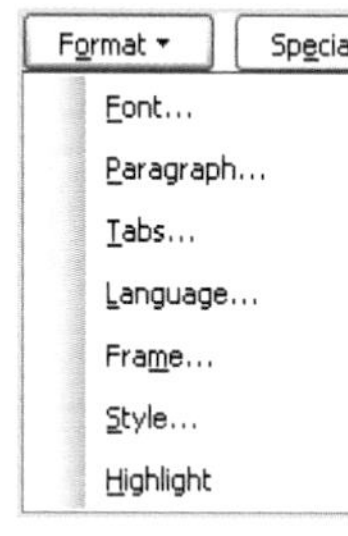

Figure 2-17: Word offers a number of advanced ways to search a document.

USING WILDCARDS

Wildcards are characters that are used to represent one or more characters in a word or phrase when searching for items with similar or unknown parts. You must select the **Use Wildcards** check box, and then type the wildcard characters along with the known characters in the Find What. For example, typing **page ?** will find both "page 4" and "page 5." The "?" stands for any single character.

Find what: page ?
Options: Use Wildcards

Word has defined the following characters as wildcard characters when used in the Find command to replace one or more characters.

REPLACE TEXT

Often, when searching for a word or phrase, you want to replace it with something else. Word lets you use all the features of Find and then replace what is found.

1. Click the **Edit** menu and click **Replace**. The Find And Replace dialog box will open.
2. Enter the word or phrase for which you want to search in the Find What text box.
3. Enter the word or phrase you want to replace the found item(s) in the Replace With text box, as you can see in Figure 2-18.

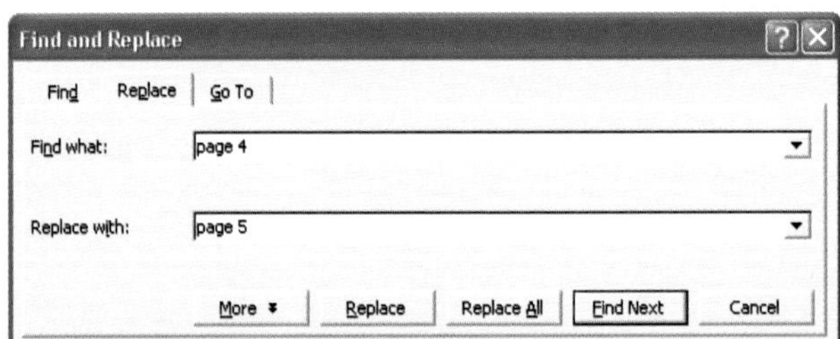

Figure 2-18: You can replace text either on a one-by-one basis or universally.

TABLE 2-3: WILDCARD CHARACTERS USED IN FIND

CHARACTER	USED TO REPLACE	EXAMPLE	WILL FIND	WON'T FIND
?	A single character	Page ?	Page 4 or Page 5	Page1
*	Any number of characters	Page *	Page 4 and Page 5	Pages 1-5
<	The beginning of a word	<(corp)	Corporate	Incorporate
>	The end of a word	(ton)>	Washington	Toner
\	A wildcard character	What\?	What?	What is
[*cc*]	One of a list of characters	B[io]b	Bib or Bob	Babe
[*c-c*]	One in a range of characters	[l-t]ook	look or took	book
[!*c-c*]	Any character except one in the range	[!k-n]ook	book or took	look
{*n*}	*n* copies of the previous character	Lo{2}	Loo or Look	Lot
{*n*,}	*n* or more copies of the previous character	Lo{1,}	Lot or Look	Late
{*n*,*m*}	*n* to *m* copies of the previous character	150{1,3}	150 to 1500	15
@	Any number of copies of the previous character	150@	15, 150, or 1500	1400

4. Click **Find Next**. The first occurrence in the document below the current insertion point will be highlighted.
5. If you want to replace this instance with the text you entered, click **Replace**. Word replaces this instance and automatically finds the next instance.
6. If you don't want to replace the text that was found, find the next occurrence by clicking **Find Next**.
7. If you want to replace all occurrences of the word you found, click **Replace All**.
8. When you are done, click **Close**.

NOTE

When searching with wildcards, both Find Whole Words Only and Match Case are turned on automatically and cannot be turned off; however, the check boxes for these features are cleared.

CAUTION

We recommend turning the Grammar checker off. It has been our experience that Word's grammar checker frequently identifies words or phrases as being in error when they aren't, and it sometimes suggests corrections that would be grammatically incorrect. Unless you can truly evaluate the Grammar checker's suggestions, this feature is not worth using. We recommend having a knowledgeable human check the document instead. The Spelling checker, however, is generally capable of making accurate yes-or-no decisions unless you have typed the wrong word (for example, "lite" instead of "light").

Complete and Save a Document

When you have completed a document or feel that you have done enough to warrant saving it and putting it aside for a while, you should go though a completion procedure that includes checking the spelling and grammar, determining where to save the document, and then actually saving it.

Check Spelling and Grammar

Unless you have a PhD in the English language, you may want Word to check your spelling and, possibly, grammar. By default, Word checks spelling and grammar as you type the document, so it might be that these functions have already been performed. You can tell if Word is checking the spelling and grammar by noticing if Word automatically places a wavy red line under words it thinks are misspelled and if a wavy green line appears beneath words and phrases whose grammar is questioned. You can turn off automatic spell and grammar checking. You can also have these features run using an array of options. You can also ask Word to perform a spell and/or grammar check whenever you want—most importantly, when you are completing a document.

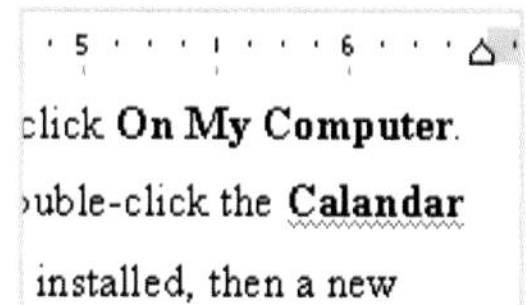

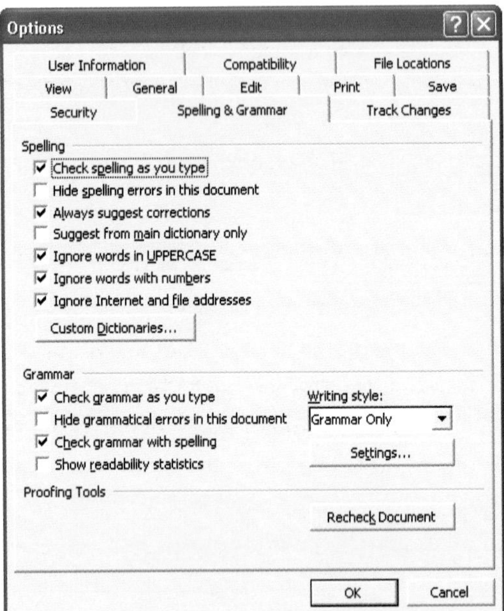

Figure 2-19: By default, Word checks spelling and grammar as you type, but you can disable those utilities in the Tools Options dialog box.

CONTROL SPELL AND GRAMMAR CHECKING

Word provides a number of settings that allow you to control how spelling and grammar checking is performed.

1. Click the **Tools** menu, click **Options**, and click the **Spell & Grammar** tab, which will open as shown in Figure 2-19.
2. If you wish to turn off automatic spell checking, uncheck **Check Spelling As You Type**.
3. If you wish to turn off the automatic grammar checking, uncheck **Check Grammar As You Type.**
4. Click **Settings** under Grammar to set the rules by which the grammar checking is done.
5. Click **OK** twice to close both the Grammar Settings and Options dialog boxes.

INITIATE SPELL AND GRAMMAR CHECKING

To manually initiate spell and grammar checking:

1. Click the **Tools** menu and click **Spelling and Grammar**. The Spelling and Grammar dialog box will open and begin checking. When a word is found that Word believes might not be correct, the dialog box will display both the perceived error and one or more suggestions for its correction (see Figure 2-20).

   –Or–

   Click the **Spelling and Grammar** icon on the Standard toolbar. The Spelling and Grammar dialog box will open as spelling and grammar checking begin.
2. If you wish not to correct the perceived error, click **Ignore Once** for this one instance, or click **Ignore All** for all instances.
3. If you wish to replace the perceived error with the highlighted suggestion, click **Change** for this one instance, or click **Change All** for all instances. If one of the other suggestions is a better choice, click it before clicking **Change** or **Change All**.

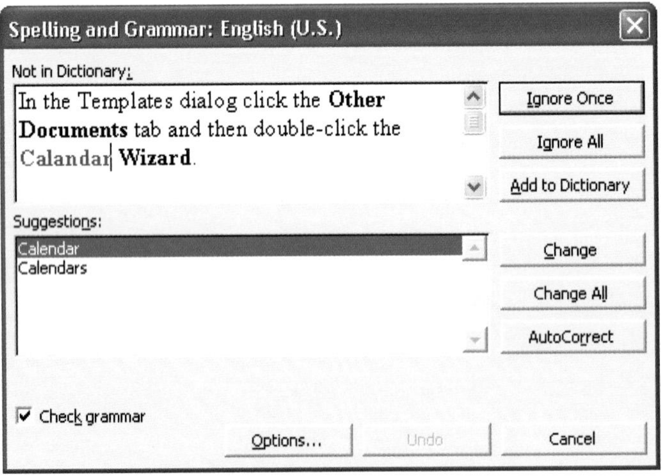

Figure 2-20: The Spelling checker is a real gift to us poor spellers!

4. If you want Word to use your spelling of the word it thinks is in error for future documents, click **Add To Dictionary**. If you want Word to automatically correct this misspelling with the selected correction every time you type the incorrect word, click **AutoCorrect**. (See Chapter 4 for more on AutoCorrect.)
5. When Word has completed checking the spelling and grammar, you'll see a message to that effect. Click **OK**.

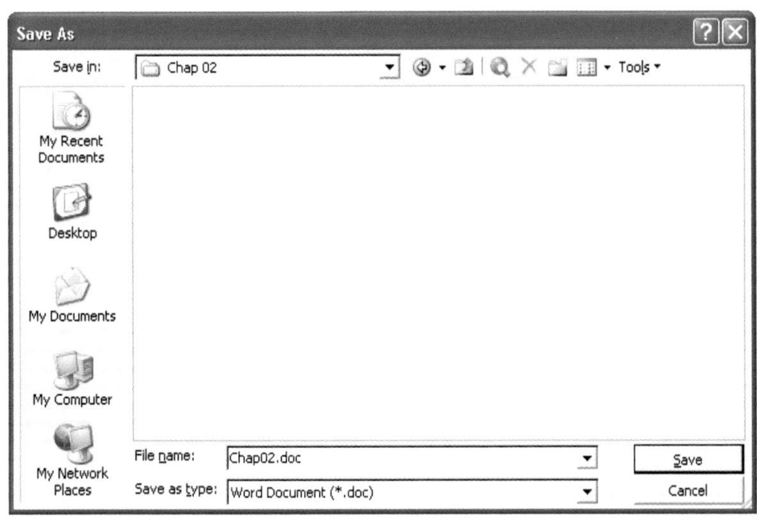

Figure 2-21: When saving a file, you don't have to enter a file extension. The ".doc" extension will be supplied by Word automatically.

Save a Document for the First Time

The first time you save a document, you have to specify where you want to save—that is, the disk drive and the folder or subfolder in which you want it saved. Since this is your first time saving the file, the Save As dialog box will open so that you can specify the location and enter a file a name.

1. Click the **File** menu, and click **Save As**.
2. Click the icon on the left for major area (for example, My Documents or My Computer) in which the file is to be saved.
3. If you want to store your new document in a folder that already exists in the major area, double-click that folder to open it.
4. If you want to store your new document in a new folder, click the **Create New Folder** icon in the toolbar, type the name of the new folder, and click **OK**. The new folder will open. (You can create yet another new folder within that folder using the same steps.)
5. When you have the folder(s) open in which you want to store the document, enter the name of the document, as shown in Figure 2-21, and then click **Save.**

TIP

As good as Word's automatic saving is, we manually save our document frequently (a couple of times an hour). We are truly paranoid about this after experiencing the frustration of working several hours on a document only to lose it.

QUICKSTEPS

SAVING A DOCUMENT

After you have initially saved a document and specified its location, you can quickly save it whenever you wish.

SAVE A DOCUMENT

To save a file:

- Open **File** and click **Save**.

  –Or–

- Click the **Save** icon in the standard toolbar. 

  –Or–

- Press **CTRL+S**.

SAVE A COPY OF YOUR DOCUMENT

When you save a document under a different name, you create a copy of it.

1. Click the **File** menu, and click **Save As**.
2. In the Save As dialog box, enter the new name in the File Name text box. Then, open the **Save In** list box and identify the path to the folder you want.
3. Click **Save.**

SAVE A DOCUMENT AS A TEMPLATE

To save a newly created document as a template from which to create new documents:

1. Click the **File** menu and click **Save As**.
2. Enter a name (without an extension) for your template in the File Name text box.
3. In the **Save As Type** drop-down list box, select **Document Template (*.dot)**.
4. Click **Save**.

Save a Document Automatically

It is important to save a document periodically as you work. Having Word save it automatically will reduce the chance of losing data in case of a power failure or other interruption.

1. Click the **Tools** menu, click **Options**, and click the **Save** tab.
2. Click **Save AutoRecover Info Every** to place a checkmark next to it.
3. In the Minutes box, use the arrows to select or enter a time for how often Word is to save your document.
4. Click **OK** to close the dialog box.

Make local copy of files stored on network or removable drives
Save AutoRecover info every: 10 minutes
Embed smart tags
Save smart tags as XML properties in Web pages

NOTE

When you first open Word, the save interval is set to a default of 10 minutes.

TIP

AutoRecover is a reserve parachute that you don't want to test unless you must. AutoRecover gives you the impression that you have lost your work. In fact, if you follow the instructions and choose to recover the AutoRecover document, you may not lose anything—at most, you might lose only the very last thing that you did.

How to...

- *Apply Character Formatting*
- *Adding Special Effects*
- *Set Character Spacing*
- *Change Capitalization*
- *Create a Drop Cap*
- *Set Paragraph Alignment*
- *Indent a Paragraph*
- *Using Indentation*
- *Determine Line and Paragraph Spacing*
- *Use Numbered and Bulleted Lists*
- *Add Borders and Shading*
- *Turning On Formatting Marks*
- *Copying Formatting*
- *Set Margins*
- *Determine Page Orientation*
- *Use Mirror Margins*
- *Specify Paper Size*
- *Using Reveal Formatting*
- *Set Vertical Alignment*

Chapter 3
Formatting a Document

Plain, unformatted text conveys information, but not nearly as effectively as well-formatted text, as you can see by the two examples in Figure 3-1. Word provides numerous ways to format your text. Most fall under the categories of text formatting, paragraph formatting, and page formatting, which are discussed in the following sections of this chapter. Additional formatting that can be applied at the document level is discussed in Chapter 4.

This chapter discusses the direct, or manual, application of formatting. Much of the character and paragraph formatting discussed in this chapter is commonly applied using styles that combine a number of different individual formatting steps, saving significant time over direct formatting. (Styles are discussed in Chapter 4.) Direct formatting is usually applied only to a small amount of text that needs formatting different from its style.

Format Text

Text formatting covers the formatting that you can apply to individual characters and includes selection of fonts, font size, color, character spacing, and capitalization.

Apply Character Formatting

Character formatting can be applied using keyboard shortcuts, the Formatting toolbar, and a menu and dialog box. Of these, clicking the **Format** menu and clicking **Font** to open the Font dialog box (see Figure 3-2) provides the most comprehensive selection of character formatting alternatives. In the sections that immediately follow, the Font dialog box can be used to accomplish the task being discussed. Keyboard shortcuts and the Formatting toolbar (see Figure 3-3) often provide a quicker way to accomplish the same task, and keyboard shortcuts (summarized in Table 3-1) allow you to keep your hands on the keyboard.

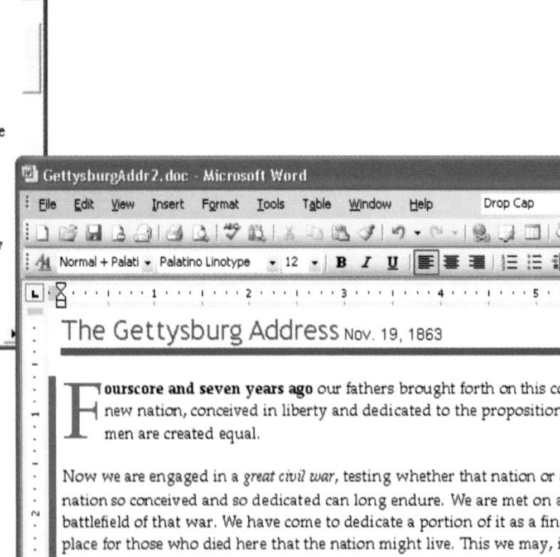

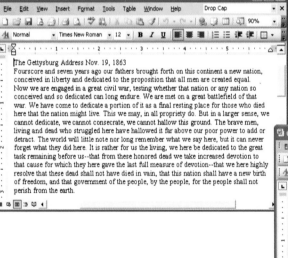

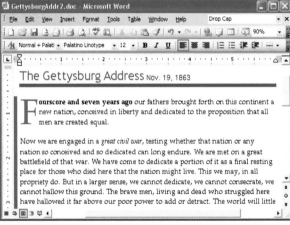

Figure 3-1: Formatting makes text both more readable and more pleasing to the eye.

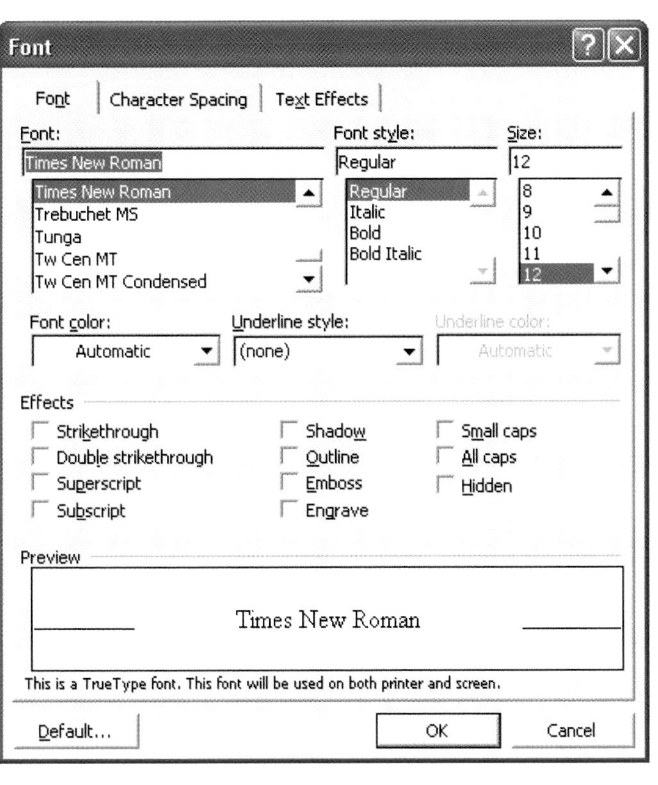

Figure 3-2: The Font dialog box provides the most complete set of character formatting controls.

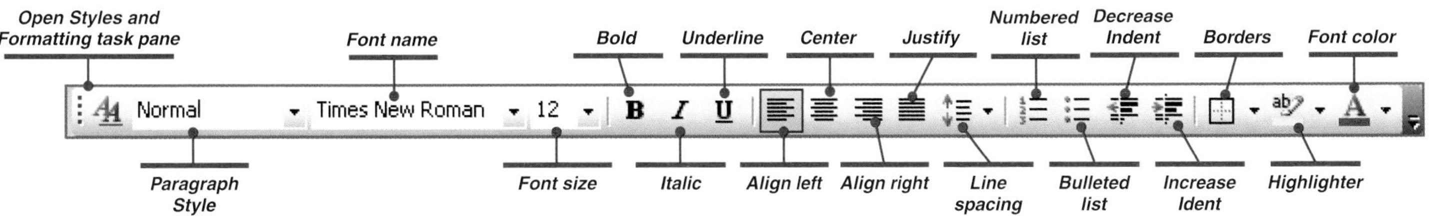

Figure 3-3: The Formatting toolbar provides fast formatting with the mouse.

NOTE

If the Formatting toolbar isn't displayed, **CTRL+SHIFT+F** and **CTRL+SHIFT+P** display the Font dialog box.

NOTE

Prior to applying formatting, you must select the text to be formatted. Chapter 2 contains an extensive section on selecting text.

TABLE 3-1: FORMATTING SHORTCUT KEYS

APPLY FORMATTING	SHORTCUT KEYS
Align left	CTRL+L
Align right	CTRL+R
All caps	CTRL+SHIFT+A
Bold	CTRL+B
Bulleted list	CTRL+SHIFT+L
Center	CTRL+E
Change case	SHIFT+F3
Copy format	CTRL+SHIFT+C
Decrease font size	CTRL+SHIFT+<
Decrease font size one point	CTRL+[
Open font dialog box	CTRL+D
Font name	CTRL+SHIFT+F
Font size	CTRL+SHIFT+P
Hanging indent paragraph	CTRL+T
Heading level 1	ALT+CTRL+1
Heading level 2	ALT+CTRL+2
Heading level 3	ALT+CTRL+3
Hidden character	CTRL+SHIFT+H
Increase font size	CTRL+SHIFT+>
Increase font size one point	CTRL+SHIFT+]
Indent paragraph	CTRL+M
Italic	CTRL+I
Justify paragraph	CTRL+J
Line space—single	CTRL+1
Line space—1.5	CTRL+5
Line space—double	CTRL+2
Normal style	CTRL+SHIFT+N
Paste format	CTRL+SHIFT+V
Reset character formatting	CTRL+SPACEBAR
Reset paragraph formatting	CTRL+Q
Small caps	CTRL+SHIFT+K
Subscript	CTRL+=
Superscript	CTRL+SHIFT+=
Symbol font	CTRL+SHIFT+Q
Un-hang paragraph	CTRL+SHIFT+T
Un-indent paragraph	CTRL+SHIFT+M
Underline continuous	CTRL+U
Underline double	CTRL+SHIFT+D
Underline word	CTRL+SHIFT+W

SELECT A FONT

A *font* is a set of characters that share a particular design, which is called a *typeface*. When you install Windows, and again when you install Office, a number of fonts are automatically installed on your computer. You can see the fonts on your computer by clicking the down arrow next to the font name in the Formatting toolbar and then scrolling the list (your most recently used fonts are at the top, followed by all fonts listed alphabetically). You can also see the list of fonts in the Font dialog box, where you can select a font in the Font list and see what it looks like in the Preview window at the bottom of the dialog box.

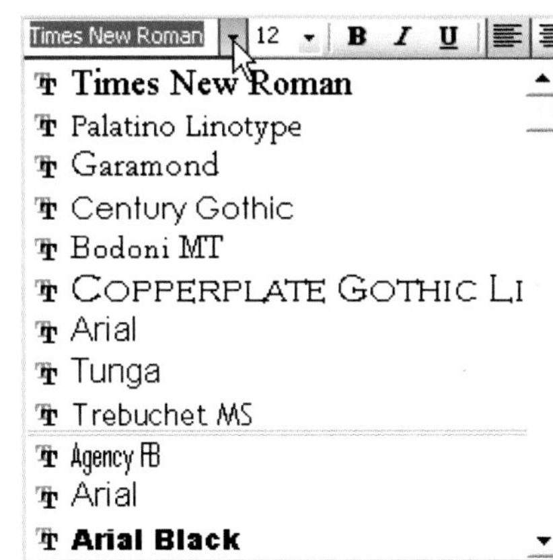

By default, the Times New Roman font is used for all text. To change this font:

1. Select the text to be formatted (see Chapter 2).
2. Press **CTRL+SHIFT+F**, press **DOWN-ARROW** until you see the font you want on the Formatting toolbar, and then press **ENTER**.

   –Or–

   Click the **down arrow** next to the font name on the Formatting toolbar, scroll the list until you see the font you want, and then click that font.

   –Or–

   Click the **Format** menu and click **Font** to open the Font dialog box. Scroll the Font list until you see the font you want. Click that font and click **OK**.

TIP

You can also open the Font dialog box by right-clicking the selected text you want to format and then clicking **Font**.

NOTE

Several types of fonts are included in the default set that is installed with Windows and Office. Alphabetic fonts come in two varieties: serif fonts, such as Times New Roman and Century Schoolbook, with the little ends or *serifs* on the ends of each of the character's lines, and *san-serif* ("without serifs") fonts, such as Arial and Century Gothic, without the ends. San-serif fonts are generally used for headings and lists, while serif fonts are generally used for body text. Finally, there are symbol fonts, such as Wingdings and Webdings, with many special characters, such as smiling faces ("smilies"), arrows, and pointing fingers.

APPLY BOLD OR ITALIC STYLE

Fonts come in four styles: regular (or "Roman"), bold, italic, and bold-italic. The default is, of course, regular, yet fonts such as Arial Black and Eras Bold appear bold. To make fonts bold, italic, or bold-italic:

1. Select the text to be formatted (see Chapter 2).
2. Press **CTRL+B** to make it bold, and/or press **CTRL+I** to make it italic.

   –Or–

   Click the **Bold** icon on the Formatting toolbar, and/or click the **Italic** icon on the Formatting toolbar.

   –Or–

   Click the **Format** menu and click **Font** to open the Font dialog box. In the Font Style list, click **Italic**, **Bold**, or **Bold Italic**, and then click **OK**.

CHANGE FONT SIZE

Font size is measured in *points*, which is the height of a character, not its width. For most fonts, the width varies with the character, the letter "i" taking less room than "w." (The Courier New font is an exception, with all characters having the same width.) There are 72 points in an inch. The default font size is 12 points for body text, with standard headings varying from 14 to 16 points. 8-point type is common for smaller print, and below 6 point is unreadable. To change the font size of your text:

1. Select the text to be formatted (see Chapter 2).
2. Press **CTRL+SHIFT+P**, press down-arrow or up-arrow until you see the font size you want on the Formatting toolbar, and then press **ENTER**.

   –Or–

   Click the **down arrow** next to the font size on the Formatting toolbar, scroll the list until you see the font size you want, and then click that font.

   –Or–

   Click the **Format** menu and click **Font** to open the Font dialog box. Scroll the Size list until you see the size you want. Click that size, and click **OK**.

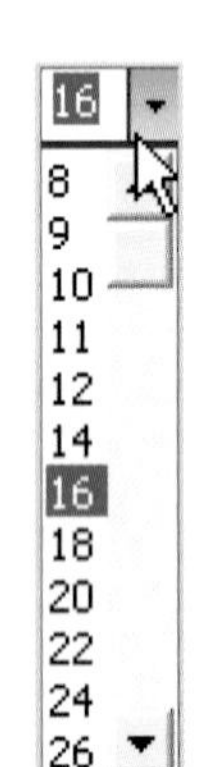

TIP

You can type in half point sizes, such as 10.5, as well as sizes that are not on the list, such as 15.

UNDERLINE TEXT

Several forms of underlining can be applied:

1. Select the text to be formatted (see Chapter 2).
2. Press **CTRL+U** to apply a continuous underline under the entire selection.

   –Or–

   Press **CTRL+SHIFT+W** to apply an underline under each word in the selection.

   –Or–

   Press **CTRL+SHIFT+D** to apply a double underline under the entire selection.

   –Or–

   Click **Underline** on the Formatting toolbar to apply a continuous underline under the entire selection.

   –Or–

   Click the **Format** menu and click **Font** to open the Font dialog box. Click the Underline Style **down arrow** and scroll the list of underline styles until you see the one you want. Click that one, and click **OK**.

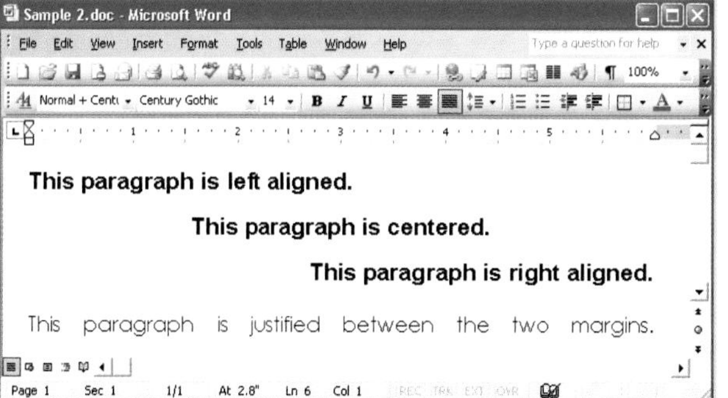

TIP

The Underline Style drop-down list in the Font dialog box contains underline choices beyond those the other methods provide—dotted, wavy, and so on.

USE FONT COLOR

To change the color of text:

1. Select the text to be formatted (see Chapter 2).
2. Click **Font Color** on the Formatting toolbar to apply the current selected color.

   –Or–

   Click the **down arrow** next to **Font Color** on the Formatting toolbar to select a color.

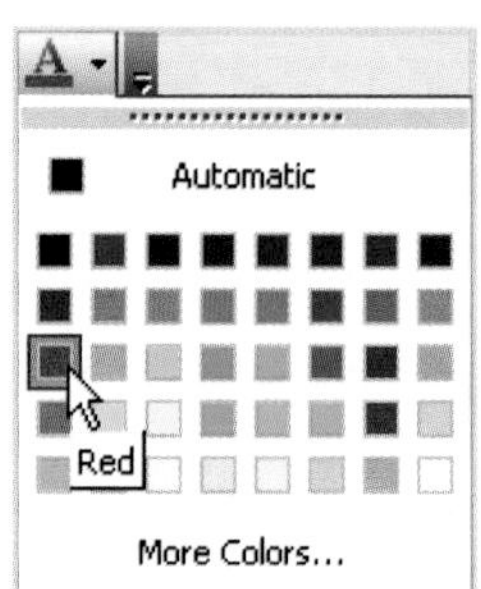

   –Or–

   Click the **Format** menu and click **Font** to open the Font dialog box. Click the Font Color **down arrow**, click the color you want, and click **OK**.
3. If, in selecting a color from either the Formatting toolbar or the Font dialog box, you do not find the color you want within the 40-color palette, click **More Colors** to open the Colors dialog box. In the Standard tab, you can pick a color from a 128-color palette, or you can use the Custom tab to choose from an almost infinite range of colors by clicking in the color spectrum or by entering the Red, Green, and Blue values, as you can see in Figure 3-4.

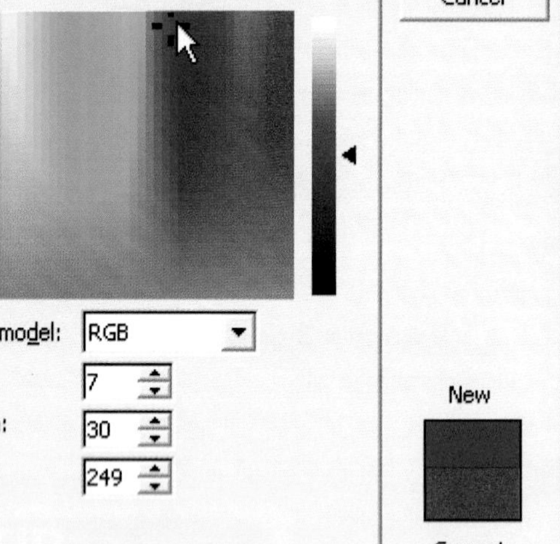

Figure 3-4: You can create any color you want in the Custom tab of the Colors dialog box.

ADDING SPECIAL EFFECTS

Word comes with two different sets of effects you can apply to text: a standard set of effects, such as superscript, emboss, and small caps; and animation effects, such as blinking background and shimmer.

APPLY STANDARD EFFECTS

1. Click the **Format** menu and click **Font** to open the Font dialog box. If it isn't already selected, click the **Font** tab.
2. In the Effects options in the middle of the dialog box, click the ones that you think you want to apply (some are mutually exclusive, such as Superscript and Subscript).
3. Check the results in the Preview area. When you are satisfied, click **OK**.

APPLY ANIMATION EFFECTS

1. Click the **Format** menu and click **Font** to open the Font dialog box. Click the **Text Effects** tab.
2. In the Animation options, click the one that you think you want to apply.
3. Check the results in the Preview area. When you are satisfied, click **OK**.

TIP

Word comes with a default set of formatting parameters comprised of Times New Roman, 12-point regular type, and black color. You can change this in the Font dialog box by selecting the font, style, size, and color you want, clicking **Default**, and then clicking **Yes** to make those settings the new default.

RESET TEXT

Figure 3-5 shows some of the formatting that has been discussed. All of those can be reset to the default formatting by:

1. Selecting the text to be formatted (see Chapter 2)
2. Pressing **CTRL+SPACEBAR** to remove all formatting not part of the default

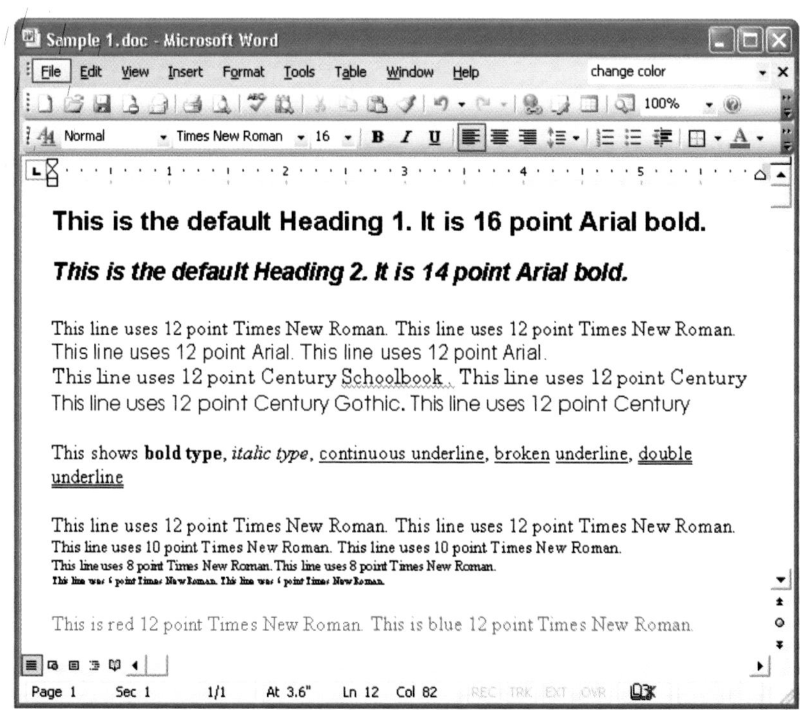

Figure 3-5: Character formatting must be applied judiciously or it will detract from the appearance of a document.

NOTE

Character spacing, especially kerning, is predominantly used when you are creating something like a brochure, flyer, or newspaper ad in which you want to achieve a typeset look.

Set Character Spacing

Character spacing in this case is the amount of space between characters on a single line. Word gives you the chance to increase and decrease character spacing as well as scale the size of selected text, raise and lower the position of text, and determine when to apply kerning (how the space for certain characters such as *A* and *V* can overlap) in the Character Spacing tab of the Font dialog box. To apply character spacing:

1. Select the text to be formatted, click the **Format** menu, and click **Font** to open the Font dialog box. Click the **Character Spacing** tab.
2. If you want, select the percentage scale factor that you want to apply. (This is not recommended. It is better to change the font size so as not to distort the font.)
3. Select the change in spacing (Expanded or Condensed) that you want and the amount of that change.
4. Select the change in position (Raised or Lowered) that you want and the amount of that change.
5. Determine if you want to apply kerning rules and the point size at which you want to do that.
6. Check the results in the Preview area, an example of which is shown in Figure 3-6. When you are satisfied, click **OK**.

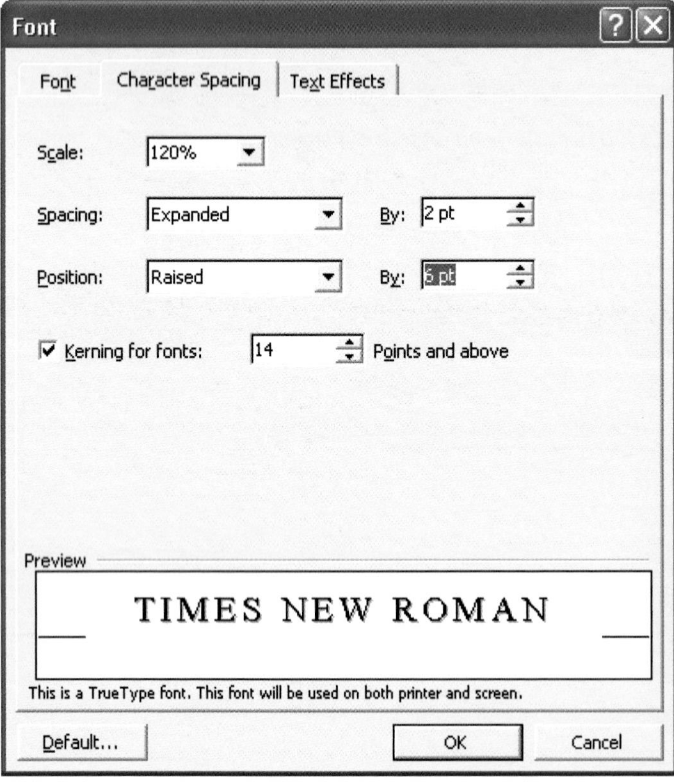

Figure 3-6: The spacing of text can have as much to do with its appearance as the choice of font.

NOTE

If you select a complete sentence with a leading capital letter and a period at the end and press **SHIFT+F3**, you will get all caps, all lowercase, and sentence caps (only the first letter of the sentence capitalized) on three successive keystrokes.

Change Capitalization

You can, of course, capitalize a character you are typing by pressing and holding **SHIFT** while you type. You can also press **CAPS LOCK** to have every letter that you type be capitalized, and then press **CAPS LOCK** again to turn off capitalization. You can also change the capitalization of existing text:

1. Select the text whose capitalization you want to change.
2. Press **SHIFT+F3**. If you started with all lowercase text (not a complete sentence), you get title case. The first character of every selected word will be capitalized.
3. Press **SHIFT+F3** a second time to get all caps. All characters of every selected word will be capitalized.
4. Press **SHIFT+F3** a third time to get all lowercase. All characters of every selected word will be lowercase.
5. Press **SHIFT+F3** a fourth time. If you started with all lowercase text, you get title case. The first character of every selected word will be capitalized.

For more options and more direct control over capitalization, use the Change Case dialog box:

1. Select the text whose capitalization you want to change.
2. Click **Format** and then click **Change Case**. The Change Case dialog box will open.
3. Select the type of capitalization you want to apply, and click OK. The options are:
   - **Sentence Case**, the first letter after a period is capitalized
   - **Lowercase**, no capitalization
   - **Uppercase**, all letters capitalized
   - **Title Case**, the first letter of every word capitalized
   - **Toggle Case**, reverse the existing capitalization

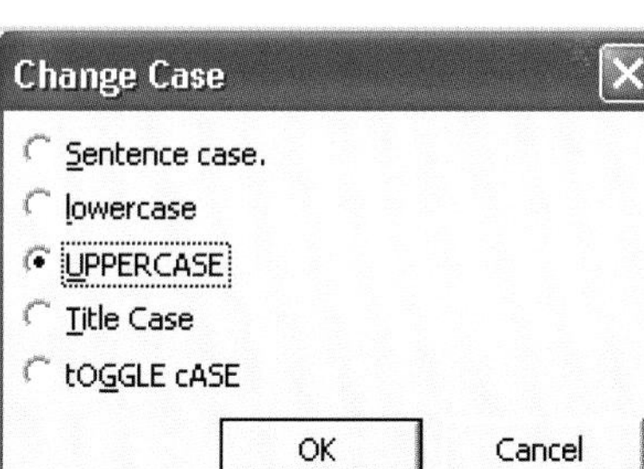

1 2 3 4 5 6 7 8 9 10

Create a Drop Cap

A *drop cap* is an enlarged capital letter at the beginning of a paragraph that extends down over two or more lines of text. To create a drop cap:

1. Select the character or word that you want to format as a drop cap.
2. Click the **Format** menu, extend the menu, and click **Drop Cap**. The Drop Cap dialog box will open.
3. Choose whether to have the paragraph wrap around the letter, as in a traditional drop cap, or to set the capital letter off in the margin.
4. Consider changing the font and other settings, and then click **OK**. The paragraph will be reformatted around the enlarged capital letter.

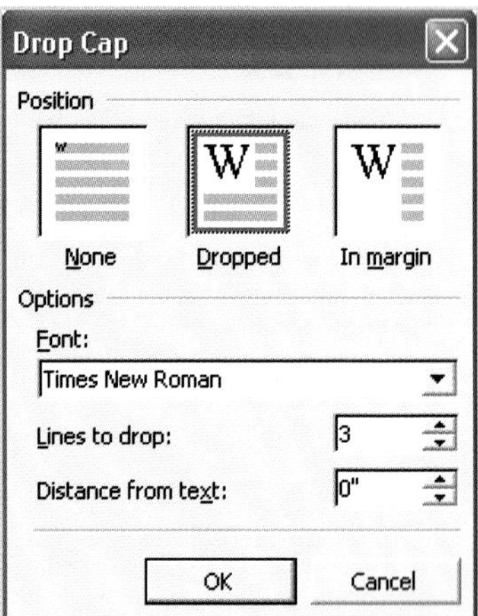

Fourscore and seven years ago our fathers brought forth on this continent a new nation, conceived in liberty and dedicated to the proposition that all men are created equal.

> **NOTE**
>
> To remove a drop cap, select the character or word, open the Drop Cap dialog box, and click **None**.

Format a Paragraph

So far, we've been looking at character formatting, formatting applied to one or more characters. The next type of formatting is *paragraph formatting*, which you can apply to any paragraph. In Word, a paragraph consists of a paragraph mark (created by pressing ENTER) and any text or objects that appear between that paragraph mark and the previous paragraph mark. A paragraph can be empty, or it can contain anything from a single character to as many characters as you care to enter. Paragraphs can be aligned; indented; have specific spacing before, within, and after it; be numbered and bulleted; and have borders placed around them.

Set Paragraph Alignment

Four types of paragraph alignment are available in Word (see Figure 3-7): left aligned, centered, right aligned, and justified. Left aligned, right aligned, and centered are self-explanatory. Justified means that the text in a paragraph is spread out between the left and right page margins. Word does this by adding space between words, which is not very attractive when applied to short segments of text. To apply paragraph alignment:

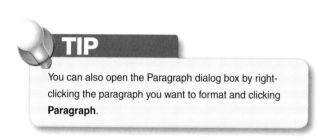

> **TIP**
>
> You can also open the Paragraph dialog box by right-clicking the paragraph you want to format and clicking **Paragraph**.

1. Click in the paragraph you want to align. (You don't need to select the entire paragraph.)
2. For left alignment, press **CTRL+L**; for right alignment, press **CTRL+R**; for centered, press **CTRL+E**; and for justified, press **H**.

   –Or–

   In the Formatting toolbar, click

   Align Left,

   Center,

   Align Right, or

   Justify

   depending on which you want to do.

   –Or–

   Click the **Format** menu and click Paragraph to open the Paragraph dialog box. In the Indents And Spacing tab, click the **down arrow** opposite Alignment, click the type of alignment you want, and click **OK**.

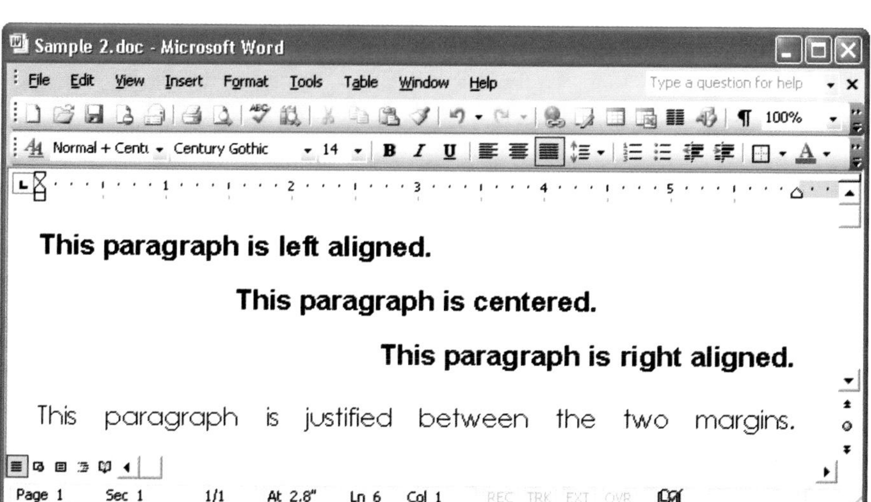

Figure 3-7: Paragraph alignment provides both eye appeal and separation of text.

Indent a Paragraph

Indenting a paragraph in Word means to:

- Move either the left or right edge (or both) of the paragraph inward towards the center
- Move the left side of the first line of a paragraph inward toward the center
- Move the left side of the first line of a paragraph leftward, away from the center, for a hanging indent

See Figure 3-8.

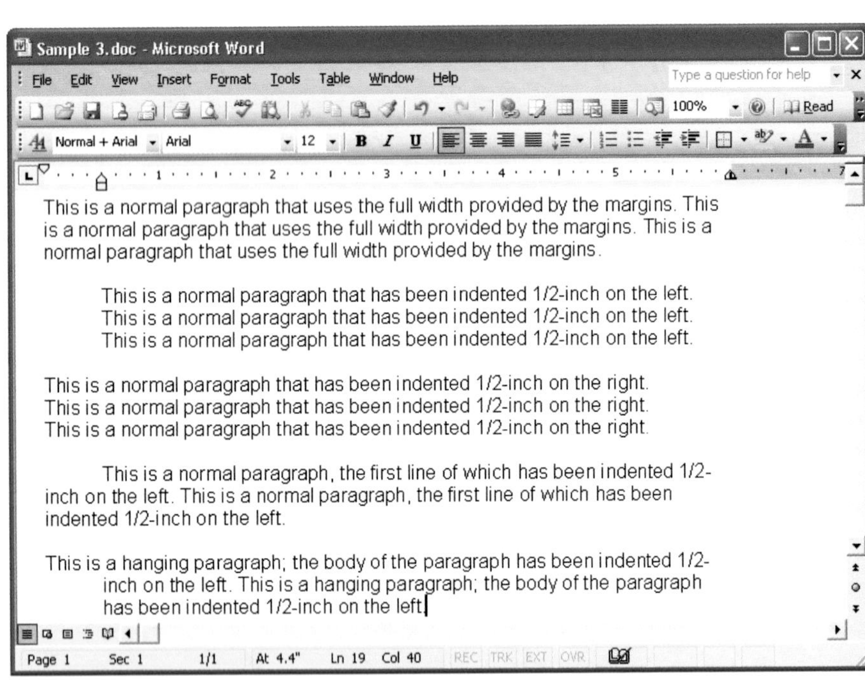

Figure 3-8: Indenting allows you to separate a block of text visually.

CHANGE THE LEFT INDENT

To move the left edge of an entire paragraph to the right:

1. Click in the paragraph to select it.
2. Press **CTRL+M** one or more times to indent the left edge 1/2-inch each time.

   –Or–

   Click **Increase Indent** in the formatting toolbar one or more times to indent the left edge 1/2-inch each time.

   –Or–

   Drag the **Left Indent** marker on the horizontal ruler to the right.

   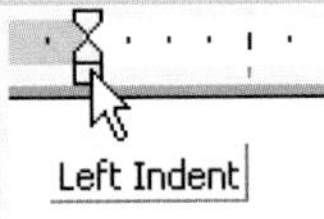

   –Or–

   Click the **Format** menu and click **Paragraph** to open the Paragraph dialog box. In the Indents And Spacing tab under Indentation, click the **increase arrow** (up) opposite Left until you get the amount of indentation you want, and then click **OK**.

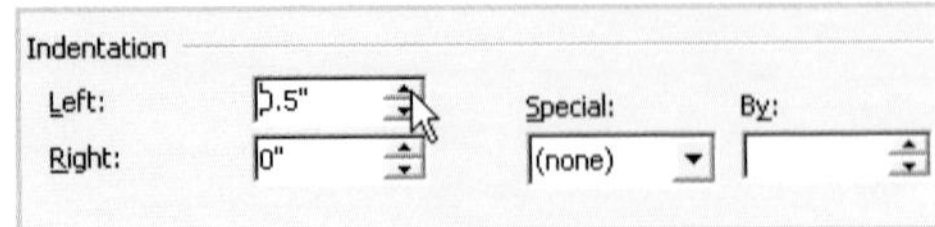

USING INDENTATION

A good question might be, "Why use indentation?" There are at least four good reasons:

- To organize and group pieces of text so they can be viewed as elements within a given topic. Bulleted and numbered lists fall into this category.
- To separate and call attention to a piece of text. An ordinary indented paragraph, either indented on the left, or on both the left and right, is done for this reason.
- To provide a hierarchical structure. An outline uses this form of indentation.
- To indicate the start of a new paragraph by indenting the first line of the paragraph.

Indentation is a powerful formatting tool when used correctly. Like other formatting, it can also be overused and make text hard to read or to understand. Ask yourself two questions about indentation: 1) Do I have a good reason for it? 2) Does it improve the readability and/or understanding of what is being written?

REMOVE A LEFT INDENT

To move the left edge of an entire paragraph back to the left:

1. Click in the paragraph to select it.
2. Press **CTRL+SHIFT+M** one or more times to un-indent the left edge 1/2-inch each time.

   –Or–

   Click **Decrease Indent** in the formatting toolbar one or more times to un-indent the left edge 1/2-inch each time.

   –Or–

   Drag the **Left Indent** marker on the horizontal ruler to the left.

   –Or–

   Click the **Format** menu and click **Paragraph** to open the Paragraph dialog box. In the Indents And Spacing tab, under Indentation, click the **decrease arrow** (down) opposite Left until you get the amount of indentation you want, and then click **OK**.

CHANGE THE RIGHT INDENT

To move the right edge of an entire paragraph to the left:

1. Click in the paragraph to select it.
2. Drag the **Right Indent** marker on the horizontal ruler to the left.

   –Or–

   Click the **Format** menu and click **Paragraph** to open the Paragraph dialog box. In the Indents And Spacing tab, under Indentation, click the **increase arrow** (up) opposite Right until you get the amount of indentation you want, and then click **OK**.

INDENT THE FIRST LINE

To indent the first line of a paragraph:

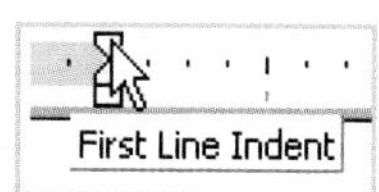

1. Click in the paragraph to select it.
2. Drag the **First Line Indent** marker on the horizontal ruler to the right.

   –Or–

   Click the **Format** menu and click **Paragraph** to open the Paragraph dialog box. In the Indents And Spacing tab, under Indentation, click the **down arrow** under Special, and select **First Line**. Enter the amount of the indent, and click **OK**.

Special: By:
(none)
(none)
First line
Hanging

1 2 3 4 5 6 7 8 9 10

MAKE A HANGING INDENT

To indent all of a paragraph except the first line:

1. Click in the paragraph to select it.
2. Press CTRL+T one or more times to indent the left edge of all but the first line 1/2-inch each time.

   –Or–

   Drag the **Hanging Indent** marker on the horizontal ruler to the right.

   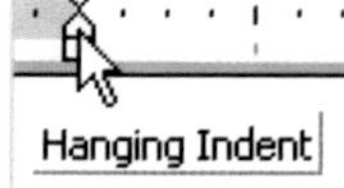

   –Or–

   Click the **Format** menu and click **Paragraph** to open the Paragraph dialog box. In the Indents And Spacing tab, under Indentation, click the **down arrow** under Special, and select **Hanging**. Enter the amount of the indent, and click **OK**.

REMOVE A HANGING INDENT

To un-indent all but the first line of a paragraph:

1. Click in the paragraph to select it.
2. Press CTRL+SHIFT+T one or more times to un-indent the left edge of all but the first line 1/2-inch each time.

   –Or–

   Drag the **Hanging Indent** marker on the horizontal ruler to the left.

   –Or–

   Click the **Format** menu and click **Paragraph** to open the Paragraph dialog box. In the Indents And Spacing tab, under Indentation, click the **down arrow** under Special, and select **None**. Click **OK**.

TIP

You can reset to the default all paragraph formatting, including indents and hanging indents, by pressing CTRL+Q.

Determine Line and Paragraph Spacing

The vertical spacing of text is determined by the amount of space between lines, the amount of space added before and after a paragraph, and where you break lines and pages.

NOTE

To specify a specific amount of space between lines other than a number of lines, select **Exactly** for the Line Spacing and then enter or select the number of points to use between lines. Single spacing is about 14 points, one and one-half line spacing (1.5) is about 21 points, and so on.

CAUTION

If you reduce the line spacing below the size of the type (below 12 points for 12 point type) the lines will begin to overlap and become hard to read.

SET LINE SPACING

The amount of space between lines is most often set in terms of the line height, with *single-spacing* being one times the current line height, *double-spacing* being twice the current line height, and so on. You can also specify line spacing in points, as you do the size of type. Single-spacing is just under 14 points for 12-point type. To set line spacing for an entire paragraph:

1. Click in the paragraph for which you want to set the line spacing.
2. Press **CTRL+1** for single-spacing, press **CTRL+5** for one and one-half line spacing, and press **CTRL+2** for double-spacing.

   –Or–

   Click the **down arrow** next to the Line Spacing icon in the Formatting toolbar, and then click the line spacing, in terms of lines, that you want to use.

   –Or–

   Click the **Format** menu and click **Paragraph** to open the Paragraph dialog box. In the Indents And Spacing tab under Spacing, click the **down arrow** under Line Spacing, and select the line spacing you want to use, as shown in Figure 3-9. Click **OK**.

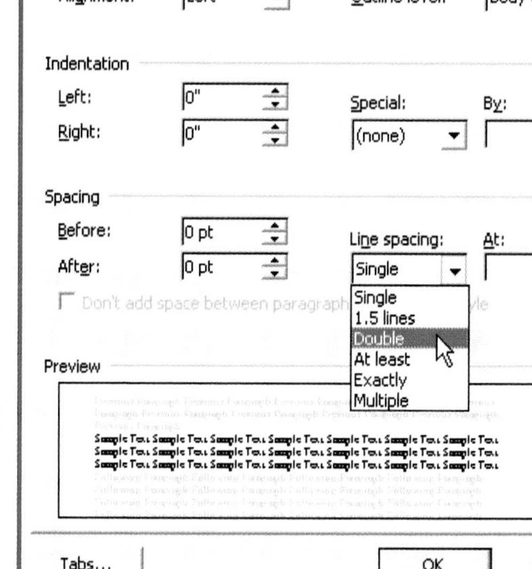

Figure 3-9: If a document is going to be edited on paper, it is a good idea to use double spacing to allow room for writing between the lines.

1 2 3 4 5 6 7 8 9 10

ADD SPACE BETWEEN PARAGRAPHS

In addition to specifying space between lines, you can add extra space at the beginning and end of paragraphs. With typewriters, many people would add an extra blank line between paragraphs. That has carried over to computers, but it does not always look that good. If you are using single spacing, leaving a blank line will leave an extra 14 points between paragraphs. Common paragraph spacing is to leave 3 points before the paragraph and 6 points afterward, so if you have two or these paragraphs one after the other you would have a total of 9 points, in comparison to the 14 points from an extra blank line. To add extra space between paragraphs:

1. Click in the paragraph to which you want to add space.
2. Click the **Format** menu and click **Paragraph** to open the Paragraph dialog box. In the Indents And Spacing tab under Spacing, click the down arrow opposite Before and either click the up arrow or enter a number in points ("pt") for the space you want to add before the paragraph. If desired, do the same thing for the space after the paragraph. When you are ready, click **OK**.

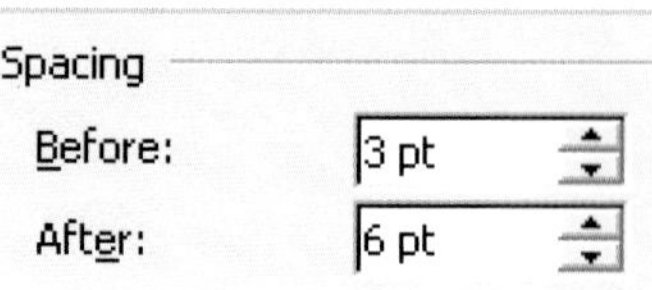

> **TIP**
>
> If you format a paragraph the way you want a group of paragraphs to look, you can often just press **ENTER** to begin a new paragraph with the same formatting. See the discussion of styles in Chapter 4.

SET LINE AND PAGE BREAKS

The vertical spacing of a document is also affected by how lines and pages are broken and how much of a paragraph you force to stay together or be with text either before or after it.

You can break a line and start a new one in two ways, depending on whether you want to create a new paragraph:

- **Create a new paragraph** by moving the insertion point to where you want to break the line and pressing **ENTER**.
- **Stay in the same paragraph** by moving the insertion point to where you want to break the line and pressing **SHIFT+ENTER**.
- Break a page and start a new one by pressing **CTRL+ENTER**.

When a paragraph is split over two pages, you have several ways to control how much of the paragraph is placed on which page.

1. Click in the paragraph you want to change.
2. Click the **Format** menu, click **Paragraph**, and click the **Line And Page Breaks** tab.
3. Click the following options that are correct for your situation, and then click **OK**.
   - **Widow/Orphan Control** adjusts the pagination to keep at least two lines on one or both pages. For example, if you have three lines, without Widow/Orphan Control one line is on the first page and two on the second. When you turn on this control, all three lines will be placed on the second page. Widow/Orphan Control is on by default.
   - **Keep Lines Together** forces all lines of a paragraph to be on the same page. Keep Lines Together is used for a multi-paragraph title where you want all of it on one page.
   - **Keep With Next** forces the entire paragraph to stay on the same page with the next paragraph. Keep With Next is used with paragraph headings, which you want to keep with the paragraph.
   - **Page Break Before** forces a page break before the start of the paragraph. Page Break Before is used with major section headings or titles, which you want to start on a new page.

Use Numbered and Bulleted Lists

Word provides the means to automatically number or add bullets to paragraphs and then format the paragraphs as hanging indents so the numbers or bullets stick out to the left (see Figure 3-10).

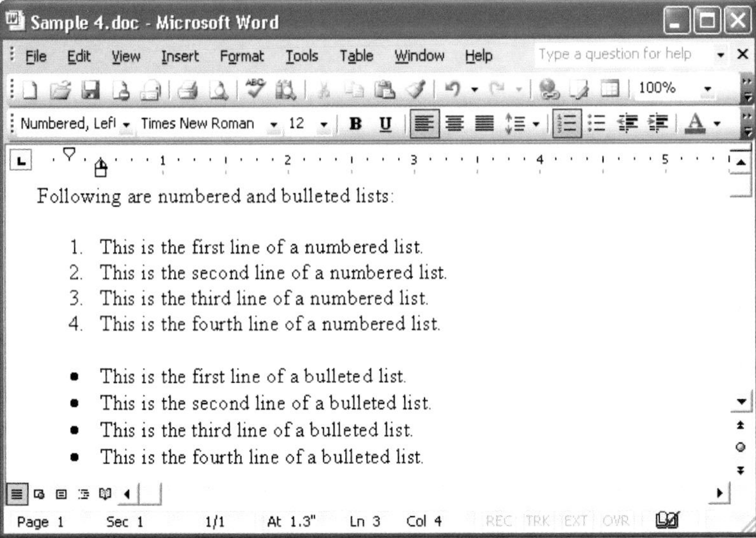

Figure 3-10: Bullets and numbering help organize thoughts into lists.

TIP

You can type 1 with or without a period, and 2 will be formatted in the same way.

CREATE A NUMBERED LIST AS YOU TYPE

Word's numbered lists are particularly handy because you can add or delete paragraphs in the middle of the list and have the list automatically renumber itself. To start a numbered list:

1. Press **ENTER** to start a new paragraph.
2. Type 1, press either **SPACE** or **TAB**, and then type the rest of what you want in the first item of the numbered list.
3. Press **ENTER**. The number "2" automatically appears, and both the first and the new line are formatted as hanging indents. Also, the AutoCorrect lightning icon appears.
4. After typing the second item in your list, press **ENTER** once again. The number "3" automatically appears. Type the item and press **ENTER** to keep numbering the list.
5. When you are done, press **ENTER** twice. The numbering will stop and the hanging indent will be removed.

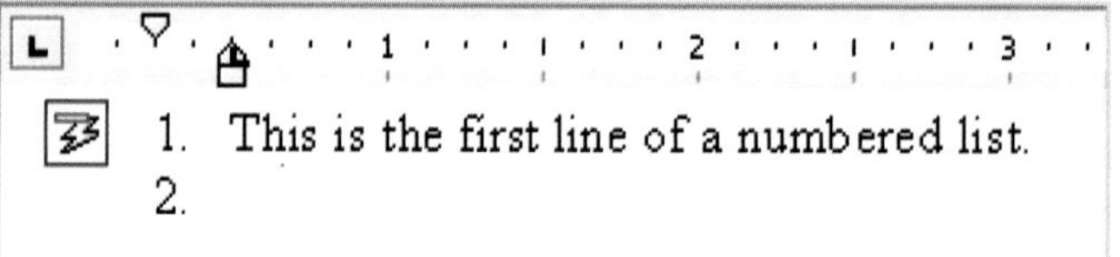

If you click on the AutoCorrect icon, you may choose to undo the automatic numbering that has already been applied, stop the automatic creation of numbered lists, and control the use of AutoCorrect (see Chapter 4 for more on AutoCorrect).

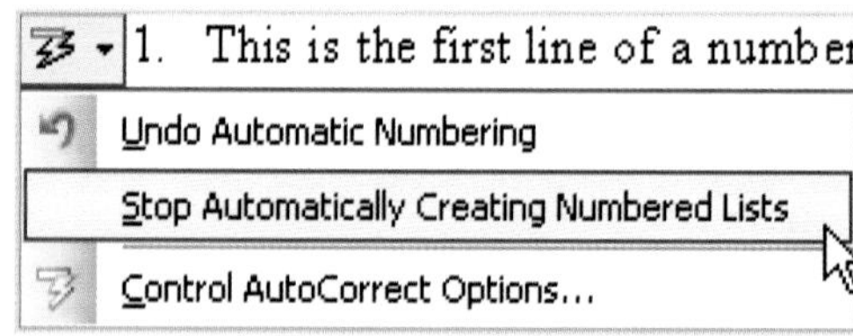

CREATE A NUMBERED OR BULLETED LIST INITIALLY

You can also create a numbered or bulleted list before you start typing the text they will contain:

1. Press **ENTER** to start a new paragraph.
2. In the Formatting toolbar, click **Numbering** to begin a numbered list, or click **Bullets** to start a bulleted list.

   –Or–

   Click the **Format** menu and click **Bullets and Numbering** to open the Bullets and Numbering dialog box (see Figure 3-11). Click either the **Bulleted** or the **Numbered** tab, click the style of bullets or number you want to use, and click **OK**.

   –Or–

   Press **CTRL+SHIFT+L** to start a bulleted list.
3. Type the first item and press **ENTER** to start the second numbered or bulleted item with the same style as the first item.
4. When you are done with the list, press **ENTER** twice to stop the automatic list.

   –Or–

   Click **Numbering** or click **Bullets** in the Formatting toolbar to stop the list.

   –Or–

   Click the **Format** menu, click **Bullets and Numbering**, click **None** to stop the list, and click **OK**.

NUMBER OR ADD BULLETS TO AN EXISTING LIST

To make an existing list into a numbered or bulleted list:

1. Select the paragraphs you want to make into a numbered or bulleted list.
2. Use any of the techniques described under "Create a Numbered or Bulleted List Initially" above to make the paragraphs numbered or bulleted.

Figure 3-11: Word provides many different styles of bullets and ways to number.

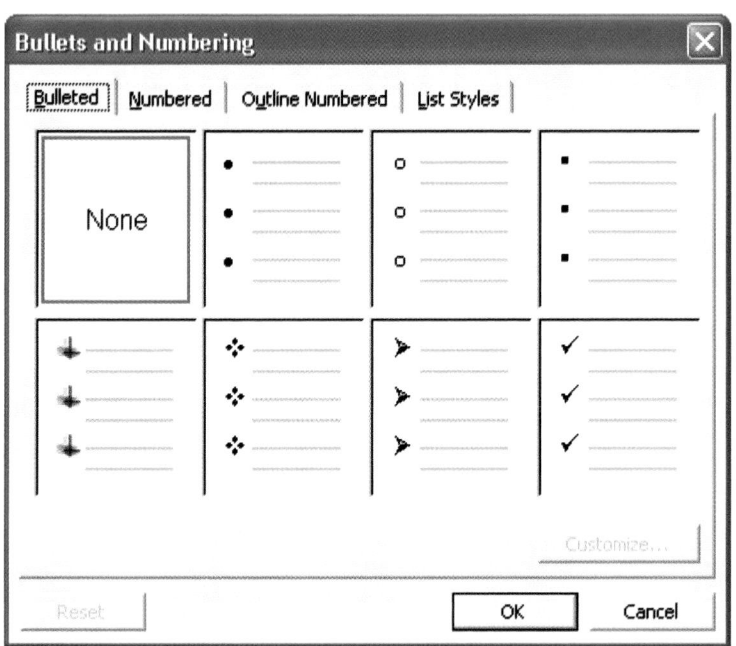

1 2 3 4 5 6 7 8 9 10

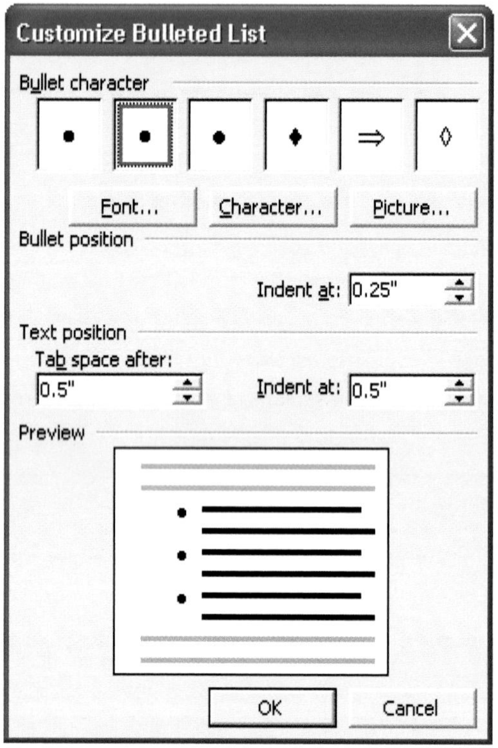

CUSTOMIZE BULLETS AND NUMBERS USED IN LISTS

You saw in Figure 3-11 that Word offers seven different types of bullets. Similarly, Word offers seven different styles for numbering paragraphs. For those to whom seven is not enough, there is a Customize option for both bullets and numbering that includes the ability to select from hundreds of pictures and import others to use as bullets. To use custom bullets or numbering:

1. Click the **Format** menu and click **Bullets and Numbering** to open the Bullets and Numbering dialog box.
2. Click either the Bulleted or Numbered tabs, and click **Customize**.
   - For bullets, the Customize Bulleted List dialog box opens (see Figure 3-12). Select a font and the character that you want to use, or, alternatively, click **Picture** to choose from a number of picture bullets that are included in Office's clip art (Figure 3-13). To use your own picture, click **Import** and select that picture. Click **OK** to close the Picture dialog box, select both the bullet and text position, click **OK** again, and use the new bullet.
   - For numbering, the Customize Numbered List dialog box opens (see Figure 3-14). If you want just the number without the period, delete the period; select the font to use, the style (numbers, capital letters, lowercase letter, Roman numerals, and so on), the starting number, and both the number and text position. Click **OK** to apply the customized numbering.

Figure 3-12: You can select any character in any font to use as a bullet.

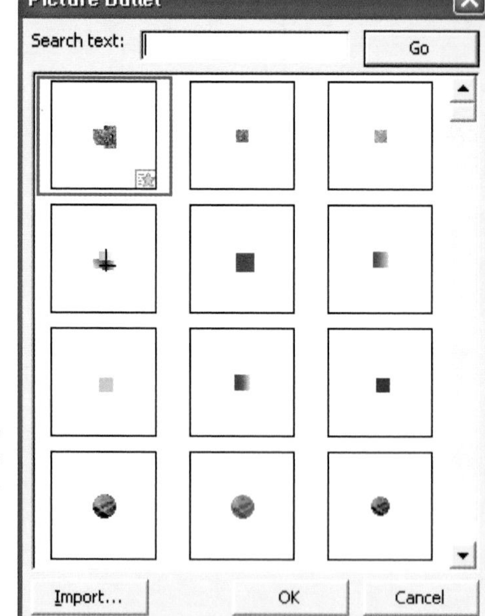

Figure 3-13: Word provides a number of pictures that can be used as bullets.

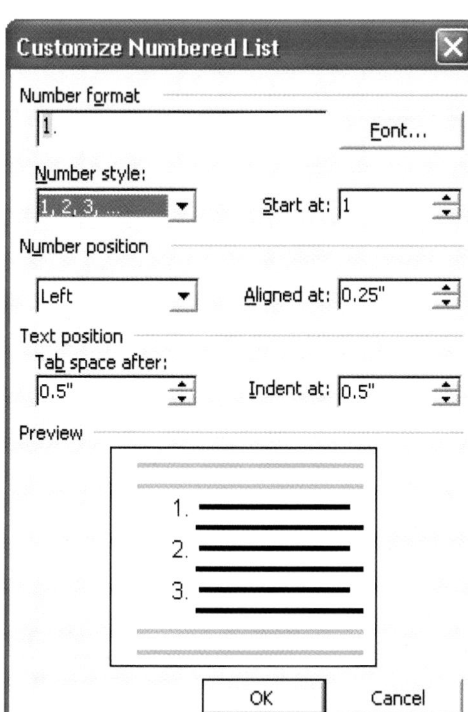

Figure 3-14: Numbered paragraphs can use numbers, letters, or even uppercase or lowercase Roman numerals.

TIP

You can switch a numbered list to a bulleted one or vice versa by selecting the list and clicking the other icon on the Formatting toolbar.

REMOVE NUMBERING AND BULLETING

To remove the numbering or bulleting formatting (both the numbers or bullets and the hanging indent):

1. Select the paragraphs from which you want to remove the numbering or bulleting.
2. Use any of the numbering or bulleting techniques described in Step 4 under "Create a Numbered or Bulleted List Initially," which when applied to an existing bulleted or numbered list will remove the bullets or numbers and the associated formatting. The easiest way to remove numbering or bulleting is to click **Numbering** or **Bullets**, as appropriate, on the Formatting toolbar.

Add Borders and Shading

Borders and shading allow you to separate and call attention to text. You can place a border on any or all of the four sides of selected text, paragraphs, and pages; and you can add many varieties of shading to the space occupied by selected text, paragraphs, and pages—with or without a border around them (see Figure 3-15). You can create horizontal lines as you type, and you can add other borders from both the Formatting toolbar and the Borders and Shading dialog box.

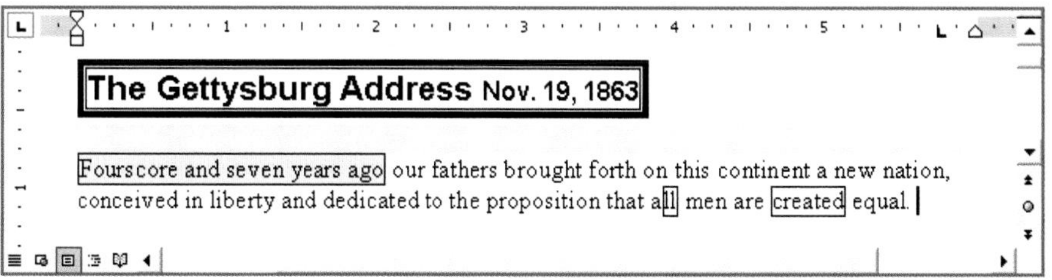

Figure 3-15: Borders and shading can be applied to text, blank paragraphs, phrases, characters, and words.

CREATE HORIZONTAL LINES AS YOU TYPE

Horizontal lines can be added as their own paragraph as you type:

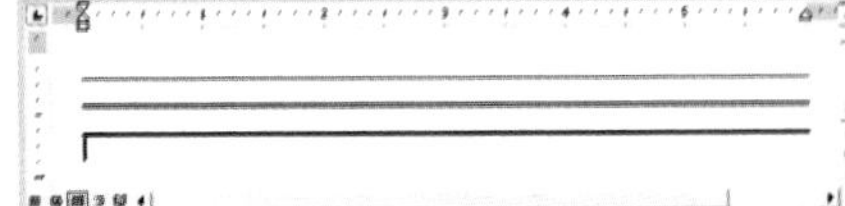

1. Press **ENTER** to create a new paragraph.
2. Type - - - (three hyphens) and press **ENTER**. A single, light horizontal line will be created between the left and right margin.

   –Or–

   Type = = = (three equal signs) and press **ENTER**. A double horizontal line will be created between the left and right margin.

   –Or–

   Type ___ (three underscores) and press **ENTER**. A single, heavy horizontal line will be created between the left and right margin.

ADD BORDERS AND SHADING TO TEXT

Borders and shading can be added to any amount of text, from a character to pages, by:

1. Selecting the text for which you want to have a border or shading.
2. Clicking the **down arrow** next to Borders in the Formatting toolbar, and then selecting the type of border you want to apply. If you have selected less than a paragraph you can only select a four-sided box (you actually can select less, but you will get a full box).

   –Or–

   Click the **Format** menu and click **Borders And shading**. The Borders and Shading dialog box will open, as shown in Figure 3-16.

Figure 3-16: Borders can be created with many different types and widths of lines.

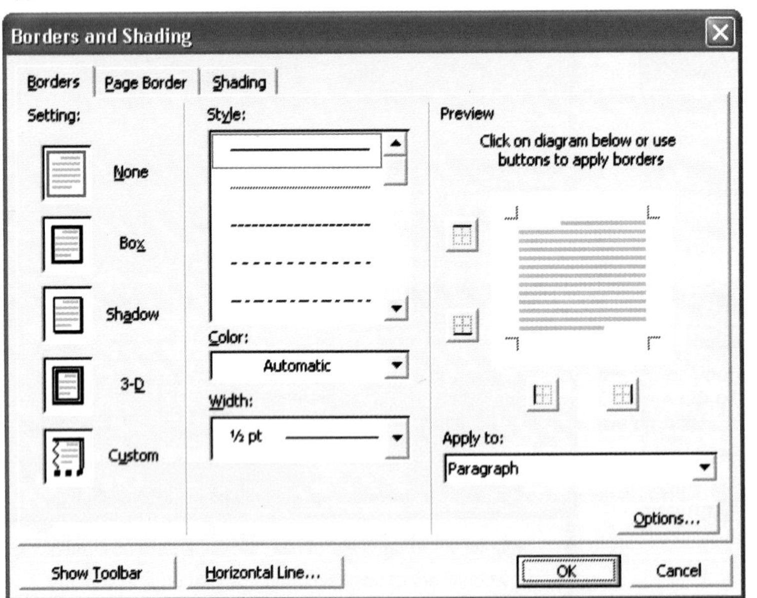

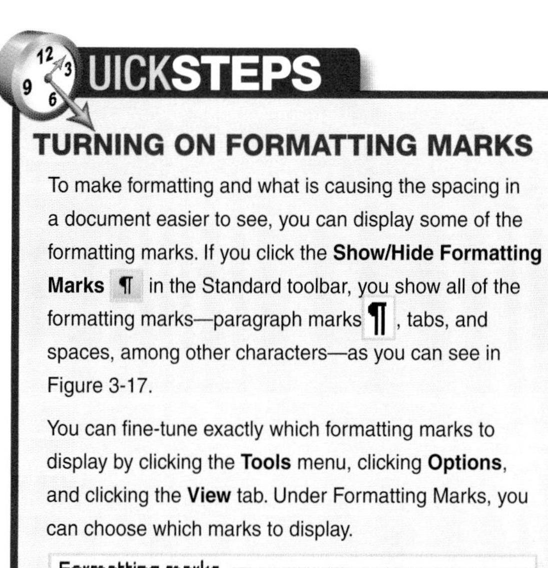

QUICKSTEPS

TURNING ON FORMATTING MARKS

To make formatting and what is causing the spacing in a document easier to see, you can display some of the formatting marks. If you click the **Show/Hide Formatting Marks** ¶ in the Standard toolbar, you show all of the formatting marks—paragraph marks ¶, tabs, and spaces, among other characters—as you can see in Figure 3-17.

You can fine-tune exactly which formatting marks to display by clicking the **Tools** menu, clicking **Options**, and clicking the **View** tab. Under Formatting Marks, you can choose which marks to display.

Formatting marks
- ☐ Tab characters
- ☐ Spaces
- ☐ Paragraph marks
- ☐ Hidden text
- ☐ Optional hyphens
- ☑ All

NOTE

Borders will be discussed further as they relate to tables in Chapter 6.

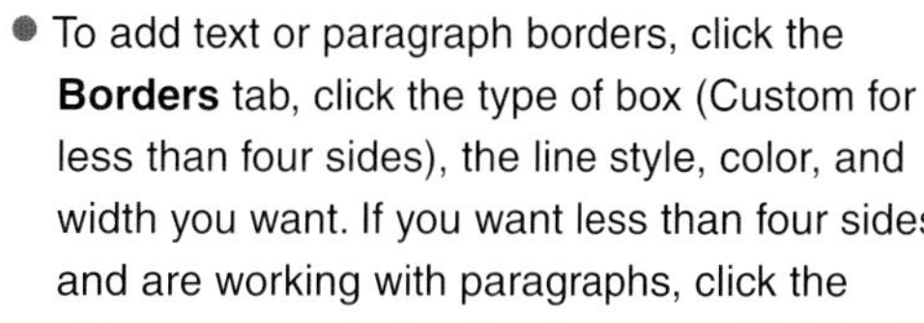

- To add text or paragraph borders, click the **Borders** tab, click the type of box (Custom for less than four sides), the line style, color, and width you want. If you want less than four sides and are working with paragraphs, click the sides you want in the Preview area. Click **Options** to set the distance the border is away from the text.
- To add page borders, click the **Page Border** tab, click the type of box (Custom for less than four sides), the line style, color, width you want, and any art you want to use for the border. If you want fewer than four sides, click the sides you want in the Preview area. Click **Options** to set the distance the border is away from either the edge of the page or the text.
- To add shading, click the **Shading** tab, click the color of shading, or *fill*, you want. If desired, select a pattern (this is independent of the fill), and choose whether to apply it to the entire paragraph or just to the selected text.
- To add a graphic horizontal line, click **Horizontal Lin**e, click the line you want, and click **OK**.
- When you are done with the Borders and Shading dialog box, click **OK**.

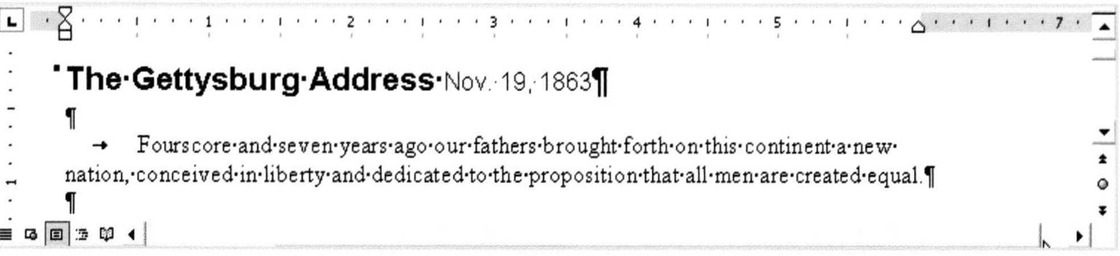

Figure 3-17: Turning on formatting marks helps you see what is making your document look the way it does.

COPYING FORMATTING

Often, you'll want a word, phrase, or paragraph formatted like an existing word, phrase, or paragraph. Word allows you to copy just the formatting.

USE THE TOOLBAR FORMAT PAINTER

1. Drag across the word, phrase, or paragraph whose formatting you want to copy. In the case of a paragraph, make sure you have included the paragraph mark (see "Turning on Formatting Marks" QuickSteps).
2. Click the **Format Painter** in the Standard toolbar. 
3. Drag across the word, phrase, or paragraph (including the paragraph mark) you want formatted.

COPY FORMATS WITH THE KEYBOARD

1. Select the word, phrase, or paragraph whose formatting you want to copy.
2. Press **CTRL+SHIFT+C** to copy the format.
3. Select the word, phrase, or paragraph (including the paragraph mark) you want formatted.
4. Press **CTRL+SHIFT+V** to paste the format.

COPY FORMATTING TO SEVERAL PLACES

If you want to copy formatting to several separate pieces of text or paragraphs:

1. Drag across the text with formatting to be copied.
2. Double-click the **Format Painter**.
3. Drag across each piece of text or paragraph that you want to format.
4. When you are done, click the **Format Painter** again, or press **ESC**.

Format a Page

Page formatting has to do with overall formatting items, such as margins, orientation, size, and vertical alignment of a page.

Set Margins

Margins are the space between the edge of the paper and the text. To set margins:

1. Open the document whose margins you want to set (see Chapter 2). If you want the margins to apply only to a selected part of a document, select that part now.
2. Click the **File** menu and click **Page Setup** to open the Page Setup dialog box shown in Figure 3-18.

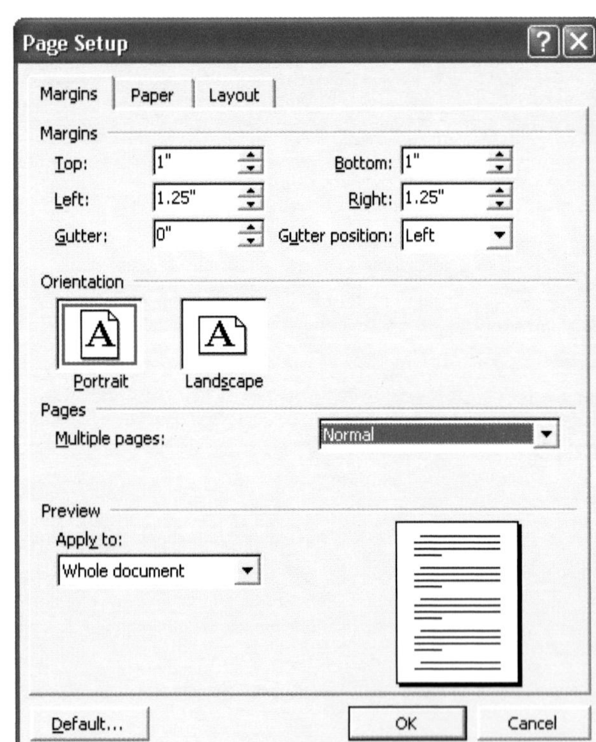

Figure 3-18: Most page formatting tasks are on the Page Setup dialog box.

TIP

If you are going to bind the document and want to add an extra amount of space on one edge for the binding, enter that amount opposite "Gutter," and select the side the gutter is on opposite "Gutter Position."

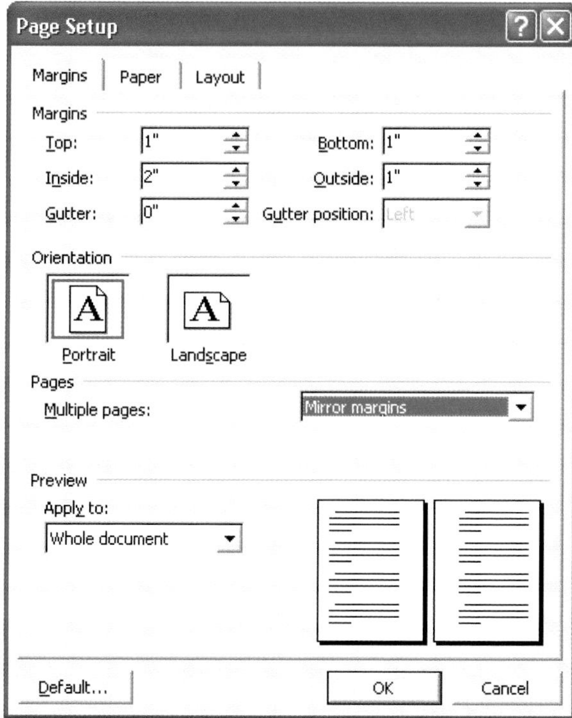

Figure 3-19: Mirror margins allow you to do a simple layout across two pages.

3. Under Margins, use the arrows or manually enter the desired distance in inches between the particular edge of the paper and the start or end of text.
4. If you want these margins to apply only to the selected part of a document, click **Selected Text** under Preview Apply To. When you are done setting margins, click **OK**.

Determine Page Orientation

Page orientation specifies whether a page is taller than it is wide, called "portrait," or wider than it is tall, called "landscape." For 8½-inch by 11-inch letter size paper, if the 11-inch side is vertical (the left and right edges), which is the standard way of reading a letter, then it is portrait. If the 11-inch side is horizontal (the top and bottom edges), then it is landscape. Portrait is the default orientation in Word. To change it:

1. Open the document whose orientation you want to set (see Chapter 2). If you want the orientation to apply only to a selected part of a document, select that part now.
2. Click the **File** menu and click **Page Setup** to open the Page Setup dialog box.
3. Under Orientation, click either **Portrait** or **Landscape**, depending on which you want.
4. When you are ready, click **OK** to close the dialog box.

Use Mirror Margins

Mirror margins allow you to have a larger "inside" margin, which would be the right margin on the left page and the left margin on the right page, or any other combination of margins that are mirrored between the left and right pages. To create mirror margins:

1 2 4 5 6 7 8 9 10

NOTE

The other options opposite Multiple Pages are used to print multiple pages on a single large piece of paper.

TIP

If you want further differentiation between the left and right pages, you need to use sections as described in Chapter 4.

1. Open the document whose margins you want mirrored (see Chapter 2).
2. Click the **File** menu and click **Page Setup** to open the Page Setup dialog box.
3. Under Pages, click the **down arrow** opposite Multiple Pages, and click **Mirror Margins**. When you do that, note that the left and right margins change to inside and outside, and the preview changes to a pair of pages, as shown in Figure 3-19.
4. Click **OK** to complete the use of mirror margins.

Specify Paper Size

Specifying the paper size gives you the starting perimeter of the area within which you can set margins and enter text or pictures.

1. Open the document for which you want to specify the paper size (see Chapter 2).
2. Click the **File** menu and click **Page Setup** to open the Page Setup dialog box.
3. Click the **Paper** tab and either choose a standard paper size from the drop-down list or enter a custom width and height.
4. Click **OK** when you are done.

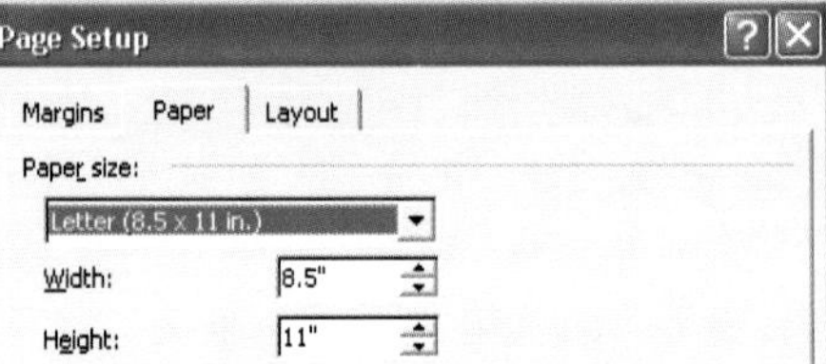

QUICKSTEPS

USING REVEAL FORMATTING

When you turned on the formatting marks (see "Turn on Formatting Marks," earlier in this chapter), you might have felt a bit disappointed that they didn't tell you more. That function is left to Reveal Formatting, which tells you every aspect of the character, paragraph, and page formatting for a selected piece of text, as shown in Figure 3-20. To open and use the Reveal Formatting task pane:

1. Select the text whose formatting you want to look at.
2. Click the **Format** menu and, after possibly extending the menu, click **Reveal Formatting**. The Reveal Formatting task pane will open.

   –Or–

   Press **SHIFT+F1**.
3. Click the down button that appears when you move your mouse pointer to the right edge of the Selected Text text box. A drop-down menu will open. From here you can select all text with similar formatting, apply the predominant format within the selection to the remainder of the selection, and clear all formatting in the selection.

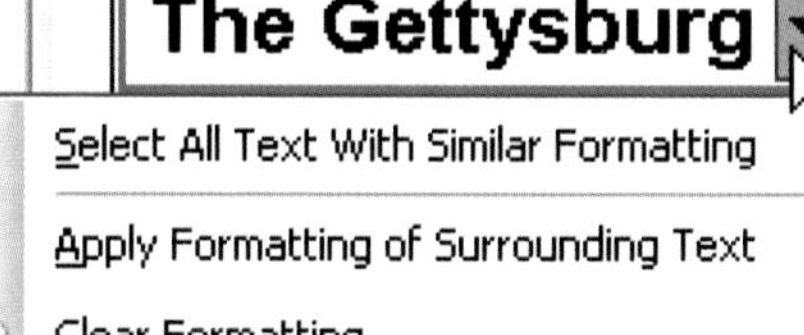

Continued...

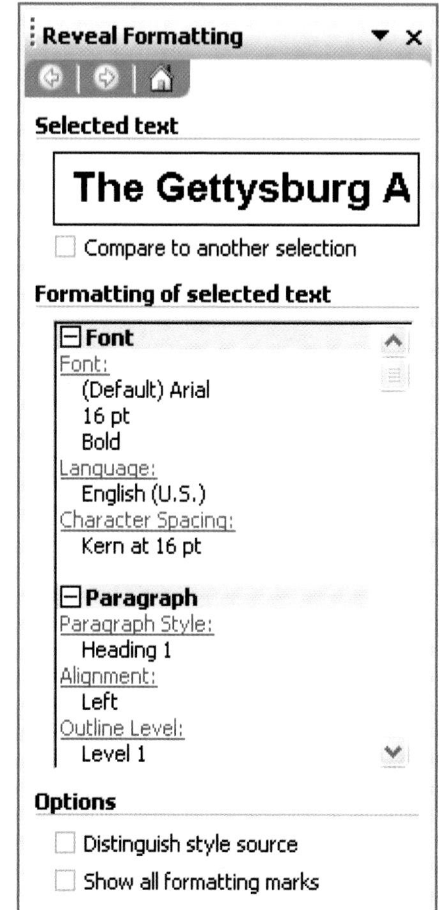

Figure 3-20: The Reveal Formatting task pane shows you all of the formatting that is being applied to a selected piece of text.

QUICKSTEPS

USING REVEAL FORMATTING

(Continued)

4. Click **Compare To Another Selection**, select another piece of text, and view the differences in the lower part of the task pane.
5. In the formatting list at the lower part of the task pane, you can click on a heading to open the dialog box where that formatting is set. For example, if you click on **Font**, the Font dialog box will be opened. Here you can make any desired changes.
6. At the bottom of the task pane, you can click **Distinguish Style Source** to see what style is being used (see Chapter 4 on the use of styles).

   Paragraph
   From Paragraph Style: Heading 1
   Paragraph Style:
   Heading 1
   Alignment:
   Left

7. Also at the bottom of the task pane, you can click **Show All Formatting Marks**.
8. When you are done with Reveal Formatting, click the task pane's **Close** button.

   –Or–

   Press **CTRL+ F1**.

Set Vertical Alignment

Just as you saw how you can right align, center, left align, and justify text between margins under "Set Paragraph Alignment," you can also specify vertical alignment, so text is aligned at the top, bottom, or center of the page, or justified between the top and bottom.

1. Open the document for which you want to set the vertical alignment (see Chapter 2).
2. Click the **File** menu and click **Page Setup** to open the Page Setup dialog box.
3. Click the **Layout** tab. Under Page, opposite Vertical Alignment, click the **down arrow**, and click the vertical alignment that you want to use.

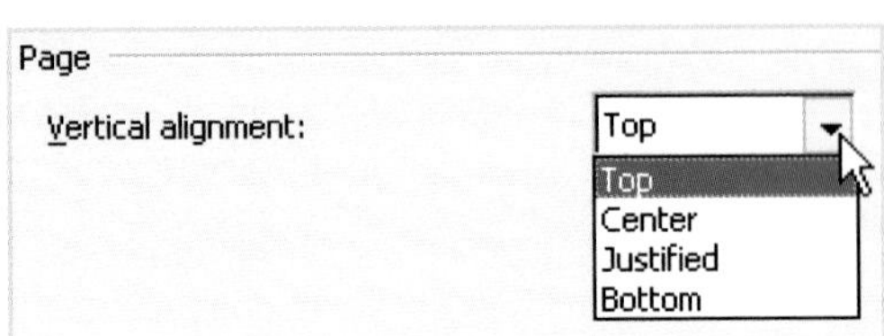

4. Click **OK** when you are done.

How to...

- *Using the Styles And Formatting Task Pane*
- *Create and Use Styles*
- *Deleting a Style*
- *Create and Use Templates*
- *Create Section Breaks*
- *Create and Use Columns*
- *Use Tabs*
- *Add Headers and Footers*
- *Using Different Left and Right Headers*
- *Add Footnotes and Endnotes*
- *Create an Index*
- *Create a Table of Contents*
- *Using View Buttons*
- *Create and Use Outlines*
- *Implement AutoCorrect*
- *Use AutoFormat*
- *Apply AutoText*
- *Use AutoSummarize*
- *Count Characters and Words*
- *Use Highlighting*
- *Add Hyphenation*
- *Exploring the Thesaurus*

Chapter 4
Customizing a Document

Microsoft Word 2003 provides a number of tools that combine text-creation, layout, and formatting features that you can use to customize your documents. Two of the most common tools used at a broad level are styles and templates. Word also provides several other features, such as AutoFormat and AutoText, that help make document creation and formatting easier.

This chapter discusses creating documents through the use of styles and templates; formatting your documents using tabs, headers and footers, and outlines; and inserting front and end matter, such as tables of contents and indexes. The chapter also discusses Word's writing aids, such as AutoText, hyphenation, and the thesaurus.

USING THE STYLES AND FORMATTING TASK PANE

The Styles And Formatting task pane includes links and options that you can select to perform common formatting tasks. For example, using the Styles And Formatting task pane, you can view and set styles for selected text.

ACCESS THE STYLES AND FORMATTING TASK PANE

To display or hide the Styles And Formatting task pane:

Click **Format** and then click **Styles And Formatting**. The Styles And Formatting task pane is displayed on the left side of the screen, as shown in Figure 4-1.

–Or–

Click the **Styles And Formatting** button on the Formatting toolbar.

APPLY A STYLE USING THE STYLES AND FORMATTING TASK PANE

To apply a style from the Styles And Formatting task pane:

1. Select the text to be formatted.
2. Open the Styles And Formatting task pane.
3. Click the name of the style you want to apply.

CHOOSE A GROUP OF STYLES

The Show drop-down list at the bottom of the Styles And Formatting task pane displays the following groups of styles:

- **Available Formatting** refers to the formats that have been used with the document you are currently working on.

Available formatting
Formatting in use
Available styles
All styles
Custom...
Show: Available styles

Continued...

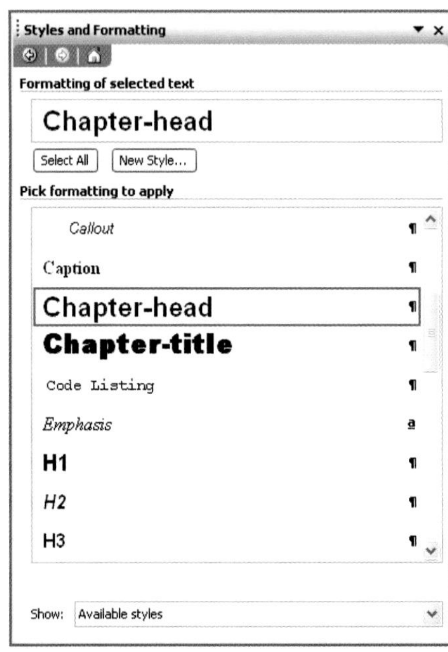

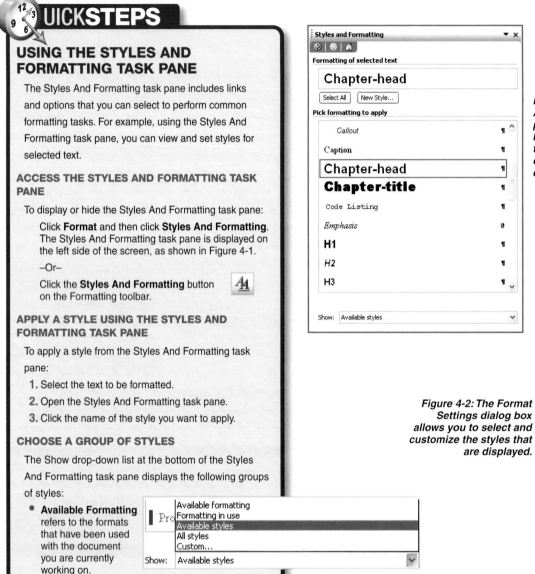

Figure 4-1: The Styles And Formatting task pane shows you how selected text is formatted and presents other formats you can choose from.

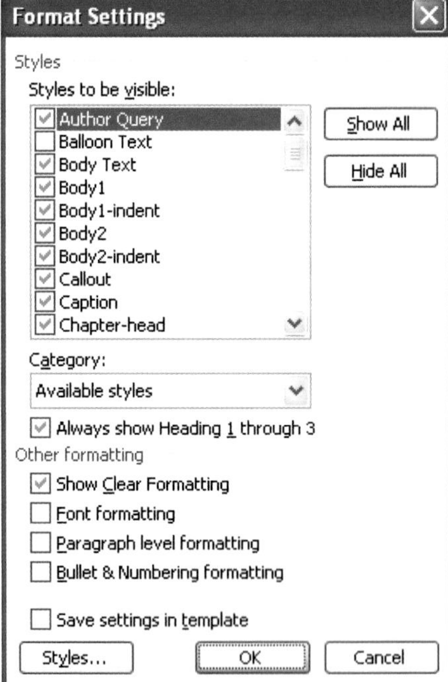

Figure 4-2: The Format Settings dialog box allows you to select and customize the styles that are displayed.

USING THE STYLES AND FORMATTING TASK PANE *(Continued)*

- **Formatting In Use** refers to the formatting currently applied to the document you are working on.
- **Available Styles** refers to the styles that have been used with the document you are currently working on.
- **All Styles** refers to the styles included in the template on which your current document is based.
- **Custom** refers to the specific styles you set. See the following section for more information.

SELECT STYLES TO DISPLAY

Use the Styles And Formatting task pane to select the styles to be displayed.

1. With the Styles And Formatting task pane displayed, click **Custom** from the Show drop-down list.
2. The Format Settings dialog box appears, as shown in Figure 4-2. Click the styles that you want to appear in the list.
3. Click **OK** when finished.

TIP

If you hover your mouse pointer over a style name, a description of the formatting included in that style is displayed.

Use Styles and Templates

Styles and templates are the primary ways that you can group and save a set of formatting specifications and easily apply those specifications to a number of documents. Styles apply to one type of formatting, such as paragraphs. Templates are broader packages of formatting that can contain a number of styles as well as text and toolbars.

Create and Use Styles

A *style* is a specific set of formatting characteristics that can be applied to individual characters or to entire paragraphs. Word provides four different types of styles:

- **Character styles** are used to format characters.
- **List styles** are used to format bulleted and numbered lists. See Chapter 3 for more information.
- **Paragraph styles** are used to format paragraphs.
- **Table styles** are used to format tables. See Chapter 6 for more information.

Styles are beneficial to document creation because they provide a consistent look and feel to all text selected for formatting.

CREATE PARAGRAPH STYLES

Usually, you will apply formatting to entire paragraphs rather than to individual characters. Furthermore, most documents have different types of paragraphs that require different styles. Body paragraphs in a document, for example, are often formatted differently from headings or lists. To create a paragraph style:

1. Click **Styles And Formatting** on the Formatting toolbar if the Styles And Formatting task pane is not already displayed.

1

2

3

4

5

6

7

8

9

10

TIP

Paragraph styles are indicated in the Style menu with the paragraph icon. ¶

Character styles are indicated with the character icon. a

NOTE

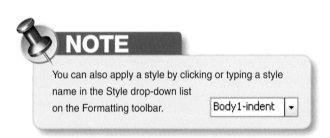

You can also apply a style by clicking or typing a style name in the Style drop-down list on the Formatting toolbar. Body1-indent

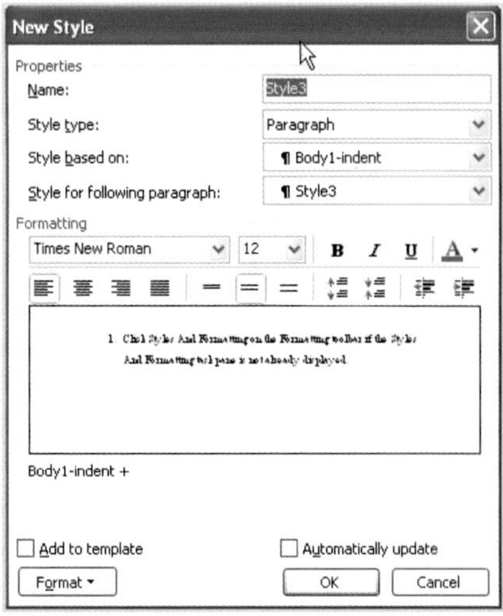

2. Click **New Style**. The New Style dialog box appears.
3. Type a name for the style in the Name text box.
4. In the Style Type box, click **Paragraph**.
5. Select the existing style, if any, you want to base the new style on from the Style Based On drop-down list.
6. Select a style from the Style For The Following Paragraph drop-down list. Doing so tells Word which style to apply to the next paragraph after you press **ENTER**.
7. Use the features in the Formatting area to determine such things as font, font size, and paragraph alignment. Click the **Format** button for additional formatting options.
8. Select the **Automatically Update** check box if you want Word to automatically update the paragraph style whenever you apply manual formatting to text using this style. (If you want to add the new paragraph style to the template on which your current document is based, select the **Add To Template** check box.)
9. Click **OK** when finished.

USE PARAGRAPH STYLES

To apply a paragraph style:

1. Select the paragraph you want to apply the style to by dragging over the text to highlight it or by clicking within the paragraph three times.
2. Click the **Styles And Formatting** button if the Styles And Formatting task pane is not already displayed.
3. Click the style you want. If the style you want is not listed, click **All Styles** in the Show box.
4. Close the Styles And Formatting task pane.

CAUTION

The Automatically Update option is available only when working with paragraph styles and is not recommended when using the Normal style. See "Use the Normal Template," later in this chapter, for more information. Automatic Update can very easily change a style that you may not want to change.

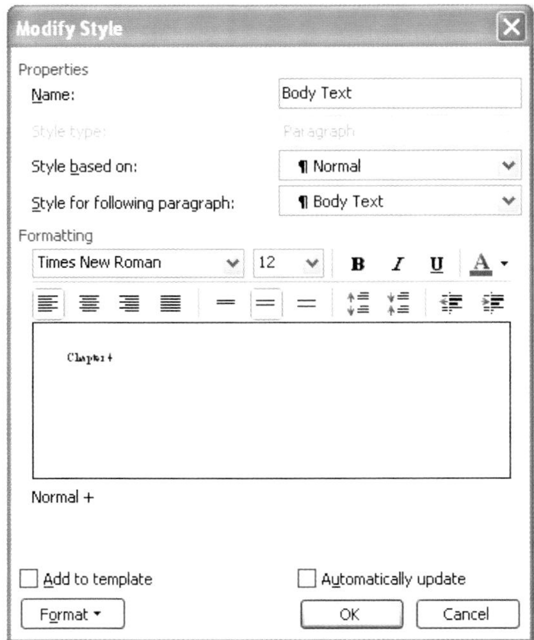

Figure 4-3: Use the Modify Style dialog box to automatically update a style.

UPDATE A PARAGRAPH STYLE

Sometimes you may make changes to a paragraph style and want those changes to be permanent. To automatically update a paragraph style:

1. Click the **Styles And Formatting** button if the Styles And Formatting task pane is not already displayed.
2. Right-click the style you want to automatically update.
3. Click **Modify**. The Modify Style dialog box appears (see Figure 4-3).
4. Select the **Automatically Update** check box. Word will automatically redefine the style you selected whenever you apply manual formatting to any paragraph with this style.

MODIFY A PARAGRAPH STYLE

To manually modify a paragraph style:

1. Click the **Styles And Formatting** button if the Styles And Formatting task pane is not already displayed.
2. Right-click the style you want to automatically update.
3. Click **Modify**. The Modify Style dialog box appears.
4. Click the **Format** button and select Paragraph. The Paragraph dialog box appears (see Figure 4-4).
5. Make the changes you want, and click **OK** when finished.

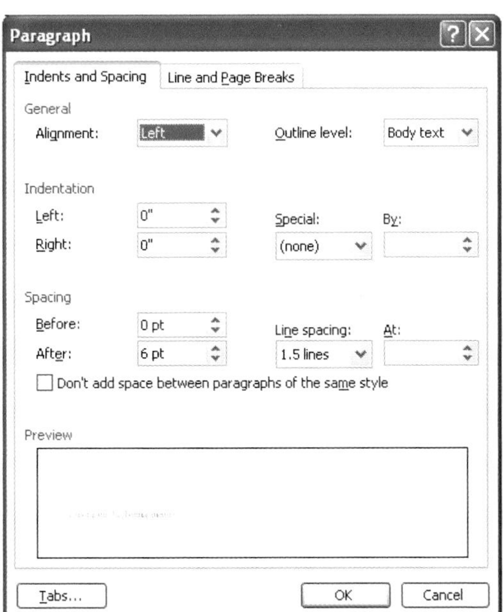

Figure 4-4: You can modify a paragraph style manually if you need to make very specific changes.

1 2 3 4 5 6 7 8 9 10

> **TIP**
>
> You can select a whole word by clicking it twice.

> **NOTE**
>
> You can also apply a style by clicking or typing a style name in the Style drop-down list on the Formatting toolbar.

CREATE CHARACTER STYLES

Character styles are used to specify how individual characters will look. They specify font and font size; whether characters are bold, italic, or underlined; and other characteristics. To create a character style:

1. Click the **Styles And Formatting** button on the Formatting toolbar if the Styles And Formatting task pane is not already displayed.
2. Click **New Style**. The New Style dialog box appears.
3. Type a name for the style in the Name text box.
4. In the Style Type box, click **Character**.
5. Select the existing style, if any, you want to base the new style on from the Style Based On drop-down list.
6. Use the features in the Formatting area to determine such things as font, font size, and paragraph alignment. Click the **Format** button for additional formatting options.
7. Click **OK** when finished.

USE CHARACTER STYLES

Character styles are used in a similar fashion as paragraph styles. You can apply a character style to selected text, modify a character style, and use the Style Gallery.

To apply a character style:

1. Select the text you want to apply the style to by dragging the cursor over the text to highlight it or by placing the insertion point at the place in the document where you will begin typing the text.
2. Click the **Styles And Formatting** button if the Styles And Formatting task pane is not already displayed.
3. Click the style you want. If the style you want is not listed, click **All Styles** in the Show box.
4. Close the Styles And Formatting task pane.

TIP

To use a modified character style in new documents based on the same template, select the **Add To Template** check box in the Modify Style dialog box. The modified style is added to the template attached to the current document.

MODIFY A CHARACTER STYLE

1. Click the **Styles And Formatting** button if the Styles And Formatting task pane is not already displayed.
2. Right-click the style you want to modify, and then click **Modify**.
3. Change any formatting options you want.
4. To display more options, click **Format** and then click the attribute—for example, **Font** or **Numbering**—you want to modify. Click **OK**.
5. Repeat step 4 for any additional attributes you want to change, clicking **OK** each time you are finished.
6. Close the Style And Formatting task pane.

Figure 4-5: Select a theme from the Style Gallery that you want to apply to your document.

USE THE STYLE GALLERY

Word 2003 contains a feature called the Style Gallery that you can use to copy styles from a different template to a document you are currently working on and apply those styles to the document. To use the Style Gallery:

1. Click **Format** and click **Theme**. The Theme dialog box appears (see Figure 4-5).
2. Click the **Style Gallery** button. The Style Gallery dialog box appears (see Figure 4-6).

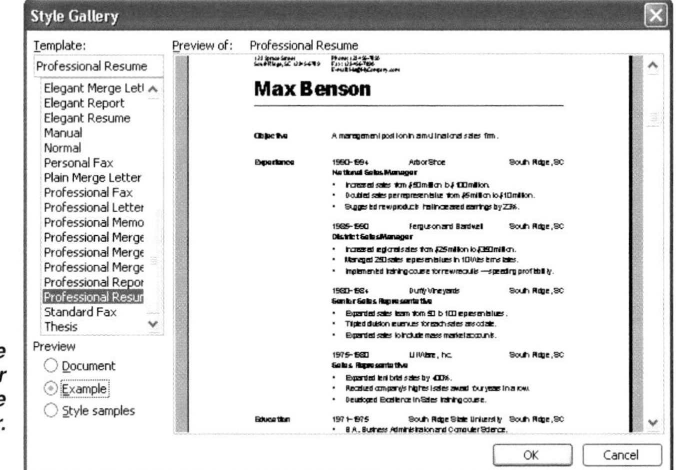

Figure 4-6: The Style Gallery is a useful tool for copying styles from one document to another.

UICKSTEPS

DELETING A STYLE

You might choose to delete a style that you created for a one-time-use document and don't ever plan to use again. To delete a style:

1. Click the **Styles And Formatting** button if the Styles And Formatting task pane is not already displayed.
2. Right-click the style you want to delete, and click **Delete**. A dialog box appears asking you to confirm the deletion.
3. Click **Yes** if you are sure you want to delete the style.
4. Close the Styles And Formatting task pane.

Keep in mind two things when deleting styles. When you delete a paragraph style, the Normal style (the default; see "Use the Normal Template" for more information) is applied to the text to which the deleted style had been applied. Furthermore, not all styles can be deleted. For example, the Normal style cannot be deleted, nor can heading styles.

TIP

You cannot preview a template unless it has been added to the Style Gallery. If you select a template that has not yet been added, a message will be displayed stating that you need to add the template. Click **OK** to add the template and apply it to your document.

CAUTION

Keep in mind that any changes you make to the Normal template will be applied to any future documents you create unless you specifically apply a different template.

3. Select a template from the Template list. An example of your document with the template's styles applied is displayed in the Preview area to the right.
4. Click **OK** if you want to apply the selected template to your document.

   –Or–

   Click **Cancel** to close the Style Gallery dialog box without applying any templates.

There are three options in the bottom-left corner of the Style Gallery dialog box:

- **Document** shows your document with the template applied to it.
- **Example** shows a sample document with the template applied to it.
- **Style Samples** shows each of your document's styles with the associated formatting applied to it.

Create and Use Templates

A *template* is a collection of styles and associated formatting features used to determine the overall appearance of a document, and it has an extension of .dot. Templates are always attached to documents, and Word 2003 comes with several templates that you can use to create letters, faxes, memos, and so on. Some of these templates include wizards to assist you in using them. The Microsoft Office web site (http://office.microsoft.com/templates/) has online templates that you can make use of as well. You can also create your own templates.

USE THE NORMAL TEMPLATE

The *Normal* template is the default template used by Word unless you tell it otherwise. It, like all templates, includes default styles, AutoText, toolbars, and other customizations that determine the general look of your document. You can customize the Normal template to the styles you want on a repetitive basis. To change the default styles of the Normal template:

1. With a Word document open, click the **File** menu, click **Open**, and then browse to C:\Documents And Settings*Your user name*\Application Data\Microsoft\Templates.

NOTE

If the Normal.dot template is renamed, damaged, or moved, Word automatically creates a new version (with the original default settings) the next time you start Word. The new version will not include any changes or modifications you made to the version that you renamed or moved.

NOTE

You can also create a new template based on a previously created document.

2. If no templates are listed in the Open dialog box, click the **Files Of Type** down arrow, and click Document Templates. If you still do not see Normal.dot, click **File**, click **File Search**, type normal.com in the Value field, click **Go**, and click **No** when asked if you want to add a property.
3. Double-click the **Normal.dot** file to open it. Ensure that you're working in the default template by verifying that that "Normal.dot" appears in the Word title bar.
4. Change the template by changing the styles using the steps described earlier in this chapter.
5. When you are finished making the changes you want, click **File** and click **Save** to resave Normal.dot.

CREATE A TEMPLATE

1. With Word open, click **File** and click **New**. The New Document task pane is displayed.
2. In the Templates area, click **On My Computer**. The Templates dialog box appears, as shown in Figure 4-7.

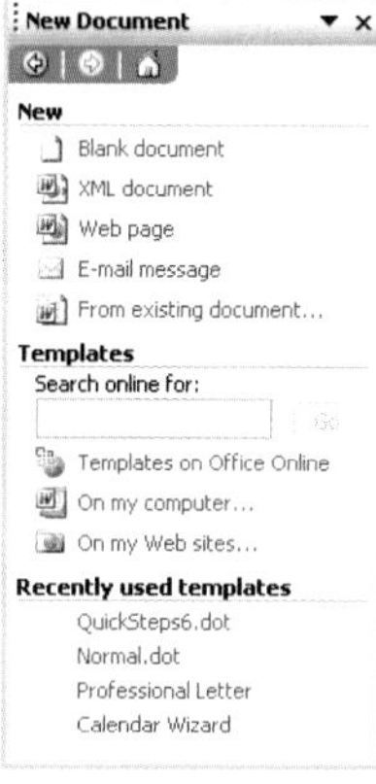

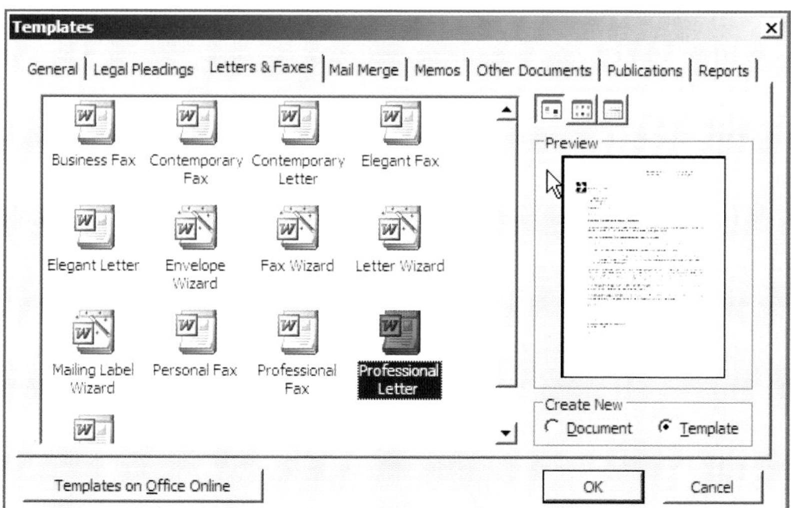

Figure 4-7: Word comes with several templates you can use to create letters, faxes, and more.

TIP

If you want to create a template based on a different type of document—for example, a web page or an e-mail message—select the relevant template instead of the Blank Document template in the Templates dialog box.

3. Verify that the **General** tab is active, and click the **Blank Document** icon.
4. Select the **Template** option in the Create New area located in the bottom-left corner of the Templates dialog box.
5. Click **OK**. A new template opens.

APPLY A TEMPLATE TO A NEW DOCUMENT

1. Click **File** and click **New** to open the New Document task pane.
2. Under Templates, click **On My Computer** to open the Templates dialog box.
3. Click the tab for the type of document you want to create, click the template you want to use, and click **OK**.

APPLY A TEMPLATE TO AN EXISTING DOCUMENT

1. With the document to which you want to apply the template open in Word, click **Tools** and click **Templates And Add-Ins**. The Templates And Add-Ins dialog box appears.

2. Click the **Attach** button. The Attach Template dialog box appears.
3. Click one of the locations on the left, or open the Look In drop-down list to locate the template you want to attach. Click the template you want, and click the **Open** button.
4. Click **OK**.

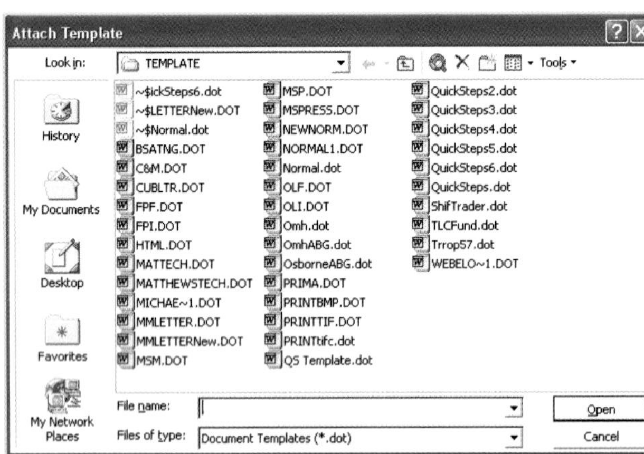

> **NOTE**
>
> In a normal or default installation, Word places its templates in two locations: Normal.dot is in C\Documents and Settings*user name*\Application Data\Microsoft\Templates\. This is also where you should store your custom templates. Many Word templates, such as Brochure.dot, Elegant Memo.dot, and Professional Letter.dot, are stored in C:\Program Files\Microsoft Office\Templates\1033\.

CUSTOMIZE WORD TEMPLATES

Word includes several ready-made templates that you can use to create such things as letters, faxes, and even legal pleadings. Some templates include a wizard that walks you through the process of customizing the template to best suit your needs (you will see the word "wizard" in the template name). You can use these templates as is (see "Apply a Template to a New Document" and "Apply a Template to an Existing Document"), or you can customize them to better fit your needs. To customize a Word template, you must open the template in Word.

1. Click **File** and click **Open**. Browse to the location of the template (see the accompanying Note) and double-click the template you want to modify. The template will open in Word. (Figure 4-8 shows the Professional Letter template.)
2. Click **Format** and click **Styles And Formatting** to open that task pane. Right-click any of the styles you want to change, and click **Modify**. Change the style as described in "Modify a Character Style." After modifying an individual style, click **OK.**

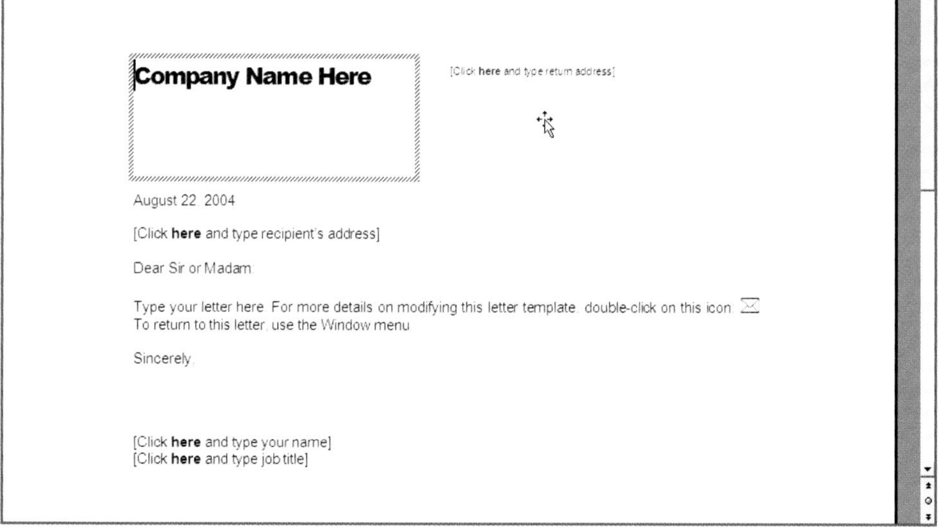

Figure 4-8: Word's templates have placeholder text indicating what and where you need to provide information.

A sample of the type of document created by each template and wizard is displayed in the Preview area of the Templates dialog box.

TIP

If you don't see section breaks displayed in your document, click the **Show/Hide** button in the toolbar. ¶

3. Modify as many of the styles as you want, and make other changes to the template to suit your needs. For example, you may want to add some recurring text. When you are done, you can close the Styles And Formatting task pane.
4. Save the template with a new name so that you can go back and use the original template in the future if you wish. You also should save the modified template to the Documents And Settings location mentioned in the accompanying Note.

Create Section Breaks

A *section break* indicates the end of a section in a document. You can use section breaks to vary the layout of a document within a page or between pages. For example, you might choose to format the introduction of a magazine article in a single column and format the body of the article in two columns. You must separately format each section, but the section break allows them to be different. Section breaks allow you to change the number of columns, page headers and footers, page numbering, page borders, page margins, and other characteristics and formatting within a section.

INSERT A SECTION BREAK

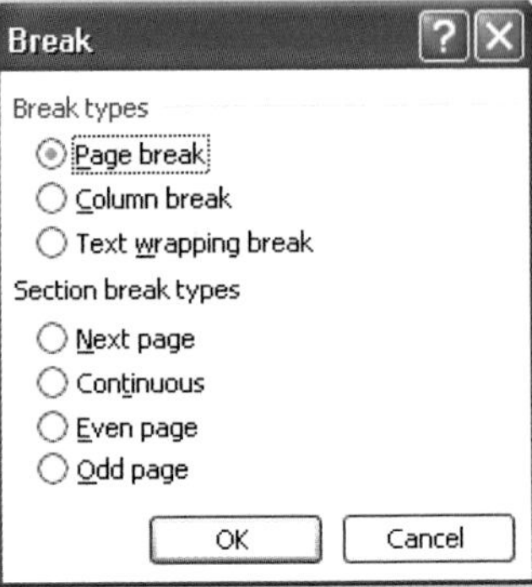

1. Open the document and click where you want to insert a section break.
2. Click **Insert** and click **Break**. The Break dialog box appears.
3. To set a simple break, in the Break Types area, select whether you want to start a new page, start a new column, or a change the way text wraps around a graphic.
4. To create a new section, in the Section Break Types area, select what comes after the break: the next page, the continuation of the current page, a new even-numbered page, or a new odd-numbered page.
5. Click **OK**. The section break is inserted.

> **NOTE**
>
> When you delete a section break, you also delete the specific formatting for the text above that break. That text becomes part of the following section and assumes the formatting of that section.

DELETE A SECTION BREAK

When a section break is inserted on a page you will see a note to that effect. You can delete the break by selecting that note.

:::::::::::::::Section Break (Next Page):::::::::::::::

1. Select the section break you want to delete.
2. Press **DELETE**.

CHANGE A SECTION BREAK

1. Click in the section of the document you want to change.
2. Click **File**, click **Page Setup**, and then click the **Layout** tab. The Page Setup dialog box appears.

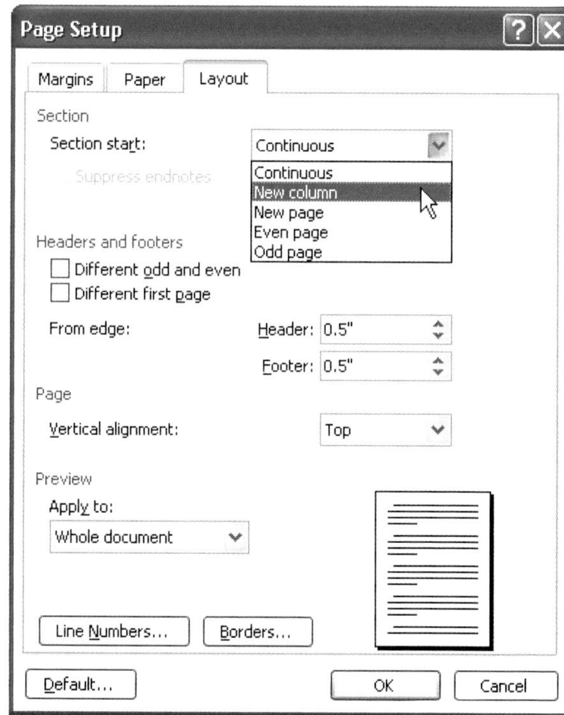

Figure 4-9: Use the Page Setup dialog box to modify a section break.

3. In the Section Start area, select the option for the section you want: Continuous, New column, New Page, Even Page, or Odd Page (see Figure 4-9).

Create and Use Columns

You can format your documents in a single column or in two or more columns, like text found in newspapers or magazines. To create columns in a document:

1. Place the insertion point at the place where you want the columns to begin.
2. Click **Format** and click **Columns** (you may have to expand the menu). The Columns dialog box appears. (See Figure 4-10.)
   - Click an icon in the Presets area, or type a number in the Number Of Columns box to set the number of columns you want.
   - Use the options in the Width And Spacing area to manually determine the dimensions of your columns and the amount of space between columns. To do this, you will have to clear the **Equal Column Width** check box.
   - Select the **Line Between** check box if you want Word to insert a vertical line between columns.
   - Use the **Apply To** list box to select the part of the document to which you want your selections to apply: Whole Document, This Section, Selected Text, or This Point Forward. Select **This Point Forward** and then select the **Start New Column** check box if you want to insert a column break at an insertion point.
3. Click **OK** when finished.

TIP

The Preview area in the Columns dialog box displays the effects of your changes as you change the various column settings.

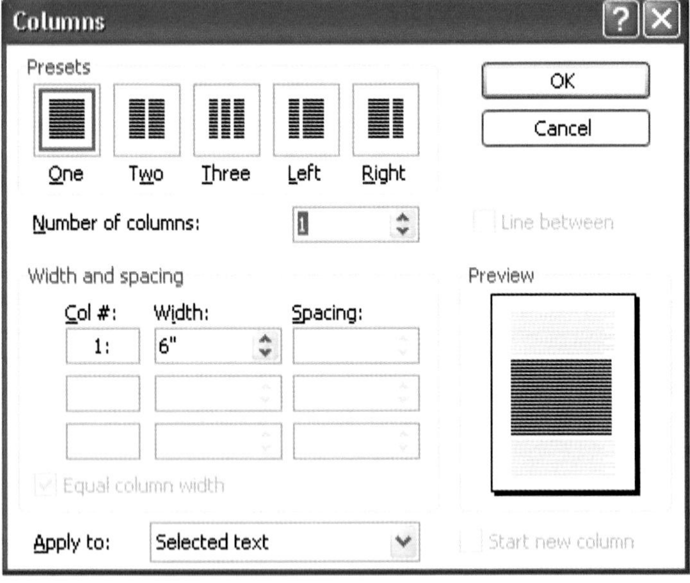

Figure 4-10: Use the Columns dialog box to create and format columns in your documents.

Work with Documents

In addition to using styles and templates to format your documents, you can use tabs, headers and footers, tables of contents, and indexes to further refine your documents.

> **TIP**
>
> Word has default tab stops set at every half-inch. To change these, click the **Format** menu and click **Tabs**. In the Default Tab Stops field, enter the amount of spacing you want between tab stops.

Use Tabs

A *tab* is a type of formatting usually used to align text and create simple tables. By default, Word 2003 has *tab stops* (the horizontal position of the insertion point when you press TAB) every half-inch. Tabs are better than space characters in such instances because tabs are set to specific measurements, while spaces may not always align the way you intend due to the size and spacing of individual characters in a given font.

Word 2003 supports five kinds of tabs:

- **Left tab** aligns text to the left of the tab stop.
- **Center tab** aligns text directly beneath the tab stop.
- **Right tab** aligns text to the right of the tab stop.
- **Decimal tab** aligns the decimal point of tabbed numbers beneath the tab stop.
- **Bar tab** aligns text with a vertical line that is displayed beneath the tab stop.

To align text with a tab, press the TAB key before the text you want aligned.

SET TABS USING THE RULER

To set tabs using the ruler at the top of a page:

1. Select the text, from one line to an entire document, in which you want to set one or more tab stops.
2. Click the **Left Tab** icon, located at the far left of the horizontal ruler until it changes to the type of tab you want:

Left Tab Right Tab Bar Tab
Center Tab Decimal Tab

3. Click the horizontal ruler where you want to set a tab stop.

1 2 3 4 5 6 7 8 9 10

TIP

When working with tabs, it's a good idea to display text formatting so that you can distinguish tabs from spaces. To display formatting, click the **Show/Hide** button.

SET TABS USING MEASUREMENTS

To set tabs according to specific measurements:

1. Click **Format** and click **Tabs**. The Tabs dialog box appears (see Figure 4-11).
2. Enter the measurements you want in the Tab Stop Position text box. Click **Set**.
3. Repeat step 2 for as many tabs as you want to set. Click **OK** to close the dialog box.

SET TABS WITH LEADERS

You can also set tabs with *tab leaders*—characters that fill the space otherwise left by a tab—for example, a solid, dotted, or dashed line.

1. Click **Format** and click **Tabs**. The Tabs dialog box appears.
2. In the Tab Stop Position text box, type the position for a new tab, or select an existing tab stop to which you want to add a tab leader.
3. In the Alignment area, select the alignment for text typed at the tab stop.
4. In the Leader area, select the leader option you want, and then click **Set**.
5. Repeat steps 2 through 4 for additional tabs. When you are done, click **OK** to close the dialog box.

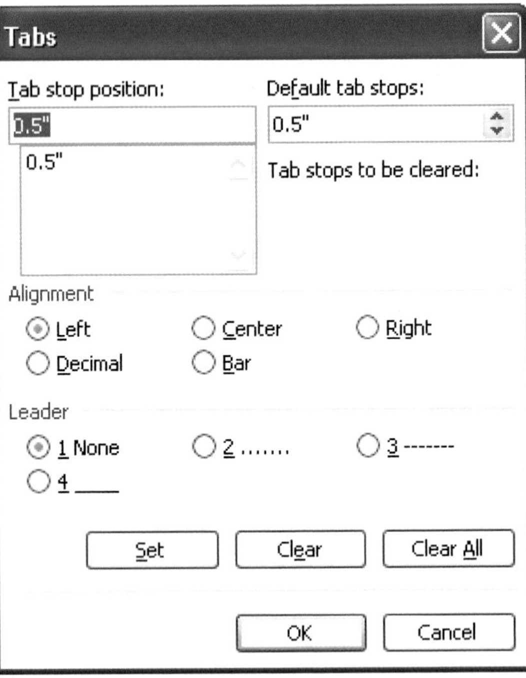

Figure 4-11: From the Tabs dialog box, you can format specific tab measurements and set tab leaders.

Add Headers and Footers

Headers and footers are parts of a document that contain information such as page numbers, revision dates, the document title, and so on. The header appears at the top of every page, and the footer appears at the bottom of every page. Figure 4-12 shows the buttons available on the Header And Footer toolbar.

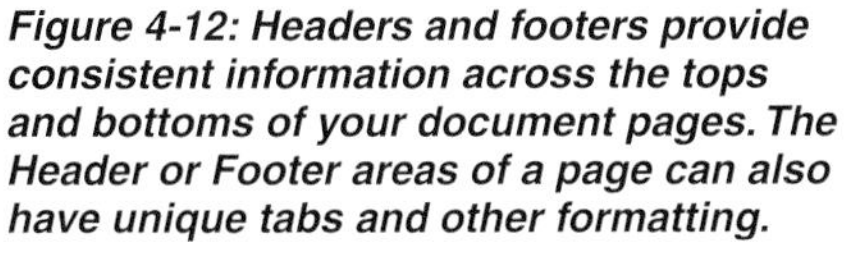

Figure 4-12: Headers and footers provide consistent information across the tops and bottoms of your document pages. The Header or Footer areas of a page can also have unique tabs and other formatting.

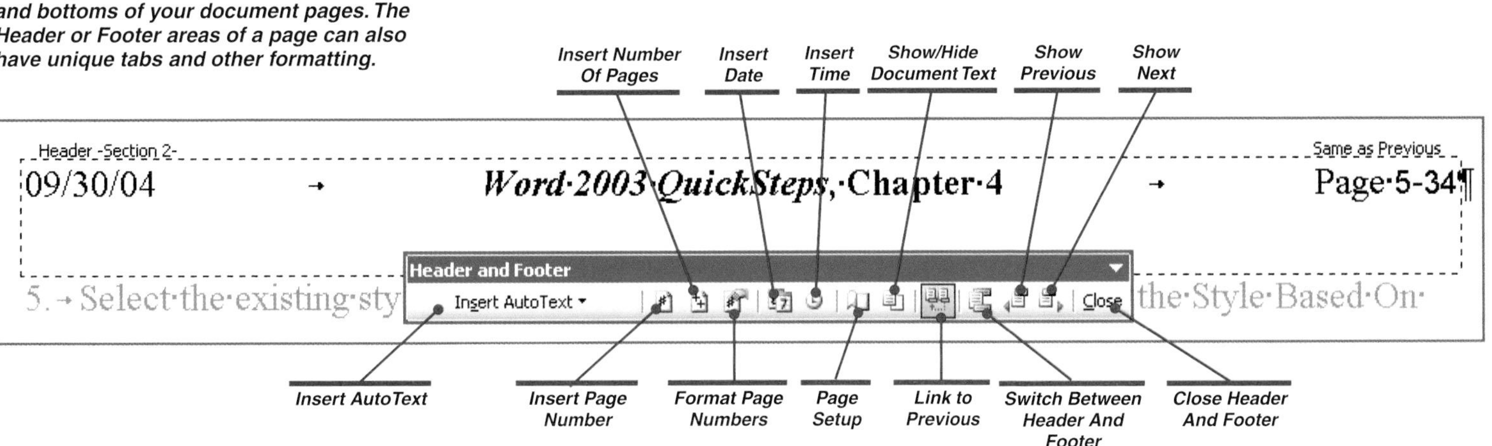

QUICKSTEPS

USING DIFFERENT LEFT AND RIGHT HEADERS

Different left and right pages use section breaks to allow different margins and tabs. Sometimes you might want to create a document that has different left and right headers and/or footers. For example, you might have a brochure, pamphlet, or manuscript in which all odd-numbered pages have a title in the header and all even-numbered pages have the author's name or other information.

To create different left and right headers and/or footers:

1. Open the document to which you want to add a different left and right header or footer (see Chapter 2).
2. Click the **View** menu and click **Header And Footer**. The header area will be displayed along with the Header And Footer toolbar. On the Header And Footer toolbar, click the **Page Setup** button. The Page Setup dialog box appears.
3. Click the **Layout** tab.
4. Select the **Different Odd And Even** check box, and then click **OK**.

Headers and footers
☐ Different odd and even
☐ Different first page
From edge: Header: 0.5"
Footer: 0.5"

5. If necessary, in the Header And Footer toolbar, click the **Show Previous** or **Show Next** buttons to move to the odd or even header or footer areas.
6. Create the header or footer for odd-numbered pages in the Odd Page Header or Odd Page Footer area, and create the header or footer for even-numbered pages in the Even Page Header or Even Page Footer area.
7. When finished, click the **Close Header And Footer** button.

CREATE A HEADER OR FOOTER

1. Open the document to which you want to add a header or footer (see Chapter 2).
2. Click the **View** menu and click **Header And Footer**. The header area will be displayed along with the Header And Footer toolbar.
3. Type the text you want displayed in the header. To type text in the footer, click the **Switch Between Header And Footer** button, and type the text you want displayed in the footer.

4. When finished, click the **Close Header And Footer** button.

EDIT A HEADER OR FOOTER

1. Open the document to which you want to add a header or footer (see Chapter 2).
2. Click the **View** menu and click **Header And Footer**. The header area will be displayed along with the Header And Footer toolbar, as shown in Figure 4-12.
3. If necessary, click the **Show Previous** or **Show Next** buttons on the Header And Footer toolbar to display the header or footer you want to edit.

4. Edit the header or footer. For example, you might revise text, change the font, apply bold formatting, or add a date or time.
5. When finished, click the **Close Header And Footer** button.

DELETE A HEADER OR FOOTER

1. Open the document from which you want to delete a header or footer (see Chapter 2).
2. Click the **View** menu and click **Header And Footer**. The header area will be displayed along with the Header And Footer toolbar.
3. If necessary, click **Show Previous** or **Show Next** on the Header And Footer toolbar to move to the header or footer you want to delete.
4. Select the text or graphics you want to delete, and press DELETE.

NOTE

When you edit a header or footer, Word automatically changes the same header or footer throughout the document unless the document contains different headers or footers in a section. When you delete a header or footer, Word automatically deletes the same header or footer throughout the entire document. To delete a header or footer for part of a document, you must first divide the document into sections and then create a different header or footer for part of a document. (See "Create Section Breaks" for more information.)

Add Footnotes and Endnotes

Footnotes and *endnotes* are types of annotations in a document usually used to provide citation information or to provide additional information for readers. The difference between the two is where they appear in a document. Footnotes appear either after the last line of text on the page or at the bottom of the page on which the annotated text appears. Endnotes appear either at the end of the section in which the annotated text appears or at the end of the document.

INSERT A FOOTNOTE OR ENDNOTE

1. Position the insertion point immediately after the text you want to annotate.
2. Click **Insert**, click **Reference**, and then click **Footnote**. The Footnote And Endnote dialog box appears (see Figure 4-13).
3. Select the **Footnotes** or **Endnotes** option.
4. In the Number Format box, select the type of numbering you want from the drop-down list.
5. Click **Insert**. Word inserts the note number and places the insertion point next to the note number.
6. Type the note text.
7. When finished, return the insertion point to the body of your document and continue typing.

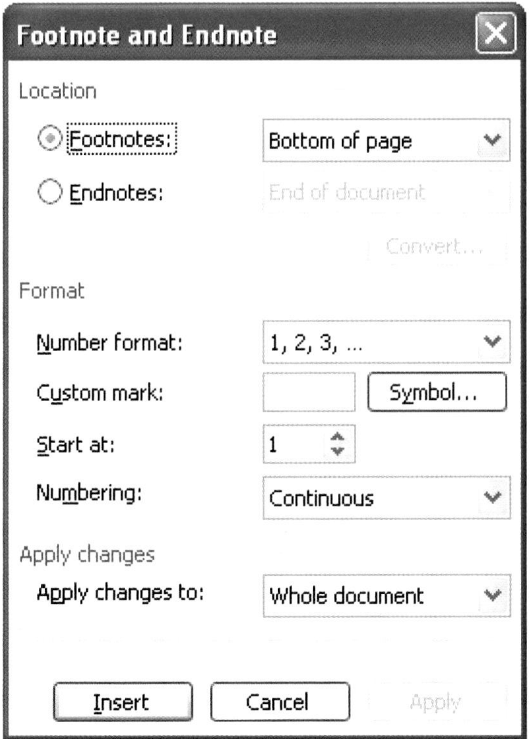

Figure 4-13: Footnotes and endnotes provide supplemental information to the body of your document.

NOTE

Word automatically places footnotes at the end of each page and endnotes at the end of the document. You can change the placement of footnotes and endnotes using the drop-down list boxes to the right of the Footnotes and Endnotes options.

NOTE

When deleting an endnote or footnote, make sure to delete the number corresponding to the annotation and not the actual text in the note. If you delete the text but not the number, the placeholder for the annotation will remain.

DELETE A FOOTNOTE OR ENDNOTE

In the document, select the number of the note you want to delete, and then press DELETE. Word automatically renumbers the notes.

CONVERT FOOTNOTES TO ENDNOTES OR CONVERT ENDNOTES TO FOOTNOTES

1. Select the reference number or symbol in the body of a document for the footnote or endnote.
2. Click **Insert**, click **Reference**, and then click **Footnote**.
3. Click the **Convert** button. The Convert Notes dialog box appears.
4. Select the option you want (if more than one is available), and then click **OK**.
5. Click **Close**.

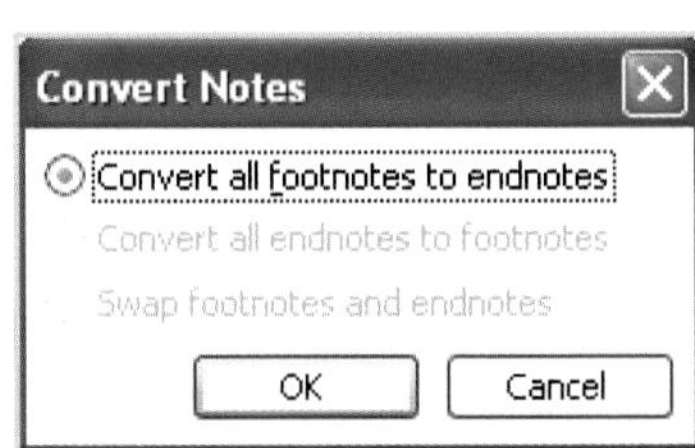

Create an Index

An *index* is an alphabetical list of words or phrases in a document and the corresponding page references. Indexes created using Word can include main entries and subentries as well as cross-references. When creating an index in Word, you first need to tag the index entries and then generate the index.

TAG INDEX ENTRIES

1. In the document in which you want to build an index, select the word or phrase you want to use as an index entry. If you want an index entry to use text that you separately enter instead of using existing text in the document as the entry, place the insertion point in the document where you want your new index entry to refer.
2. Press **ALT+SHIFT+X**. The Mark Index Entry dialog box appears (see Figure 4-14).
3. Type or edit the text in the Main Entry box. Customize the entry by creating a subentry or by creating a cross-reference to another entry, if desired.
4. Select the **Bold** or **Italic** check box in the Page Number Format area to determine how the page numbers will appear in the index.
5. Click **Mark**. To mark all occurrences of this text in the document, click **Mark All**.

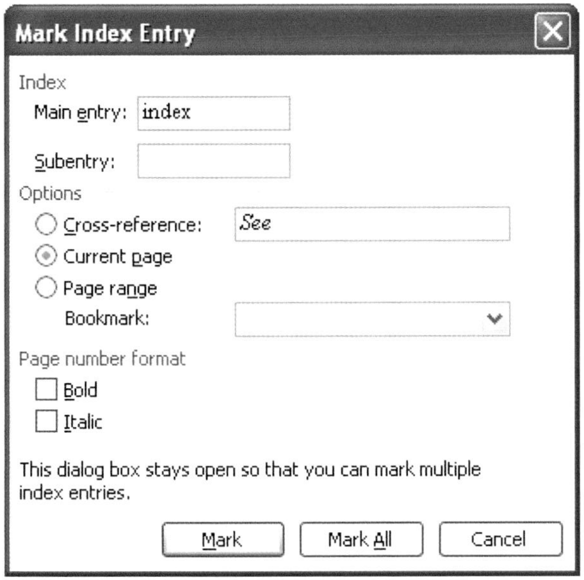

6. Repeat steps 3 through 5 to mark additional index entries on the same page.
7. Close the dialog box when finished.
8. Repeat steps 1 through 7 for the remaining entries in the document.

Figure 4-14: You need to tag index entries before you can generate an index.

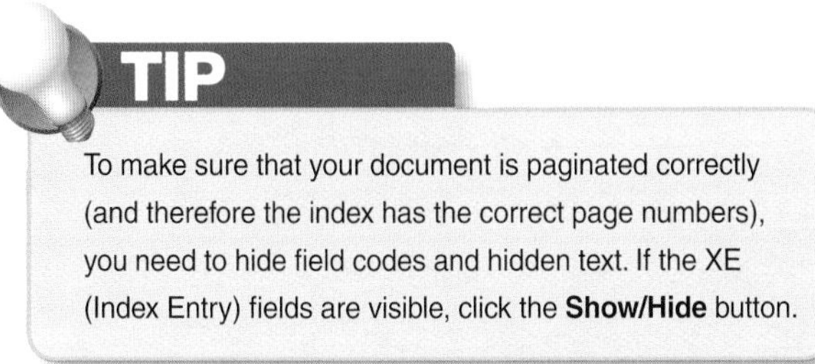

TIP

To make sure that your document is paginated correctly (and therefore the index has the correct page numbers), you need to hide field codes and hidden text. If the XE (Index Entry) fields are visible, click the **Show/Hide** button.

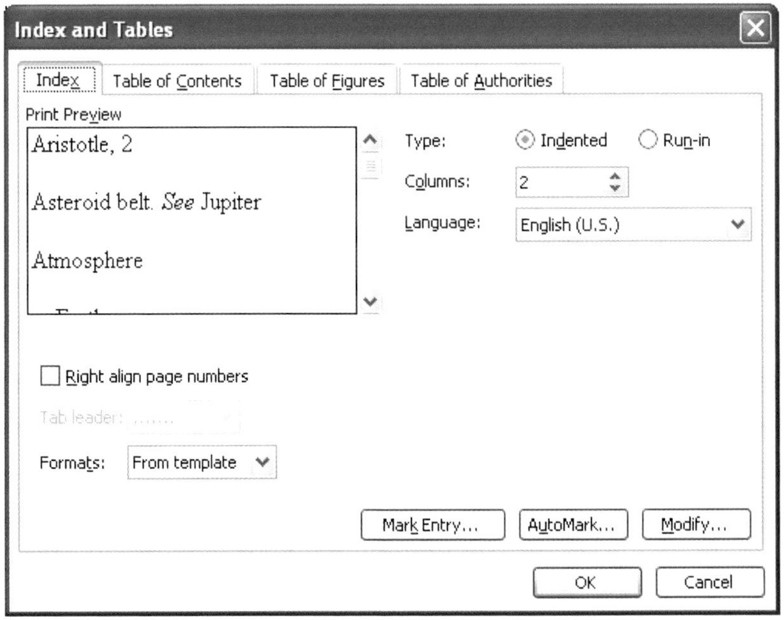

GENERATE AN INDEX

1. Position the insertion point where you want to insert the finished index (this will normally be at the end of the document).
2. Click **Insert**, click **Reference**, click **Index And Tables**, and then, if needed, click the **Index** tab (see Figure 4-15).
3. Select a design in the Formats box to use one of the available designs, such as Classic or Fancy.
4. Select whether to right-align page numbers, the type of leader to use, whether to indent entries with multiple lines, the number of columns to use, and, if you're building an index for text in another language, select the language.
5. Click **OK** when finished. Word generates the index.

Figure 4-15: Use the options and settings in the Index And Tables dialog box to determine how your index will look.

Create a Table of Contents

A *table of contents* is a list of the headings in the order in which they appear in the document. If you have formatted paragraphs with heading styles, you can automatically generate a table of contents based on those headings. If you have not used the heading styles, then, as with indexes, you must first tag table of content (or TOC) entries and then generate the table of contents.

TAG TABLE OF CONTENTS ENTRIES

1. Click **View**, click **Toolbars**, and click **Outlining**. The Outlining toolbar is displayed (see Figure 4-16).
2. Select the first piece of text (remember that headings, formatted as such, are automatically in the TOC) that you want to appear in the table of contents.
3. On the Outlining toolbar, select the outline level that you want to associate with the selected paragraph.
4. Repeat steps 2 and 3 for each heading that you want to include in the table of contents.

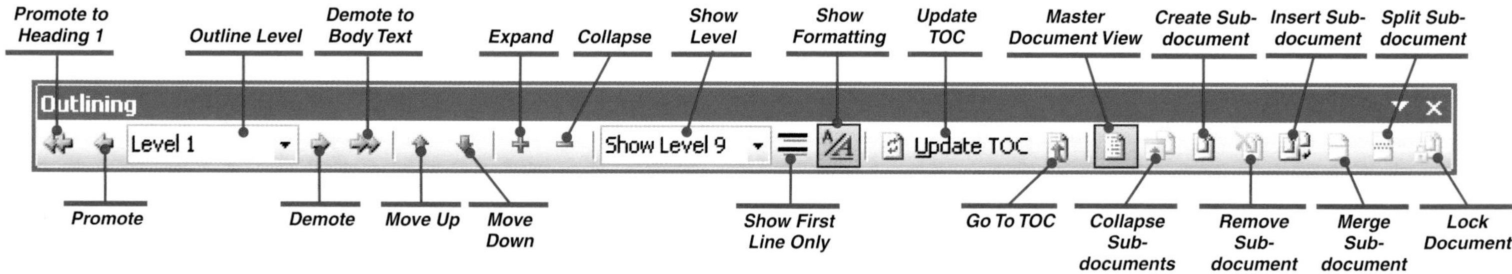

Figure 4-16: Use the Outlining toolbar to mark entries for a table of contents. The Outlining toolbar also provides a number of ways to work with outlines.

TIP

You can also tag TOC entries by selecting the text that you want to include in your table of contents. Press ALT+SHIFT+O. The Mark Table Of Contents Entry dialog box appears. In the Level box, select the level and click **Mark**. If you have multiple tables of contents, you can identify to which table the current entry belongs by using the Table Identifier. To mark additional entries, select the text, click in the Entry box, and click **Mark**. When you have finished adding entries, close the dialog box.

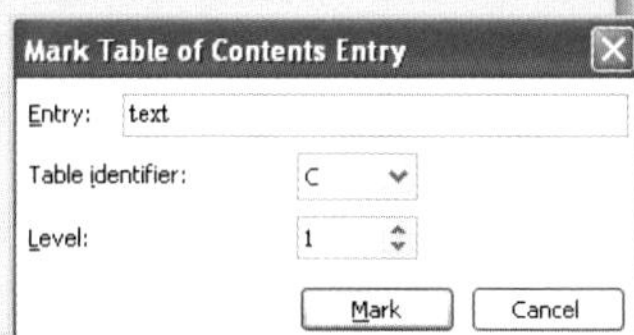

TIP

It is a good idea to place a table of contents in its own section where you can have separate formatting, margins, and page numbers. If you want to do this, create the section before creating the TOC. See "Create Section Breaks" earlier in this chapter.

TIP

If you want to create a special TOC with just your manual entries, click the **Options** button on the Table Of Contents tab. Clear the **Style** and **Outline Levels** check boxes, and select the **Table Entry Fields** check box.

GENERATE A TABLE OF CONTENTS

1. Place the insertion point where you want to insert the table of contents (normally at the beginning of the document).
2. Click **Insert**, click **Reference**, and click **Index And Tables**.
3. Click the **Table Of Contents** tab (see Figure 4-17).
4. To use one of the available designs, select a design in the Formats box.
5. Select any other table of contents options you want.
6. Click **OK** when finished.

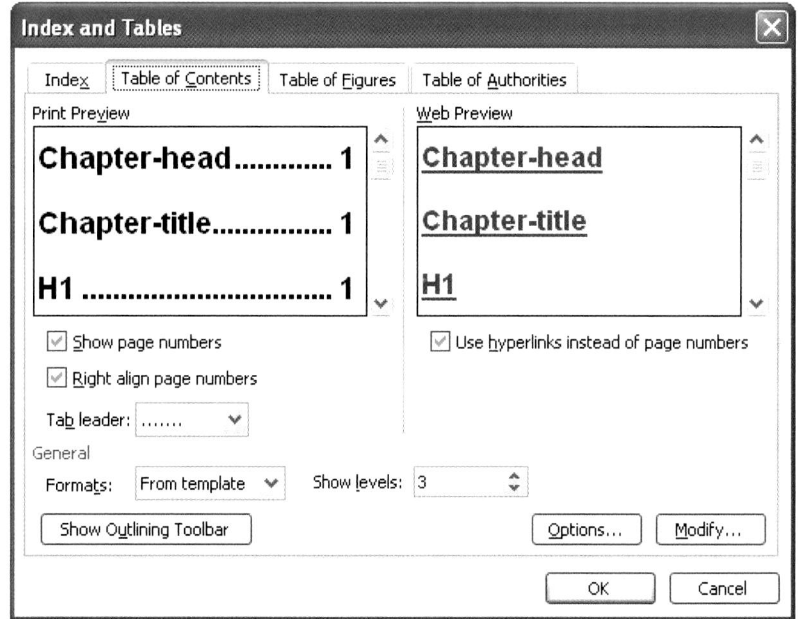

Figure 4-17: Use the options and settings in the Index And Tables dialog box to determine how your table of contents will look.

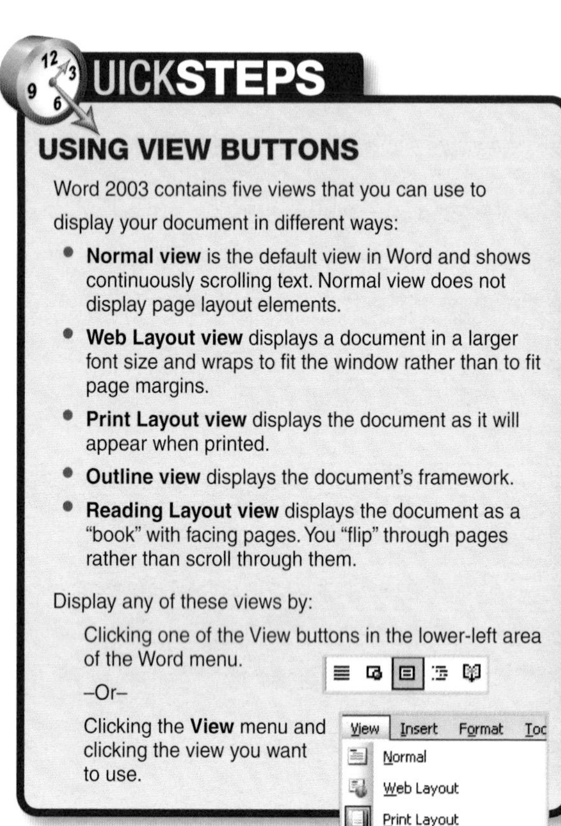

QUICKSTEPS

USING VIEW BUTTONS

Word 2003 contains five views that you can use to display your document in different ways:

- **Normal view** is the default view in Word and shows continuously scrolling text. Normal view does not display page layout elements.
- **Web Layout view** displays a document in a larger font size and wraps to fit the window rather than to fit page margins.
- **Print Layout view** displays the document as it will appear when printed.
- **Outline view** displays the document's framework.
- **Reading Layout view** displays the document as a "book" with facing pages. You "flip" through pages rather than scroll through them.

Display any of these views by:

Clicking one of the View buttons in the lower-left area of the Word menu.

–Or–

Clicking the **View** menu and clicking the view you want to use.

Create and Use Outlines

An *outline* is a framework upon which a document is based. It is a hierarchical list of the headings in a document. You might use an outline to help you organize your ideas and thoughts when writing a speech, a term paper, a book, or a research project. The Outline view in Word makes it easy to build and refine your outlines.

1. Open a new blank document (see Chapter 1). Click **View** and click **Outline**. Word switches to Outline view, and the Outlining toolbar is displayed (see Figure 4-16).
2. Type your heading text and press ENTER. Word formats the headings using the built-in heading style Heading 1.
3. To assign a heading to a different level and apply the corresponding heading style, place the insertion point in the heading, and then click the **Promote** or **Demote** buttons on the Outlining toolbar until the heading is at the level you want.
4. To move a heading to a different location, place the insertion point in the heading, and then click the **Move Up** or **Move Down** buttons on the Outlining toolbar until the heading is where you want it. (If a heading is collapsed, the subordinate text under the heading moves with the heading.)
5. When you're satisfied with the organization, switch to Normal view, Print Layout view, or Web Layout view to add detailed body text and graphics. (See the QuickSteps "Using View Buttons" for more information.)

Use Word Writing Aids

Word 2003 provides several aids that can assist you in not only creating your document, but also in making sure that it is as professional-looking as possible. These include AutoCorrect, AutoFormat, AutoText, AutoSummarize, character and word counts, highlighting, hyphenation, and a thesaurus.

Implement AutoCorrect

The AutoCorrect feature automatically corrects common typographical errors when you make them. While Word 2003 comes preconfigured with hundreds of AutoCorrect entries, you can also manually add entries.

CONFIGURE AUTOCORRECT

1. Click **Tools**, expand the menu if necessary, and click **AutoCorrect Options**. The AutoCorrect: <Language> dialog box appears.
2. Click the **AutoCorrect** tab (if it is not already displayed), and select the following options, according to your preferences (see Figure 4-18):

   - **Show AutoCorrect Options Buttons** displays a small blue button or bar beneath text that was automatically corrected. Click this button to see a menu where you can undo the correction or set AutoCorrect options.

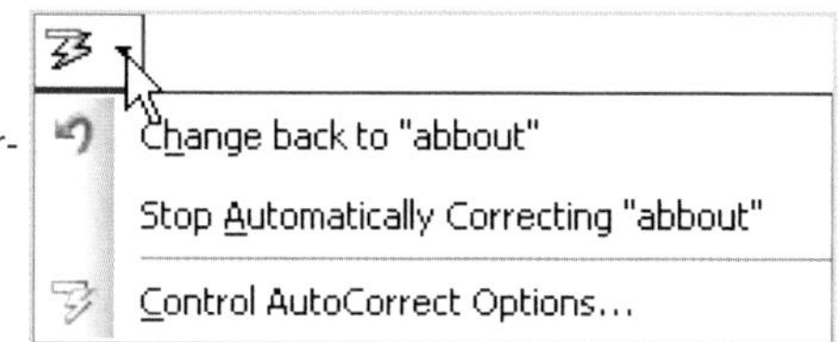

   - **Correct TWo INitial CApitals** changes the second letter in a pair of capital letters to lowercase.
   - **Capitalize the first letter of sentences** capitalizes the first letter following the end of a sentence.
   - **Capitalize the first letter of table cells** capitalizes the first letter of a word in a table cell.
   - **Capitalize names of days** capitalizes the names of the days of the week.
   - **Correct accidental usage of cAPS LOCK key** corrects capitalization errors that occur when you type with the CAPS LOCK key depressed and turns off this key.
   - **Automatically use suggestions from the spelling checker** tells Word to replace spelling errors with words from the dictionary as you type.

3. Click **OK** when finished.

Figure 4-18: Use the AutoCorrect tab to determine what items Word will automatically correct for you as you type.

ADD AN AUTOCORRECT ENTRY

1. Click **Tools** and click **AutoCorrect Options**. The AutoCorrect: <Language> dialog box appears.
2. Click the **AutoCorrect** tab (if it is not already displayed).
3. Type the text that you want to automatically replace in the Replace box. Type the text that you want to replace it with in the With box.
4. Click **Add** and click **OK**.

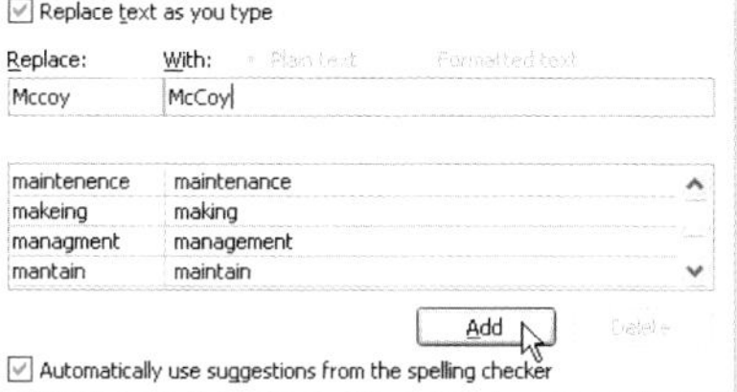

DELETE AN AUTOCORRECT ENTRY

1. Click **Tools** and click **AutoCorrect Options**. The AutoCorrect: <Language> dialog box appears.
2. Click the **AutoCorrect** tab (if it is not already displayed).
3. Scroll through the list of AutoCorrect entries, and click the entry you want to delete.
4. Click **Delete** and click **OK**.

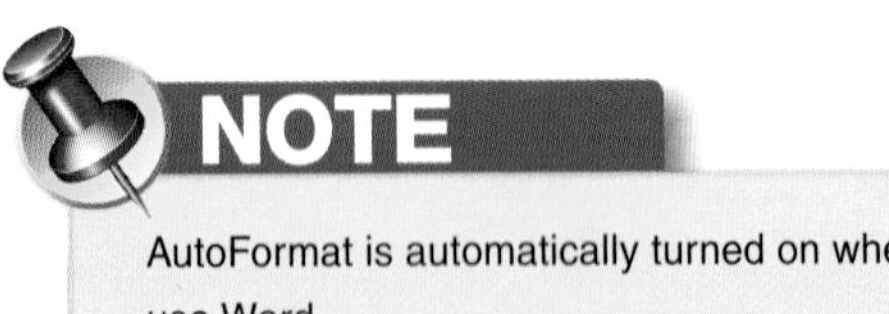

NOTE

AutoFormat is automatically turned on when you first use Word.

Use AutoFormat

AutoFormat automatically formats a document—as you type it or when the document is complete—by applying the associated styles to text depending on how it is used in the document. For example, Word will automatically format two dashes (--) into an em dash (—) or will automatically format Internet and e-mail addresses as hyperlinks.

To use AutoFormat on a completed document:

1. Click **Format** and click **AutoFormat**. An AutoFormat dialog box appears.
2. Select **AutoFormat Now** to use AutoFormat without reviewing the changes, or select **AutoFormat And Review Each Change** to review each change individually as you use AutoFormat.
3. Click **OK**. If you selected AutoFormat Now, AutoFormat runs and the process is complete.
4. If you selected AutoFormat And Review Each Change, AutoFormat runs. Another AutoFormat dialog box appears. Click one of the following four buttons:
   - **Accept All** accepts all the changes in the document.
   - **Reject All** rejects all the changes in the document.
   - **Review Changes** gives you the opportunity to review the changes individually using the Review AutoFormat Changes dialog box.
   - **Style Gallery** displays the Style Gallery dialog box so you can select a different template (see "Use the Style Gallery" for more information). Upon selecting a template, you are returned to the AutoFormat dialog box.

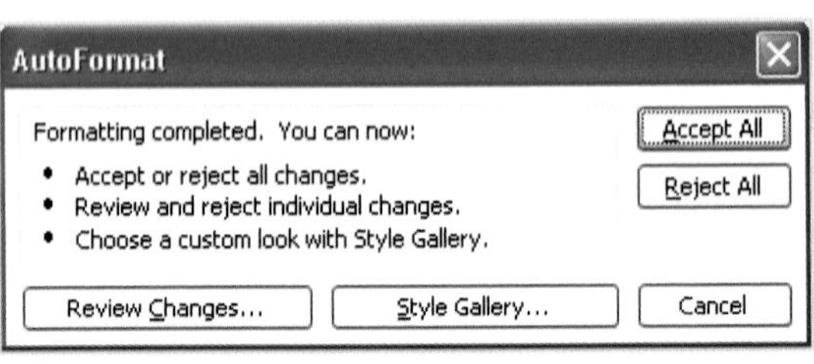

5. If you click **Review Changes**, The Review AutoFormat Changes dialog box appears. To start the review, click the **Find** button with the right-pointing arrow. The first change is selected and explained.

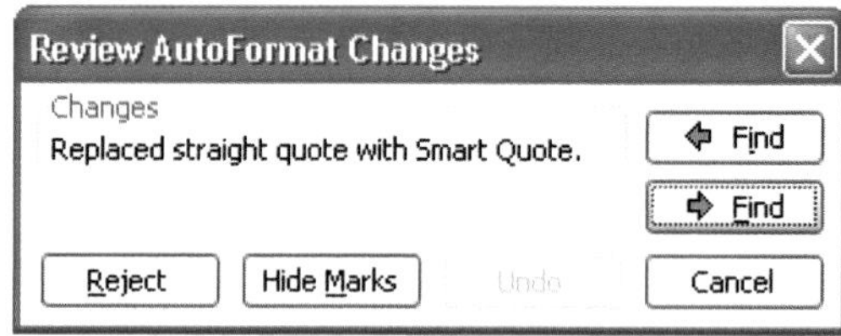

6. To accept a change, click the **Find** button with the right-pointing arrow. To reject a change, click **Reject**. After you accept or reject a change, Word moves to the next correction in the document.
7. When you reach the end of the document, a dialog box is displayed asking if you want to continue searching from the beginning. Click **Cancel** twice.
8. Click **Accept All** to accept any changes you did not reject.

SET AUTOFORMAT OPTIONS

1. Click **Format** and click **AutoFormat**. An AutoFormat dialog box appears.
2. Click the **Options** button. The AutoCorrect dialog box appears. Click the **AutoFormat** tab if it is not already selected.
3. Select from among the following options, depending on your preferences (see Figure 4-19):
   - **Built-In Heading Styles** applies heading styles to heading text.
   - **List Styles** applies list and bullet styles to numbered and bulleted lists.
   - **Automatic Bulleted Lists** applies bulleted list formatting to paragraphs beginning with *, o, or – followed by a space or tab character.
   - **Other Paragraph Styles** applies other styles.
   - **"Straight Quotes" With "Smart Quotes"** replaces plain quotation characters with curly quotation characters.
   - **Ordinals (1st) With Superscript** formats ordinal numbers (numbers designating items in an ordered sequence) with a superscript. For example, 1st becomes 1st.
   - **Fractions (1/2) With Fraction Character (½)** replaces fractions typed with numbers and slashes with fraction characters.
   - **Hyphens (--) With Dash (—)** replaces a single hyphen with an en dash (–) and two hyphens with an em dash (—).

Figure 4-19: Use the AutoFormat tab to determine what items Word will automatically format for you as you type.

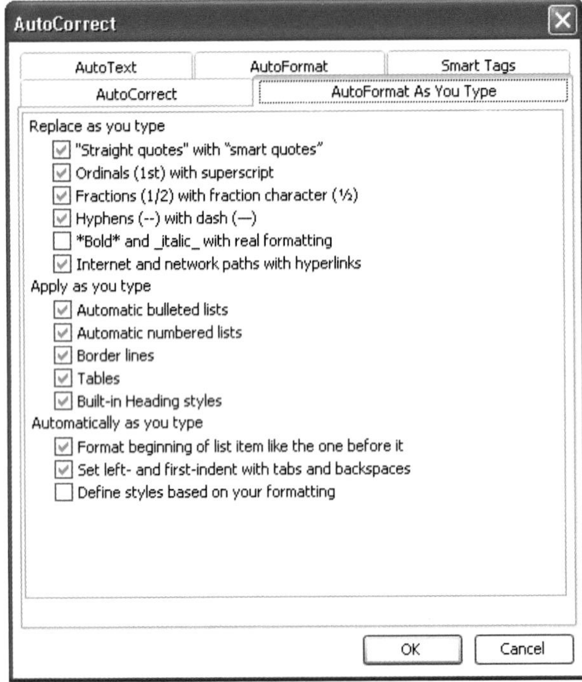

Figure 4-20: Use the AutoFormat As You Type tab to further determine what items Word will automatically format for you as you type.

- ***Bold* And _Italic_ With Real Formatting** formats text enclosed within asterisks (*) as bold and text enclosed within underscores (_) as italic.
- **Internet And Network Paths With Hyperlinks** formats e-mail addresses and URLs (Uniform Resource Locator—the address of a Web page on the Internet or an intranet) as clickable hyperlink fields.
- **Styles** prevents styles already applied in your document from being changed.
- **Plain Text WordMail Documents** enables you to format e-mail messages when using Word as your e-mail editor.

4. Click **OK** when finished.

SET AUTOMATIC FORMATTING OPTIONS

1. Click **Format** and click **AutoFormat**. An AutoFormat dialog box appears.
2. Click the **Options** button. The AutoCorrect dialog box appears. Click the **AutoFormat As You Type** tab.
3. Select from among the options, depending on your preferences (some of which are already explained in the previous section) (see Figure 4-20):
   - **Automatic Numbered Lists** applies numbered list formatting to paragraphs beginning with a number or letter followed by a space or a tab character.
   - **Border Lines** automatically applies paragraph border styles when you type three or more hyphens, underscores, or equal signs (=).
   - **Tables** creates a table when you type a series of hyphens with plus signs to indicate column edges.
   - **Format Beginning Of List Item Like The One Before It** repeats character formatting that you apply to the beginning of a list item. For example, if you format the first word of a list item in bold, the first word of all subsequent list items are formatted in bold.
   - **Set Left- And First-Indent With Tabs And Backspaces** sets left indentation on the tab ruler based on the tabs and backspaces you type.
   - **Define Styles Based On Your Formatting** automatically creates or modifies styles based on manual formatting that you apply to your document.
4. Click **OK** when finished.

Apply AutoText

The AutoText feature automatically inserts blocks of text that you type often, such as a greeting or closing or boilerplate text.

INSERT AN AUTOTEXT ENTRY

1. Place the insertion point in the document where you want to insert the AutoText entry.
2. Click the **Insert** menu, click **AutoText**, and then select the type of entry you want to insert, for example, **Salutation**. (See Figure 4-21.)

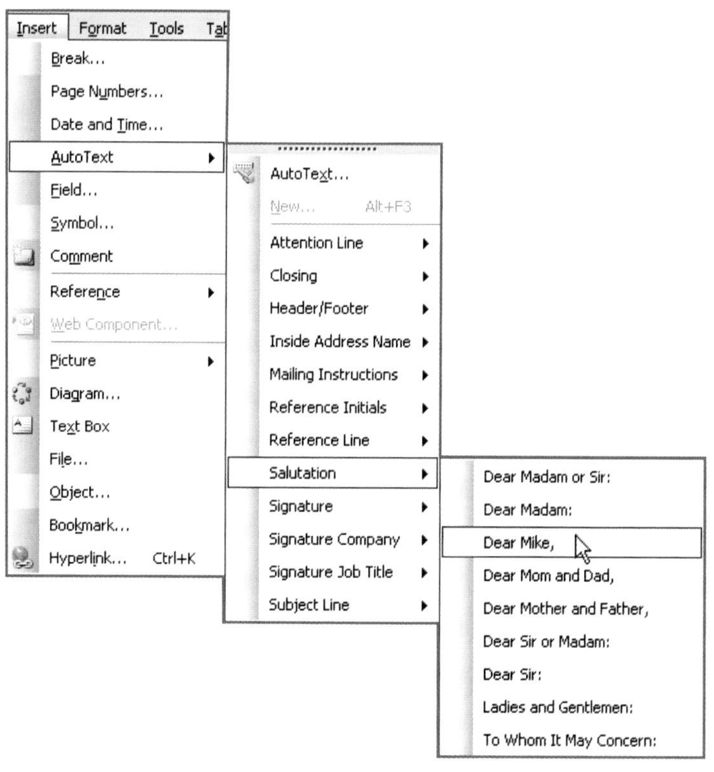

Figure 4-21: Word provides certain AutoText entries that you can use when composing documents.

CREATE AN AUTOTEXT ENTRY

1. Select the text or graphic you want to store as an AutoText entry. (Include the paragraph mark in the selection if you want to store paragraph formatting.)
2. Click the **Insert** menu, click **AutoText**, and then click **New**.
3. The Create AutoText dialog box appears. Accept the suggested name for the AutoText entry, or type a short abbreviation for a new one.
4. Click **OK**.

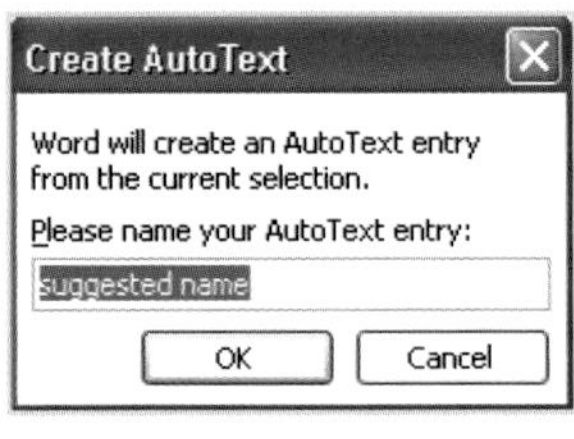

–Or–

1. After selecting the text or graphic you want as an AutoText entry, click the **Insert** menu, click **AutoText**, and click **AutoText** again. The AutoCorrect dialog box appears with the AutoText tab selected.
2. Type the text that you want to use to recall the AutoText entry in the Enter AutoText Entries Here text box (see Figure 4-22).
3. Click **Add**. The entry is added to the list.
4. Repeat steps 2 and 3 to create additional entries. Click **OK** when finished.

NOTE

You cannot undo the deletion of an AutoText entry. The only way to restore an AutoText entry is to re-create it.

Figure 4-22: You can create your own AutoText entries for use with custom documents.

DELETE AN AUTOTEXT ENTRY

1. Click the **Insert** menu, click **AutoText**, and click **AutoText** again. The AutoCorrect dialog box appears.
2. In the Enter AutoText Entries Here list, select the name of the AutoText entry you want to delete.
3. Click **Delete** and click **OK**.

NOTE

AutoSummarize, in most cases, only gives you a start at a summary and normally requires a fair amount of effort to transform the results into a usable summary.

Use AutoSummarize

Word can automatically create a summary of a document for you. You can see what Word thinks are the key points of a document, create a new document with just the summary, or place the summary at the beginning of the document. You can also choose how long you want the summary to be. Once you have the summary, you can edit and expand it as you wish. To create a summary of a document:

1. Open the document you want to summarize in Word.
2. Click **Tools** and click **AutoSummarize**. The AutoSummarize dialog box appears, as shown in Figure 4-23.
3. Choose whether you want to look at what Word thinks are the highlights, create a separate document, or add the summary to the existing document.
4. Choose how long you want the summary to be, and observe the statistics.
5. Determine if you want to update the document statistics for the added words and length, and then click **OK**.

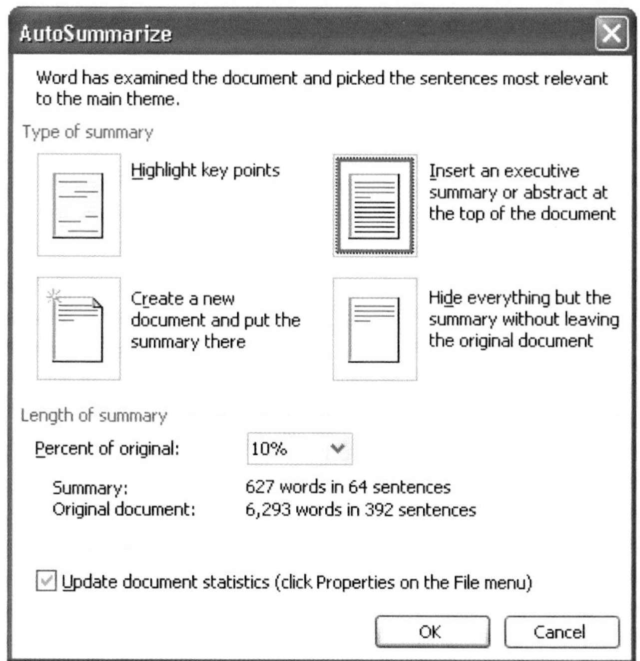

Figure 4-23: AutoSummarize provides an automated way to generate a document summary.

Count Characters and Words

Word can tell you the number of characters and the number of words in a document or in just a portion of the document you select.

1. Click the **Tools** menu (expand the menu if necessary), and click **Word Count**. The Word Count dialog box appears displaying the following information about your document (see Figure 4-24):
   - Number of pages
   - Number of words
   - Number of characters (not including spaces)
   - Number of characters (including spaces)
   - Number of paragraphs
   - Number of lines
2. Click the **Show Toolbar** button if you want the Word Count toolbar displayed at the top of your document.

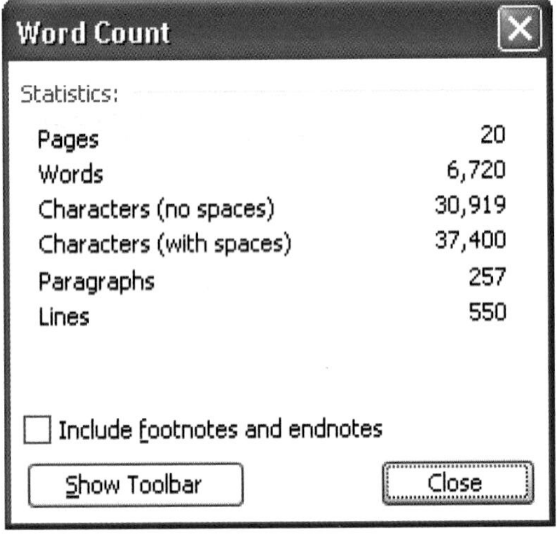

Figure 4-24: The Word Count feature is a quick and easy way to view the specifics of your document.

Use Highlighting

The Highlight feature is useful for marking important text in a document or text that you want to call to a reader's attention. Keep in mind, however, that highlighting parts of a document works best when the document is viewed online. When printed, the highlighting marks often appear gray and may even obscure the text you're trying to call attention to.

APPLY HIGHLIGHTING

1. On the Formatting toolbar, click the **Highlight** button.
2. Select the text or graphic you want to highlight. The highlighting is applied to your selection. (See Figure 4-25.)
3. To turn off highlighting, click the **Highlight** button again or press **ESC**.

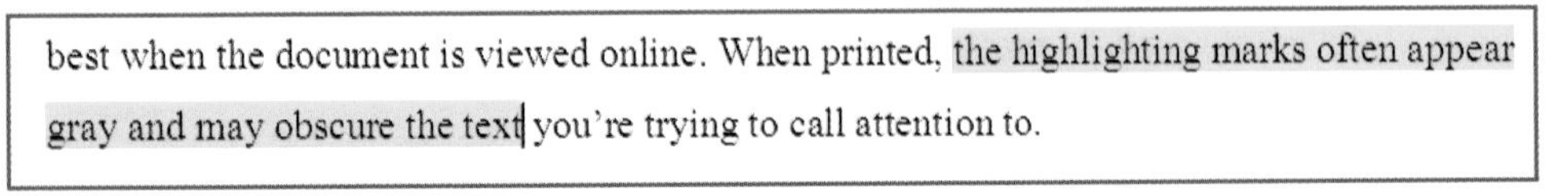

best when the document is viewed online. When printed, the highlighting marks often appear gray and may obscure the text you're trying to call attention to.

Figure 4-25: Highlighting is a great way to call attention to specific sections or phrases of your document.

TIP

You can also apply highlighting by selecting the text first and then clicking the **Highlight** button on the Formatting toolbar.

TIP

You can also hyphenate existing text by selecting the text, opening the Hyphenation dialog box, clicking **Automatically Hyphenate Document**, and clicking **OK**.

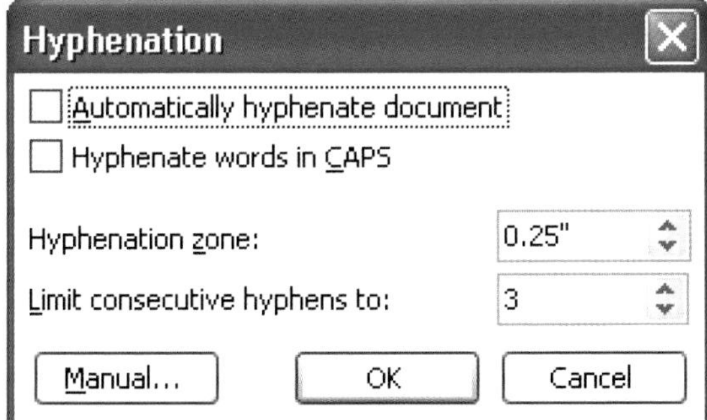

Figure 4-26: You can determine how Word will automatically hyphenate words.

REMOVE HIGHLIGHTING

1. Select the text you want to remove highlighting from, or press CTRL+A to select all of the text in the document.
2. On the Formatting toolbar, click the **Highlight** button drop-down arrow, and then click **None**.

FIND HIGHLIGHTED TEXT IN A DOCUMENT

1. Click the **Edit** menu and click **Find**.
2. If you don't see the Format button, click the **More** button.
3. Click the **Format** button and then click **Highlight**.
4. Click **Find Next** and repeat this until you reach the end of the document.
5. Click **OK** when the message box is displayed indicating that Word has completed the search.

Add Hyphenation

The Hyphenation feature automatically hyphenates words based on hyphenation rules. You can use it to make words fit better on a line, or avoid uneven margins or large gaps between words. (See Chapter 3 for information on text alignment.)

AUTOMATICALLY HYPHENATE TEXT

To automatically hyphenate text as you type:

1. Click the **Tools** menu (expand the menu if needed), click **Language**, and click **Hyphenation**. The Hyphenation dialog box appears.
2. Select the options you want from the following (see Figure 4-26):
   - **Automatically Hyphenate Document** enables automatic hyphenation as you type or after the fact for selected text (this option is turned off in Word by default).
   - **Hyphenate Words in CAPS** hyphenates words typed in all uppercase letters.
   - **Hyphenation Zone** sets the distance from the right margin within which you want to hyphenate the document (the lower the value, the more words are hyphenated).
   - **Limit Consecutive Hyphens** sets the maximum number of hyphens that can appear in a row.
3. Click **OK** when finished.

QUICKSTEPS

EXPLORING THE THESAURUS

A *thesaurus* is a book or list of synonyms (words that have similar meanings), and Word contains a Thesaurus feature that will help you find just the right word to get your message across.

1. Click the **Tools** menu, expand it if necessary, and click **Research**. The Research task pane is displayed. (See Figure 4-28.)
2. If **Thesaurus** is not displayed in the Reference Book drop-down list, click the down arrow and select it.
3. Type the word you want to find synonyms for in the Search For field.
4. Click the **green arrow** button to start searching.
5. A list of possible words is displayed. Point to the word you want to use. Click the arrow that appears, and click **Insert**.
6. Close the Research pane when finished.

TIP

You can also open the Thesaurus by selecting the word you want to look up and pressing **SHIFT+F7**.

MANUALLY HYPHENATE TEXT

1. Click the **Tools** menu, click **Language**, and click **Hyphenation**. The Hyphenation dialog box appears.
2. Make sure that the **Automatically Hyphenate Document** check box is clear.
3. Click the **Manual** button.
4. Word searches for possible words to hyphenate. When it finds one, the Manual Hyphenation dialog box appears. (See Figure 4-27.)
5. Do one of the following:
   - Click **Yes** to hyphenate the word at the suggested break.
   - Click the hyphen where you want to break the word, and click **Yes**.
   - Click **No** to continue without hyphenating the word.
6. Word will continue searching for words to hyphenate and display the Manual Hyphenation dialog box until the entire document has been searched. A message box is displayed to that effect. Click **OK**.

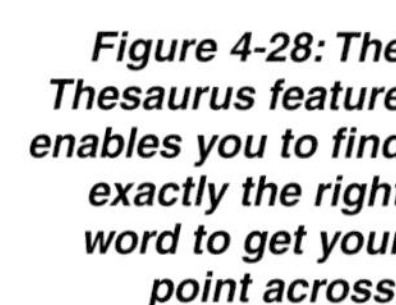

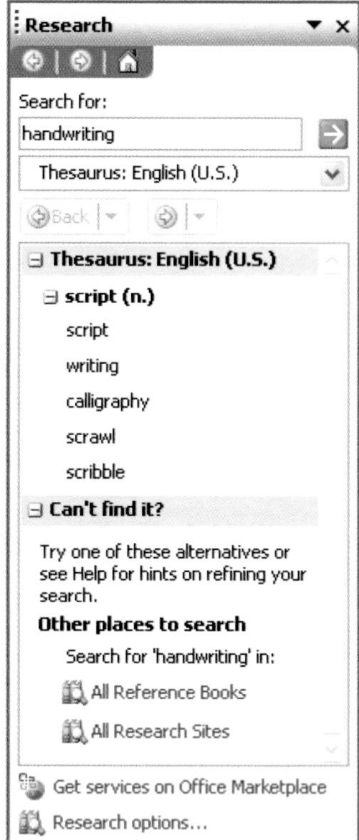

Figure 4-28: The Thesaurus feature enables you to find exactly the right word to get your point across.

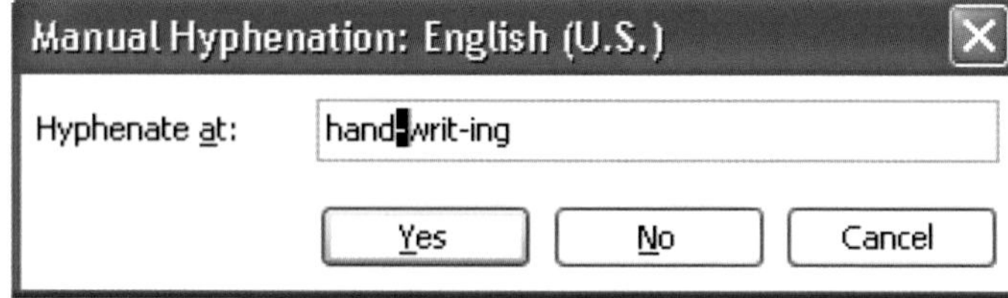

Figure 4-27: You can choose where a word should be hyphenated rather than accepting the automatic suggestions provided by Word.

How to...

- *Set Up Your Printer*
- *Define How a Document Is Printed*
- *Preview What You'll Print*
- *Print a Document*
- *Print an Envelope*
- *Print Labels*
- *Faxing*
- *Create a Merge Document*
- *E-Mailing*
- *Set Up a Name and Address List*
- *Insert Merge Fields*
- *Using Variable Fields*
- *Preview a Merge*
- *Complete a Merge*

Chapter 5

Printing and Using Mail Merge

The printing capabilities provided by Word 2003 go beyond just printing a document. You can preview your document before printing it and set specific parameters with regards to what is printed. Word also includes a convenient feature called Mail Merge that you can use to merge mailing lists into documents, including letters or envelopes.

This chapter covers these topics and more, including how to print envelopes and labels and how to set up a name and address list.

Print Documents

While printing documents may seem like a fairly basic function, there are several tasks associated with it that deserve attention, including setting up your printer, using Print Preview, and printing envelopes and labels.

> **NOTE**
>
> Due to the wide variety of printers available, this chapter cannot cover them all. The examples and figures in this chapter use a Lexmark Z11 printer. Depending on your printer model and how it's configured, you may see differences between your screen and what is shown in the figures and illustrations here.

> **NOTE**
>
> If there is a check mark next to the Printer icon, that printer is set as the default printer.

Set Up Your Printer

Your printer will come with documentation that specifically tells you how to set it up, but there are two basic areas that you need to consider when setting up a printer: installing it on your computer and setting a default printer.

INSTALL A PRINTER

Follow the manufacturer's instructions to unpack, ready, and connect the printer to your computer, or identify the network printer you want to use. If you install a Plug and Play printer, it will automatically install itself and you can ignore the following instructions. Otherwise, to install a printer:

1. With Windows XP Professional, click the **Start** button and then click **Printers And Faxes**.

   –Or–

   With Windows XP Home Edition, click the **Start** button, click **Control Panel**, and then click **Printers And Faxes** (in Classic view). The Printers And Faxes page is displayed.

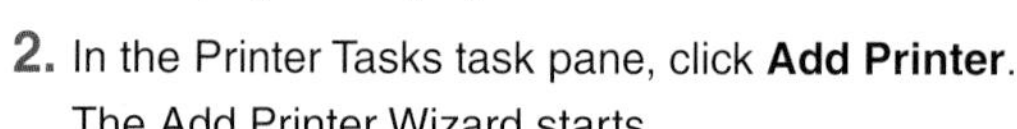

2. In the Printer Tasks task pane, click **Add Printer**. The Add Printer Wizard starts.
3. Follow the instructions in the Add Printer Wizard.
4. If you are using a local printer and you want to print a test page, make sure the printer is turned on and ready to print.

SET A DEFAULT PRINTER

1. In Windows XP Professional, click the **Start** button and then click **Printers And Faxes**.

   –Or–

   In Windows XP Home Edition, click the **Start** button, click **Control Panel**, and then click **Printers And Faxes** (in Classic view).
2. Right-click the icon for the printer you want to use as the default printer, and then click **Set As Default Printer** from the shortcut menu that appears. A check mark is displayed next to the icon you have selected.

Define How a Document Is Printed

The Properties dialog box for your printer is where you define how your document will be printed. From here, you can set such things as orientation, number of copies to print, effects, and so on. An example of a Properties dialog box for a Lexmark Z11 printer is shown in Figure 5-1. Keep in mind that the Properties dialog box for your printer will probably have some different options. Consult the documentation that came with your printer for specific instructions.

Figure 5-1: Use the Properties dialog box for your printer to define how your documents will be printed.

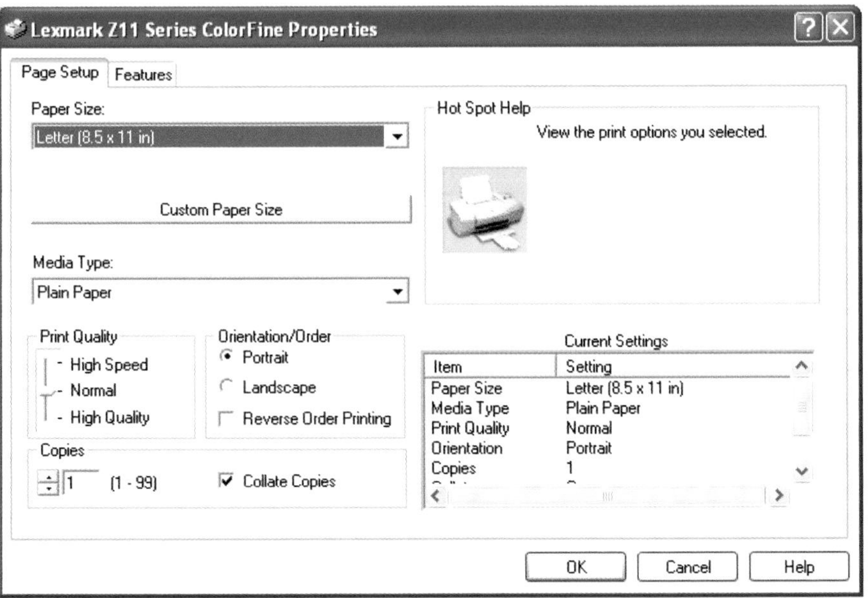

To open the Properties dialog box for your printer:

1. In Word, click the **File** menu and click **Print**. The Print dialog box appears.
2. Click the **Properties** button. The Properties dialog box for your printer appears.

   This particular printer model has two tabs in this dialog box: Page Setup and Features.
3. The Page Setup tab for the Lexmark Z11 has the following options, as shown in Figure 5-1. Other printers will have different tabs and different options, but within the Properties dialog box, they will need to cover the same functions. Make your selections accordingly.
   - **Paper Size** indicates the size of the paper you are printing on, for example, letter, legal, or postcard.
   - **Media Type** indicates the type of paper you are printing on, for example, plain or glossy.
   - **Print Quality** determines the quality of your print job. You can choose speed over quality or quality over speed.
   - **Orientation/Order** determines how the document is aligned on the page and the order in which the pages will be printed.
   - **Copies** determines the number of copies to be printed.

- **Collate Copies** determines whether multiple copies of a document are printed one at a time. In other words, one copy is printed from start to finish and then the next copy is printed, and so on.
- **Hot Spot Help** provides an instant description of an option when the mouse is hovering over it.
- **Current Settings** details the settings most recently selected for this printer.

4. The Features tab for the Lexmark Z11 has the following options, as shown in Figure 5-2. Again, a different printer will have different options and tabs. Make your selections accordingly.

   - **Cartridge Maintenance** opens a dialog box from where you can clean your print nozzles and make sure your cartridge is aligned properly, among other things.
   - **Clean Rollers** opens a dialog box from where you can clean your printer's rollers, provided your printer has them.
   - **Defaults** restores the default settings on all available tabs.
   - **About Lexmark** provides the printer software version number and copyright information.

5. When you have the settings the way you want them, click **OK** to close the dialog boxes.

Figure 5-2: The Properties dialog box for different printers will have different tabs, but similar types of printers—color inkjet, for example—will have similar options.

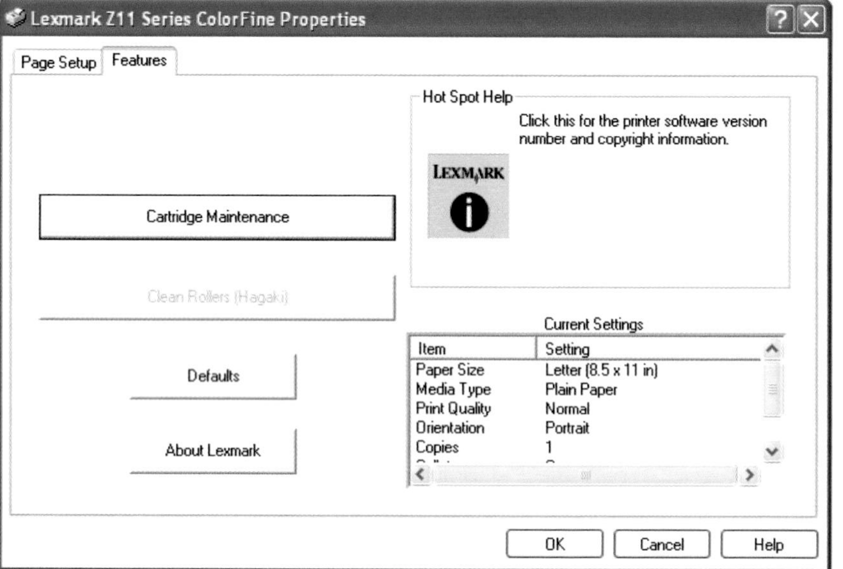

Preview What You'll Print

You can use the Print Preview feature to view your document on the screen before you print it. Print Preview displays the page(s) of your document exactly as they will appear when printed. You can also set page breaks and margins using this feature (see Chapter 3 for more information).

To use Print Preview:

1. Click the **File** menu and click **Print Preview**.

   –Or–

   Click the **Print Preview** button on the Standard toolbar. 
   Your document is displayed in Print Preview view, as shown in Figure 5-3.

2. The Print Preview toolbar (see Figure 5-4) is displayed at the top of the screen when you use the Print Preview feature.

Figure 5-3: By displaying your document in Print Preview, you can see how it will look when printed.

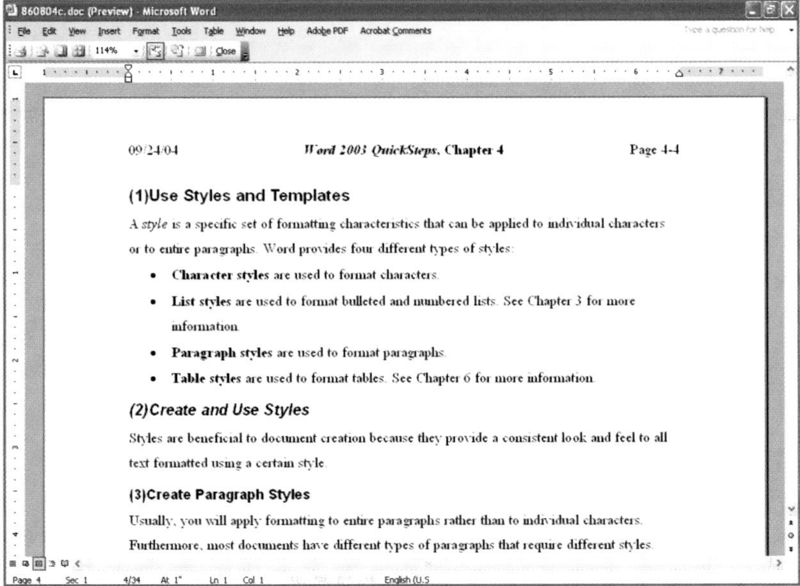

09/24/04 *Word 2003 QuickSteps*, **Chapter 4** Page 4-4

(1)Use Styles and Templates

A *style* is a specific set of formatting characteristics that can be applied to individual characters or to entire paragraphs. Word provides four different types of styles:

- **Character styles** are used to format characters.
- **List styles** are used to format bulleted and numbered lists. See Chapter 3 for more information.
- **Paragraph styles** are used to format paragraphs.
- **Table styles** are used to format tables. See Chapter 6 for more information.

(2)Create and Use Styles

Styles are beneficial to document creation because they provide a consistent look and feel to all text formatted using a certain style.

(3)Create Paragraph Styles

Usually, you will apply formatting to entire paragraphs rather than to individual characters. Furthermore, most documents have different types of paragraphs that require different styles.

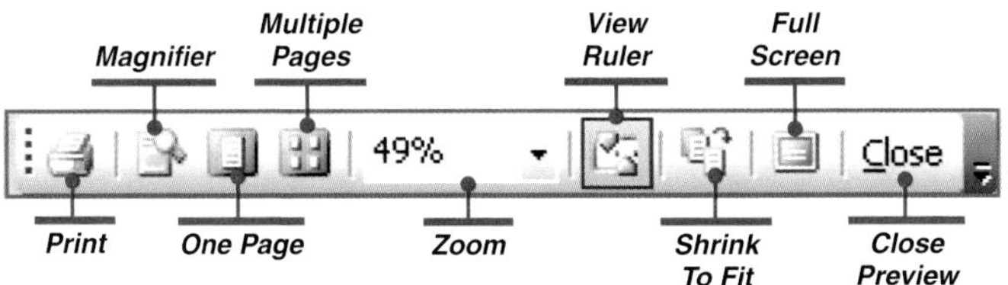

Figure 5-4: Use the Print Preview toolbar to modify your document before printing.

TIP

You can also type a number for whatever value you want in the Zoom percentage field by clicking directly in the field, typing a number, and pressing **ENTER**.

NOTE

When using Print Preview, your document is automatically displayed one page at a time. To return to a single-page view from multiple-page view, click the **One Page** button on the Print Preview toolbar.

ZOOM IN AND OUT

1. Click the **Magnifier** button on the Print Preview toolbar. The cursor changes to a magnifying glass.

2. Click anywhere on the page. The first click causes the document to increase to 100 percent in size. Click again, and the document shrinks back to the amount displayed in the Zoom percentage field on the Print Preview toolbar.

   –Or–

   Click the down arrow next to the Zoom percentage list box, and select a value.

VIEW MULTIPLE PAGES

Click the **Multiple Pages** button on the Print Preview toolbar, and select the page layout that you want.

CHANGE MARGINS

1. Click the **View Ruler** button on the Print Preview toolbar. A ruler is displayed on the left and on the top of the document, as you saw in Figure 5-3.
2. Position the mouse pointer over the margin you want to change. The cursor changes to a double-headed arrow.

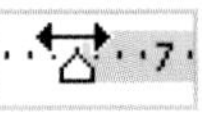

3. Drag the cursor until the margin is where you want it. As you drag, a dotted line indicates the margin's position (see Figure 5-5).

Figure 5-5: You can change the margins of a page from within Print Preview. The dotted line indicates the margin's position.

NOTE

You can also change page margins using the Margins tab of the Page Setup dialog box (see Chapter 3 for more information).

MOVE FROM PAGE TO PAGE

Click **Previous Page** or **Next Page** (the up or down arrows below the vertical scroll bar) to move forward or backward one page at a time.

REDUCE THE NUMBER OF PAGES

If, for example, you have a report that absolutely cannot be more than four pages and a line or two—or even several paragraphs—has caused the document to be five pages, click the **Shrink To Fit** button on the Print Preview toolbar. Word reformats the document onto one less page by making slight adjustments to font size and paragraph spacing. You can keep doing this to reduce the number of pages one at a time. Obviously, after a while, the document is no longer very attractive, if it is even readable.

USE FULL-SCREEN VIEW

Click the **Full Screen** button on the Print Preview toolbar. The document is displayed without scroll bars or margins present, as shown in Figure 5-6. Click the **Close Full Screen** button on the Full Screen toolbar to return to the regular Print Preview view.

Full Screen
Close Full Screen

EXIT PRINT PREVIEW

Click the **Close Preview** button on the Print Preview toolbar.

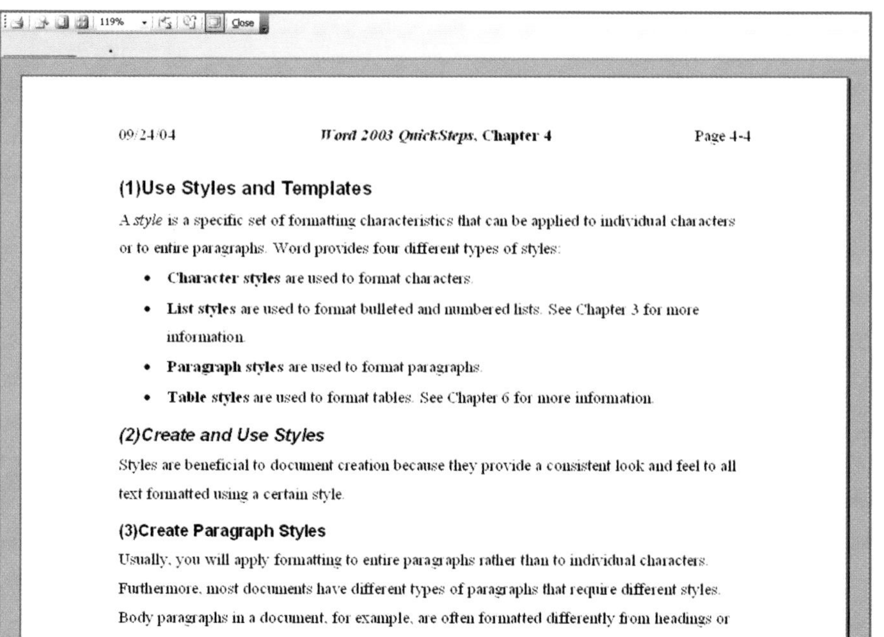

09/24/04 *Word 2003 QuickSteps*, **Chapter 4** Page 4-4

(1)Use Styles and Templates

A *style* is a specific set of formatting characteristics that can be applied to individual characters or to entire paragraphs. Word provides four different types of styles:

- **Character styles** are used to format characters.
- **List styles** are used to format bulleted and numbered lists. See Chapter 3 for more information.
- **Paragraph styles** are used to format paragraphs.
- **Table styles** are used to format tables. See Chapter 6 for more information.

(2)Create and Use Styles

Styles are beneficial to document creation because they provide a consistent look and feel to all text formatted using a certain style.

(3)Create Paragraph Styles

Usually, you will apply formatting to entire paragraphs rather than to individual characters. Furthermore, most documents have different types of paragraphs that require different styles. Body paragraphs in a document, for example, are often formatted differently from headings or lists. To create a paragraph style:

Figure 5-6: Use Full-Screen view to view your document without margins or scroll bars.

Print a Document

If you're in a hurry or don't care about changing margins, then printing a document is as easy as clicking the **Print** button on the standard toolbar.  To set specific options before printing your document, however, you need to use the Print dialog box, as shown in Figure 5-7.

1. Click the **File** menu and click **Print**. The Print dialog box appears.
2. If more than one printer is available to you, select the printer you want to use from the Name drop-down list. Usually, the default printer is displayed automatically in the Name list box.
3. Select an option in the Page Range area.
   - **All** prints all the pages in your document.
   - **Current Page** prints the currently selected page or the page in which the insertion point is active.
   - **Selection** prints only the content you have selected. Select text to print by dragging over it to highlight it.
   - **Pages** prints the range of pages you select. To print contiguous pages, use a hyphen (for example, 1-4); to print noncontiguous pages, use commas (for example, 1, 3, 5).
4. Select an option from the Print What drop-down list:

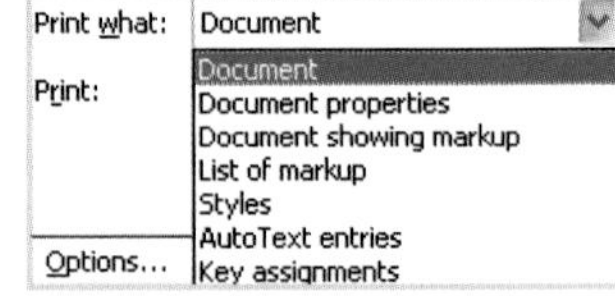

   - **Document** prints the document.
   - **Document Properties** prints the information about the document, such as the file name, the date the document was created, and when it was last saved.
   - **Document Showing Markup** prints the document with any revision marks present. (See Chapter 10 for more information on revision marks.)
   - **List Of Markup** prints a list of the edits, insertions, and other markups or changes made to a document.

Figure 5-7: The Print dialog box provides further options for printing your document.

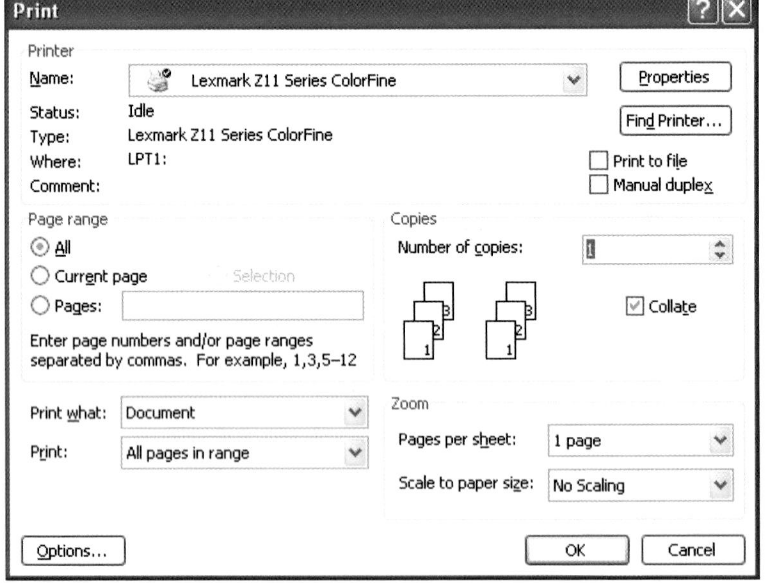

- **Style** prints style information. (See Chapter 4 for more information on styles.)
- **AutoText Entries** prints a list of AutoText entries. (See Chapter 4 for more information on AutoText.)
- **Key Assignments** prints a list of shortcut keys defined by the user and available in Word. (See Chapter 8 for more information on shortcut keys.)

Print: All pages in range
All pages in range
Odd pages
Even pages

5. Select an option from the Print drop-down list:
   - **All Pages In Range** prints all pages, either all the pages in the document or in the range you specify (see step 3).
   - **Odd Pages** prints all the odd-numbered pages in the document or in the range you specify (see step 3).
   - **Even Pages** prints all the even-numbered pages in the document or in the range you specify (see step 3).

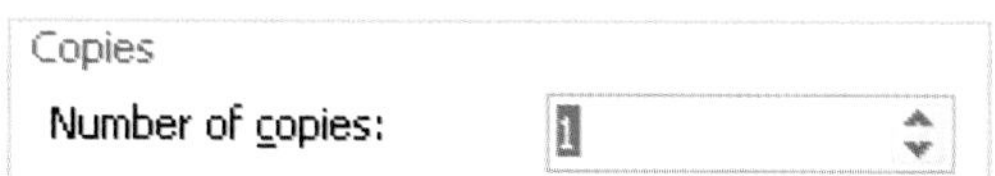

6. Type the number of copies you want to print in the Number Of Copies box, or use the spinner to select the number of copies you want.
7. Click the **Pages Per Sheet** down arrow, and select a number to print if you want more than one page on a sheet of paper.
8. Click the **Scale To Paper Size** down arrow, and select a paper size to which your document needs to be scaled. For example, you might select **Legal (8.5 x 14 in)** if you are printing documents on legal-sized paper.
9. When you have selected all the options you want and are ready to print your document, click **OK**. Your document is printed.

Print an Envelope

You can print a mailing address on an envelope to give your correspondence a more professional look.

To print an envelope:

1. Click the **Tools** menu, click **Letters And Mailings**, and then click **Envelopes And Labels**. The Envelopes And Labels dialog box appears, as shown in Figure 5-8.
2. Click the **Envelopes** tab.
3. In the Delivery Address box, enter or edit the mailing address.
4. In the Return Address box, accept the default return address, or enter or edit the return address. (If you are using preprinted envelopes, you can omit a return address by selecting the **Omit** check box.)
5. Select the **Add Electronic Postage** check box if you have separately installed electronic postage software and want to add it to your envelope.
6. To set options for the electronic postage programs that are installed on your computer, click **E-Postage Properties**. (See the Note regarding electronic postage.)
7. To select an envelope size, the type of paper feed, and other options, click **Options**, select the options you want, and then click **OK**.
8. To print the envelope now, insert an envelope in the printer as shown in the Feed box, and then click **Print**.
9. To attach the envelope to a document you are currently working on and print it later, click **Add To Document**. The envelope is added to the document in a separate section.

NOTE

If you do not have an electronic postage program installed, Microsoft Word prompts you to install one when you select Add Electronic Postage and offers to connect you to the Microsoft Office Online Web site. There you can get more information and view links to other sites that offer electronic postage, such as www.stamps.com.

Figure 5-8: Printed envelopes give your correspondence a professional look.

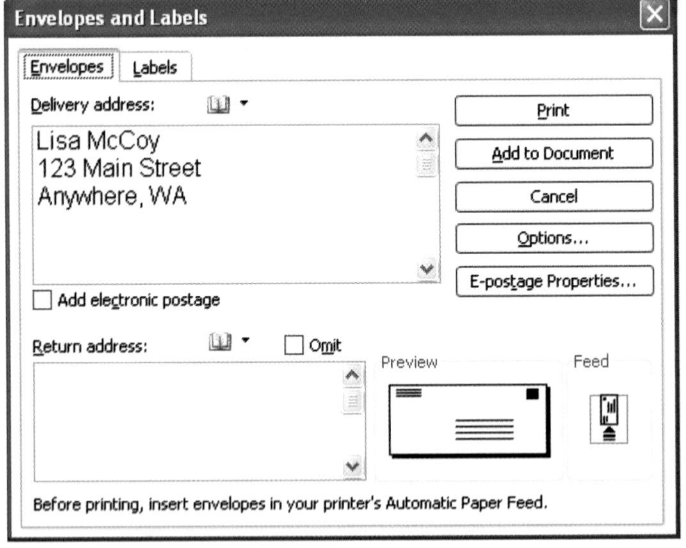

Print Labels

You can print labels for a single letter or for a mass mailing, such as holiday cards, invitations, or for marketing purposes. See the section "Merge to Labels," later in this chapter, for instructions on how to create labels for a mass mailing.

To print a single label:

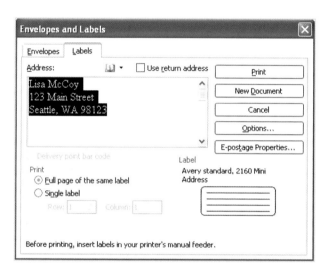

1. Click the **Tools** menu, click **Letters And Mailings**, and then click **Envelopes And Labels**. The Envelopes And Labels dialog box appears.
2. Click the **Labels** tab.
3. In the Address box, do one of the following:
   - If you are creating a mailing label, enter or edit the address.
   - If you want to use a return address, select the **Use Return Address** check box, and then edit the address if necessary.
   - If you are creating another type of label, type the text you want.
4. In the Print area, do one of the following:
   - Select the **Single Label** option to print a single label. Then type or select the row and column number on the label sheet for the label you want to print.
   - Select **Full Page Of The Same Label** to print the same information on a sheet of labels.
5. To select the label type, the type of paper feed, and other options, click **Options**, select the options you want, and then click **OK**. If the type of label you want to use is not listed in the Product Number box, you might be able to use one of the listed labels, or you can click **New Label** to create your own custom label.

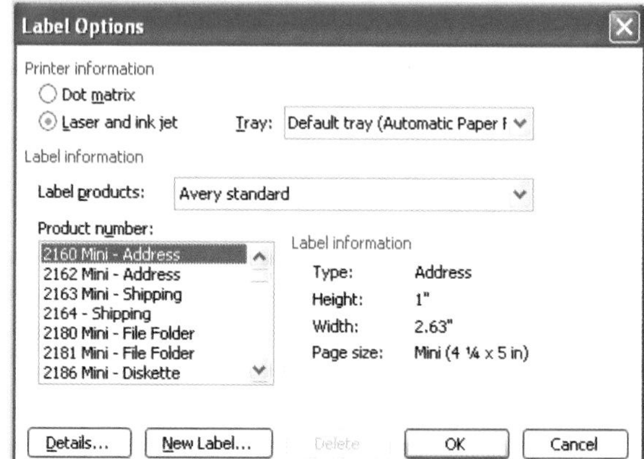

QUICKSTEPS

FAXING

You can send faxes directly from your computer. There are two ways to send faxes: via a faxing service and via a fax modem.

USE A FAX SERVICE

To send a fax using a fax service:

1. Click the **File** menu, expand the menu if necessary, click **Send To**, and then click **Recipient Using Internet Fax Service**.
2. The first time you use fax services, you will be prompted to sign up with a provider. Click **OK** to open your Web browser, and then follow the signup instructions on the Web site.

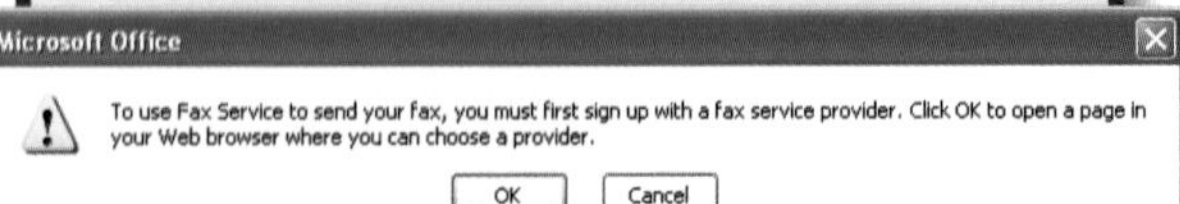

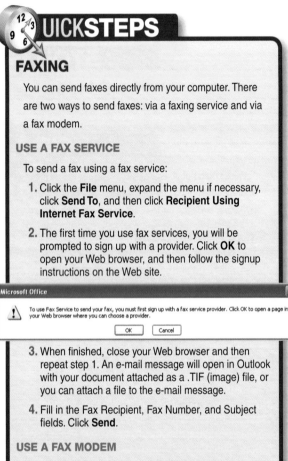

3. When finished, close your Web browser and then repeat step 1. An e-mail message will open in Outlook with your document attached as a .TIF (image) file, or you can attach a file to the e-mail message.
4. Fill in the Fax Recipient, Fax Number, and Subject fields. Click **Send**.

USE A FAX MODEM

This procedure requires that your fax modem be set up as a printer on your system. To send a fax using a fax modem:

1. Click the **File** menu, click **Send To**, expand the menu if necessary, and then click **Recipient Using a Fax Modem**.
2. Follow the steps in the Fax Wizard to send your fax.

6. To print one or more labels, insert a sheet of labels into the printer, and then click **Print**.
7. To save a sheet of labels for later editing or printing, click **New Document** and save the labels document.

Merge Lists with Letters and Envelopes

Mail Merge allows you to combine a mailing list with a document by following the steps in the Mail Merge task pane. You can merge a mailing list to letters, envelopes, and labels. A mail merge combines two kinds of documents: the *main document*, which is the text of the document—for example, the body of a letter; and the *data source*, which is the information that changes with each version of the document—for example, the individual names and addresses of the people who will be receiving the letter. The following sections will show you how to create a main document, create a data source, and then merge them together.

Create a Merge Document

The first thing you need to do for a mail merge is create the main document (also known as the merge document). The main document has two parts: static text and merge fields. *Static text* is text that does not change—for example, the body of a letter. *Merge fields* are indicators as to where information from the list or data source goes. For example, in a form letter, "Dear" would be static text while <<First Name>> <<Last Name>> are merge fields. When the main document and the data source are combined, the result is "Dear John Doe," "Dear Jane Smith," and so on.

You can compose the static text in a document first and then insert the merge fields, or you can compose the static text and insert the merge fields as you go. Keep in mind that you cannot insert merge fields into a main document until you have created the data source and associated it with your main document.

E-MAILING

You can e-mail documents that you create in Word as attachments to your e-mail messages. To attach and send a document in an e-mail:

1. Click the **File** menu, click **Send To**, expand the menu if necessary, and then click **Mail Recipient** to send your Word document in the body of the e-mail message; or click **Mail Recipient As Attachment** to send your Word document as an attachment to your e-mail message.
2. A new e-mail message is opened with your document title automatically filled in the Subject line and the document automatically embedded or attached to the e-mail.

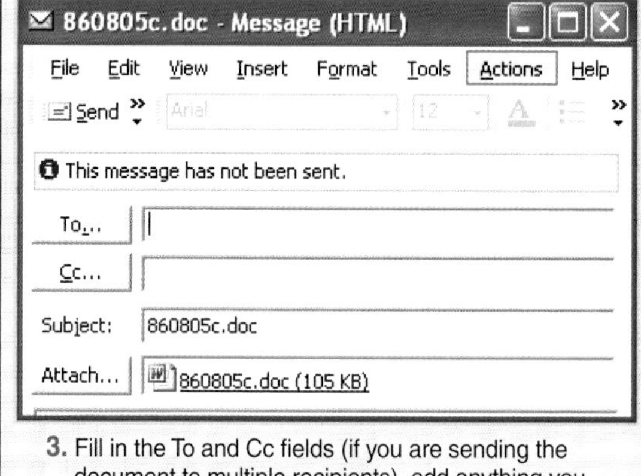

3. Fill in the To and Cc fields (if you are sending the document to multiple recipients), add anything you want to the body of the message, and click **Send**. Your e-mail message with the document attached is sent.

To create a merge document:

1. Open the document you want to use as your primary document, or open a new document (see Chapter 2).
2. Click the **Tools** menu, click **Letters And Mailings**, and click **Mail Merge**. The Mail Merge task pane is displayed, as shown in Figure 5-9.
3. In the Select Document Type area, select one of the following options:
   - **Letters** are form letters designed to be sent to multiple people.
   - **E-Mail Messages** are form letters designed to be sent to multiple people via e-mail.
   - **Envelopes** are envelopes addressed to multiple people.
   - **Labels** are labels addressed to multiple people.
   - **Directory** is a collection of information regarding multiple items, such as a mailing list or phone directory.

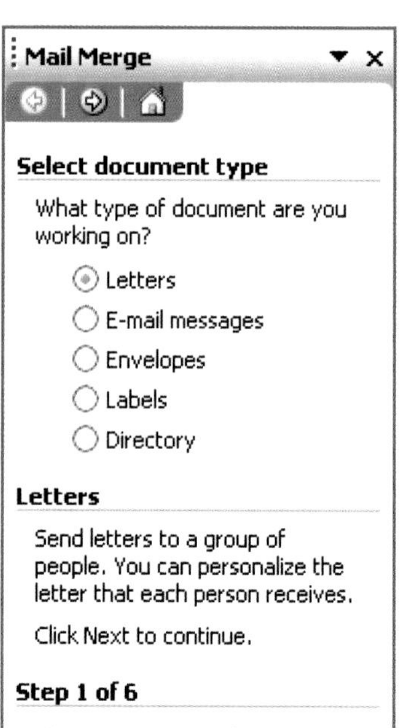

Figure 5-9: The Mail Merge task pane is where you begin the merge process.

4. Click the **Next: Starting Document** link at the bottom of the task pane.
5. In the Select Starting Document area, select one of the following options:
   - **Use The Current Document** uses the currently open document as the main document for the mail merge.
   - **Start From A Template** uses a template you designate as the main document for the mail merge.

   Select starting document
   How do you want to set up your letters?
   Use the current document
   Start from a template
   Start from existing document

   - **Start From Existing Document** uses an existing document you designate as the main document for the mail merge.
6. See the following section, "Set Up a Name and Address List," to create a data source.

NOTE

You can e-mail documents as attachments to people who are reviewing a document. See Chapter 10 for more information on reviewing documents in Word.

TIP

You cannot use the Mail Merge task pane unless a document is open.

NOTE

Word also allows you to take a list other than a mailing list—a parts list, for example—and merge it with a document to create a catalog or directory.

NOTE

You can also use Word as your editor when composing and sending e-mails. To do so, open Microsoft Outlook, click the **Tools** menu, click **Options**, and then click the **Mail Format** tab. Select the **Use Microsoft Word To Edit E-Mail Messages** check box, click **Apply** and then click **OK**.

Set Up a Name and Address List

A name and address list is an example of a data source. A data source has two parts: fields and records. A *field* is a category of information. For example, in a mailing list, First Name, Last Name, and Street Address are examples of fields. A *record* is a set of fields for an individual. For example, in a mailing list, the record for John Doe would include all the relevant fields for this individual—his first and last name, street address, city, state, and ZIP code.

To set up a name and address list:

1. Follow steps 1-6 in the previous section, "Create a Merge Document."
2. Click the **Next: Select Recipients** link at the bottom of the task pane. In the Select Recipients area, select **Type A New List**.
3. Click the **Create** link in the middle of the pane in the Type A New List area. The New Address List dialog box appears, as shown in Figure 5-10.

Select recipients
Use an existing list
Select from Outlook contacts
Type a new list

New Address List
Enter Address information
Title
First Name
Last Name
Company Name
Address Line 1
Address Line 2
City
New Entry | Delete Entry | Find Entry... | Filter and Sort... | Customize...
View Entries
View Entry Number | First | Previous | 1 | Next | Last
Total entries in list 1
Cancel

Figure 5-10: Use the New Address List dialog box to create your mailing list.

TIP

Sort the merge recipients by clicking the field name at the top of the list that will provide the sort order. For example, if you want the list ordered alphabetically by last name, click **Last Name**.

4. Enter the information for the first record in the fields you want to use. Press **TAB** to move to the next field, or press **SHIFT + TAB** to move back to the previous field.
5. When you have completed all the fields you want for the first record, click the **New Entry** button, and provide information for the second record.
6. Repeat steps 4 and 5 until you have added all the records you want to your list. Click the **Close** button.
7. A Save Address List dialog box appears. Type a file name for the list, and select the location on your computer where you want to save it.
8. The Mail Merge Recipients dialog box appears, as shown in Figure 5-11. Select the check boxes next to the recipients you want to include in the list.
9. Click **OK** when finished. See the following section, "Insert Merge Fields."

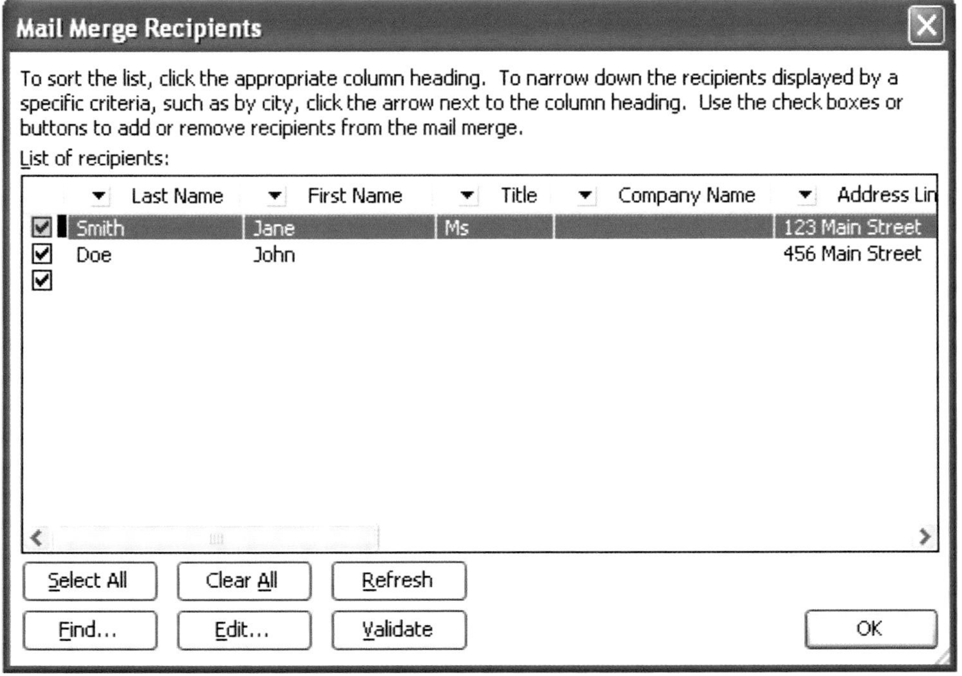

Figure 5-11: Use the Mail Merge Recipients dialog box to manage your mailing list prior to completing the merge.

1 2 3 4 5 6 7 8 9 10

Insert Merge Fields

After composing your main document and creating a data source, you need to insert the merge fields. This section will tell you how to insert merge fields in general; the example uses a letter; additional sections will show you how to use merge fields when creating envelopes and labels.

To insert merge fields:

1. Follow steps 1-9 in the previous section, "Set Up a Name and Address List."
2. Click the **Next: Write Your Letter** link at the bottom of the Mail Merge task pane. (This section assumes that the letter has already been written.)
3. Place the cursor in the document where you want to insert a merge field. Do one of the following:
   - Select one of the four items in the top of the Mail Merge task pane if you want to insert a predefined block of merge fields, such as an address or a greeting. If you select anything other than More Items, a dialog box will appear and ask you to select options and formatting for that item.

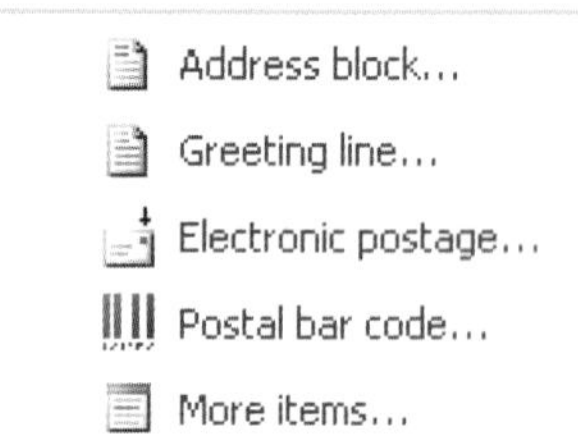

   - Click the **More Items** link (the fifth item in the list) to insert an individual merge field. The Insert Merge Field dialog box appears. Verify that **Database Fields** is selected, and then select the field you want to insert (for example, First Name and Last Name). Click the **Insert** button to insert the merge field into your document. Click the **Close** button when you are done inserting all the fields you need.
4. Add commas, spaces, and other punctuation to the address as needed. Figure 5-12 shows an example of a letter with merge fields inserted. See the following section, "Preview a Merge."

Figure 5-12: Merge fields are a convenient way to create a form letter designed for multiple recipients.

«First_Name» «Last_Name»
«Address_Line_1»
«City», «State» «ZIP_Code»

Dear «First_Name»,

The purpose of this letter is to notify you of our upcoming move. We are very excited to offer you a larger space, a greater selection, and even lower prices.

USING VARIABLE FIELDS

Variable fields, also known as Word fields, are merge fields that are applied if certain conditions are met. One of the most common variable fields is the IF field. The IF field performs one of two alternative actions, depending on a condition you specify. For example, the statement "If the weather is sunny, we'll go to the beach; if not, we'll go to the museum," specifies a condition that *must* be met (sunny weather) for a certain action to take place (going to the beach). If the condition is not met, an alternative action occurs (going to the museum).

Look at an example of using an IF variable field in Word:

> {IF { MERGEFIELD City } = "Seattle" "Please call our office." "Please call our distributor."}

This works as follows: If the current data record contains "Seattle" in the City field, then the first text in quotation marks ("Please call our office.") is printed in the merged document that results from that data record. If "Seattle" is not in the City field, then the second set of text in quotation marks ("Please call our distributor.") is printed. Using a variable field is easy and doesn't require writing such a complex statement.

To insert a variable field into a merge document:

1. Position the insertion point where you want the variable field.
2. Click the **Insert Word Field** button on the Mail Merge toolbar. Insert Word Field ▾
   If the Mail Merge toolbar isn't displayed, click the **Tools** menu, click **Letters And Mailings**, and click **Show Mail Merge Toolbar**.

Continued…

Preview a Merge

Prior to actually completing the merge, the Mail Merge task pane presents you with an opportunity to review what the merged document will look like. This way, you can go back and make any last-minute changes to fine-tune your merge.

To preview a merge:

1. Follow steps 1-4 in the previous section, "Insert Merge Fields."
2. Click the **Next: Preview Your Letters** link at the bottom of the Mail Merge task pane.
3. Use the right and left arrow buttons in the Mail Merge task pane to scroll through the recipient list.
4. If you want to exclude a particular recipient from the merge, click the **Exclude This Recipient** button. Exclude this recipient

   –Or–

   Click the **Edit Recipient List** link to edit a particular recipient's information. If you click this link, the Mail Merge Recipients dialog box appears again (see Figure 5-11). Click the **Edit** button, modify the information, and click the **Close** button. Click **OK** to close the Mail Merge Recipients dialog box.

Preview your letters

One of the merged letters is previewed here. To preview another letter, click one of the following:

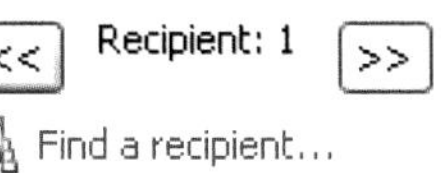

Complete a Merge

The last step in performing a mail merge is to complete the merge; that is, to accept the preview of how the merge will look and direct Word to perform the merge.

To complete a merge:

1. Follow steps 1-4 in the previous section, "Preview a Merge."
2. Click the **Next: Complete The Merge** link at the bottom of the Mail Merge task pane.

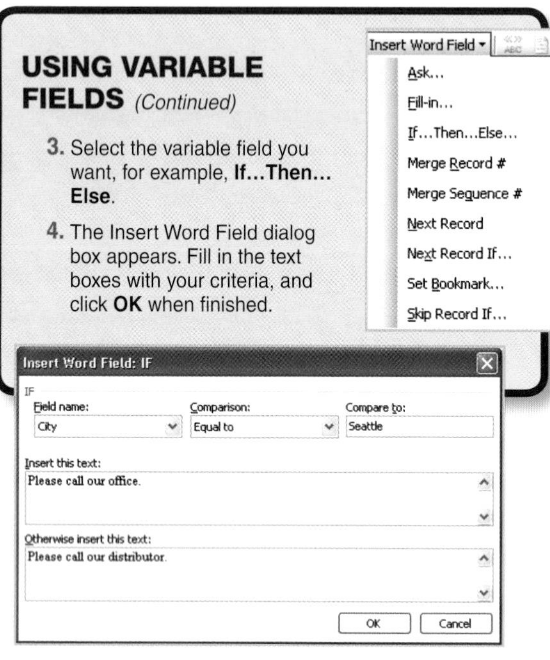

USING VARIABLE FIELDS *(Continued)*

3. Select the variable field you want, for example, **If...Then... Else**.
4. The Insert Word Field dialog box appears. Fill in the text boxes with your criteria, and click **OK** when finished.

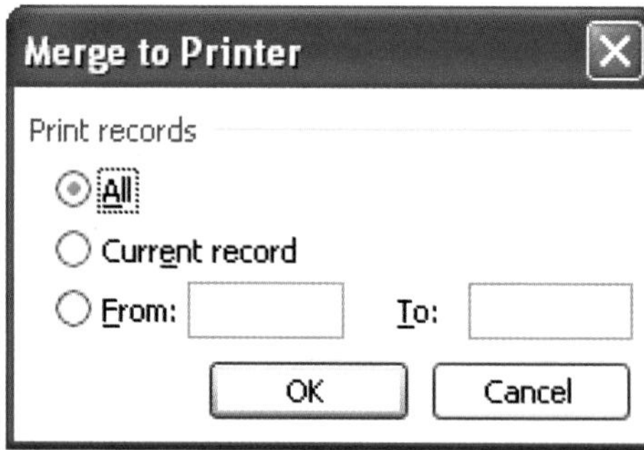

Figure 5-13: Specify the records to be printed prior to actually completing the merge.

3. Click the Print link in the Merge area. The Merge To Printer dialog box appears, as shown in Figure 5-13.
4. Select one of the following options:
   - **All** prints all records in the data source that have been included in the merge.
   - **Current Record** prints only the record that is displayed in the document window.
   - **From/To** prints a range of records you specify. Enter the starting and ending numbers in the text boxes.
5. Click **OK** when finished. The Print dialog box appears.
6. Select the print options you want, and click **OK**. Your merged document is printed.

MERGE TO ENVELOPES

The process for merging to envelopes is similar to that for merging to letters.

1. Follow steps 1-2 in the section "Create a Merge Document." In the Select Document Type area, select **Envelopes**.
2. Click the **Next: Starting Document** link at the bottom of the Mail Merge task pane. Select one of the following options:
   - **Change Document Layout** lets you modify the current document.
   - **Start From Existing Document** lets you use a different existing document.
3. If you selected Start From Existing Document, select the main document you want to use from the displayed list, and click **Open.** If you want to use a document that is not listed, click **Open** and locate and select the document you want from the Open dialog box that appears.
4. If you selected Change Document Layout, click the **Envelope Options** link in the middle of the Mail Merge task pane. The Envelope Options dialog box appears.
5. Select the options you want from the Envelope Options and Printing Options tabs. Click **OK** when finished.
6. Click the **Next: Select Recipients** link at the bottom of the Mail Merge task pane. Follow steps 2-9 in the section "Set Up a Name and Address List."
7. Click the **Next: Arrange Your Envelope** link at the bottom of the Mail Merge task pane.

1 2 3 4 5 6 7 8 9 10

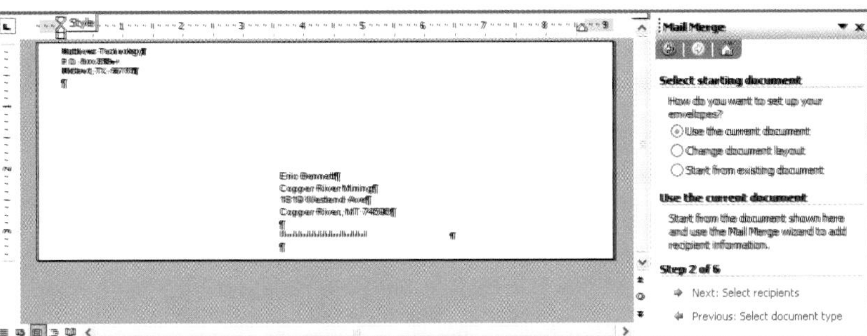

Figure 5-14: You can see how your merged envelope will look when completed prior to printing.

8. Select one of the first four options to insert a predefined block of merge fields, such as an address block or a postal bar code.

   –Or–

   Click the **More Items** link to insert an individual mail merge field.
9. Repeat step 8 for each merge field that you want to insert.
10. Click the **Next: Preview Your Envelopes** link at the bottom of the Mail Merge task pane. Follow steps 3-4 in the section "Preview a Merge."
11. Click the **Next: Complete The Merge** link at the bottom of the Mail Merge task pane. Follow steps 3-6 in the section "Complete a Merge." Your completed envelope may look similar to Figure 5-14.

MERGE TO LABELS

The process for merging to labels is similar to that for merging to letters and envelopes.

1. Follow steps 1-2 in the section "Create a Merge Document." In the Select Document Type area, select **Labels**.
2. Click the **Next: Starting Document** link at the bottom of the Mail Merge task pane. Select one of the following options:
   - **Change Document Layout** lets you modify the current document.
   - **Start From Existing Document** lets you use a different existing document.
3. If you selected Start From Existing Document, select the main document you want to use from the displayed list, and click **Open.** If your want to use a document that is not listed, click **Open** and locate and select the document you want from the Open dialog box that appears.
4. If you selected Change Document Layout, click the **Label Options** link in the middle of the Mail Merge task pane. The Label Options dialog box appears, as shown in Figure 5-15.
5. Select the options you want. Click **OK** when finished.
6. Click the **Next: Select Recipients** link at the bottom of the Mail Merge task pane. Follow steps 2-9 in the section "Set Up a Name and Address List."

7. Click the **Next: Arrange Your Labels** link at the bottom of the Mail Merge task pane.
8. Select one of the first four options to insert a predefined block of merge fields, such as an address block or a postal bar code.

   –Or–

   Click the **More Items** link to insert an individual mail merge field.
9. Repeat step 8 for each merge field that you want to insert.
10. Click the **Next: Preview Your Labels** link at the bottom of the Mail Merge task pane. Follow steps 3-4 in the section "Preview a Merge."
11. Click the **Next: Complete The Merge** link at the bottom of the Mail Merge task pane. Follow steps 3-6 in the section "Complete a Merge."

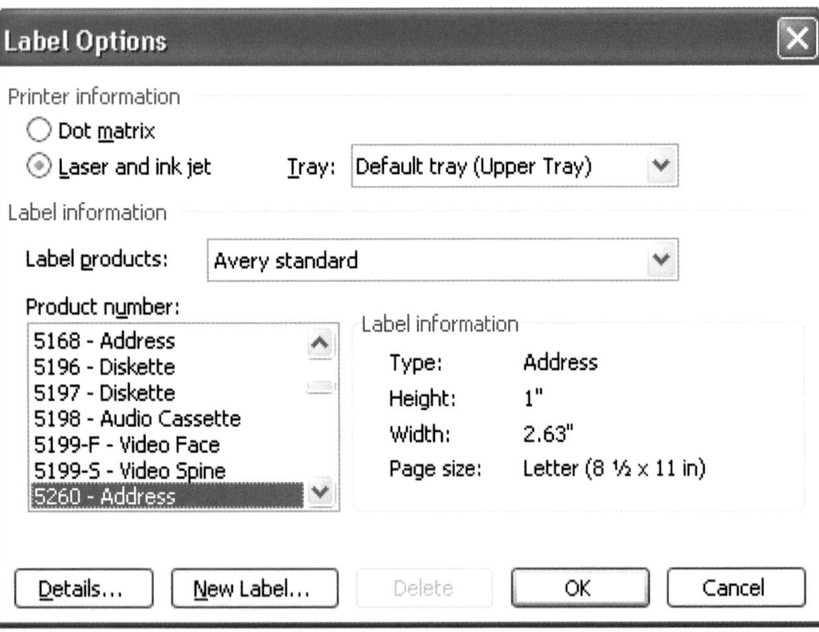

Figure 5-15: Choose how your labels will look prior to completing the merge.

How to...

- *Dissecting a Table*
- *Insert a Table*
- *Draw a Table*
- *Selecting Tables, Rows, Columns, or Cells*
- *Change the Table Size*
- *Change Column Width and Row Height*
- *Entering Information*
- *Sort Data*
- *Moving and Copying Tables, Columns, and Rows*
- *Calculate with Formulas*
- *Working with Formulas*
- *Convert Tables to Text and Text to Tables*
- *Repeat Heading Rows*
- *Remove a Table*
- *Formatting Content*
- *Merge and Split Cells*
- *Changing a Table's Alignment*
- *Wrap Text around a Table*
- *Change Cell Margins*
- *Apply Shading and Borders*
- *Format a Table Automatically*

Chapter 6

Using Tables

Documents can be comprised of text only, but using visual elements to support information helps emphasize, organize, and clarify your written words. *Tables* provide a familiar column and row matrix that lets you easily define terms, list items, and lay out data in a convenient and organized manner. Word provides extensive features that support creating, using, and formatting tables to accomplish a variety of purposes. (See Chapters 7 and 8 for more information on working with Word's other features that provide visual enhancements to text. Chapter 7 covers graphics and Chapter 8 describes using charts.)

Create Tables

Tables allow you to divide a portion of a page into rows and columns that create *cells* by their intersection. Tables can be used to systematically arrange information in rows and columns, or they can be used to lay out text and graphics in a document.

1 2 3 4 5 6 7 8 9 10

DISSECTING A TABLE

A table comes with an extensive vocabulary of terms that describe many of its elements, features, and usage, as shown in Figure 6-1.

A few of the ways that you can use tables are:

- Displaying tabular data, with and without cell borders
- Placing side-by-side columns of text
- Aligning labels and boxes for forms
- Presenting text on one side, graphics on the other
- Placing borders around text or graphics
- Placing text on both sides of graphics or vice versa
- Adding color to backgrounds, to text, and to graphics

Columns
Row headings
Hidden (non-printing) grid lines
Selected cell
Split table
Move handle
Centered content, horizontal and vertical
Cell
Rows
Shading
Grid lines
Sizing a column
Merged cells

Chapter 6 Examples.doc - Microsoft Word

Word Feature	Illustration	Description
Scroll button		Moves the contents of the pane in the direction it is dragged
Scroll bar		Moves the contents of the pane in the direction it is clicked

Browse buttons		Enables you to specify an object to use for navigation (for example, pages, tables, or headings) and navigate quickly to the previous or next instance of that object
Status bar	Page 3 Sec 1 3/3	Displays information about the open document
View buttons		Controls the current view of the document being displayed
Rulers	$48.45 $26.98	Enables you to see the precise position of text and other objects in a document
Document pane	Displays the contents of the document being created or edited	

Page 3 Sec 1 3/4 At 2.2" Ln 3 Col 1 REC TRK EXT OVR English (U.S

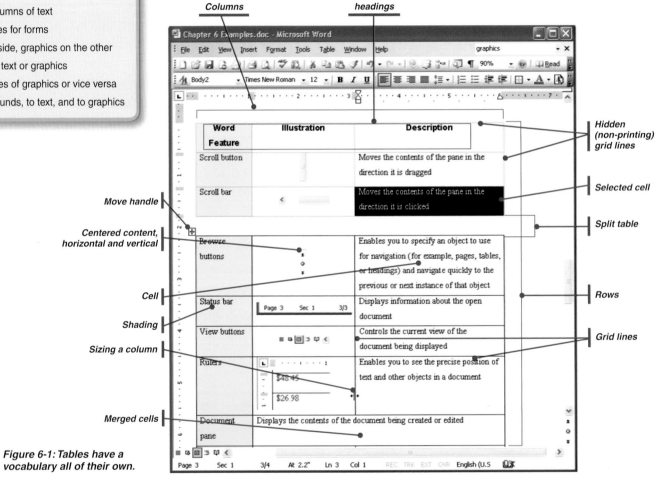

Figure 6-1: Tables have a vocabulary all of their own.

TIP

If you want to insert a table larger than the four rows by five columns shown in the Insert Table drop-down table, simply drag the lower right corner of the drop-down table to the size you want. The box will expand to display the number of rows and/or columns you select.

NOTE

You can easily add rows or columns to an existing table as you need. See "Change the Table Size" later in this chapter.

TIP

Although screen real estate is a commodity not to be wasted, docking the Tables And Borders toolbar under the typically displayed Standard and Formatting toolbars is a reasonable investment when you are working with tables. The time you save by not having to open menus and dialog boxes generally outweighs the loss of displayed information.

Insert a Table

When you create a table, you can determine the number of rows and columns in the table. Additionally, depending on how you create the table, you can select how the columns' width is determined and choose a table style. In all cases, you can easily modify the table attributes after the original table displays in your document. In Word, place the insertion point at the appropriate location in the document where you want a table.

INSERT A TABLE QUICKLY

The Insert Table button on the Standard toolbar offers the quickest method for creating a table using the table defaults.

1. Click the **Insert Table** button on the toolbar. In the drop-down table that opens, click the lower-right cell needed to give you the number of rows and columns you want.
2. Type the information you want in the table, pressing **TAB** as needed to move from cell to cell (see the QuickSteps "Entering Information" later in this chapter).

3 x 3 Table

INSERT A TABLE FROM A DIALOG BOX

The Insert Table dialog box provides a number of initial table-setup options.

1. Click the **Tables And Borders** button on the Standard toolbar. The floating Tables And Borders toolbar displays, as shown in Figure 6-2. Click the **Insert Table** button in the new toolbar.

   –Or–

   Click the **Table** menu, click **Insert**, and click **Table**.

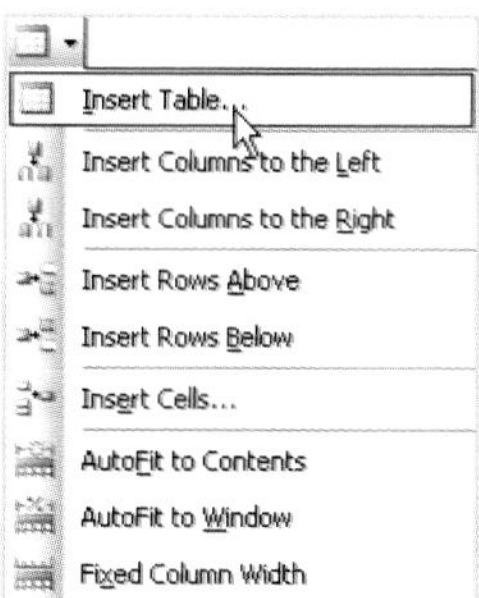

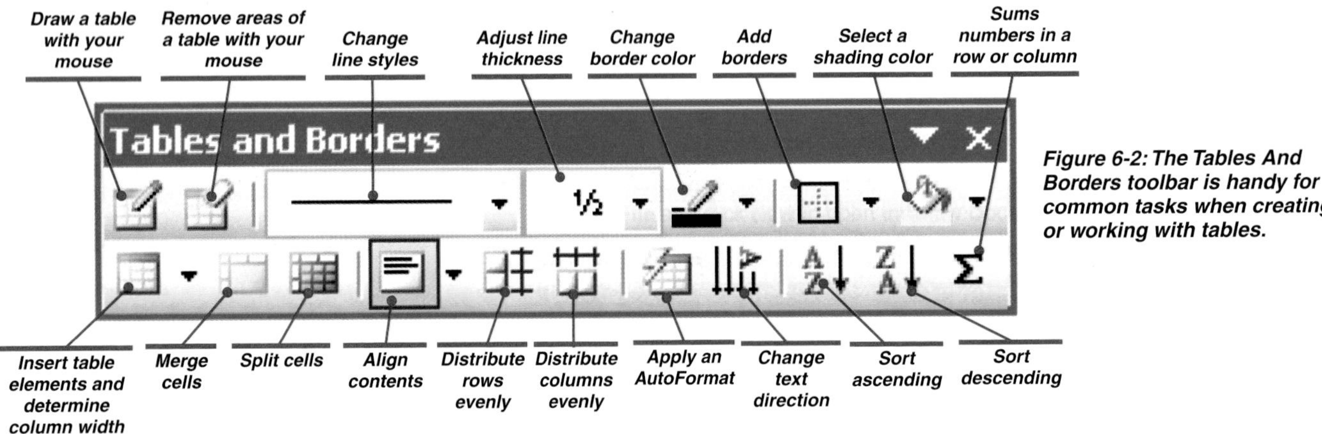

Figure 6-2: The Tables And Borders toolbar is handy for common tasks when creating or working with tables.

Insert Table

Table size

Number of columns: 3

Number of rows: 2

AutoFit behavior

Fixed column width: Auto

AutoFit to contents

AutoFit to window

Table style: Table Grid AutoFormat...

Remember dimensions for new tables

OK Cancel

Figure 6-3: You can determine several table attributes when creating a table using the Insert Table dialog box.

2. The Insert Table dialog box displays, as shown in Figure 6-3.
   - Under Table Size, click the respective spinners, or enter a value to determine the number of rows and columns in the table.
   - Under AutoFit Behavior, choose a fixed column width by clicking the spinner or entering a value (*Auto*, the default, sizes each column equally so they fill the available width of the table), have Word set each column's width to fit the contents in each column, or have Word size the columns to fit the window the table is in (see "Change Column Width and Row Height" later in the chapter for more ways to adjust column width after a table is created).
   - Click **AutoFormat** to apply a preformatted style (see "Format a Table Automatically" later in the chapter for details on choosing and modifying table styles). AutoFormat...
3. If you want to keep the size settings you chose to apply to future tables you create, select the **Remember Dimensions For New Tables** check box.
4. Click **OK** to display the table in your document.

Draw a Table

The most hands-on way to create a table is to draw it:

1. With the document in which you want a table open in Word, scroll to the page where you want to draw a table.
2. Click the **Table** menu and click **Draw Table**. The Tables And Borders toolbar will be displayed.

   –Or–

   If the Tables And Borders toolbar is already displayed, click **Draw Table**.

   In either case, the mouse pointer turns into a pencil.

3. Place the pencil-mouse pointer within the blank lines you created, and drag it horizontally across the page and then vertically down the page. This creates an outline that is the height and width of the outer border of the table you want, as shown in Figure 6-4.
4. Place the pencil-mouse pointer on the top border at the location of the right edge of the leftmost column you want and drag down to the bottom border. Repeat this for the other columns you want.

   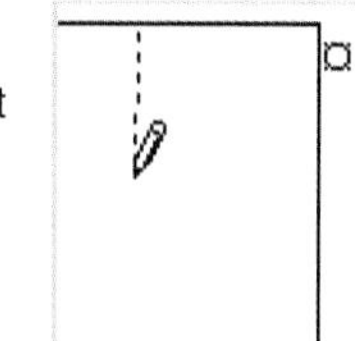
5. Place the pencil-mouse pointer on the left border of the bottom of the top-most row you want and drag to the right outer border. Repeat that for the other rows you want.

NOTE

It is not important to get the initial size and grid perfectly aligned. You can adjust them after the table has been drawn.

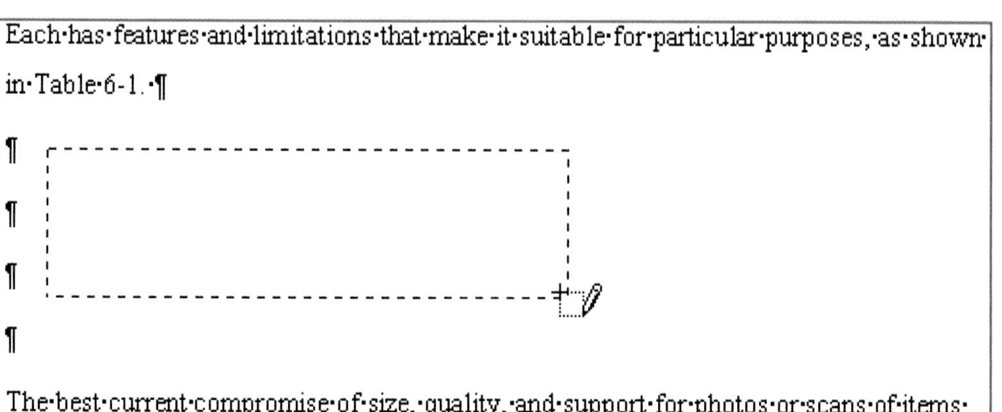

Each·has·features·and·limitations·that·make·it·suitable·for·particular·purposes,·as·shown·
in·Table·6-1.·¶
¶
¶
¶
¶
The·best·current·compromise·of·size,·quality,·and·support·for·photos·or·scans·of·items·

Figure 6-4: Drawing a table is as simple as dragging a rectangular marquee.

1 2 3 4 5 6 7 8 9 10

SELECTING TABLES, ROWS, COLUMNS, OR CELLS

Before you can perform many actions in a table, you must select the element you are working with. With the table open in Word:

SELECT A TABLE

1. Click anywhere in the table you want to select.
2. Click the **Table** menu, click **Select**, and click **Table**.

SELECT ROWS OR COLUMNS BY CLICKING

- Move the mouse pointer to the left border, if selecting rows, so that the pointer becomes an angled rightward-pointing arrow, and double-click.

- Move the mouse pointer to the top border, if selecting columns, so that the pointer becomes a black arrow, and click.

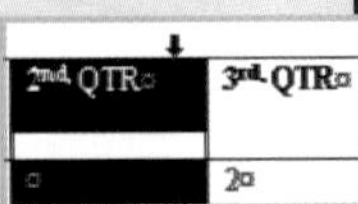

SELECT ROWS OR COLUMNS BY DRAGGING

Move the mouse to the first cell of the row or column and drag it to the last cell. You can easily select multiple rows and/or columns this way.

SELECT ROWS OR COLUMNS FROM THE MENU

1. Click any cell in the row or column you want to select.
2. Click the **Table** menu, click **Select**, and click either **Row** or **Column**.

SELECT A CELL BY CLICKING

1. Move the mouse pointer to the left border of the cell, so that the pointer becomes an angled rightward-pointing black arrow.
2. Click the mouse to select the cell.

SELECT A CELL FROM THE MENU

1. Place your mouse pointer in the cell you want selected.
2. Click the **Table** menu, click **Select**, and click **Cell**.

Continued...

6. When you are done drawing, press **ESC** to turn off the pencil-mouse pointer and return to the I-beam pointer.
7. If you want to adjust the location of any of the outer borders or the row or column borders, point on the border you want to adjust. The mouse pointer will turn into a double-headed resize arrow. Drag the selected border to the location you want it.
8. Enter the information you want in the table, pressing **TAB** as needed to move from cell to cell.

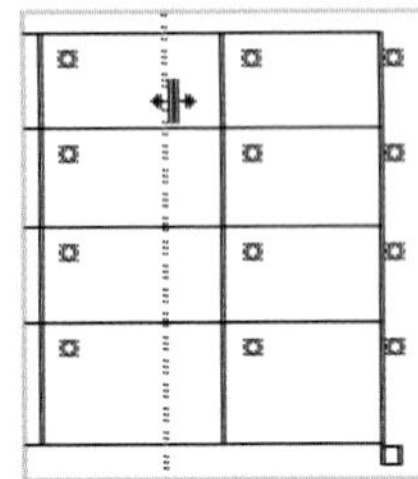

Change the Table Size

Rows, columns, and cells can be added to a table using the Table menu, context menus, or the Tables And Borders toolbar. You can also change a table's size by removing elements, splitting a table, or resizing the overall dimensions.

Figure 6-5: The fast way to select contiguous cells is to drag across them.

Superior Office Supplies	1st Qtr	2nd Qtr	3rd Qtr	4th Qtr
Revenue				
--Paper Supplies	$[illegible]3,567	$35,938	$38,210	$39,876
--Writing Instruments	$5,4[illegible]	$5,834	$5,923	$6,082
--Cards and Books	$14,986	$1[illegible]043	$16,975	$16,983
--Other Items	$25,897	$26,72[illegible]	$[illegible]27,983	$28,721
Total Revenue	$69,887	$8[illegible],544	$89[illegible]	$91,662
Expenses				
--Wages	$8,345	$8,598	$9,110	$9,301
--Income tax	$1,252	$1,290	$1,367	$1,395

Click here and... *...drag...* *...to here to select a range of cells*

SELECTING TABLES, ROWS, COLUMNS, OR CELLS *(Continued)*

SELECT CELLS BY DRAGGING

Place your mouse pointer in the upper-leftmost cell you want to select and drag down and to the right across the remaining cells in the range you want selected, as shown in Figure 6-5. (If you are left handed, you might find it easier to click in the upper-rightmost cell and drag down and to the left).

TIP

It's usually better to add entire rows or columns instead of individual cells, especially when adding cells to a row. You can wind up with cells hanging to the right of your table that appear to be in a column of their own. Also, if your table contains data in a spreadsheet or list format, adding cells can easily jumble the data organization.

ADD CELLS

Cells can be added to a table below or to the right of existing cells.

1. Select the cells adjacent to where you want to add the new cells. (To add a single cell, select only the cell above or to the left of where you want the new cell. If adding more than one cell, select the number of cells you want added and an equal number will be added below or to the right of your selection.) See the QuickSteps "Selecting Tables, Rows, Columns, or Cells."
2. Click the **Table** menu, click **Insert**, and click **Cells**.

   –Or–

   Click the **Insert Table** down arrow on the Tables And Borders toolbar, and click **Insert Cells**.
3. In the Insert Cells dialog box, click **Shift Cells Right** (existing cells are "pushed" to the right of the rightmost column).

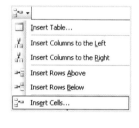

   –Or–

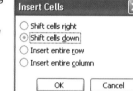

   Click **Shift Cells Down** (new rows are added to the bottom of the table equal to the number of cells added).
4. Click **OK**.

RESIZE BY DRAGGING

1. Click the **View** menu and click **Print Layout** (the sizing handle doesn't display in Normal view).
2. Place your mouse over the table whose size you want to change, and drag the sizing handle that appears in the lower right corner of the table to increase or decrease the table size. The rows and columns increase or decrease proportionately within the constraints of the cell contents.

1 2 3 4 5 6 7 8 9 10

CAUTION

Removing cells also deletes any text or graphics contained in the affected table elements.

ADD ROWS AT THE BOTTOM OF A TABLE

As you are entering information into a table and you reach the bottom-rightmost cell, simply pressing **TAB** will add another row to the table.

INSERT ROWS OR COLUMNS

You can quickly add rows or columns from menu choices available on the menu bar or Tables and Borders toolbar.

1. Select the rows or columns in the table next to where you want to add rows or columns (the number of rows or columns added will equal the number of rows or columns selected).
2. Click the **Table** menu, and then click **Insert**.

   –Or–

   Click the **Insert** down arrow on the Tables and Borders toolbar.
3. Click the appropriate option on the menus to:
   - **Add columns** to the left or right of the selected columns

     –Or–
   - **Add rows** above or below the selected rows

REMOVE CELLS, ROWS, OR COLUMNS

1. Select the cells, rows, or columns you want to remove (see the QuickSteps “Selecting Tables, Rows, Columns, or Cells”).
2. Right-click the selection and:
   - Click **Delete Columns** to remove selected columns.

     –Or–
   - Click **Delete Rows** to remove selected rows.

     –Or–
   - Click **Delete Cells** to open the Delete Cells dialog box. Choose whether to fill the vacant area of the table by shifting cells to the left or up. Click **OK**.

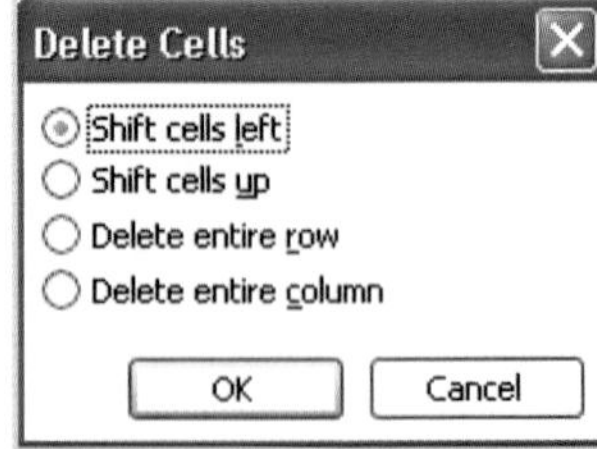

NOTE

You can also remove parts of a table by erasing the elements you don’t want. Click **Eraser** on the Tables And Borders toolbar. Drag a rectangle with the eraser pointer over the elements you want removed. The borders of the elements to be removed within the red rectangular selection are bolded. Release the mouse button to remove the selected elements (when cells are removed within the interior of the table, the “hole” that remains is one larger, merged cell). Press **ESC** to return to the standard pointer, or click the **Eraser** button.

$8,345	$8,508	$9,110	$9,301
$1,252	$1,290	$1,367	$1,395
$1,035	$1,066	$1,130	$1,153
$242	$249	$264	$270

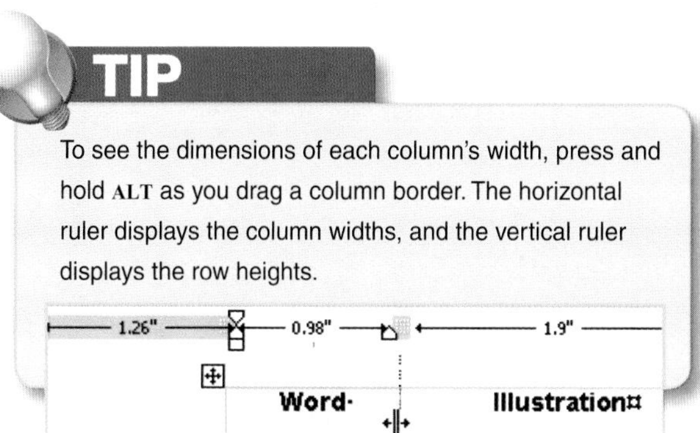

TIP

To see the dimensions of each column's width, press and hold ALT as you drag a column border. The horizontal ruler displays the column widths, and the vertical ruler displays the row heights.

Figure 6-6: *You can set exact dimensions for each column's width or as a percentage of the table width.*

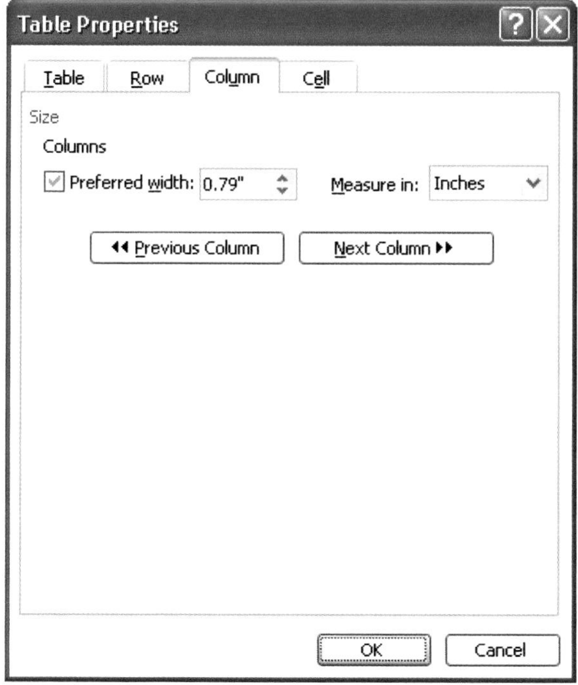

SPLIT A TABLE

You can divide a table along any of its rows to split it into segments. Word will divide longer tables when it creates automatic page breaks, though you might find it handy to be able to control exactly where the break occurs in the table.

1. Click a cell in the row below where you want the split to occur.
2. Click the **Table** menu and click **Split Table**. A blank paragraph is inserted between the two tables (see Figure 6-1).

Change Column Width and Row Height

By default tables are created with equal column widths spanning the width of the table (margin-to-margin across document). You can change each column to a specific width you set, or use AutoFit to adjust the width to fit the longest entry in the column. Row heights change vertically as needed to accommodate lines of text or larger font size (all cells in a row increase to match the highest cell in the row).

CHANGE COLUMN WIDTH AND ROW HEIGHT BY DRAGGING

1. Place the mouse pointer on the right border of the column whose width you want to change or the bottom border of the row height you want to change. The mouse pointer changes to a resize pointer showing the opposing directions you can drag.

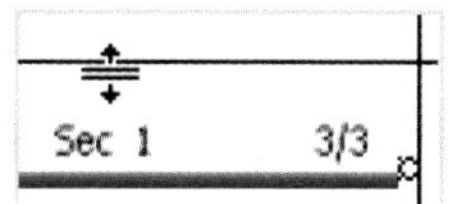

2. Drag the border to increase or decrease the size.

CHANGE COLUMN WIDTH PRECISELY

1. Right-click the table that contains the columns whose widths you want to change, and click **Table Properties** from the context menu.
2. In the Table Properties dialog box, click the **Column** tab, shown in Figure 6-6.
3. Use the **Previous Column** and **Next Column** buttons to select the initial column you want to set.
4. Select the **Preferred Width** check box, and set a width in inches or as a percent of the table width.
5. Repeat steps 3 and 4 to change the width of other columns.
6. Click **OK**.

TIP

You can manually adjust column widths and row heights to fit contents by selecting the columns or rows you want to adjust, pointing at the columns' rightmost border or the rows' lowermost border, and double-clicking when the pointer changes to a resizing icon.

TIP

Distribute Columns or Rows Evenly buttons are particularly useful when you draw a table by hand.

CHANGE COLUMN WIDTH TO FIT CONTENTS

You can use AutoFit to dynamically adjust the column widths to fit the longest single-line entry in that column.

Right-click a table with columns you want to adjust to fit the content, click **AutoFit**, and click **AutoFit To Contents**. (To return to the default text-wrapping behavior, right-click the table, click **AutoFit**, and click **Fixed Column Width**. You will need to manually narrow any column widths to wrap text that extends full-cell length.)

SPACE COLUMN WIDTHS OR ROW HEIGHTS EQUALLY

Select the columns or rows that you want to make the same size. On the Tables And Borders toolbar:

- Click **Distribute Columns Evenly** to space selected column widths equally.
- Click **Distribute Rows Evenly** to space selected row heights equally.

Work with Tables

Tables can be set up for many purposes, and Word provides features to support many uses. You can use special shortcut key combinations to move through the cells, sort lists, and work with formulas. Also, you can move, copy, and delete tables.

TABLE 6-1: MOVE AROUND A TABLE FROM THE KEYBOARD

TO MOVE TO...	PRESS...
cells to the right and down at row end (cell contents selected)	TAB
cells to the left and up at row end (cell contents selected)	SHIFT+TAB
first cell in a column	ALT+PAGE UP
last cell in a column	ALT+PAGE DOWN
first cell in a row	ALT+HOME
last cell in a row	ALT+END

ENTERING INFORMATION

Typing text in table cells is very similar to tying text elsewhere in the document. You can use familiar tools such as bullets, tabs, and other options found on the Standard and Formatting toolbars and in the Font and Paragraph dialog boxes. See Chapters 2 through 4 for basic techniques when working with text.

TYPE TEXT ABOVE A TABLE

Place the insertion point in the upper-leftmost cell in the table (to the left of any text in the cell) and press **SHIFT+CTRL+ENTER**. A new paragraph is created above the table.

MOVE AROUND A TABLE

The most straightforward way to move between cells in a table is to simply click the cell where you want to add text or graphics. However, if you're adding a lot of data to a table, it's more efficient to keep your hands on the keyboard. See Table 6-1 for several keyboard shortcuts you can use.

MOVE CONTENT AROUND

You can cut and copy text and other content using the same techniques for basic text. Just select the content in the cells you want, and for example, press **CTRL+C** to copy the content. When pasting the content into other cells in the table, place the insertion point in the cell where you want the content to appear. Press **CTRL+V** or use menu or toolbar options. Any content in existing cells to the right and below the range of pasted cells will be overwritten with the new content.

Sort Data

You can sort information in ascending or descending order according to the values in one or more columns. You can sort an entire table or selected cells (all data in the table or range is realigned so that the data in each row remains the same, even though the row might be placed in a different order than it was originally), or just a column (data in columns outside the sorted column does not change order).

SORT A TABLE OR SELECTED CELLS

1. Place your insertion point in the table you want to sort, or select a range of cells to sort.
2. Click the **Table** menu and click **Sort**. The Sort dialog box opens, as shown in Figure 6-7.

Figure 6-7: You can reorganize information in a table by sorting by one or more columns in ascending or descending order.

1

2

3

4

5

6

7

8

9

10

NOTE

Sorting in Word is determined by a specified *sort order*. Each of the three types of information recognized by Word contains its own sort order. For example, Text entries beginning with punctuation characters are sorted first, followed by entries beginning with numbers, and then entries starting with letters. When sorting is based on the Numbers type, all other characters are ignored. Dates are recognized by the separators used to define days, months, and years. Periods, hyphens (-), forward slashes (/), and commas are valid date separators.

TIP

You can sort by four columns, but you have to "trick" Word a bit by doing the sort in two steps. First, sort on the least specific column in the Sort dialog box, and click **OK**. Next, complete a second sort in the Sort dialog box as you normally would, from the most to the least specific column, using the three sorting sections. Click **OK** to close the Sort dialog box a second time.

3. Click the **Sort By** down arrow, and click the column of primary importance in determining the sort order in the drop-down list (if the columns have headings, select one of the titles; if there are no headings, select a column based on the displayed numbers that start with the leftmost column).
4. Click the **Type** down arrow, and click whether the column contains numbers, dates, and anything else (the Text option is the catch-all sort type). Click **Ascending** or **Descending**.

Text
Text
Number
Date

5. Click the first **Then By** down arrow, and click the column you want to base the sort on that is of secondary importance in the drop-down list. Select the type of information in the column, and click **Ascending** or **Descending**.
6. Repeat, if necessary, for the second Then By section to sort by a third column of information.
7. Under My List Has, click whether the table or selection has a heading row.
8. Click **OK** when finished. An example of a table sorted by two columns is shown in Figure 6-8.

Primary sort, on Price, arranges list in ascending price order
Secondary sort, on Category, determines order of entries that have same price

Title	Price	Category	Author
2010	$3.95	Sci. Fic.	Clarke
A Thief of Time	$4.95	Mystery	Hillerman
Dragon	$5.95	Mystery	Cussler
Final Flight	$5.95	Thriller	Coonts
Hawaii: A Paradise Family Guide	$5.95	Travel	Penisten
Fatherhood	$14.95	Children	Cosby
Classic Italian Cookbook	$15.95	Cooking	Hazan
A Brief History of Time	$16.95	Science	Hawking

Figure 6-8: Sort by multiple columns to arrange entries that have the same next higher-level sort value.

You can also use the Sort Ascending and Sort Descending buttons on the Tables And Borders toolbar to sort selected columns. Sorting using these two buttons assumes the first cell in a column is a heading and doesn't include it in the sort.

SORT A SINGLE COLUMN

1. Select the column you want to sort (see the QuickSteps "Selecting Tables, Rows, Columns, or Cells").
2. Click the **Table** menu and click **Sort**.
3. In the Sort dialog box, click **Options**.
4. In the Sort Options dialog box, click the **Sort Column Only** check box.
5. Click **OK** twice.

SORT BY MORE THAN ONE FIELD IN A COLUMN

If you combine two or more fields of information, such as city, county, and state (for example, Everett, Snohomish, WA) in a single column instead of splitting them out into separate columns, you can sort your list by choosing which fields to sort by.

1. Place your insertion point in the table.
2. Click the **Table** menu and click **Sort**.
3. In the Sort dialog box, click **Options**. In the Sort Options dialog box, under Separate Fields At, click the character used to separate the fields in a single column, or click **Other** and type the separator character. Click **OK** to close the Sort Options dialog box.

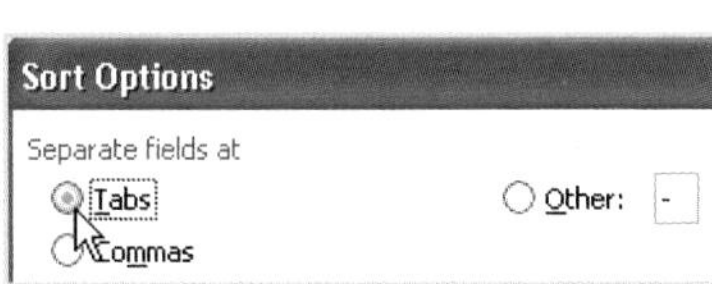

4. In the Sort dialog box, click the **Sort By** down arrow, and click the primary column that contains multiple fields. Click the **Type** down arrow, click an information type, and click **Ascending** or **Descending**. Click the **Using** down arrow, and click the field you want to sort by.
5. Use the Then By sections if you want to sort by additional columns or fields.
6. Click **OK** when finished.

1
2
3
4
5
6
7
8
9
10

MOVING AND COPYING TABLES, COLUMNS, AND ROWS

A table is easily moved or copied by dragging its move handle (the move handle is only displayed when viewing the document in Print Layout view). Columns and rows can also be dragged into new positions.

MOVE A TABLE

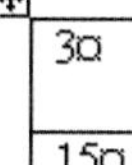

1. Hover the mouse pointer over the table you want to move to display its move handle, above and to the left of the upper-leftmost cell in the table.
2. Drag the table into the position you want.

COPY A TABLE

Press and hold **CTRL,** and then drag the table's move handle to position where you want the copy of the table.

–Or–

Click the **Table** menu, click **Select**, and click **Table**. Press **CTRL+C** to copy the table to the clipboard. Place your insertion point where you want the new table, and press **CTRL+V**.

MOVE COLUMNS AND ROWS

1. Select the columns or rows you want to move (see the QuickSteps "Selecting Tables, Rows, Columns, or Cells" earlier in the chapter).
2. Drag the selection where you want the elements moved.

- Selected columns display to the left of the column where you end the drag.
- Selected rows display above the row where you end the drag.

COPY COLUMNS AND ROWS

To leave selected elements in place while adding a copy of them to a new location, use the previous procedure for moving columns and rows, except press and hold **CTRL** while dragging.

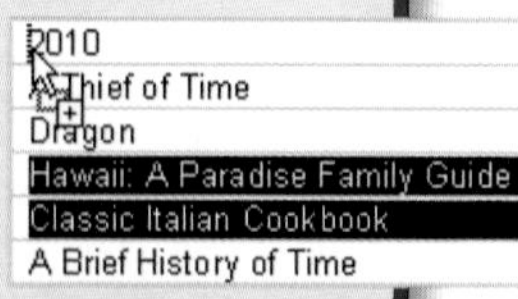

Calculate with Formulas

You can use formulas in tables to perform arithmetic calculations and provide results, by either putting together your own or using an AutoSum feature.

ASSEMBLE YOUR OWN FORMULAS

1. Place your mouse pointer in the cell where you want the result displayed.
2. Click the **Table** menu and click **Formula**. The Formula dialog box opens, as shown in Figure 6-9.
3. In the Formula text box, keep the Word-suggested formula, apply a number format, and click **OK** to display the result.

   –Or–

   Delete everything except the equal (=) sign.

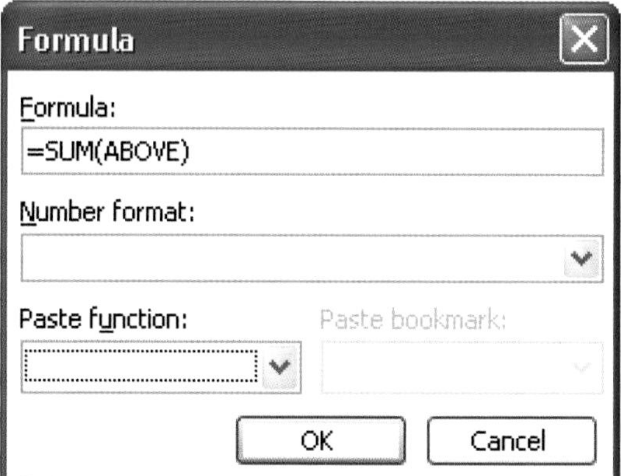

Figure 6-9: The Formula dialog box provides tools to set up formulas for basic calculations.

TIP

You must manually update formulas after changing an underlying cell value. To recalculate a formula, select the resulting value and press **F9**.

WORKING WITH FORMULAS

Word provides a rudimentary spreadsheet capability in tables to perform calculations on numeric entries. Knowing a number of terms and concepts associated with working with formulas will make using them in tables much easier. See *Microsoft Office Excel 2003 QuickSteps*, published by McGraw-Hill/Osborne, for more information on working with formulas, functions, and worksheets.)

- **Syntax** is the set of rules Word uses for you to communicate how to perform calculations with formulas. For instance, to identify to Word that a series of characters in a cell are to be calculated, they must be preceded with an equal sign. Also, the cell references to be acted upon must be enclosed in parentheses.
- **Cell reference** is a scheme formulas you can use to provide a unique address for each cell consisting of its column and row intersection. Columns are designated alphabetically starting with the leftmost column as *A*; rows are sequentially numbered from top to bottom with the topmost row as *1*. For example, the third cell from the left in the second row would be identified as cell C2.
- **Cell reference operators** are the syntax to identify multiple cells in a formula. For example, to add the values in cell A1, A2, B1, and B2, you use commas to list the cells the function is to sum: =SUM(A1,A2,B1,B2). Use a colon (:) operator to identify a *range* of contiguous cells: =SUM(A1:B2).
- **Functions** are prewritten formulas that you can use to perform specific tasks. For example, some functions perform arithmetic calculations, such as SUM and AVERAGE; some apply Boolean logic, such as AND, TRUE, and NOT; others are used for unique purposes, such as to COUNT the number of values in a list.
- **Attributes** communicate instructions to a function to perform an action. For example, if you click the bottom cell in a column and open the Formula dialog box, Word suggests a formula, =SUM(ABOVE). The ABOVE attribute eliminates the need for you to reference each cell in the column above the cell.

4. Click the **Paste Function** down arrow, and choose the function you want to use.

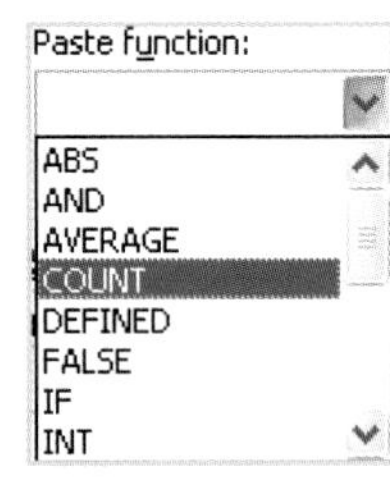

5. In the Formula text box, between the parentheses following the function, type the cell references or attribute the function applies to.
6. Click the **Number Format** down arrow, and click the style you want applied to the result.

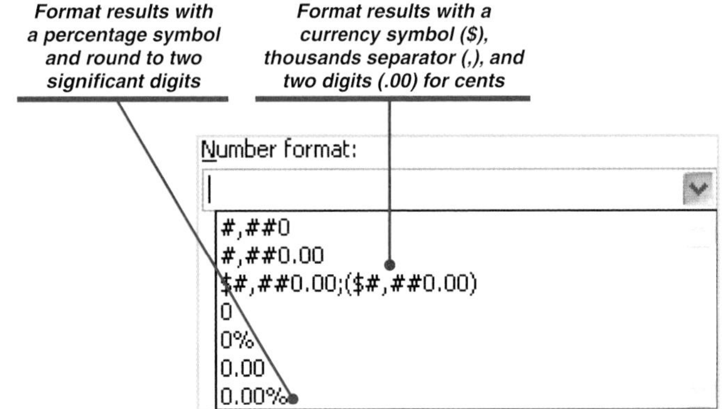

7. Click **OK** to display the result.

TIP

To convert the result of a formula into plain text (remove the underlying formula and associated field code), select the field code containing the formula's result, and press **CTRL+SHIFT+F9.**

NOTE

AutoSum sums contiguous values. If you have a blank cell within a series of values in a row or column, AutoSum will only sum to the blank cell. To include all values, enter a zero in the blank cell.

NOTE

If you see a field code in a cell containing the code for the formula instead of the formula's result, select the field code, and press **SHIFT+F9**. The code syntax is replaced by a numeric value.

{ =SUM(a1:a2) }

TIP

The best choice for column and row separators is to use tabs to separate columns of text and paragraph marks to separate rows. Other characters you can use, such as commas, are often used within the text and can cause unpredictable results during the conversion.

SUM NUMBERS AUTOMATICALLY

You can quickly sum values in a row or column by using the AutoSum tool.

1. Place your insertion point in the cell where you want the result. Contiguous values in a row to the left of the cell will be summed; contiguous values in a column above the cell will be summed (if you have numbers both to the left and above a cell, the column wins!).
2. Click **AutoSum** on the Tables And Borders toolbar. Σ

Convert Tables to Text and Text to Tables

If you have information in text format, Word has the means to convert it to a table and similarly to convert information in a table to ordinary text.

CONVERT TEXT TO A TABLE

Converting text to a table requires that the text be appropriately formatted with tabs, commas, or another character between columns and a separate character, such as a paragraph mark, between rows.

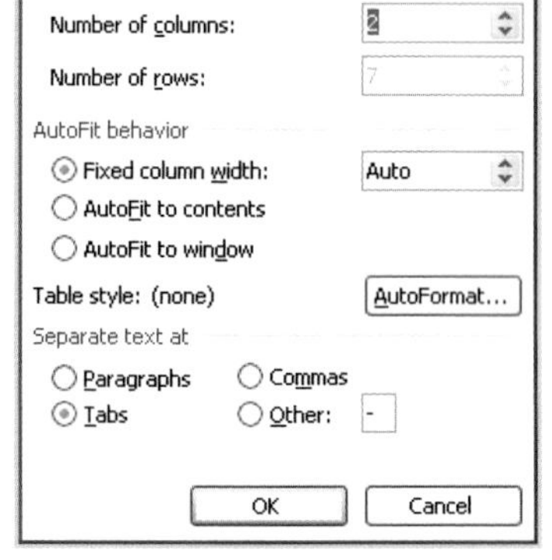

1. Drag across all the text to select it. Click the **Table** menu, click **Convert**, and click **Text To Table**. The Convert Text To Table dialog box opens. Do not be concerned if the number of rows and columns do not yet match your expectations.
2. Under Separate Text At, click the formatting character used to separate columns of text, or click **Other** and type the character. The number of columns and rows values should now reflect how you formatted the text to be displayed in a table.
3. Under AutoFit Behavior, choose a fixed column width by clicking the spinner or entering a value (*Auto*, the default, sizes each column equally so they fill the available width of the table). Decide whether to have Word set each column's width to fit its contents or have Word size the columns to fit the window the table is in. (AutoFit To Window is primarily used when sizing tables in web pages. See Chapter 9 for more information on saving Word documents as web pages.)

4. Click **AutoFormat** to apply a preformatted style (see "Format a Table Automatically" later in the chapter for details on choosing and modifying table styles). Click **OK** to close Table AutoFormat.

5. Click **OK** when finished. The table that was created from the data in Figure 6-10 shows text "before and after" being converted to a table.

Title bar → Contains the name of the open document and the controls for the window¶
Menu bar → Contains the primary controls for Word, divided into categories¶
Standard toolbar → Allows direct access to many of the basic functions for Word¶
Formatting toolbar → Allows direct access to many of the formatting features in Word¶
Minimize button → Minimizes the window to an icon on the taskbar¶
Maximize button → Maximizes the window to fill the screen¶
Close → Exits Word and closes the window¶
Task pane → Displays options for your current task, such as getting started¶
Scroll arr

Title bar	Contains the name of the open document and the controls for the window
Menu bar	Contains the primary controls for Word, divided into categories
Standard toolbar	Allows direct access to many of the basic functions for Word
Formatting toolbar	Allows direct access to many of the formatting features in Word
Minimize button	Minimizes the window to an icon on the taskbar
Maximize button	Maximizes the window to fill the screen
Close	Exits Word and closes the window
Task pane	Displays options for your current task, such as getting started
Scroll arrow	Moves the contents of the pane in the direction of the arrow

Figure 6-10: Text properly formatted with separators is easily converted to a Word table.

CONVERT A TABLE TO TEXT

Converting a table into text converts the table information into text with the contents of each cell separated by a character you choose; each row becomes a separate paragraph.

1. Select the table that you want to convert to text (see the QuickSteps "Selecting Tables, Rows, Columns, or Cells"). Click the **Table** menu, click **Convert**, and click **Table To Text**. The Convert Table To Text dialog box displays.

2. Under Separate Text With, click the formatting character you want to be used to separate text in columns, or click **Other** and type the character you want.

3. If you have a table within a table, click the **Convert Nested Tables** check box to convert them as well.

4. Click **OK** when finished.

1

2

3

4

5

6

7

8

9

10

Repeat Heading Rows

Headings are the column identifiers placed in the first rows of a table (see Figure 6-1) to distinguish different categories of information. In tables, so they can span multiple document pages, heading rows can be repeated at the top of each page. The reader, then, does not have to remember the column category or keep returning to the beginning of the table (repeated headings only apply to Word-generated page breaks, not to those you create manually).

1. Click the **View** menu and click **Print Layout** so you can see the headings displayed.
2. Select the heading rows (see the QuickSteps "Selecting Tables, Rows, Columns, or Cells").
3. Click the **Table** menu, extend the menu, and click **Heading Rows Repeat** to place a check mark next to the option.

TIP

You can remove a table using your mouse. Click **Eraser** on the Tables And Borders toolbar. Drag a rectangle with the eraser pointer over the table border, and release the mouse button. Press ESC to return to the standard pointer.

Remove a Table

Removing a table removes the rows and columns of the table along with any text or data.

1. Place the insertion point in the table you want to remove.
2. Click the **Table** menu, click **Select**, and click **Table**. Press DELETE.

   –Or–

   Select the table and click **Cut** on the toolbar. The table is removed but available to be pasted elsewhere (see Chapter 2 for information on using the Office Clipboard to paste material in Word documents and Chapter 10 for pasting into other applications).

FORMATTING CONTENT

Tables provide several formatting features specifically focused on working with content in cells.

ALIGN CONTENT WITHIN A CELL

By default, content is aligned to start at the top left corner of a cell. You can change this to several other configurations.

1. Select the cells whose content alignment you want to change.
2. Right-click the selected cells, click **Cell Alignment** on the context menu, and click one of the nine alignment options.

   –Or–

   Click the cell alignment down arrow on the Tables And Borders toolbar, and click an alignment option.

CHANGE TEXT WRAPPING IN A CELL

By default, text is wrapped in a cell to the next line when it extends to the right border of the cell. (You can override this behavior by using AutoFit to adjust column widths to the content. See "Change Column Width to Fit Contents" earlier in this chapter.) To remove text wrapping in cells:

1. Select the cells that you do not want to wrap text.
2. Right-click the selected cells, click **Table Properties** on the context menu, and click the **Cell** tab.
3. Click **Options** to open the Cell Options dialog box. Under Options, deselect the **Wrap Text** check box.
4. Click **OK** twice to close the Cell Options and Table Properties dialog boxes.

Options

☐ Wrap text

Continued...

Change a Table's Appearance

A table chock full of data is informative but not necessarily appealing. Word offers special features including text wrapping and orientation options. You can also change the look of the table structure by merging and splitting cells; adjusting margins surrounding cells; aligning the table on the document page; and applying color, shading, and emphasis to backgrounds and borders.

Merge and Split Cells

Cells can be *merged* by combining two or more cells into one cell. Merged cells can be used to create a banner that spans the width of a table, as a placeholder for larger inserted graphics, and for other special effects. You can also accomplish the opposite effect by subdividing a cell into multiple columns and/or rows by splitting the cell.

NOTE

You can apply most of the formatting features to text within a table as you do to narrative text outside a table—for example, you can add numbered and bulleted lists and color text. Use the Format menu options and Formatting toolbar to add spice to your table contents!

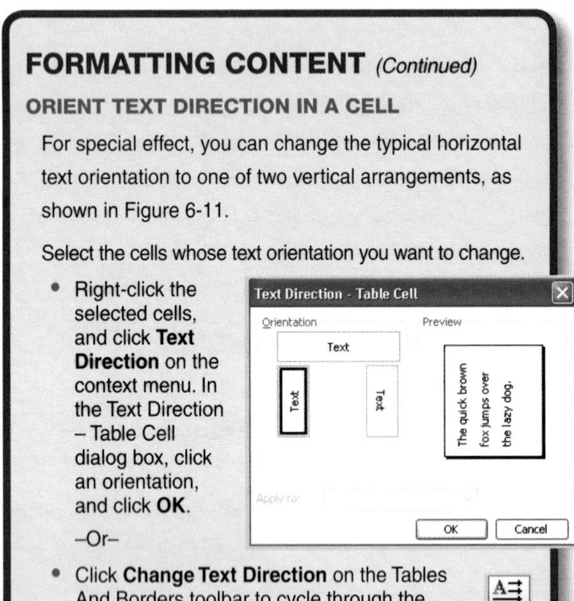

FORMATTING CONTENT *(Continued)*

ORIENT TEXT DIRECTION IN A CELL

For special effect, you can change the typical horizontal text orientation to one of two vertical arrangements, as shown in Figure 6-11.

Select the cells whose text orientation you want to change.

- Right-click the selected cells, and click **Text Direction** on the context menu. In the Text Direction – Table Cell dialog box, click an orientation, and click **OK**.

  –Or–

- Click **Change Text Direction** on the Tables And Borders toolbar to cycle through the three orientation options.

TIP

Check out the alignment, lists, and indent buttons on the Formatting and Tables And Borders toolbars after you click a cell whose text direction has changed. The button faces become oriented vertically as well!

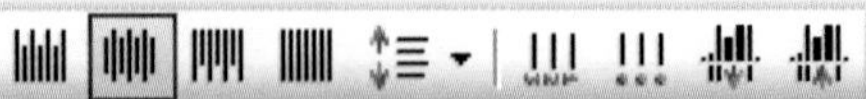

MERGE CELLS

1. Select the cells you want to combine into one cell (see the QuickSteps "Selecting Tables, Rows, Columns, or Cells").

Document· pane¤	¤	Displays·the·contents·of·the·document· being·created·or·edited¤

2. Right-click the selection and click **Merge Cells**.

   –Or–

   Click **Merge Cells** on the Tables And Borders toolbar.

Any content spans the merged cell.

Document· pane¤	Displays·the·contents·of·the·document·being·created·or·edited¤

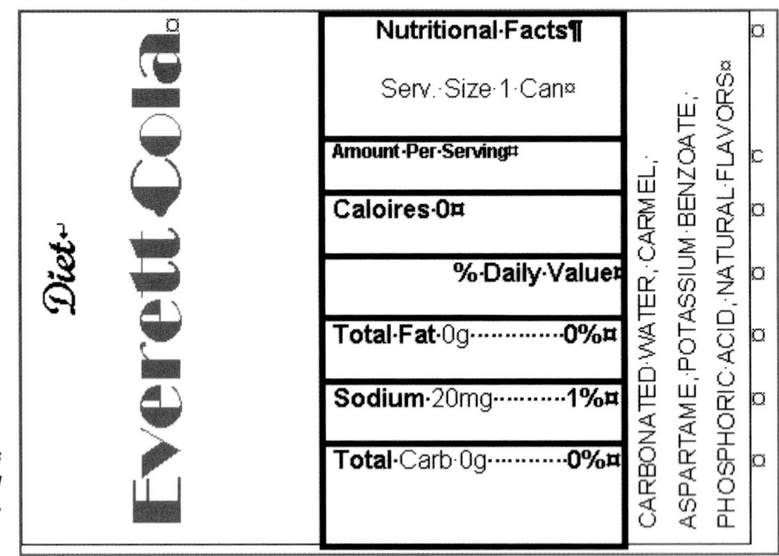

Figure 6-11: Vertical text provides interesting opportunities for laying out logos and other advertising.

CHANGING A TABLE'S ALIGNMENT

ALIGN A TABLE QUICKLY

1. Place the insertion point in the table you want to align.
2. Click the **Table** menu, click **Select**, and click **Table**.
3. Click **Align Left**, **Center**, or **Align Right** on the Formatting toolbar.

ALIGN AND INDENT A TABLE

1. Right-click the table you want to align, click **Table Properties** on the context menu, and click the **Table** tab, as shown in Figure 6-12.
2. Click the **Left** alignment icon. Click the **Indent From Left** spinner, or enter a value to shift the indent to the right of the margin on the left side of the page (enter a negative number to move the indent to the left of the margin on the left side of the page).
3. Click **OK**.

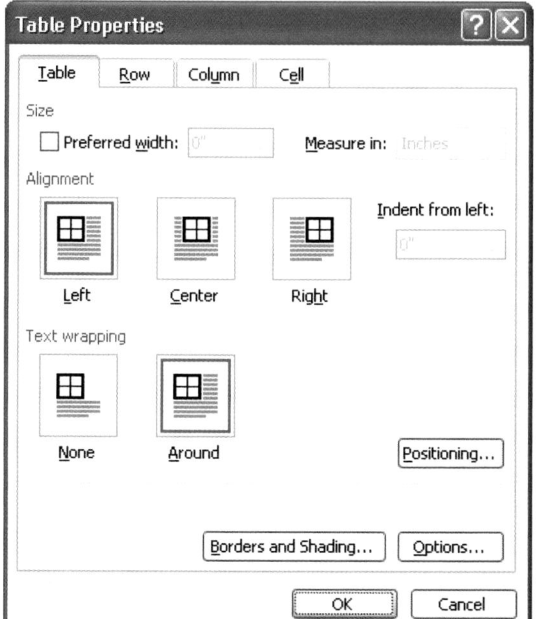

Figure 6-12: The Table tab of a table's properties dialog box lets you align and indent a table, as well as size and determine text wrapping options.

SPLIT CELLS

1. Select the cells you want to split into more columns or rows.
2. Click the **Table** menu and click **Split Cells**. The Split Cells dialog box opens.

   –Or–

   Right-click the cells and click **Split Cells**.

   –Or–

   Click **Split Cells** on the Tables And Borders toolbar.

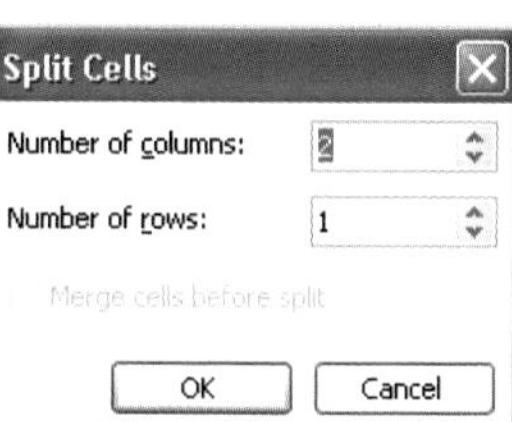

3. Click the **Number Of Columns** spinner, or enter a value, to divide the selected cells vertically.
4. Click the **Number Of Rows** spinner, or enter a value, to divide the selected cells horizontally (other cells in the rows being split increase their height to accommodate the increase).
5. To split each selected cell into the number of rows or columns entered, deselect the **Merge Cells Before Split** check box.

   –Or–

   To split the merged block of selected cells into the number of rows or columns entered, select the **Merge Cells Before Split** check box.
6. Click **OK**.

Wrap Text around a Table

Tables are inserted *inline*, with other text and objects in the document, so the other content is either above or below the table's position. You can choose to have adjacent text wrap on either side of the table, as well as adjust how the table is positioned relative to the text.

1. Right-click the table you want to align, click **Table Properties** on the context menu, and click the **Table** tab (see Figure 6-12).
2. Under Text Wrapping, click the **Around** icon to wrap text around the sides of the table (the table's width must be less than the margin width for text to appear on the sides).

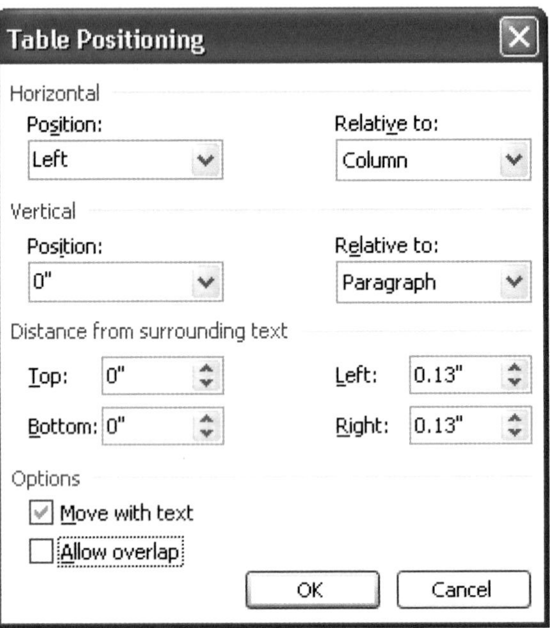

Figure 6-13: You can lock a table's position relative to the document's elements and set options for how the text displays near the table.

3. Click **Positioning** to open the Table Positioning dialog box, shown in Figure 6-13.
   - Under Horizontal and Vertical, set values to position the table relative to other elements on the page.
   - Under Distance From Surrounding Text, determine how much of a gap you want to exist between the table and surrounding text.
   - Select the **Move With Text** check box if you want the table to move with text flow; deselect it to keep the table in a fixed position regardless whether content is added to or removed from the page.
   - Select **Allow Overlap** to let text flow in front of the table.
4. Click **OK** twice.

Change Cell Margins

You can change the distance between content and cell borders, both for an entire table and for selected cells.

SET MARGINS FOR ALL CELLS IN A TABLE

1. Right-click the table whose default cell margins you want to change, and click **Table Properties** on the context menu.
2. On the Table tab, click **Options**. In the Table Options dialog box, under Default Cell Margins, change the **Top**, **Bottom**, **Left**, and **Right** values as needed by clicking their respective spinners or entering numbers.
3. Click **OK** twice.

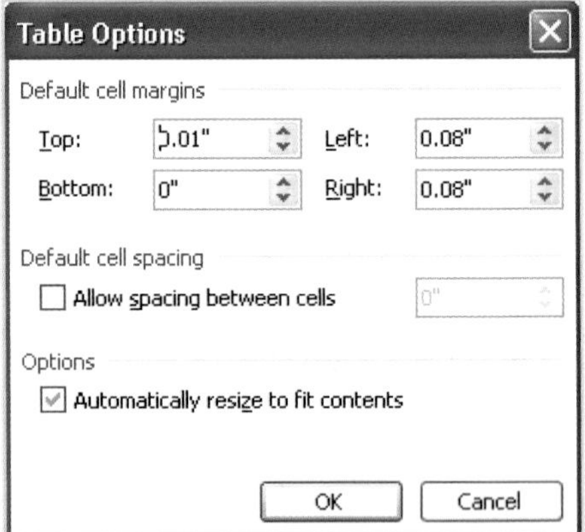

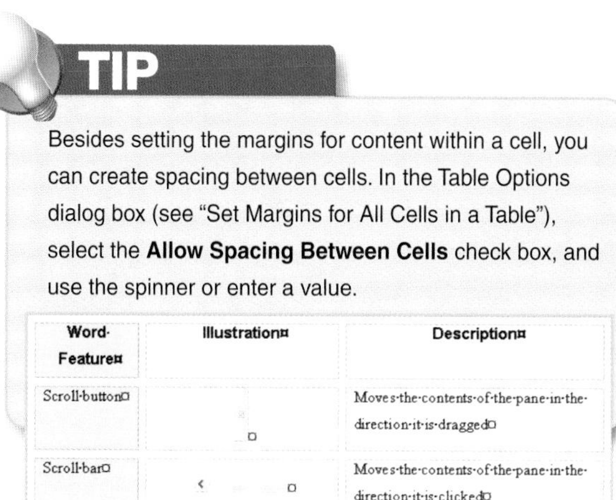

TIP

Besides setting the margins for content within a cell, you can create spacing between cells. In the Table Options dialog box (see "Set Margins for All Cells in a Table"), select the **Allow Spacing Between Cells** check box, and use the spinner or enter a value.

Word Feature	Illustration	Description
Scroll button		Moves the contents of the pane in the direction it is dragged
Scroll bar		Moves the contents of the pane in the direction it is clicked

SET MARGINS FOR SELECTED CELLS

1. Select the cells whose default cell margins you want to change, and click **Table Properties** on the context menu.
2. On the Cell tab, click **Options**.
3. In the Cell Margins dialog box, deselect the **Same As The Whole Table** check box, and change the **Top**, **Bottom**, **Left**, and **Right** values as needed by clicking their respective spinners or entering numbers.
4. Click **OK** twice.

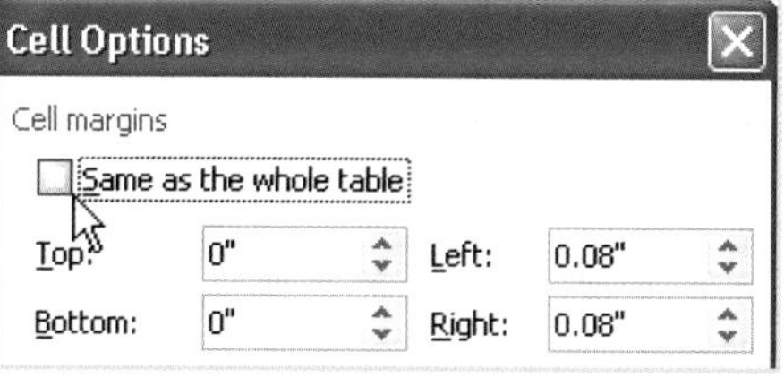

Apply Shading and Borders

Tables and individual cells can be emphasized with Word's broad set of tools to apply shading and border outlines.

1. Select the table or cells which you want to apply a shading or border effect.
2. Open the Borders And Shading dialog box, shown in Figure 6-14, by one of several means:
   - Right-click the selected element, and click **Borders And Shading** on the context menu.
   - Click the **Format** menu and click **Borders and Shading**.
   - Click **Borders And Shading** on the Table tab of the Table Properties dialog box.

     Borders and Shading...

     –Or–

     Use the border tools on the Tables and Borders toolbar (see Figure 6-2).

(See Chapter 3 for information on how to apply borders and shading to text.)

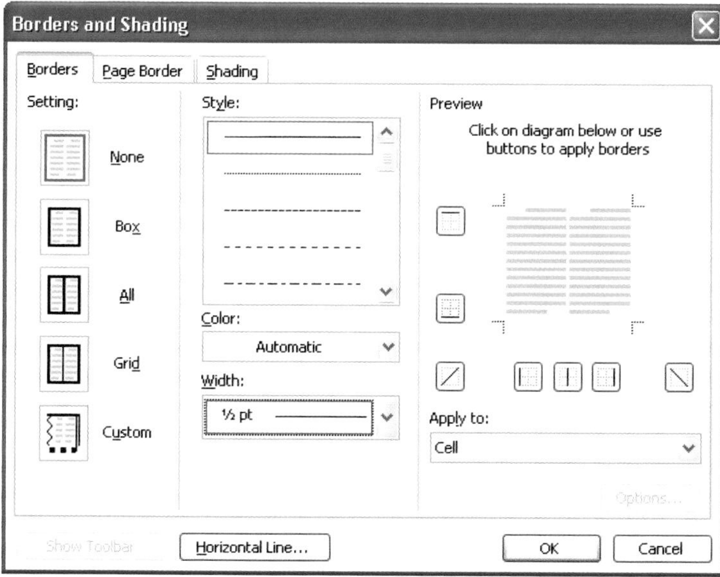

Figure 6-14: You can choose borders for each side of the cells and the table, as well as provide background fills and patterns.

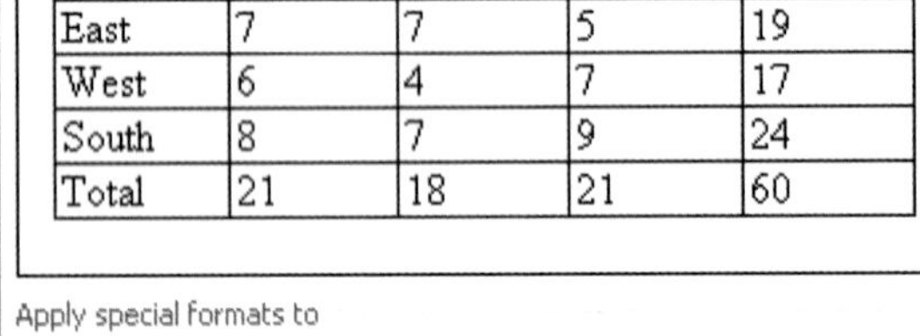

	Jan	Feb	Mar	Total
East	7	7	5	19
West	6	4	7	17
South	8	7	9	24
Total	21	18	21	60

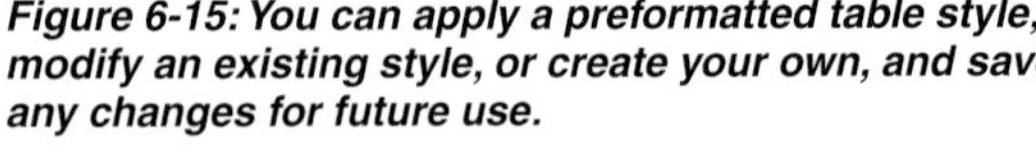

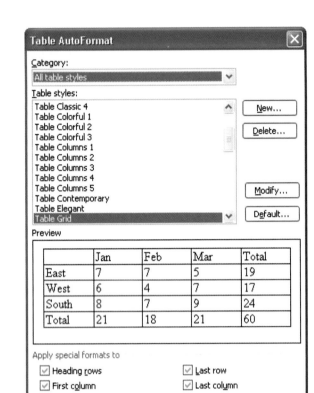

Figure 6-15: You can apply a preformatted table style, modify an existing style, or create your own, and save any changes for future use.

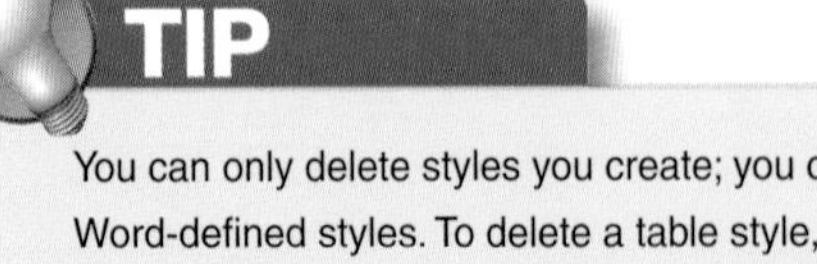

TIP

You can only delete styles you create; you cannot delete Word-defined styles. To delete a table style, in the Table AutoFormat dialog box (see Figure 6-15), click the **Category** down arrow, and click **All Table Styles**. Click the style you want to delete, click **Delete**, and click **Yes** confirm your decision.

Format a Table Automatically

Tables are easily changed after they are created, but when you are in a hurry (or when visually challenged), it is often helpful to give Word the first crack at applying a consistent look to a table. You can always modify the formatting as you want, or just start over with a different appearance. Additionally, you can create a format style from scratch and save it, or modify an existing format style and save it.

1. Click the table whose format you want to apply automatically. (You can also automatically format a table as you create it in the Insert Table dialog box. See "Insert a Table from a Dialog Box" earlier in the chapter.)
2. Click the **Table** menu and click **Table AutoFormat**. The Table AutoFormat dialog box opens, as shown in Figure 6-15.

APPLY A TABLE FORMAT STYLE

1. In the Table AutoFormat dialog box, scroll through the Table Styles list, and select each to see its preview.
2. Under Apply Special Formats, select whether the formatting applies to the listed table elements.
3. Click **Apply**.

CHANGE OR CREATE A TABLE STYLE

The Modify Style and New Style dialog boxes provide a similar set of options and tools to change or create a table style as do the analogous dialog boxes that are used to create and change paragraph and character styles. See Chapter 4 for more information on working with styles. In the Table AutoFormat dialog box (see Figure 6-15), click **Modify** to change an existing style, or click **New** to create a new style.

How to...

- Linking Picture Files
- Add Pictures
- Use the Clip Art Organizer
- Using the Picture Toolbar
- Remove Unwanted Areas
- Reduce a Picture's File Size
- Positioning Pictures Like Text
- Position a Picture Absolutely
- Using the Drawing Toolbar
- Add AutoShapes
- Add Special Effects to Text
- Working with Curves
- Create a Diagram
- Adding Objects from Other Programs
- Use Color Effects
- Resize and Rotate Graphics Precisely
- Position Graphics
- Use Handles and Borders to Change Graphics
- Working with Graphics
- Combine Graphics by Grouping

Chapter 7 Working with Graphics

Graphics is a term used to describe several forms of visual enhancements that can be added to a document. In this chapter you will learn how to insert, format, and manage graphic files (*pictures*), such as digital photos and clip art images. You will see how to create your own basic renderings (*drawings*) directly on a document and how to combine them with built-in drawings (*shapes*). Additionally, you will see how to embed products of other programs (*objects*) alongside your text and how to produce organizational charts and other business-oriented *diagrams*.

Work with Pictures

Pictures can be manipulated in a number of ways once you have them within Word. You can organize your clip art collections, resize the images, and move them into the positions you want.

QUICKFACTS

LINKING PICTURE FILES

Pictures are *embedded* by default when inserted in a document. Embedding adds the file size of the picture file to the size of the saved Word document. In a document with several high resolution pictures (the greater the number of pixels in a picture, the higher the resolution, and the larger the file size), the document's size can quickly rise into several megabytes. To dramatically reduce the size of a document that contains pictures, you can *link* to the picture files instead. (Alternatively, you can also reduce the resolution and compress embedded pictures, though the reduction in file size won't be as large as with linked files. (See "Reduce a Picture's File Size" later in the chapter.) Another characteristic of linking picture files is that any changes made and saved in the source file will be updated in the Word document. Linking does have the downside of requiring the picture files to remain in the same folder location they were in when the link was created. Additionally, documents with linked files are not suitable for sharing outside your local network.

To link a picture file, open the **Insert Picture** dialog box (see "Browse for Pictures" in this chapter), click the **Insert** down arrow, and click **Link To File** on the context menu.

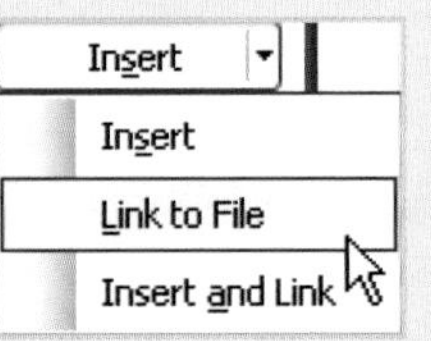

Add Pictures

You can browse for picture files, use the Clip Art task pane to assist you, drag and drop pictures from other locations, or import them directly from a scanner or digital camera.

TABLE 7-1: PICTURE FILE FORMATS ACCEPTED BY WORD

FILE TYPE	EXTENSION
AutoCAD 2-D	DXF
Computer Graphics Metafile	CGM
CorelDRAW	CDR
Encapsulated PostScript	EPS
FPX	FPX
Graphics Interchange Format	GIF, GFA
Joint Photographic Expert Graphics	JPG, JPEG, JFIF, JPE
Macintosh PICT/Compressed	PCT, PICT/PCZ
Micrografx Designer/Draw	DRW
Picture It!	MIX
Portable Network Graphics	PNG
Tagged Image File Format	TIF, TIFF
Windows Bitmap	BMP, BMZ, RLE, DIB
Windows Enhanced Metafile/Compressed	EMF/EMZ
Windows Metafile/Compressed	WMF/WMZ
WordPerfect Graphics	WPG

NOTE

Pictures are files that are produced by a device, such as a digital camera or scanner, or are created in a painting or drawing program, such as Microsoft Paint or Adobe Illustrator. In either case, the files are saved in a graphic format, such as JPEG or GIF (popular formats used on the Internet), or TIF (used in higher-end printing applications). Table 7-1 lists the graphic file formats supported by Word. You might need to install filters from your Office CD or the Microsoft Office web site before you can use some of the formats.

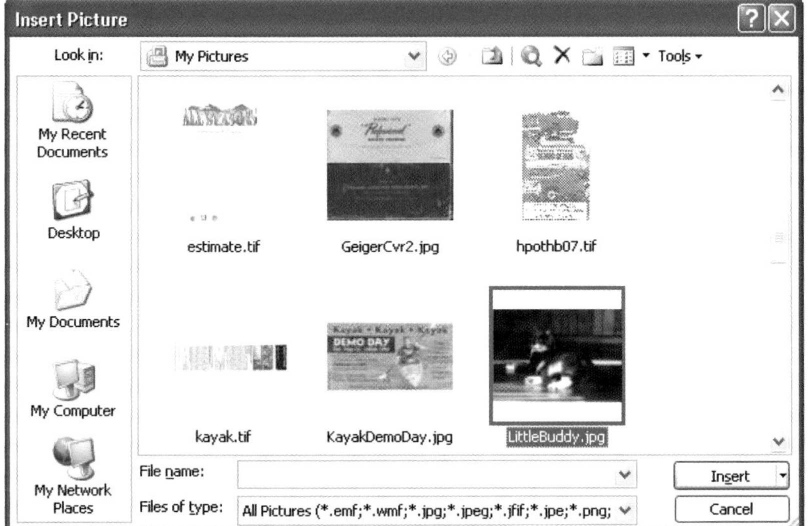

Figure 7-1: The Insert Picture dialog box displays thumbnails of picture files accepted by Word.

BROWSE FOR PICTURES

1. Place your insertion point in the paragraph or table where you want the picture.
2. Click **Insert**, click **Picture**, and click **From File**.

   –Or–

   Click **Insert Picture** on the Picture or Drawing toolbars (see the respective QuickSteps later in this chapter for more details on each toolbar).

   The Insert Picture dialog box opens, as shown in Figure 7-1.
3. Browse to the picture you want and select it. (If you do not see your pictures, click the **Views** down arrow on the dialog box toolbar, and click **Thumbnails**.)

   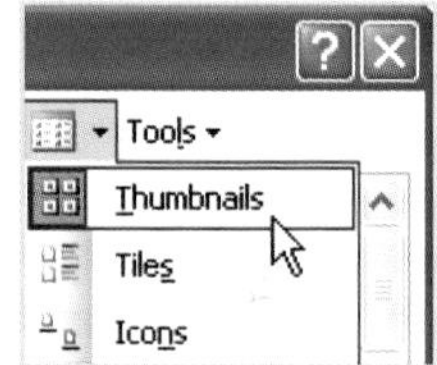

4. Click **Insert**. The picture displays in the document.

ADD CLIP ART

1. Place your insertion point in the paragraph or table where you want the picture.
2. Click **Insert**, click **Picture**, and click **Clip Art**.

   –Or–

   Click **Insert Clip Art** on the Drawing toolbar.

3. The Clip Art task pane opens.
4. In the Search For text box, type a keyword.
5. Click the **Search In** down arrow and refine your search to specific collections. (The Web Collections category includes thousands of clips maintained at Office Online; therefore, it can take considerable time to find what you're looking for.)

   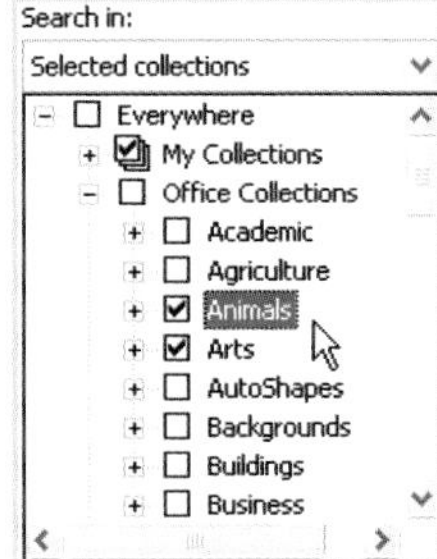

6. Click the **Results Should Be** down arrow and deselect all file types besides Clip Art.
7. Click **Go**. In a few moments thumbnails of the search results will appear, as shown in Figure 7-2.
8. Double-click the thumbnail to insert it in your document.

ADD PICTURES DIRECTLY

1. Place your insertion point in the paragraph or table where you want the picture.
2. Make sure the device, scanner, or digital camera is connected to your computer and is turned on.
3. Click **Insert**, click **Picture**, and click **From Scanner Or Camera**. The Insert Picture From Scanner Or Camera dialog box opens.

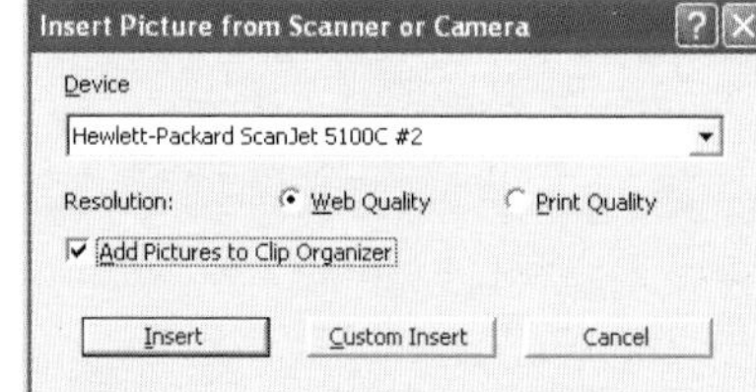

4. Select the device you want to use.
5. **Click Web Quality** for a lower resolution (and smaller file size).

   –Or–

   Click **Print Quality** for a higher resolution image (and larger file size). Click **Add Pictures To Clip Organizer** if you think you might use the image again.
6. Click **Insert** to add the image from the device with its default setting.

   –Or–

   Click **Custom Insert** to choose from custom settings such as saving the resolution in dpi (dots per inch), adjusting brightness and contrast, and choosing to display the image in color, grayscale, or black and white. Figure 7-3 shows the advanced properties for a scanner.

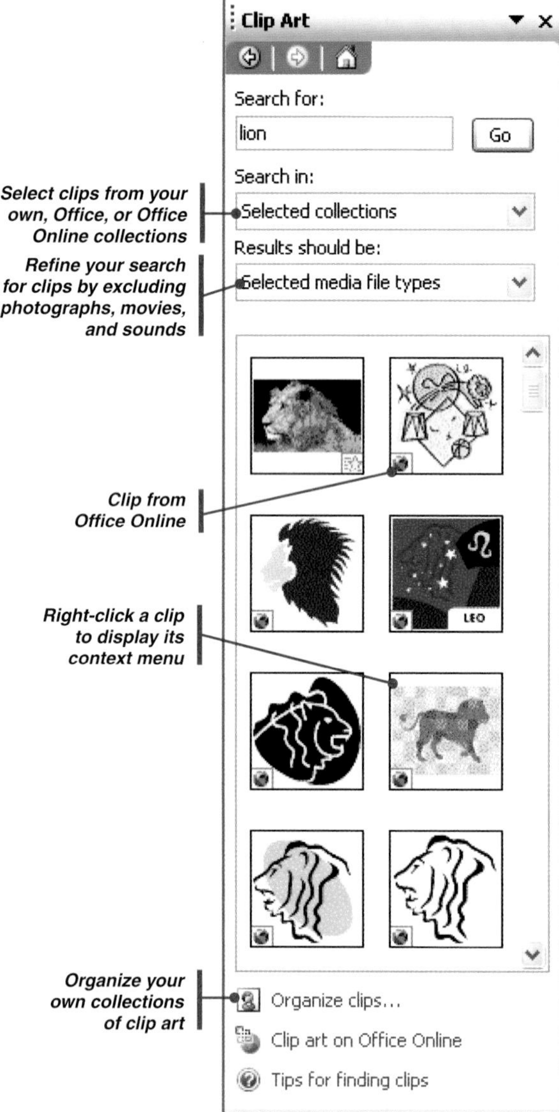

Figure 7-2: The Clip Art task pane helps you find clips on your computer and on Office Online and then assists you in organizing them.

TIP

Besides using the Insert Pictures command in Word to add pictures, you can drag and drop picture files from the desktop or Windows Explorer into an open document. To best use Explorer, close or minimize all windows other than Word and Explorer. Right-click a blank area of the Windows taskbar, and click **Tile Windows Vertically** on the context menu. Locate the picture file you want in the right pane of Explorer, and drag it to the location in the document where you want it.

TIP

If you have plugged in and turned on your camera or scanner, and everything looks like it should be working but you can't see the image, open **Start**, click **Control Panel**, and, in Classic View, double-click **Scanners and Cameras**. If your camera is not listed, click **Add An Imaging Device**. Click **Next**, select the manufacturer and model, click **Next**, click **Automatic Port Detection**, click **Next**, and click **Finish**.

CAUTION

Material you copy from the Internet, books, magazines, and other sources is normally protected by copyright; therefore, before you put it on your web site or use it for any commercial purpose, be sure to check the licensing agreement or contact the copyright owner.

Use the Clip Art Organizer

You can organize the clip art located on your hard disks into collections, entirely or by folders you choose. Keywords are automatically added to the clips so you can easily find them. Start by opening a document.

OPEN THE ORGANIZER

1. If necessary, display the task pane by clicking the **View** menu and clicking **Task Pane**, or by pressing **CTRL+F1**.

2. Click the task pane title bar down arrow, and select **Clip Art**. The Clip Art task pane opens, as shown in Figure 7-2.
3. Click **Organize Clips**. The Add Clips To Organizer dialog box opens telling you the Microsoft Clip Organizer can search your hard disks and catalog any media files it finds. You can choose to do it now or later, and you can optionally pick the folders on your disks to be cataloged.

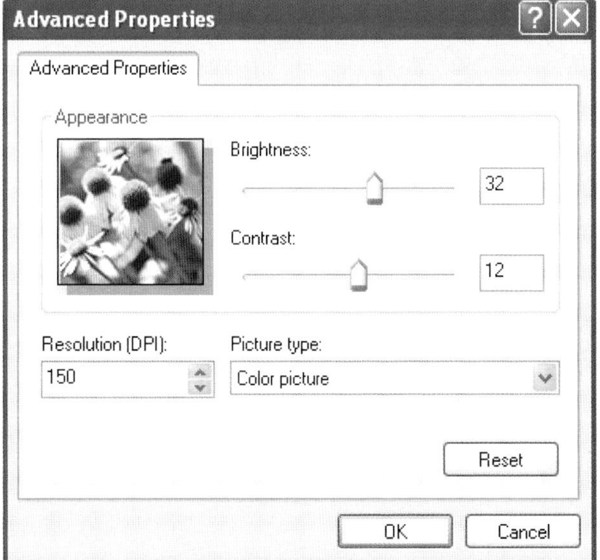

Figure 7-3: Depending on your device, you can set several image properties before you insert the image onto your document.

1 2 3 4 5 6 7 8 9 10

> **TIP**
>
> You can add clip art manually, from a camera or scanner, or automatically at any time. In the Clip Organizer, open **File**, select **Add Clips To Organizer**, and click the method of adding clips you want to use.

4. Click **Now**. After several moments of cataloging and adding keywords, the Microsoft Clip Organizer opens. Open a collection and then open a folder of clips in the Collection List pane—the clips display in the right pane, similar to Figure 7-4.

FIND CLIP ART

1. Click **Search** on the Clip Organizer toolbar. A portion of the Clip Art task pane displays in the left pane of the window.
2. Add keywords in the Search For text box, and refine the search in the Search Options drop-down list boxes.
3. Click **Go**. Clips meeting your search criteria display in the right pane.

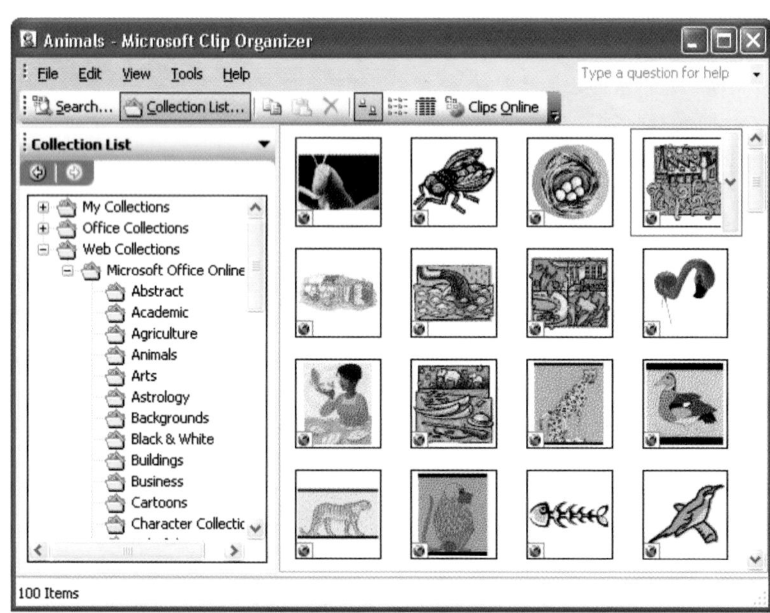

Figure 7-4: The Clip Organizer searches your hard disk and creates collections of clips similar to your folder structure.

MOVE AND COPY CLIPS IN A DIALOG BOX

1. Select a clip in the right pane of the Clip Organizer. To move and copy multiple clips, press and hold **CTRL** and click noncontiguous clips to select them, or press and hold **SHIFT** and click the first and last clip in a contiguous series. Click the down arrow of the clip or one of the selected clips, or click the **Edit** menu.
2. Click **Copy To Collection** or **Move To Collection** depending on what you want to do.

   –Or–

   Click **Make Available Offline** if transferring an online clip.
3. In the Copy Or Move dialog box, either browse to and select the collection where you want the clip and click **OK**, or put the clip into a new collection by clicking **New**, naming the collection, browsing to and selecting where you want the new collection, and clicking **OK** twice.

TIP

Actions you perform on clips in the Clip Organizer only affect what you see in the Organizer; that is, the actual picture files located on your hard disks are not affected, and what you see in the Organizer are simply shortcuts to the files and folders themselves.

NOTE

You cannot delete clips from Office Online.

MOVE AND COPY CLIPS BY DRAGGING

1. Click a clip in the right pane of the Clip Organizer. To move and copy multiple clips, press and hold **CTRL** and click non-contiguous clips to select them, or press and hold **SHIFT** and click the first and last clip in a contiguous run.
2. Copy the selected clips either by dragging them from the right pane to the destination collection in the left pane or by pressing and holding **SHIFT** while dragging them from the right pane to the destination collection in the left pane. Release the mouse before you release **SHIFT**.

DELETE CLIPS

1. Select a clip in the right pane of the Clip Organizer. To delete multiple clips, press and hold **CTRL** while clicking noncontiguous clips to select them, or press and hold **SHIFT** and click the first and last clip in a contiguous run. Click the down arrow of the clip or one of the selected clips, or click the **Edit** menu.
2. Click **Delete From** collection name to remove the clips from the current collection.(If a clip was originally in My Collections, it is moved to the Unclassified Clips collection for future use; if the clip was added after your My Collection was created, it's removed from all collections.)

   –Or–

   Click **Delete From Clip Organizer** to remove the clips from all collections.

EDIT KEYWORDS AND CAPTIONS

1. Select a clip in the right pane of the Clip Organizer. Click its down arrow and click **Edit Keywords**. For adding keywords to multiple clips, select them, click the **Edit** menu, and click **Keywords**.
2. In the Keywords dialog box, shown in Figure 7-5, click the **Clip By Clip** tab to address clips individually, or click the **All Clips At Once** tab to make changes to all selected clips.
3. Type keywords, separated by commas. Click **Add**. To delete a keyword, select it and click **Delete**.
4. Type a caption or select one from the drop-down list box. To delete a caption, select it and press **DELETE**.

Figure 7-5: Add keywords for easier searching and add captions to better describe your clip art.

USING THE PICTURE TOOLBAR

Pictures are manipulated primarily by the Picture toolbar and the Format Picture dialog box. To display the Picture toolbar, as shown in Figure 7-6, right-click the picture that you want to work with, and click **Show Picture Toolbar** on the context menu. A floating Picture toolbar will display.

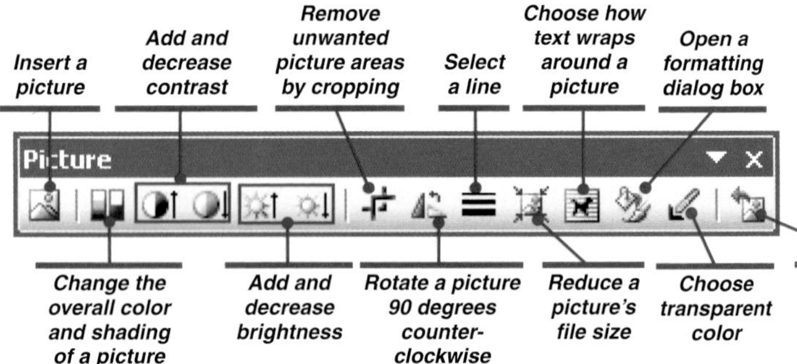

Figure 7-6: The Picture toolbar is your one-stop shopping venue for accessing picture-related options.

Remove Unwanted Areas

You can remove areas you do not want by using the Crop tool on the Picture toolbar.

1. Select the picture you want to crop.
2. Display the Picture toolbar (see the QuickSteps "Using the Picture Toolbar").
3. Click the **Crop** tool to turn it on. The mouse pointer displays with the cropping icon when placed over the picture.
4. Place the cropping tool over one of the eight sizing handles surrounding the picture, and drag the tool so that the dashed marquee borders the area of the picture you want to keep, as shown in Figure 7-7.
5. Release the mouse button. The areas of the picture outside the marquee are removed and the Crop tool is turned off.

Figure 7-7: Cropping removes the area of a picture outside the dashed marquee.

TIP

You can add a caption to inserted pictures to give a uniform appearance to your picture identifiers. Right-click a picture and click **Caption**. In the Caption dialog box, choose a label (create your own labels by clicking **New Label**) where you want the caption, and a numbering format. You can also have Word, using AutoCaption, automatically add a caption based on the type of picture or object inserted.

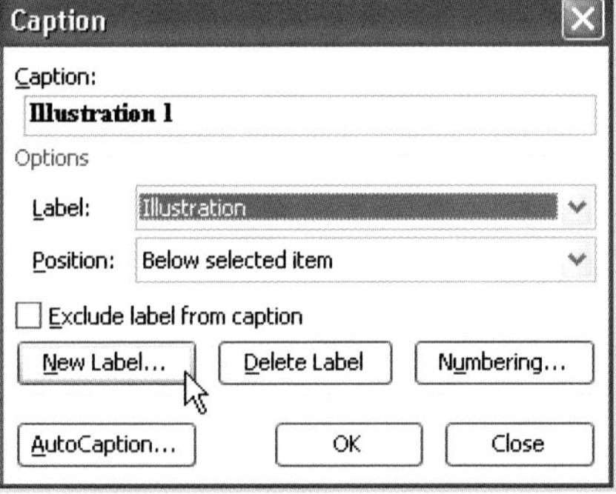

Reduce a Picture's File Size

Pictures embedded in a document add to the document's file size. Just a few high resolution pictures or several lower resolution pictures can quickly increase a document's file size beyond the threshold established by many e-mail servers and network administrators. To mitigate against file size "bloat" you have a few options available to you. (An alternative method of reducing the impact of inserted pictures is to link the pictures to the document. See the QuickFacts "Linking Picture Files" earlier in this chapter for information on linking pictures.)

1. Select the pictures whose file sizes you want to reduce.
2. Right-click a selected picture and click **Format Picture** on the context menu.
3. Click the **Picture** tab of its Format Picture dialog box, and click **Compress**. Compress...
4. Figure 7-8 shows the Compress Pictures dialog box where you can choose which pictures to reduce and by which method:
   - Under **Apply To**, choose whether to apply the changes to selected or all pictures in the document.
   - Under **Change Resolution**, choose whether to change to an appropriate resolution for online use or printing. Resolution is the number of dots per inch (dpi) comprising the picture. Choosing No Change retains the picture's native resolution.
   - Under **Options**, select **Compress Pictures** to reduce the file size by software compression, if it's possible, and/or select **Delete Cropped Areas Of Pictures**, which removes any cropped areas not only from view but totally from the document.
5. Click **OK** twice to close the Compress Pictures and Format Picture dialog boxes.

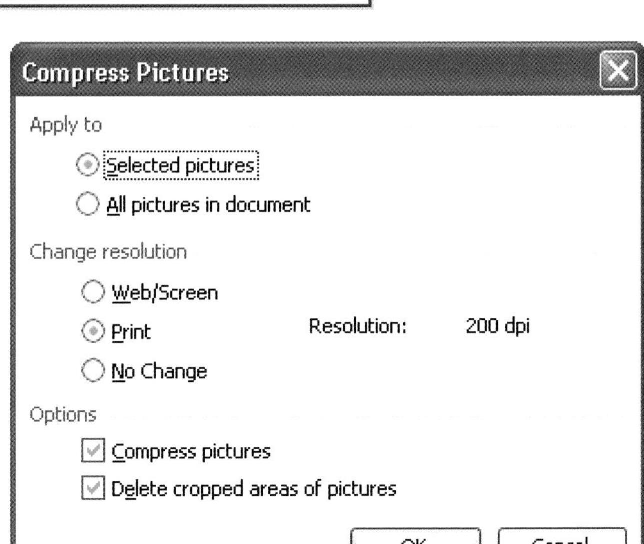

***Figure 7-8:** You can reduce the impact of adding pictures to a document by reducing their file sizes.*

QUICKSTEPS

POSITIONING PICTURES LIKE TEXT

When you insert a picture, by default the image is positioned in a paragraph similar to a character you enter from the keyboard; that is, the bottom of the image is aligned with the bottom of the text line at the insertion point (the bottom of characters, like *e*, without a descender). The paragraph will expand vertically the height of the picture and "push" any other text or objects down the page. The picture is "in line with text" and maintains its *relative* position to surrounding content as text and other objects are added or removed from the page.

ALIGN PICTURES

Use one or more of the following paragraph formatting techniques to align pictures (see Chapter 3 for details on how to format paragraphs):

- Alignment buttons on the Formatting toolbar
- Alignment, indentation, and spacing options in the Paragraph dialog box
- Tabs and indents from the horizontal ruler or the Tabs dialog box

MOVE PICTURES

1. Click the picture you want to move to select it.
2. Drag the picture to a new paragraph or table cell.

TIP

Pictures with paragraph formatting characteristics can be identified by the square sizing handles that surround them. Pictures that can be positioned absolutely, either by dragging or by references to other objects, display round sizing handles similar to drawings.

Position a Picture Absolutely

Absolute positioning pictures offers three features that the default paragraph positioning feature does not. You can:

- Place a picture in a document so that it keeps its position regardless whether other content shifts on the page.
- Drag a picture to any location on a page regardless of paragraph considerations.
- Place the picture according to distances or positions relative to document areas.

To position a picture absolutely:

1. Double-click the picture, and click the **Layout** tab of its Format Picture dialog box.
2. Click a wrapping style except In Line With Text, and click **OK**. You can now drag and place the picture anywhere in the document.

   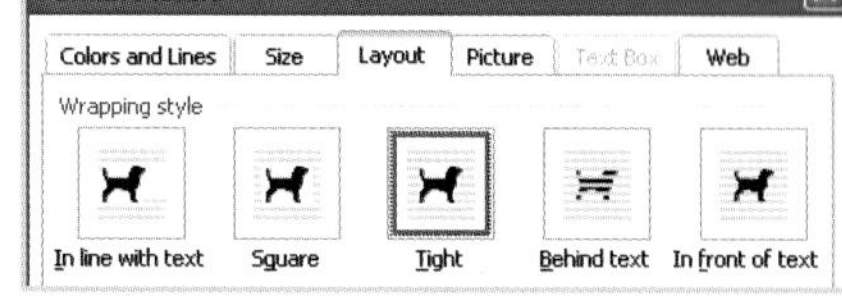

   –Or–

   Click the **Advanced** button if you want to want to place the picture relative to other document objects or lock the picture to a fixed location. See "Position Graphics" later in the chapter for positioning options you can apply to absolutely positioned pictures and drawings.

Create Drawings

Drawings may be comprised of prebuilt shapes, text you add effects to, and renderings you put together using one or more drawing tools. You can manipulate drawings by altering their position, size, color, shape, and other characteristics.

Drawings are created within a drawing canvas, which is a rectangular area where you can move and size multiple drawings as one object. Add a drawing canvas by clicking the **Insert** menu, clicking **Picture**, extending the menu, and clicking **New Drawing**. (Or simply add a graphic from the Drawing toolbar and a drawing canvas will be created for you.)

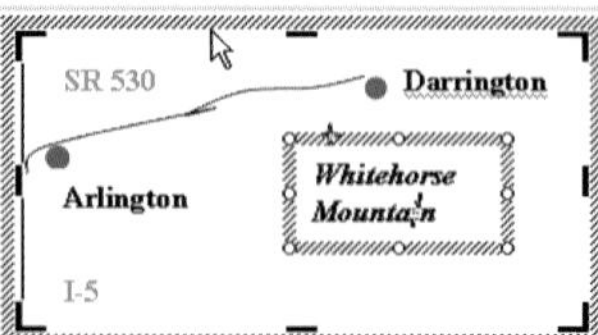

QUICKSTEPS

USING THE DRAWING TOOLBAR

You can choose pre-made graphics (AutoShapes or just *shapes*), add effects to text (using WordArt), or create your own graphics with the tools available from the Drawing toolbar (see Figure 7-9). Display the Drawing toolbar by clicking **Drawing** on Word's Standard toolbar or right-clicking an existing toolbar and clicking **Drawing**.

TIP

Display a Drawing Canvas toolbar to help you size the canvas and determine how text wraps around the canvas by right-clicking the canvas and clicking **Show Drawing Canvas Toolbar**.

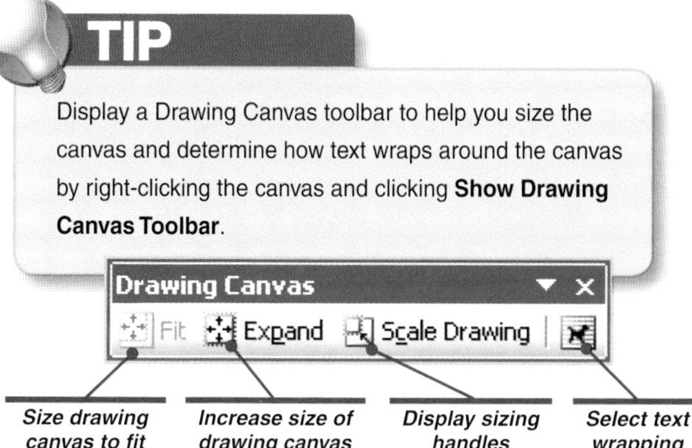

Add AutoShapes

AutoShapes are small, prebuilt drawings you can select, or you can create your own by modifying existing shapes or drawing your own freeform. The prebuilt AutoShapes and tools for creating your own are located together on the Drawing toolbar.

1. Click **Drawing** on the Standard toolbar to display the Drawing toolbar.
2. Choose an AutoShape:
   - Click **AutoShapes** and select a shape from one of the several categories.

   –Or–

   - Click one of the four buttons to the right of AutoShapes to create lines, rectangles, or ellipses.
3. Drag the mouse cross-pointer to the approximate location and size you want. In the case of freeform tools, see the QuickSteps "Working with Curves."

AutoShapes
Lines
Connectors
Basic Shapes
Block Arrows
Flowchart
Stars and Banners
Callouts
More AutoShapes...

Select objects
Opens several categories of shapes
Use WordArt to add special effects to text
Search for clip art
Add color to areas, lines, and text
Add shadows and 3-D effects
Drawing
Draw
AutoShapes
Group, position, change shapes and drawings
Create your own graphics and add text
Create organization charts and other diagrams
Browse for pictures and drawings
Select lines

Figure 7-9: The Drawing toolbar provides tools to create and insert drawings and apply effects.

Add Special Effects to Text

Special effects, as shown in Figure 7-10, can be easily added to text using WordArt to simulate a graphic artist's professional touch.

APPLY A WORDART EFFECT

1. Click **Drawing** on the Standard toolbar to display the Drawing toolbar.
2. Click the **WordArt** button to display the WordArt gallery of text styles. 
3. Click a style that's close to what you want (you can "tweak" it later), and click **OK**. The Edit WordArt Text dialog box opens.
4. Type the text you want styled, and click **OK**. The text is displayed with the effect you have selected.

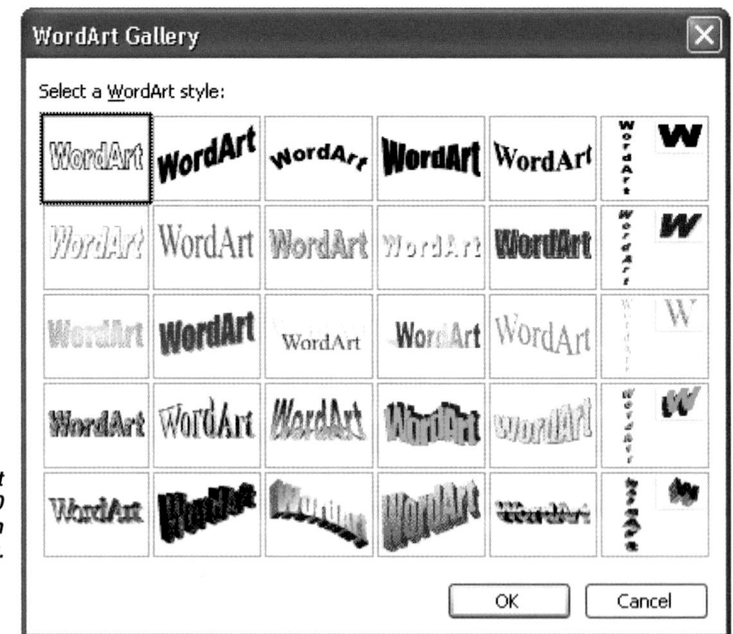

Figure 7-10: The WordArt Gallery provides 30 special effects that can be applied to text.

TIP

The Draw menu on the left of the Drawing toolbar has two options that are very handy when working with the placement of several objects: Nudge and Align Or Distribute. Nudge allows you to move an object by very small amounts that may be difficult to do with a mouse. Align Or Distribute allows you to align a common edge of several objects or to evenly distribute them.

TIP

Several AutoShapes are available from clip art collections. Type autoshapes in the Clip Art task pane **Search For** text box. Choose to search in all collections, and click **Go** (see "Add Clip Art" earlier in the chapter).

TIP

If a curve doesn't have an edit point where you need one, right-click the curve where you want one, and click **Add Point** on the context menu.

QUICKSTEPS

WORKING WITH CURVES

Freeform tools, used to draw curved AutoShapes, are available under AutoShapes on the Drawing toolbar.

CREATE A CURVE

On the Drawing toolbar, click **AutoShapes**, and click **Lines**. You may choose to:

- Click **Curve**, and click the cross pointer to establish the curve's starting point. Move the pointer and click at each change in direction to continue creating other curvatures. Click to set the end point and complete the drawing.
- Click **Freeform**, and use a combination of curve and scribble techniques. Click the cross pointer to establish curvature points, and/or drag the pencil pointer to create other designs. Click to set the end point and complete the drawing.
- Click **Scribble**, and drag the pencil icon to create the shape you want. Release the mouse button to complete the drawing.

ADJUST A CURVE

1. Right-click the curve and click **Edit Points**. Black rectangles (*vertices*) appear at the curvature points.
2. Drag a vertex to reconfigure its shape.
3. Change any other vertex and click outside the curve when finished.

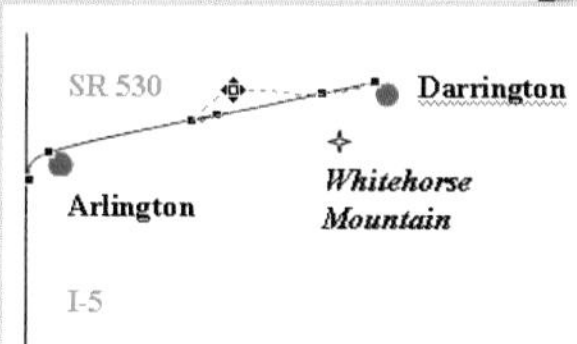

CLOSE A CURVE

Right-click the curve and click **Close Path**.

OPEN A CURVE

Right-click a closed curve and click **Open Path**.

WORK WITH WORDART

The WordArt toolbar, shown in Figure 7-11, displays when you select text that has a WordArt effect applied to it. Use its buttons to edit, apply different styles, and change the contour of the effect.

- Click **Insert WordArt** to apply a WordArt effect to text (see "Apply a WordArt Effect" earlier in this chapter).
- Click **Edit Text** to change the text and the font characteristics that the effect is applied to.
- Click **WordArt Gallery** to apply a different effect to your text (see Figure 7-10).

- Click **Format WordArt** to change formatting properties.
- Click **WordArt Shape** to recontour the WordArt effect to one of 40 different shapes.

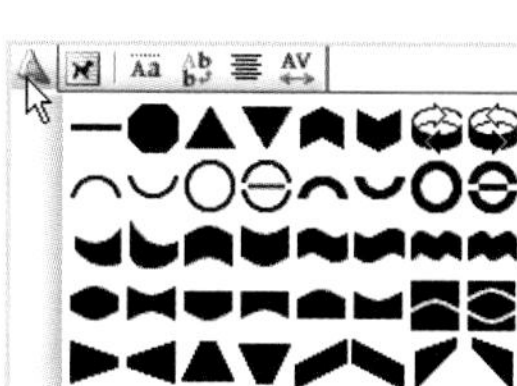

- Click **Text Wrapping** to change to an absolute positioning model, and choose from several text wrapping styles (see "Position Graphics" later in this chapter for more information on wrapping text and absolute positioning options).
- Click **WordArt Same Letter Heights** to adjust all WordArt characters to the same vertical size.
- Click **WordArt Vertical Text** to shift the positioning of WordArt characters to a vertical orientation from the typical horizontal orientation.
- Click **WordArt Alignment** to choose from several alignment formats.
- Click **WordArt Character Spacing** to choose from several spacing options.

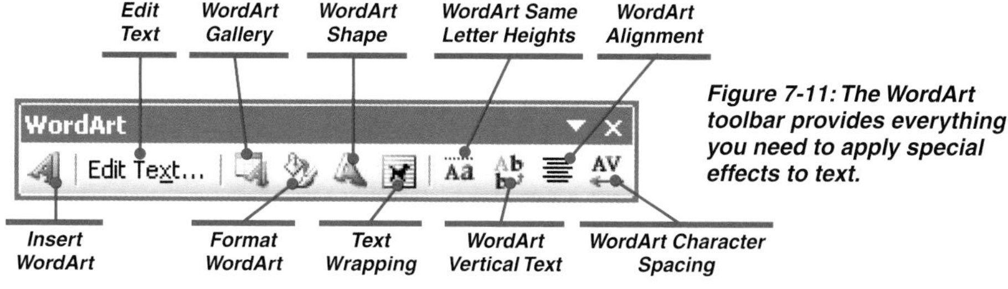

Figure 7-11: The WordArt toolbar provides everything you need to apply special effects to text.

Create a Diagram

You can quickly create and modify several different types of diagrams, five of which are easily interchangeable. The sixth, an organization chart, provides special tools and features that streamline the structuring of this popular form of charting.

> **NOTE**
>
> Diagrams are really just combinations of AutoShapes that fit a specific need. As such, you can, for example, delete an element of a diagram by selecting it and pressing **DELETE**, or delete the entire diagram by selecting its border and pressing **DELETE**. See "Modify Graphics" to learn how to format the overall diagram as well as how to change various AutoShapes components.

1. Click **Drawing** on the Standard toolbar to open the Drawing toolbar. Click **Insert Diagram Or Organizational Chart**, or open **Insert** and click **Diagram**. A gallery of diagrams opens.
2. Double-click the upper-leftmost diagram to display the start of an organization chart and the Organization Chart toolbar. Then personalize your chart by doing one or more of the following:

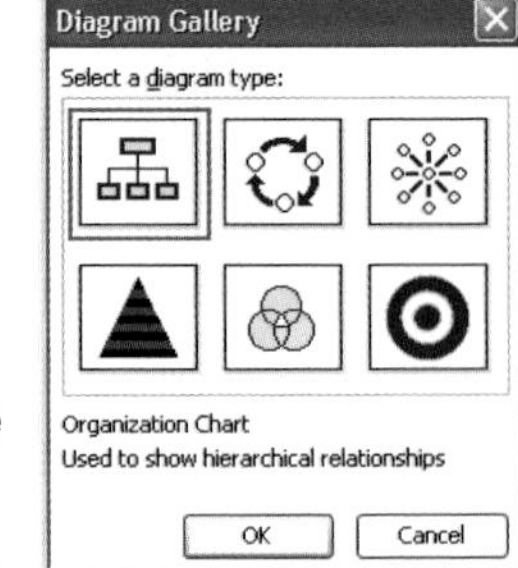

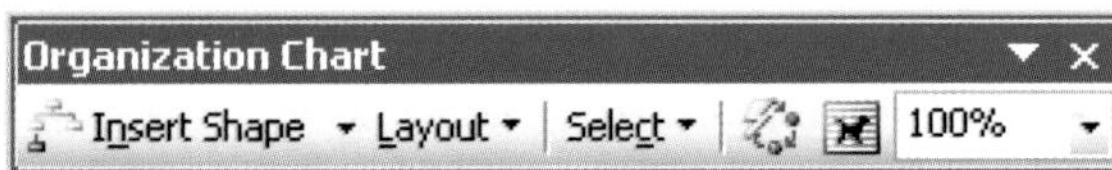

- Click the highest level, or *manager* position, and click **Layout** in the Organizational Chart toolbar to open a menu of hierarchical options. Click the structure that best matches your organization.
- Click a current box on the chart, click the **Insert Shape** down arrow, and select the type of new position you want to add to the current structure.
- To place text in a shape, place the insertion point in its text box. Type the name, title, or other identifier for the position. Press **ENTER** after each line of text to add multiple lines. Format text in the shapes as you would standard text, using the Formatting toolbar and dialog boxes. Figure 7-12 shows the start of a chart.
- Click **Select** to assist in selecting groups of positions that can be acted upon together.

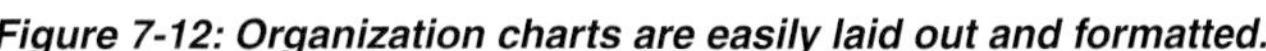

Figure 7-12: Organization charts are easily laid out and formatted.

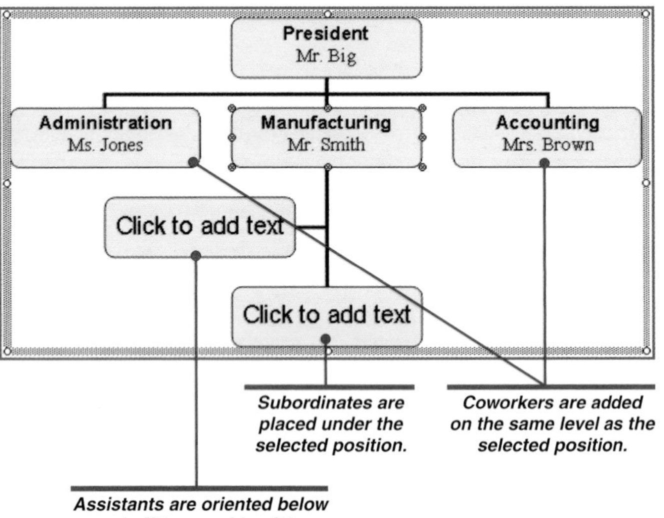

QUICKSTEPS

ADDING OBJECTS FROM OTHER PROGRAMS

You might want to include the product of another program in a document as a graphic. The major difference between adding the graphic as an *object* (these are technically *OLE objects*, named for "object linking and embedding," which is the technology involved) as opposed to copying and pasting it is that an object maintains a link to the program that created it. This means that in addition to formatting and other general appearance changes you can make with all the other graphics formats, you can make *content* changes using the menus, task panes, and other tools of the originating program while still in Word.

1. Click the **Insert** menu, extend the menu, and click **Object**.
2. Choose whether to create a new object or use an existing one.
   - Click the **Create New** tab, select an object type, and click **OK**.

     –Or–

   - Click the **Create From File** tab, browse to an existing object, and click **OK**.

   Depending on the object, a blank object opens either in its originating program within Word, or with the toolbars, menus, and other tools taking on those of the object's originating program, as shown in Figure 7-14.
3. Add content, and apply design and formatting. If you need to return to Word, open the **File** menu, and click **Close And Return To *object type* In *document name***; if you are already in Word, just click the page outside the object.

- Click **AutoFormat** to open the Organization Chart Style Gallery, where you can change the overall appearance of the chart, as shown in Figure 7-13.
- Click **Text Wrapping** to select how you want surrounding text to appear.
- Click the **Zoom** down arrow, and click a magnification factor to view the page and organization chart at a more macro and micro scale.

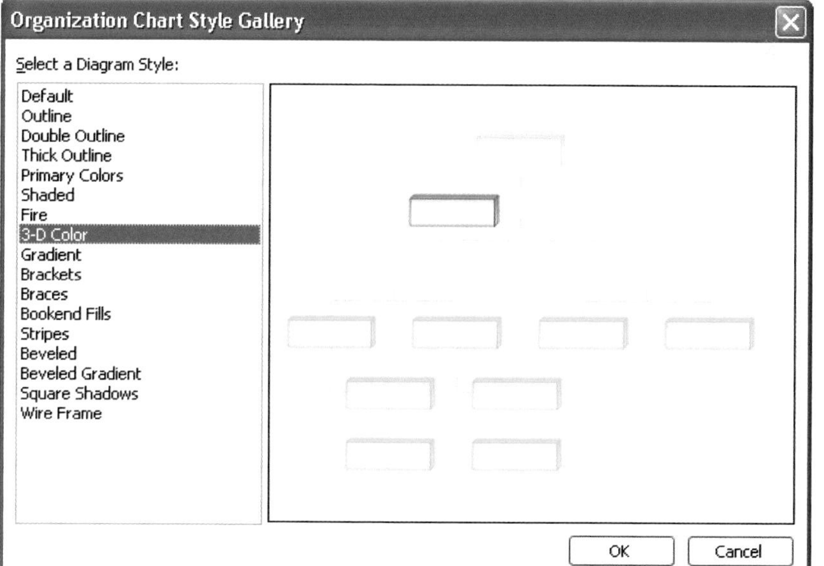

Figure 7-13: Quickly redesign the overall appearance of your organization chart.

TIP

If you create an object from an existing file using the Create From File tab, you can create a *link* between the object in Word and the file. To create the link, click **Link To File** in the **Create From File** tab. See the QuickFacts "Linking Picture Files" for more information on linking files.

Use Color Effects

Color in various shades, gradients, textures, and patterns can be added to interior fills, to borders, and to text. Click a drawing to select it, and click the **Fill Color**, **Line Color**, or **Font Color** down arrow on the **Drawing** toolbar. A menu of coloring options displays (make the menu float by dragging the dotted line in its title bar from the toolbar). Depending on what attribute you want to format, you will see all or part of the these options.

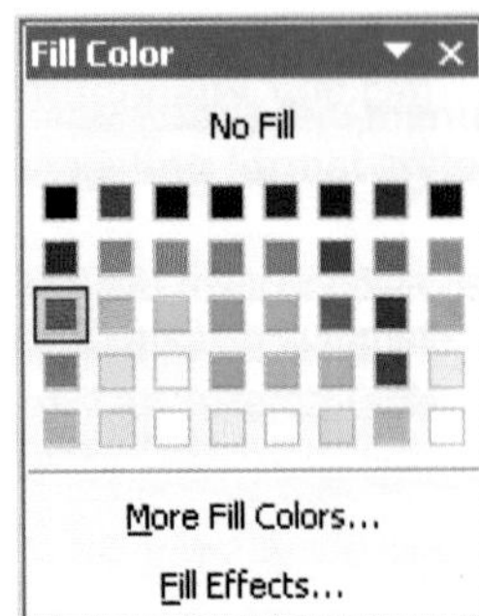

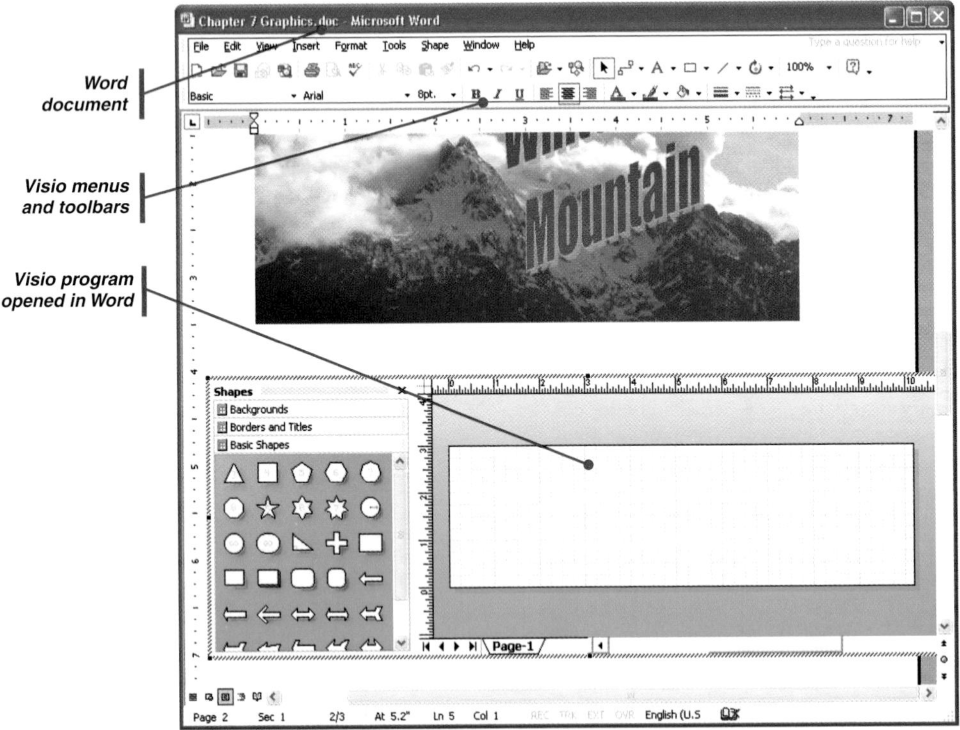

Figure 7-14: Many objects inserted in a document allow you to use their menus and toolbars within Word.

SET A COLOR QUICKLY

Click one of the 40 standard colors in the color matrix on the Fill Color, Line Color, or Font Color drop-down menu.

–Or–

Click **More (*Fill* or *Line*) Colors** to have access to over 200 standard colors and even more custom colors.

SET GRADIENTS

1. Click **Fill Effects** on the Fill Color drop-down menu, and click the **Gradient** tab.
2. Select a Colors option, as shown in Figure 7-15:

Figure 7-15: You can blend colors to create gradient fills.

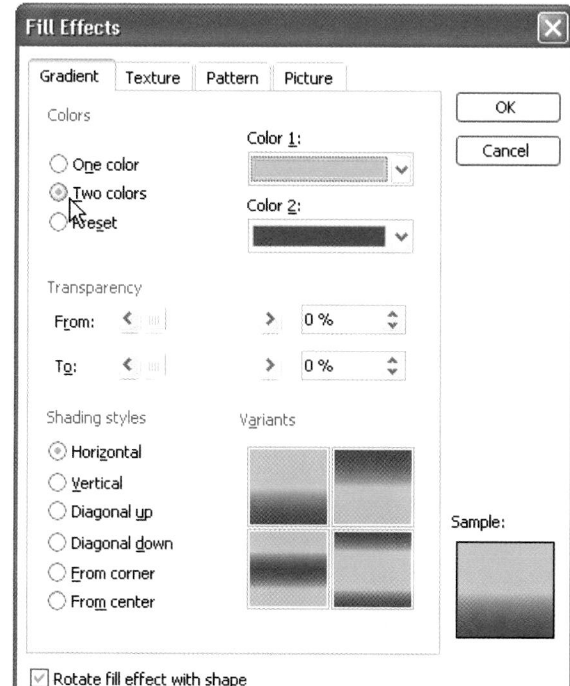

   - **One Color** gives you a one-color gradient result.
   - **Two Colors** gives you a gradient resulting from one color blending into another color.
   - **Preset** allows you to select one of the gradient color schemes from the Preset Colors drop-down list box.
3. Select a Transparency percentage to set the degree of transparency:
   - Click the **From** and **To** horizontal arrows to change the relative extent to which each extreme of the two colors will be transparent.

     –Or–

   - Click the spinners to set the degree of transparency more precisely.
4. Select a shading style to determine which direction the shading will fall across the drawing. To see the differences, click each option and see the results.
5. When you are done, click **OK**.

USE A PICTURE TO FILL YOUR DRAWING

1. Click **Fill Effects** on the Fill Color drop-down menu, and click the **Picture** tab.
2. Click **Select Picture**. The Select Picture dialog box will open.
3. Browse for the picture you want, select it, click **Insert**, and then click **OK**. The picture will be inserted into the background of the drawing shape.

NOTE

Much like adding effects to fills, you can apply arrows to lines, change the thickness of a line, add shadows and 3-D effects to drawings, and introduce other enhancements. The tools work similarly: select the drawing by clicking it, and then click the tool whose effect you want.

CAUTION

Do not remove the line around a drawing unless you have first added a fill. Without the line and a fill, the drawing is invisible except for the handles that display when it's selected.

TIP

Double-click a graphic to open a common properties dialog box that makes available only the options that pertain to the type of graphic. For example, if you double-click a rectangle you drew, the Arrows area of the Colors And Line tab is unavailable, as shown in Figure 7-16.

COLOR TEXT BOX TEXT

1. Select the text to be colored by double-clicking or dragging. If you have trouble selecting the text you want, set your insertion point at the beginning or end of the selection, and press and hold **CTRL+SHIFT** while using the arrow keys to select the remaining characters.
2. Click the **Font Color** down arrow, and click the color you want from the color matrix. Your selected text is colored, and the toolbar button displays the selected color so you can apply that same color to additional objects by just clicking the button.

REMOVE EFFECTS

- To **remove a fill**, select the drawing, click the **Fill Color** down arrow on the Drawing toolbar, and click **No Fill**.
- To **remove the outline border** around a drawing, select the drawing, click the **Line Color** down arrow on the Drawing toolbar, and click **No Line**.
- To **remove text coloring**, select the text, click the **Font Color** down arrow, and click **Automatic** to display black.

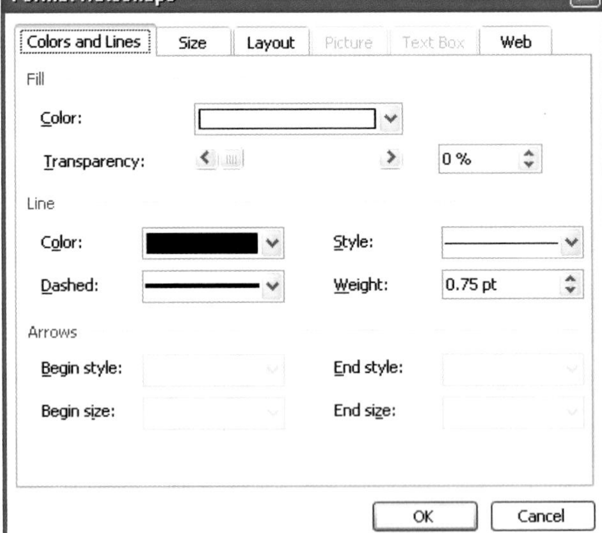

Figure 7-16: Each type of graphic has a properties dialog box that's tuned to its unique characteristics.

Pictures, such as photos and clip art, have more formatting options available to them and more closely behave like drawings, when they are provided with an absolute positioning layout. To change the default paragraph-like formatting behavior of pictures to a more flexible layout, double-click the picture to open its Format Picture dialog box. Click the **Layout** tab, click one of the four wrapping styles on the right, and click **OK**.

Enlarging an image beyond the ability of the pixels to span it causes undesirable effects.

Modify Graphics

Pictures (those that use an absolute positioning layout) and drawings share a common Format dialog box, though many of the features and options are not available for every type of graphic you can add to a Word document. This section describes formatting and other modifications you can apply to graphics.

Resize and Rotate Graphics Precisely

You can change the size of graphics by setting exact dimensions and rotating them. (You can also drag handles to change them interactively. See "Use Handles and Borders to Change Graphics" for ways to resize and rotate graphics with a mouse.)

1. Double-click the graphic you want to resize.
2. Click the **Size** tab, shown in Figure 7-17, and select the **Lock Aspect Ratio** check box to size the graphic proportionally when entering either width or height values:
   - **Under Size And Rotate**, enter either the Height or the Width dimension or use the spinners to increase or decrease one of the dimensions from its original size.

   –Or–

   - **Under Scale,** enter percentages to indicate how much to increase or decrease Height and/or Width of the picture from its original size, or use the spinners to do this.
3. To rotate the graphic, under Size And Rotate, enter a positive (rotate clockwise) or negative (rotate counterclockwise) number of degrees of rotation you want.
4. Click **OK**. The picture will resize and/or rotate according to your values.

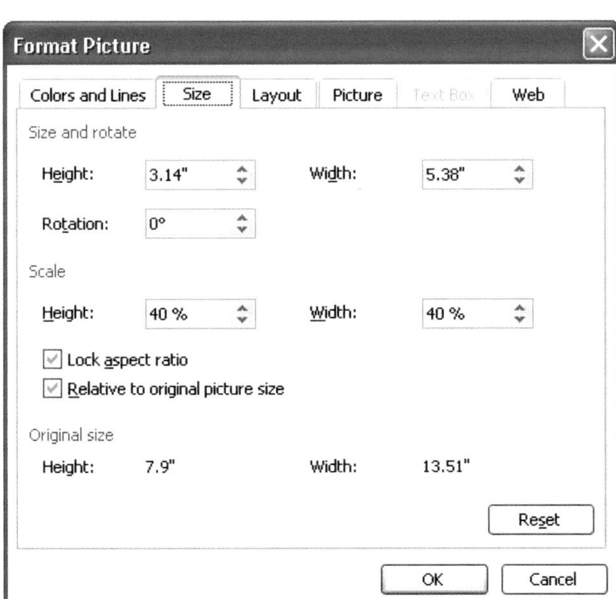

Figure 7-17: You can size a graphic to exact dimensions in its Format dialog box.

TIP

Display the Word rulers to help you draw, align, and arrange drawings. Click the **View** menu, extend the menu, and click **Ruler** to display the horizontal ruler. To display a vertical ruler (Print Layout view only), click the **Tools** menu, click **Options**, and click the **View** tab. Under Print And Web Layout Options, select the **Vertical Ruler** check box. Click **OK**.

TIP

After you change a picture from its default text wrapping style to a style that supports absolute positioning, it is difficult to return to the default style. It's easiest to just delete the picture and reinsert it.

Position Graphics

Graphics (including pictures that use absolute positioning layout) are positioned anywhere in the document you want by dragging or setting values. In either case, the graphic retains its relative position within the document as text and other objects are added or removed. You can override this behavior by anchoring the graphic to a fixed location. You can also change how text and other objects "wrap" around the graphic. Figure 7-18 shows several of these features.

CHANGE HOW CONTENT DISPLAYS AROUND A GRAPHIC

By default, text and other objects don't flow, or *wrap*, on the sides of, in front of, or behind an inserted picture. You can change this behavior:

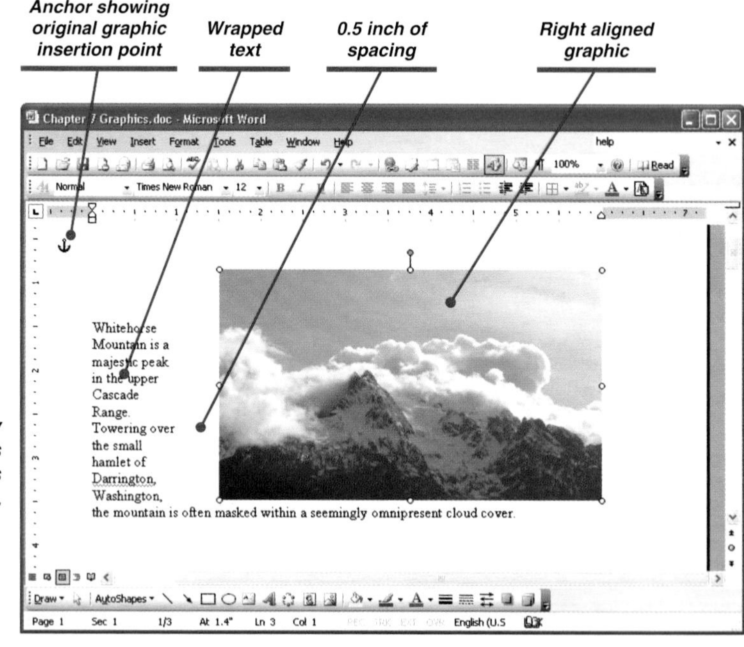

Figure 7-18: You can easily arrange text and graphics in several configurations using dialog box options.

NOTE

The default In Line With Text wrapping style is the only style that provides paragraph-like formatting to position pictures. If you change to any of the other wrapping styles, you will position the picture absolutely, that is, by dragging it into position or by selecting positions relative to document areas such as margins or paragraphs.

TIP

There are two additional wrapping styles you can use besides those offered on the Layout tab in the Format Picture dialog box. From the Layout tab, click **Advanced**, and click the **Text Wrapping** tab. The Through and Top And Bottom styles are additional.

TIP

Maybe you can determine where on a page a graphic that uses absolute positioning was originally placed. Click the **Tools** menu, click **Options**, and click the **View** tab. Under Print And Web Layout Options, select the **Object Anchors** check box. Click **OK** to display anchor icons in the document.

1. Double-click the graphic that you want to wrap text around.
2. Click the **Layout** tab of its Format Picture dialog box, and, under Wrapping Style, click one of the styles to wrap as the icons indicate (if you select the In Line With Text style, the graphic will lose its absolute positioning ability and can only be positioned using paragraph-like options—tabs, text, and spaces on the left).

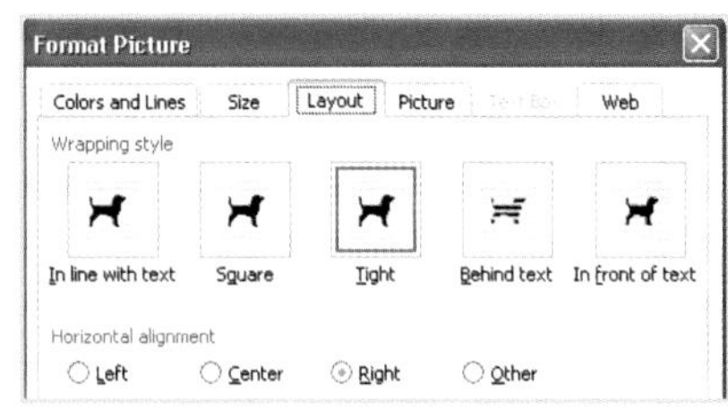

3. Click a horizontal alignment option.
   - Click **OK** to accept the wrapping style and close the dialog box.

   –Or–

   - To see or change other wrapping styles and options, click **Advanced** (see the Tip on Advanced Layout).

POSITION A GRAPHIC RELATIVE TO AREAS IN A DOCUMENT

Besides dragging a graphic into position, you can select or enter values that determine where the graphic is placed in relation to document areas.

1. Double-click the graphic that you want to position.
2. Click the **Layout** tab of its Format Picture dialog box, and click **Advanced**.
3. In Advanced Layout dialog box, click the **Picture Position** tab. Select or enter the horizontal and vertical positioning entries by selecting them from the drop-down menus, entering the values, or using the spinners to increase or decrease distances, as shown in Figure 7-19.
4. To anchor a graphic in place independent of whether other content is added or removed—for example, a graphic you want in the upper-left corner of a specific page—select the **Lock Anchor** check box, and deselect all other options.
5. Click **OK** twice to close the Advanced Layout and Format Picture dialog boxes.

ADD SPACING AROUND A GRAPHIC

1. Double-click the graphic whose spacing you want to change.
2. Click the **Layout** tab of its Format Picture dialog box, and click **Advanced**.
3. Click the **Text Wrapping** tab, and select one of the wrapping styles in the first row.
4. Under Distance From Text, click the appropriate spinners to enter the spacing distance you want.
5. Click **OK**.

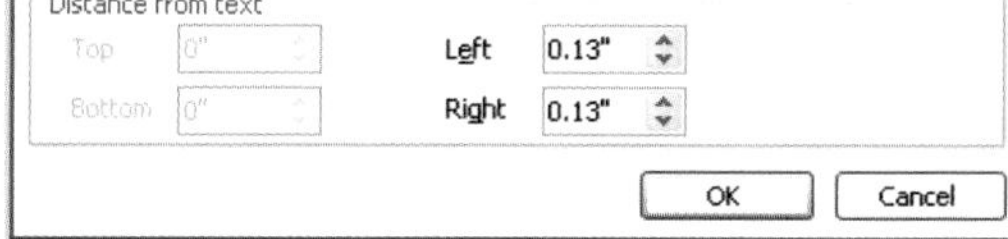

Advanced Layout
Picture Position | Text Wrapping
Horizontal
Alignment Right relative to Column
Margin
Page
Column
Character
Book layout Inside of
Absolute position 0" to the right of
Vertical
Alignment Top relative to Page
Absolute position 0.38" below Paragraph
Options
Move object with text
Allow overlap
Lock anchor
Layout in table cell
OK Cancel

Figure 7-19: Using absolute positioning, you can choose where to place a graphic relative to other objects in the document.

Use Handles and Borders to Change Graphics

Graphics are easily manipulated using their sizing handles and borders.

SELECT A GRAPHIC

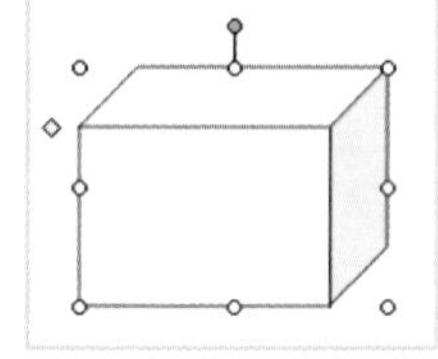

You select a graphic by clicking it. Handles appear around the graphic and allow you to perform interactive changes. Two exceptions include text boxes and text in text boxes.

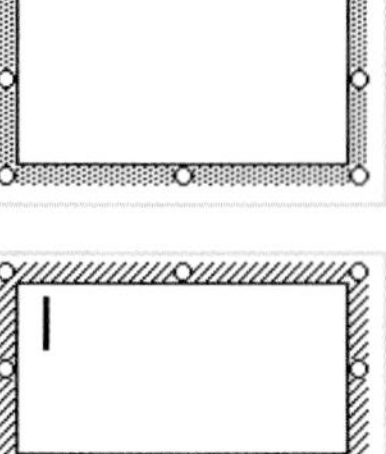

- Click the border of a text box. A dotted border appears around the perimeter of the text box.
- Double-click existing text in a text box to select it for making formatting changes, or click once in the text box where you want to place the insertion point for adding or editing text. In either case, the border becomes hatched.

WORKING WITH GRAPHICS

While graphics can be positioned absolutely by simply dragging them or choosing placement relative to other objects in a document, Word also provides a number of other techniques that help you adjust where a graphic is in relation to other graphics.

MOVE GRAPHICS INCREMENTALLY

- Select the graphic or group (see "Combine Graphics by Grouping"), press and hold **CTRL**, and press the arrow key in the direction you want to move the graphic by very small increments (approximately .01 inch).

  –Or–

- Click **Draw** on the Drawing toolbar, extend the menu, click **Nudge**, and click the direction you want the graphic moved. It will move by about an eighth of an inch, or .125 inch.

REPOSITION THE ORDER OF STACKED GRAPHICS

You can stack graphics by simply dragging one on top of another. Figure 7-20 shows an example of a three-graphics stack. To reposition the order of the stack, right-click the graphic you want to change, click **Order** on the context menu, and click:

- **Bring To Front** to move the graphic to the top of the stack
- **Send To Back** to move the graphic to the bottom of the stack
- **Bring Forward** to move the graphic up one level (same as Bring To Front if there are only two graphics in the stack)
- **Send Backward** to move the graphic down one level (same as Send To Back if there are only two graphics in the stack)

Continued...

RESIZE A GRAPHIC

Drag one of the square or round (if using absolute positioning) sizing handles surrounding the graphic—or at either end of it, in the case of a line—in the direction you want to enlarge or reduce the graphic. Press and hold **SHIFT** when dragging a corner sizing handle to change the height and length proportionately (if you have Lock Aspect Ratio selected in the Size tab of Format Pictures, the picture will remain proportionally sized without pressing **SHIFT**).

ROTATE A GRAPHIC

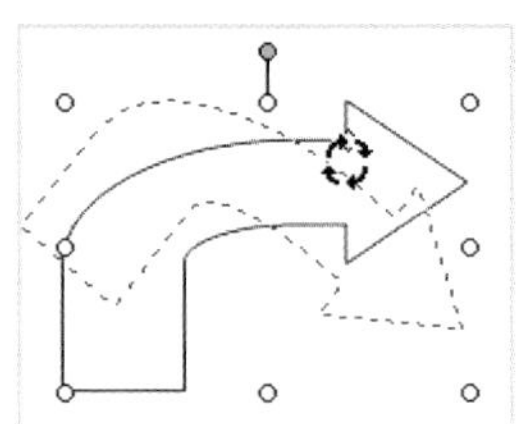

Drag the green dot in the direction you want to rotate the graphic. Press and hold **SHIFT** when dragging to rotate in 15-degree increments.

CHANGE A GRAPHIC'S PERSPECTIVE

If the graphic supports interactive adjustment, a yellow diamond adjustment handle is displayed. Drag the **yellow diamond** toward or away from the graphic to get the look you want.

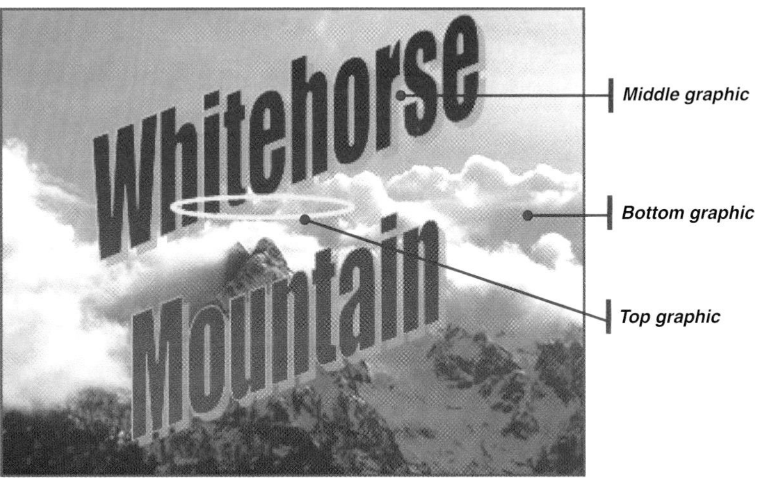

Figure 7-20: You can change the order of stacked graphics to achieve the look you want.

WORKING WITH GRAPHICS
(Continued)

- **Bring In Front of Text** to move the graphic on top of overlapping text
- **Send Behind Text** to move the graphic behind overlapping text

ALIGN GRAPHICS

To align graphics relative to one another, select the graphic, click **Draw** on the Drawing toolbar, extend the menu, click **Align Or Distribute**, and click one of the alignment choices.

EVENLY SPACE GRAPHICS

Select the graphics, click **Draw** on the Drawing toolbar, extend the menu, click **Align Or Distribute**, and click **Distribute Horizontally** or **Distribute Vertically**, depending on their orientation.

NOTE

You can "tear off" the Nudge direction submenu to make it much easier to use the directions multiple times.

Combine Graphics by Grouping

You can combine graphics for any number of reasons, but you typically work with multiple graphics to build a more complex rendering. To prevent losing the positioning, sizing, and other characteristics of the individual components, you can group them so that they are treated as one object.

GROUP GRAPHICS

1. Select the graphics to be grouped by clicking the first graphic and then pressing and holding **SHIFT** while selecting other drawings and pictures.
2. Click **Draw** on the Drawing toolbar, extend the menu, and click **Group**; or right-click one of the selected graphics, click **Grouping**, and click **Group**. A single set of selection handles surrounds the perimeter of the graphics. Coloring, positioning, sizing, and other actions now affect the graphics as a group instead of individually.

UNGROUP GRAPHICS

To separate a group into individual graphics, select the group, click **Draw** on the Drawing toolbar, and click **Ungroup**; or right-click the group, click **Grouping**, and click **Ungroup**.

RECOMBINE A GROUP AFTER UNGROUPING

After making a modification to a graphic that was part of a group, you don't have to reselect each component graphic to reestablish the group. Select any graphic that was in the group, click **Draw** on the Drawing toolbar, extend the menu, and click **Regroup**; or right-click a member graphic, click **Grouping**, and click **Regroup**.

How to...

- *Use Speech Recognition*
- *Working with Speech Recognition*
- *Scan Text into Word*
- *Understanding Document Imaging*
- *Translate to and from Another Language*
- *Create a Chart*
- *Use Data from Other Programs*
- *Use Chart Types*
- *Selecting Chart Items*
- *Work with Chart Items*
- *Understanding Data Series and Axes*
- *Format Chart Items*
- *Working with the Datasheet*

Chapter 8 Using Special Features

Microsoft Office Word is complemented with several programs that are a part of Office. These programs, once installed, work within Word to give you added value. You can use speech recognition to enter text in a Word document by talking into a microphone. You can even have Word "talk" to you by reading text in a document. You can use OCR (optical character recognition) technology to scan printed documents into a Word file. Language is no barrier as Word can translate words and even entire documents. When working with data, you can use Microsoft Graph to display *charts* that provide a more visual representation of data than a table, grid, or other forms of displayed data. You can provide the underlying data for a chart from several sources, including directly adding values to its own matrix, selecting data from a Word table, or importing data from a text file or spreadsheet program such as Microsoft Excel.

Add Text from Other Sources

You are not limited to the mouse and keyboard when entering text into a Word document. This section shows you several ways, using companion programs and newer technologies, that you can work smarter, not harder.

Use Speech Recognition

You can use your voice to enter text (dictation) and use voice commands to perform basic navigation and editing duties. While not quite yet a replacement for the mouse and keyboard, speech recognition fulfills a niche in the overall computing experience.

INSTALL SPEECH RECOGNITION

1. Start Word, click the **Tools** menu, extend the menu if needed, and click **Speech**.
2. If you haven't installed the speech recognition files previously, you will be asked if want to install them now. Click **Yes**.

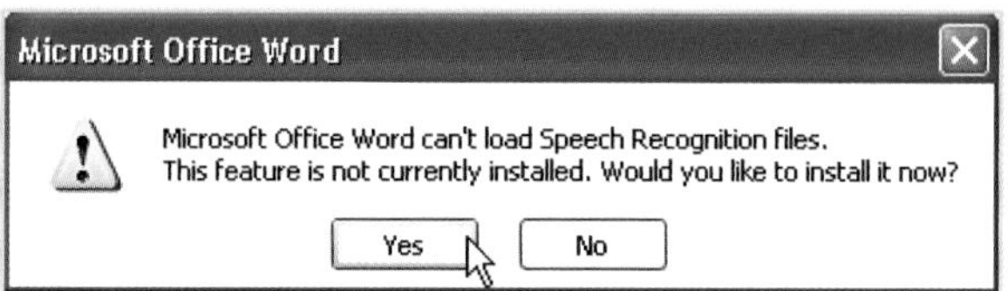

TRAIN SPEECH RECOGNITION

In order for the speech recognition software to understand your speech, you must first set up your microphone and then "train" the software by providing reading samples.

1. If the Control Panel is not already open, click the Windows **Start** button, and click **Control Panel**.
2. In Windows Classic view, double-click **Speech**. In Category view, click **Sounds, Speech, and Audio Devices**, and then click **Speech**. The Speech Properties dialog box will open.

NOTE

You will need supporting hardware to use the features described in this section, including speakers, a sound card, a microphone, and a scanner. See *Windows XP QuickSteps*, published by McGraw-Hill/Osborne, for more information on setting up and using sound and scanners with your computer.

NOTE

The speech recognition features installed by using the Speech command in Word work with other Office programs such as Microsoft Excel.

NOTE

The first time you try to use speech in Word, you might see a Welcome To Office Speech Recognition dialog box. This opens the Microphone Wizard that leads you through a similar training regimen as the Windows one described here. The training provided in Windows provides more options, and we find it a better choice. If you've done the training as described in this chapter, you can repeat the training offered in Word (the more training the better); however, you won't need to install the recommended Flash program.

Figure 8-1: The Speech Recognition tab provides the tools for you to "train" the software to your voice and adjust your microphone volume.

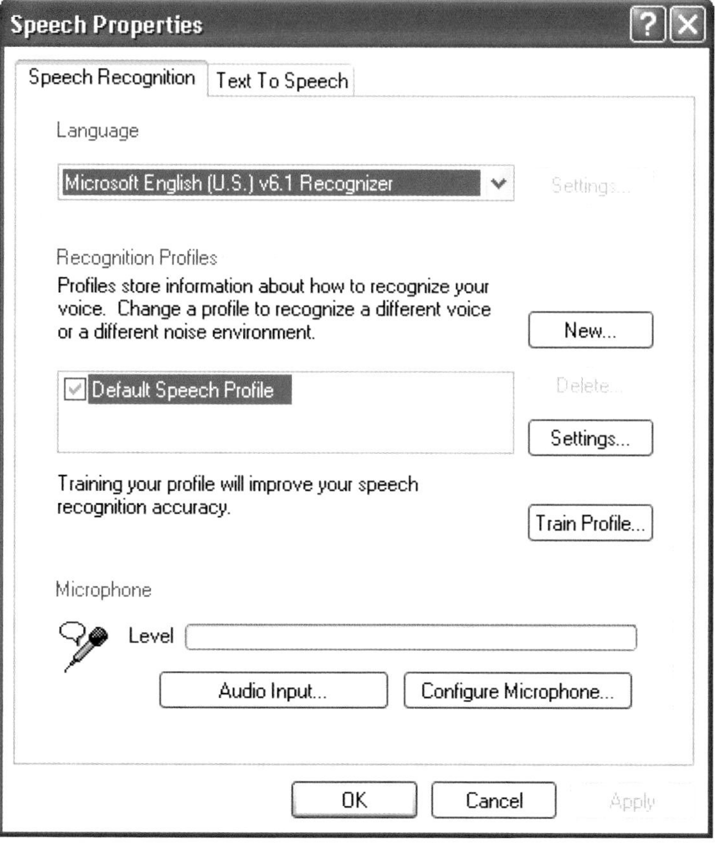

3. In the Speech Recognition tab, shown in Figure 8-1, you can set up and improve speech recognition features:

- Click **Configure Microphone** to start the Microphone Wizard. which provides volume settings for the speech recognition software. Read the two sample passages, clicking **Next** after completing each. Click **Finish** to return to the Speech Recognition dialog box. The Level volume indicator on the Speech Recognition tab will now display your speaking level when the microphone is turned on.
- Click **Train Profile** to provide the speech recognition software an opportunity to "learn" your voice for the default speech profile. You need to perform at least one reading and will need about 10 minutes to do so. Click **Next** twice and start reading the sample text. The sample text is highlighted as you read, and a bar tracks your progress, as shown in Figure 8-2. When finished with the reading, click **More Training** to perform additional readings (the more you read, the more accurate the speech recognition software becomes), or click **Finish** to return to the Speech Recognition tab.
- Click **New** if you need to create a voice profile other than the default speech profile (for another user). Name the profile and click **Next** to start the training (same as described for Train Profile). When done, ensure the correct profile is selected for subsequent use of speech recognition.
- Click **Settings** to tweak the speech recognition software if it seems to be working erratically. The defaults should work well unless you run into problems when using Word.
- Click **Audio Input** if you need to select from multiple audio hardware on your computer.
- Click **Delete** after selecting any profiles you want to remove from the system.

4. Click **OK** to close the Speech Properties dialog box. Leave the Control Panel open.

1 2 3 4 5 6 7 8 9 10

Figure 8-2: The time invested to "train" the speech recognition software will pay for itself by causing fewer mistakes when trying to decipher your voice.

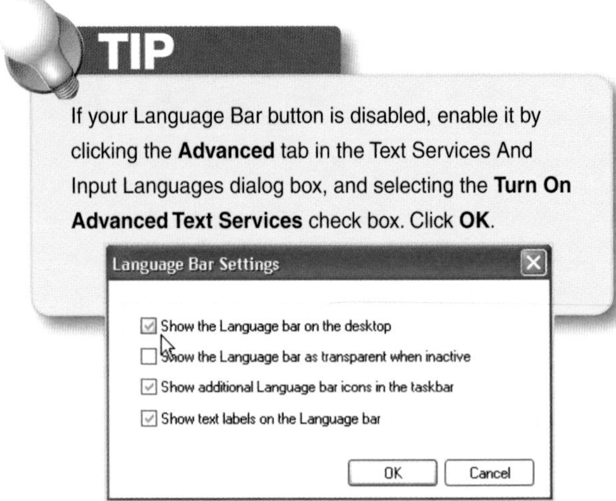

TIP

If your Language Bar button is disabled, enable it by clicking the **Advanced** tab in the Text Services And Input Languages dialog box, and selecting the **Turn On Advanced Text Services** check box. Click **OK**.

DISPLAY THE LANGUAGE BAR

1. If the Control Panel is not already open, click the Windows **Start** button, and then click **Control Panel**.
2. In Windows Classic view, double-click **Regional And Language Options**. In Category view, click **Date, Time, Language, and Regional Options**, and then click **Regional And Language Options**. The Regional and Language Options dialog box will open.
3. Click the **Languages** tab and click **Details**. In the Text Services And Input Languages dialog box, click the **Language Bar** button, and select **Show The Language Bar On The Desktop**. Leave the other selected check boxes checked until you've spent some time using the features.
4. Click **OK** three times to close the open dialog boxes, and click the **Close** button to close the Control Panel. The Language bar displays on your screen, on top of all displayed windows and objects.

SET DICTATION AND COMMAND OPTIONS

You can use speech recognition for dictation (adding text to a Word document) and for executing commands normally done by using the mouse or keyboard (for example, "Select *Gettysburg*"). There are features and options you can use for both:

1. If the Control Panel is not already open, click the Windows **Start** button, and then click **Control Panel**.
2. In Windows Classic view, double-click **Regional And Language Options**. In Category view, click **Date, Time, Language, and Regional Options**, and then click **Regional And Language Options**. The Regional and Language Options dialog box will open.
3. Click the **Languages** tab, and click **Details**. In the Text Services And Input Languages dialog box, under Installed Services, click **Speech Recognition**, and click **Properties**.

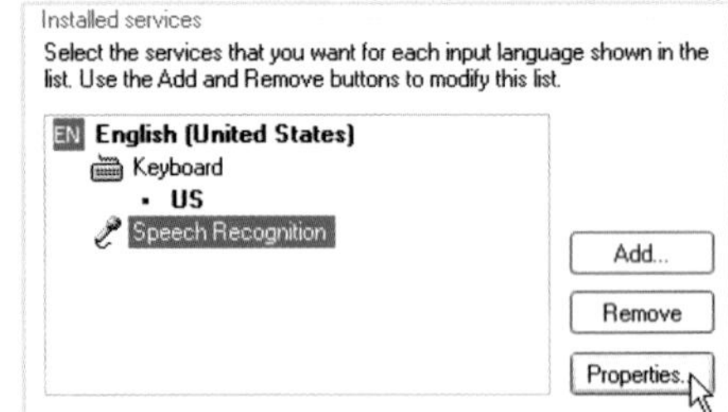

TIP

To close the Language bar, right-click the bar and click **Close The Language Bar**. Click **OK** in the Language Bar dialog box, which tells you how to display the bar when you want to use it again (repeating the steps described in this section).

NOTE

The Language bar can be integrated into the taskbar as well as display as a stand-alone toolbar. Click the **Language Bar** button in the Text Services And Input Languages dialog box, and select the **Show Additional Language Bar Icons In The Taskbar** check box in the Language Bar Settings dialog box. Click **OK**.

Show additional Language bar icons in the taskbar

Show text labels on the Language bar

TIP

With the Language bar displayed, you can open the Text Services And Input Languages dialog box by clicking the **Options** down arrow at the right end of the Language bar, and clicking **Settings**.

4. In the Speech Input Settings dialog box, shown in Figure 8-3:
   - Select the **Assign Mode Keys** check box to display buttons on a language toolbar allowing you to switch between dictation and voice command modes. Click **Settings** to see the keyboard keys used to toggle between the two modes. Click **OK** to close the Mode Button Configuration dialog box.
   - Under Advanced Speech, select or deselect any options that would improve your speech recognition experience. Click **OK** when you are finished.
   - Click **Voice Commands** to display the Voice Command Settings dialog box where you can select which options you want available (fewer is often better to improve overall accuracy). Click **OK** when finished.
5. Click **OK** three times to close the Speech Input Settings dialog box, the Text Services And Input Languages dialog box, and the Regional And Languages Options dialog box (if you entered from the Control panel), and then click **Close** on the Control Panel.

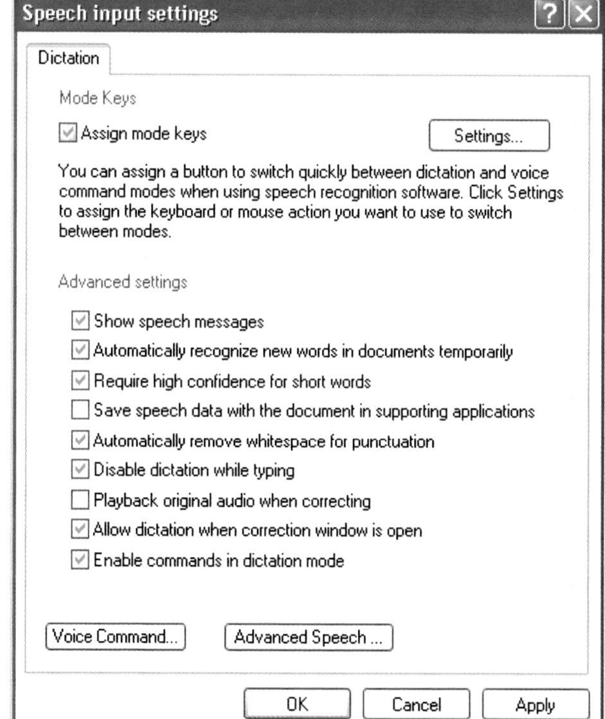

Figure 8-3: The Speech Input Settings dialog box provides options to work in Dictation and Voice Command modes.

1 2 3 4 5 6 7 8 9 10

NOTE

Besides the Dictation mode commands that help you enter text, there are additional commands you can use to format and select text as well as correct mistakes. Click the **Voice Command** button on the Language bar, and use the commands in Table 8-1 as well as those in Table 8-2.

DICTATE TO WORD

Dictating text is as simple as, well, speaking. Along with adding text, you can also give Word limited instructions to assist you in entering the text correctly.

1. Start Word, open a document, and place the insertion point in the paragraph where you want the dictated text to be displayed.
2. On the Language bar, click **Microphone** to turn it on (if your microphone has a switch, ensure it is turned on as well). The Language bar expands and includes a Dictation balloon (if the balloon displays "Voice Command," click the Dictation button).
3. Start speaking and the Speech balloon changes to "Dictating" as it adds text to the page. Use the commands in Table 8-1 to assist you in entering text. See the QuickSteps "Working with Speech Recognition" for other options.
4. When finished, turn off your microphone and click the **Microphone** button on the Language bar.

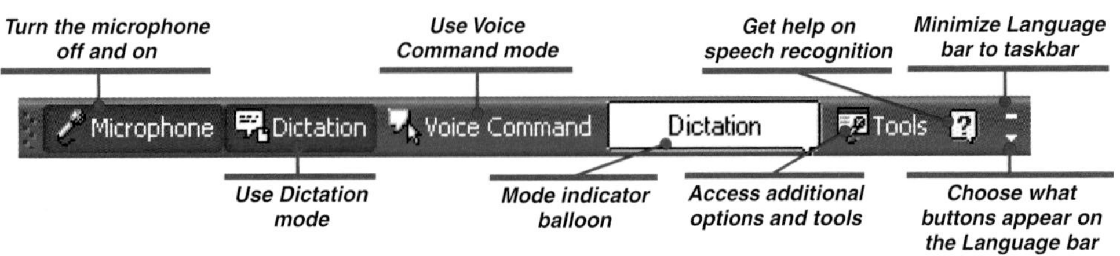

TABLE 8-1: DICTATION MODE COMMANDS

DICTATION COMMAND	ACTION PERFORMED
Backspace	Deletes character to the left of the insertion point
Delete	Deletes character to the right of the insertion point
Enter	Same as pressing ENTER
Force-num	Displays a numeral instead of the text version of a number—for example, saying "five" spells "five;" saying "Force-num five" spells "5"
Microphone	Turns the microphone off
New line	Moves text to next line
New paragraph	Inserts blank paragraph and moves text below it
Space	Adds a blank space
Spelling mode	Allows you to spell out uncommon words to follow. Pause after spelling out the words to return to standard dictation.
Spell it	Allows you to select the previous word and spell it out. Pause after spelling out the word to return to standard dictation.
Tab	Same as pressing TAB

WORKING WITH SPEECH RECOGNITION

The Tools button's drop-down menu on the Language bar provides a number of features you can use to improve your use of speech recognition.

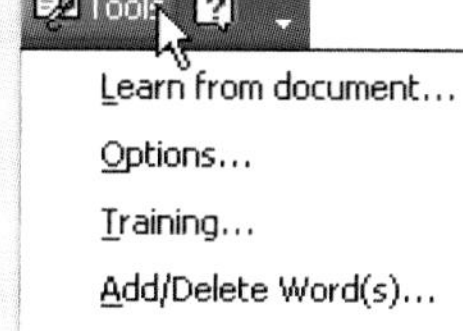

ADD OR REMOVE UNCOMMON WORDS TO DICTIONARY

1. Click **Learn From Document**. A list of uncommon words used in the document is shown.
2. Click any words you do not want to add, and click **Delete**.
3. Click **Add All** to add the remaining words.

INCREASE ACCURACY BY READING PASSAGES

1. Click **Training**.
2. Click a passage you want to read, as shown in Figure 8-4, and click **Next** to start reading.
3. Click **Finish** when done.

IMPROVE ACCURACY OF INDIVIDUAL WORDS

You can "teach" the speech recognition software individual words that the software might have trouble recognizing.

1. Add any uncommon words (see "Add or Remove Uncommon Words to Dictionary" above).
2. Click **Add/Delete Words(s)**.
3. Type the word in the Word text box, or click one from the Dictionary list.
4. Turn your microphone on, click **Record Pronunciation**, and speak the word.
5. Click **Close** when done.

CHANGE SPEECH RECOGNITION PROFILES

Click **Current User** and click the profile you want to use.

POSITION THE LANGUAGE BAR

- Place the mouse pointer on the left end of the Language bar. When the pointer changes to a four-sided move arrow, drag the Language bar to where you want it on the screen.
- Click the **Minimize** button to place the Language bar on the taskbar (click the **Restore** button on the Language bar on the taskbar, or right-click the Language bar and click **Restore Language Bar** on the context menu to display the bar on the screen).

TABLE 8-2: VOICE COMMAND MODE COMMANDS

VOICE COMMAND	ACTION PERFORMED
Copy	Same as pressing **CTRL+C**
Correct [*words*]	Deletes the spoken words
Correction	Deletes selected text or last recognized words
Correct that	Deletes the last word or phrase
Cut	Same as pressing **CTRL+X**
Delete	Deletes selected text or last recognized words
Delete that	Deletes the last phrase
Insert after [*words*]	Moves the insertion point to the right of the last word or words
Insert before [*words*]	Moves the insertion point to the left of the word or words spoken
Next cell	Moves the insertion point to the cell to the right of the current cell
Paste	Same as pressing **CTRL+V**
Scratch that	Deletes last phrase
Select word	Selects the last word displayed
Select [*words*]	Selects the spoken words
Undo	Same as pressing **CTRL+Z**
Unselect that	Deselects selected words

TIP

You can change the default voice (Michael) that reads back text to "Michelle" or "Sam." Click **Tools** on the Language bar, click **Options** on the drop-down menu, and click **Advanced Speech**. In the Speech Properties dialog box, click the **Text To Speech** tab. In the Voice Selection area, select a voice and click **OK** twice.

LISTEN TO TEXT

You can have Word read back to you text in a document. For instance, instead of trying to read that report in traffic before your status meeting (along with balancing a cup of coffee, fielding a few cell phone calls, and futzing with the radio), you could have Word running on a laptop in your front seat reciting the report to you.

1. Display the Language bar. If necessary, display the **Speak** and **Pause** buttons by clicking the **Options** down arrow at the right-end of the bar and selecting **Speak Text** and **Pause Speaking**.
2. Select the text you want read back to you, and click **Speak**. Click the same button to stop the playback, or use the Pause/Resume button to temporarily stop and restart the playback.

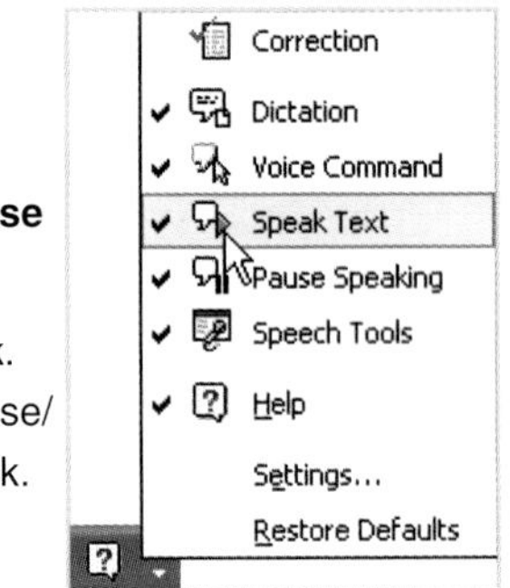

Figure 8-4: You can increase the speech recognition's ability to understand your voice by reading additional passages.

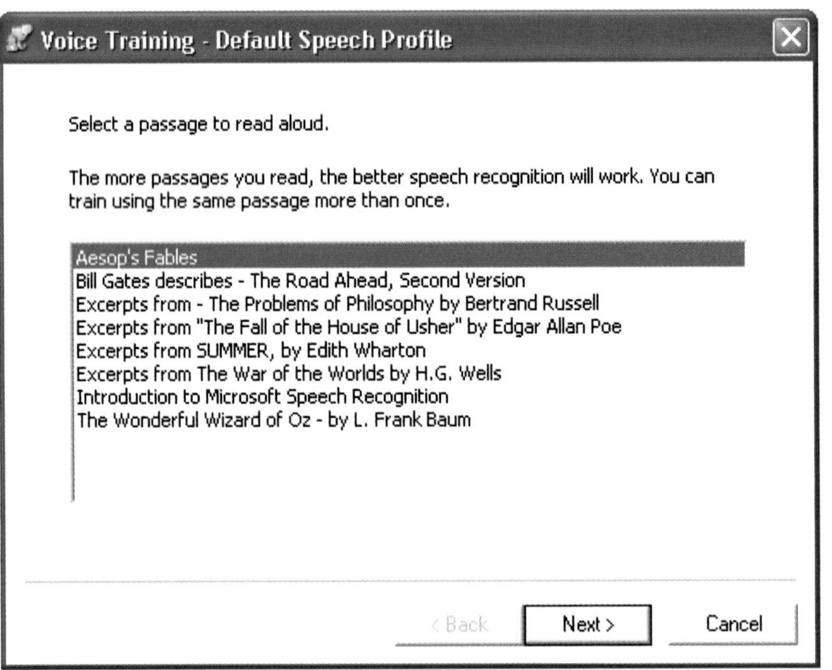

Scan Text into Word

Using a companion Office application, Microsoft Office Document Imaging, you can get information from hard-copy documents into a Word document without having to retype it. It's basically a three-step process:

1. Scan the material into Document Imaging where thumbnail pages are created that you can view, rotate, search for text, and otherwise manage, as shown in Figure 8-5.
2. Create editable text from optical character recognition (OCR) software.
3. Transfer the editable text into a new Word document.

UNDERSTANDING DOCUMENT IMAGING

Document Imaging is a powerful program that can become your central manager for working with all manner of information contained in scanned documents or faxes. Documents from other sources are added to Document Imaging where they are saved in TIFF (Tagged Image File Format) or MDI (Microsoft Document Imaging) format if not already in those formats. Once within Document Imaging, the pages of the documents can be reorganized; annotated with text, pictures, and highlights; transferred between documents; and have OCR software applied to create editable text for transfer to a Word document. The procedures in this book focus on getting scanned information into Word.

USE TIFF OR MDI FORMAT

TIFF is a widely used image file format, recognized by image editing, drawing, desktop publishing, and many other programs. If you plan to use your Document Imaging files with other programs, TIFF is a better choice. MDI is a new format, specifically created for use in Document Imaging. If compatibility with other programs is not a concern, MDI files have greater compression than TIFF files, resulting in smaller file sizes, and the images are generally of better quality.

GET INFORMATION

- Files containing one or more pages that can be opened in their programs on your computer can be imported into Document Imaging (the original file is not affected; the pages are "printed" into Document Imaging). In Document Imaging, click the **File** menu, click **Import**, navigate to and select the file, and click the **Import** button.
- You can insert files that are already in TIFF or MDI format from other sources into a Document Imaging document. Click the **File** menu, click **Insert File**, navigate to and select the file, and click **Insert**.

SCAN A PAGE

1. Click **Start**, click **All Programs**, click **Microsoft Office**, click **Microsoft Office Tools**, and click **Microsoft Office Document Imaging**. The program opens with a menu bar, toolbars, and two blank panes (if you only see the Page pane, click the **View** menu and click **Thumbnail** pane).
2. Place the document in your scanning device.
3. Click the **File** menu and click **Scan New Document**.
4. If you have more than one scanner, click the one you want to use in the Microsoft Office Document Scanning dialog box, and click **OK**.

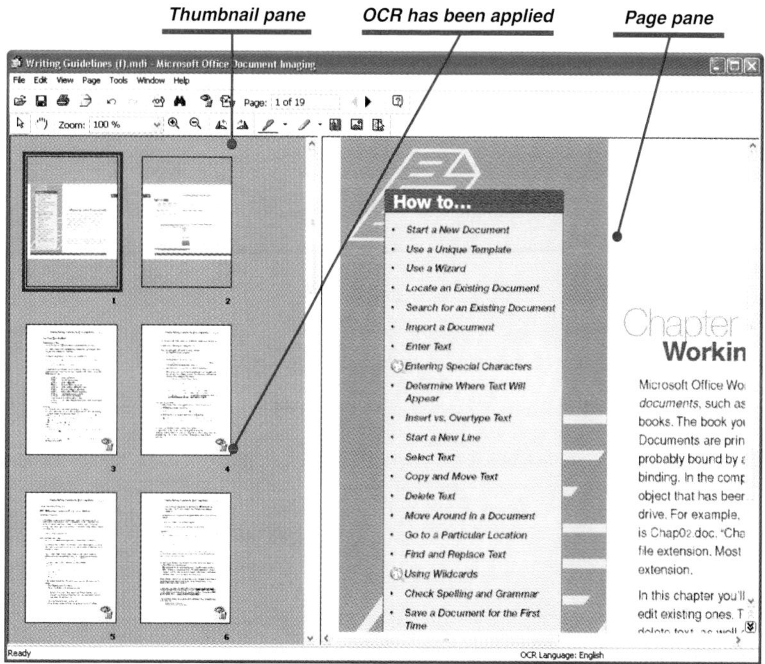

Figure 8-5: Images are created in Document Imaging by scanning, importing files from other programs, or inserting TIFF or MDI files.

1 2 3 4 5 6 7 8 9 10

NOTE

Both Document Imaging and the OCR feature may have to be installed upon your first use. You will need your Office CD or its location on your network for the installation files.

TIP

You can skip applying OCR manually by going directly from "Scan a Page" to "Transfer Text Into a Word Document" and perform the OCR during the transfer process.

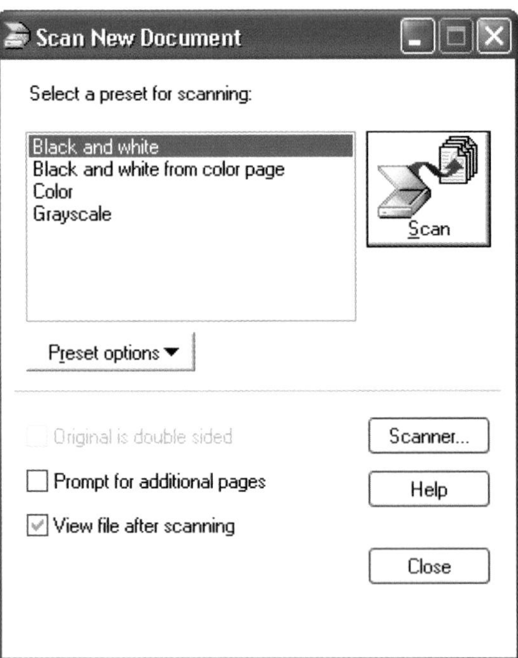

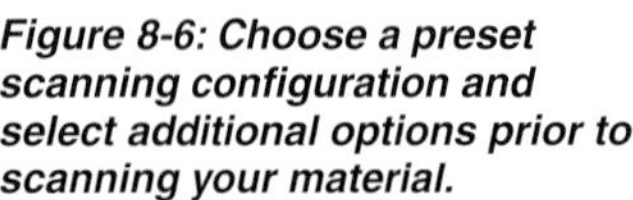
Figure 8-6: Choose a preset scanning configuration and select additional options prior to scanning your material.

5. In the Scan New Document dialog box, shown in Figure 8-6, select one of the preset configurations that best matches your source document. To fine-tune the scan, click **Preset Options** and/or select one of the check boxes at the bottom of the dialog box. Click **Scan** when finished. The page is displayed in the Document Imaging Thumbnail pane.

APPLY OCR

OCR software interprets scanned material and attempts to convert text into editable characters and identify pictures and other images. You can apply OCR to selected pages, all pages in the document, or just those that don't display the Display OCR Information tag (meaning they haven't been through an OCR process yet).

1. Select one or more pages in the Thumbnail pane (use **CTRL+CLICK** to select noncontiguous page and **SHIFT+CLICK** to select contiguous pages), click the **Tools** menu, and click **Recognize Text Using OCR**.
2. In the Recognize Text Using OCR dialog box, choose which pages to OCR, and click **OK**. Each page you identified to be processed will be checked and the Display OCR Information tag added to its thumbnail when finished.

TRANSFER TEXT INTO WORD

After a page has been "OCR-ed," you can transfer text (and graphics) into Word by selected text, selected pages, or all pages in the Document Imaging document.

1. Select a page whose text you want to transfer to Word in the Thumbnail pane. If you want to transfer a selection from the page, select the text in the Page pane by dragging a red, rectangular marquee.

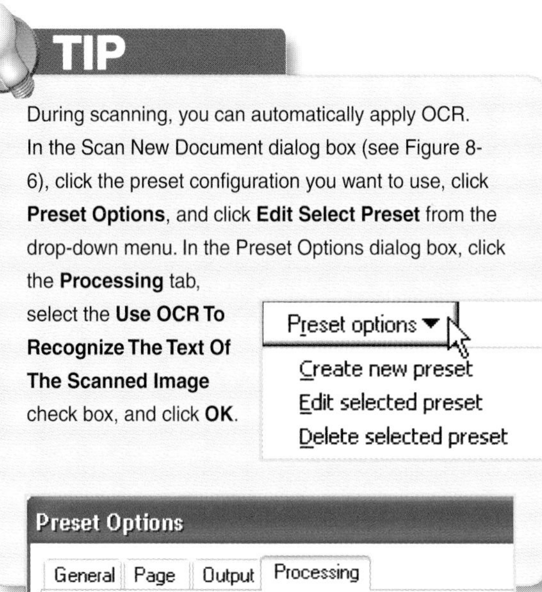

TIP

During scanning, you can automatically apply OCR. In the Scan New Document dialog box (see Figure 8-6), click the preset configuration you want to use, click **Preset Options**, and click **Edit Select Preset** from the drop-down menu. In the Preset Options dialog box, click the **Processing** tab, select the **Use OCR To Recognize The Text Of The Scanned Image** check box, and click **OK**.

2. Click the **Tools** menu and click **Send Text To Word**.
3. In the Send Text To Word dialog box, verify that the portion of the document you want to transfer is selected, choose whether to include any pictures, and browse to a folder where you want a Word document stored with the editable text.

4. Click **OK** when finished. A new Word document is placed in your chosen folder with the same file name as the Document Imaging document. Figure 8-7 shows what a page with text and graphics in Document Imaging looks like after it's been recognized by OCR and transferred to a Word document.

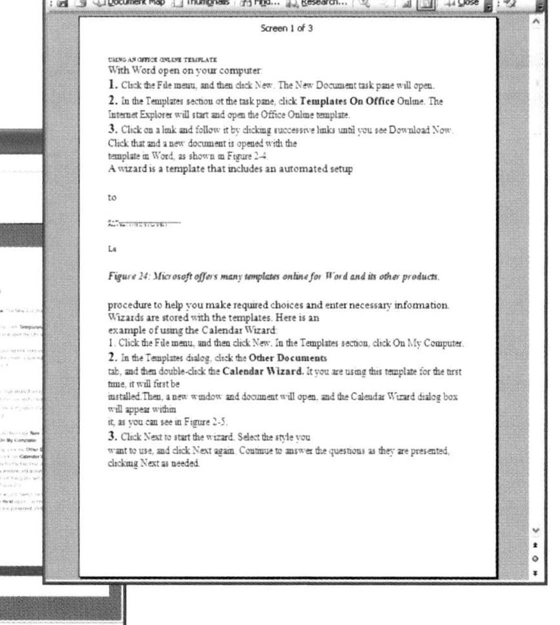

Figure 8-7: Text transfers to a Word document reasonably well, though the original layout and graphics are all but lost.

NOTE

The OCR engine that is included with Document Imaging does not contain all of the functionality and features of the original product. You can upgrade to a more robust OCR experience by clicking the **Help** menu and clicking **OCR Upgrade Information**.

NOTE

If you choose a language that does not display its translated words correctly, you might have to install additional language-supported software. Go to the Microsoft web site (www.microsoft.com), and search for "proofing tools." You can purchase a CD online that contains language support for over 50 languages.

NOTE

The bilingual translation provided by the local dictionaries is fine for short translations, but the literal translation may lose the "sense" of the words. For a "truer" translation, use the online machine translation services offered. You can adjust how the translation takes place by clicking **Translation Options** in the Translation section of the Research pane and making changes in the Translation Options dialog box.

Translate to and from Another Language

You can translate words, or even entire documents, into several languages using the translation services offered by Word (and other Office products). First you must install a local dictionary on your computer, which also provides the means to use more powerful online services.

INSTALL TRANSLATION SUPPORT

1. Click the **Tools** menu, extend it if needed, click **Language**, and click **Translate**. The Research task opens and you will be asked if you want to install the translation dictionaries.
2. Click **Yes**. (You may need your Office CD or network location for Office installation files.)

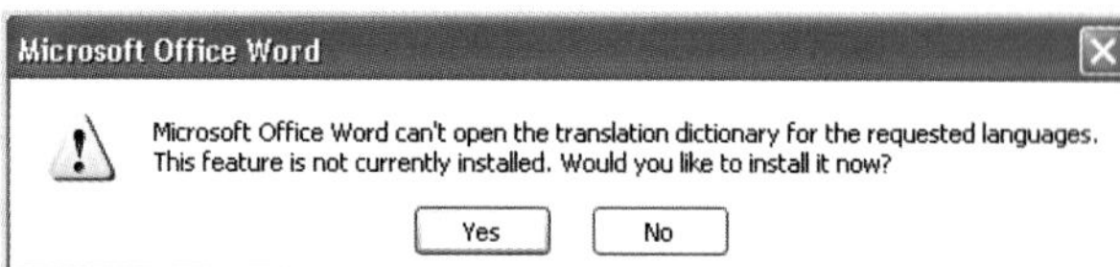

TRANSLATE A WORD OR PHRASE

1. Display the Research task pane (see Chapter 1 for information on displaying task panes).

   –Or–

   Click the **Tools** menu, click **Language**, and click **Translate**.
2. Under Translation, click the **From** and **To** down arrows, and click the languages the text is in (From) and the language you want it translated into (To).
3. Press **ALT** and click a word or select a short phrase you want translated.

   –Or–

   Type the word or phrase in the Search For text box, and click the green button.

   In either case, the results display in the Translation section of the Research task pane.

TRANSLATE AN ENTIRE DOCUMENT

You will need to be connected to the Internet for a full-document translation.

1. Display the Research task pane (see Chapter 1 for information on displaying task panes).

   –Or–

   Click the **Tools** menu, click **Language**, and click **Translate**.
2. Under Translation, click the **From** and **To** down arrows, and click the languages the text is in (From) and the language you want it translated into (To).
3. Below the From/To drop-down boxes, click the green button below the Send Document For Translation. Your browser opens to a MSN web page with the document translated, similar to Figure 8-8. You can then copy and paste text into your Word document.

Send document for translation over the Internet in unencrypted HTML format

Translation options...

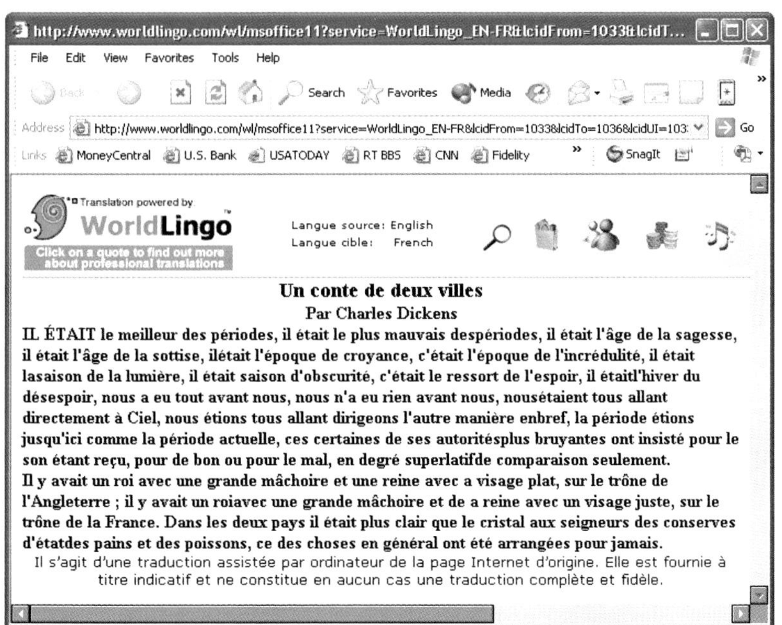

Figure 8-8: A document containing the first chapter of a classic is quickly translated by WorldLingo.

NOTE

The terms *chart* and *graph* are used interchangeably; they mean the same thing.

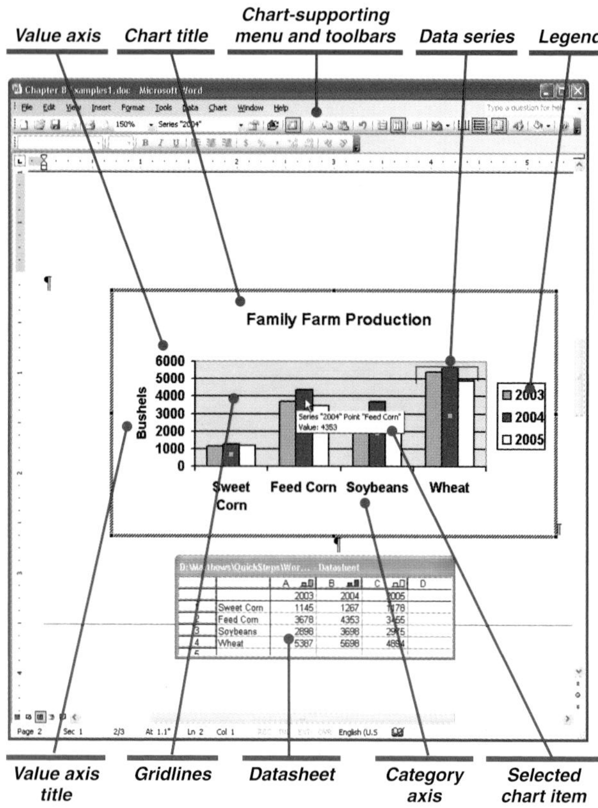

Figure 8-9: Word integrates Microsoft Graph tools so you can easily chart your data.

Working with Charts

Charts are inserted in a document using Microsoft Graph, a companion program that works within Word and your current document. You have the full functionality of Graph available to you, including its menus, toolbars, and dialog boxes as you work with your chart, as shown in Figure 8-9. After the chart is created, you can change how your data is displayed—for example, switching from the default column representation to a pie chart. Additionally, you can add or remove chart items such as titles, axes, legends, and gridlines, as well as format text and several of the chart items with color and other attributes.

Create a Chart

Charts are created in two ways, each of which allows for easy formatting and reconfiguring the chart to your needs:

- You select data in an existing Word table and create a *datasheet* (fancy name for a table or spreadsheet) from which a chart that presents the information is built.
- You start with a sample datasheet and replace the sample data with your own from which a chart that presents the information is built.

CREATE A CHART FROM A WORD TABLE

1. Select the range of cells in the table that contain the data you want to chart, including headings but omitting any titles or other non-data cells. Remove any blank rows or columns and any rows used as subheadings (see Chapter 6 for more information on working with tables in Word).
2. Click the **Insert** menu, extend the menu if needed, and click **Object**.
3. In the Object dialog box, click the **Create New** tab, scroll down the Object Type list, and double-click **Microsoft Graph Chart**. A datasheet appears, displaying the data in table form, and a column chart displays the data graphically.

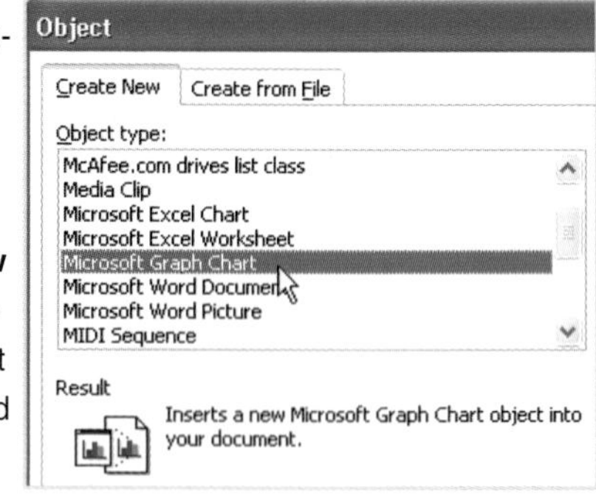

> **TIP**
>
> After you've created a chart, anytime you are in the standard Word document you can double-click the chart to reopen the Graph window and its associated datasheet.

CREATE A SAMPLE CHART

1. Place the insertion point in the Word paragraph where you want the chart to be displayed.
2. Click the **Insert** menu and click **Object**.
3. In the Object dialog box, click the **Create New** tab, scroll down the Object Type list, and double-click **Microsoft Graph Chart**. A separate document appears with a datasheet displaying sample data in table form, and a column chart displays the sample data graphically, as shown in Figure 8-10.
4. Customize the data: (see the QuickSteps "Working with the Datasheet" later in the chapter).
5. To return to the document with Word menus and toolbars, click a blank area of the document page. The chart, without its datasheet, displays in the document as a graphic (see Chapter 7 for information on working with graphics). To reopen the chart (and its datasheet) in Graph, double-click the chart.

Figure 8-10: Microsoft Graph provides sample data when creating a new chart.

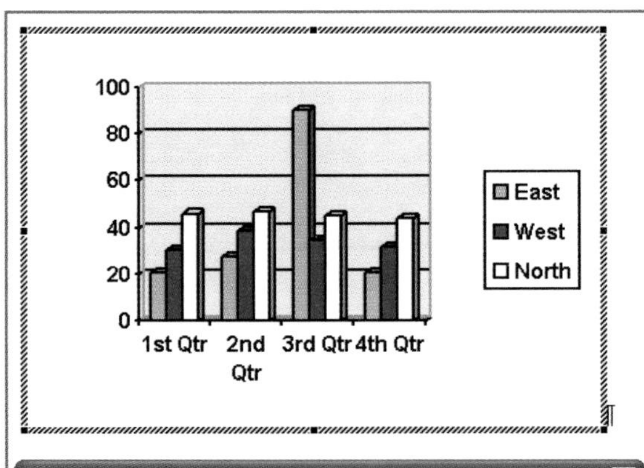

Use Data from Other Programs

You can import data into a datasheet from text files, spreadsheet files such as from Microsoft Excel or Lotus 1-2-3, as well as by pasting or linking.

IMPORT FILES

1. In Microsoft Graph, click the datasheet to make it active. (If the datasheet isn't displayed, click **View Datasheet** on the Graph toolbar.)
2. Click the cell where you want the upper-left corner of the data to start (usually the upper-leftmost cell in the datasheet).
3. Click the **Edit** menu and click **Import File**, or click **Import File** on the Graph toolbar. In the Import File dialog box, click the **Files Of Type** down arrow, and click the file type you are importing. Use the Look In drop-down list to navigate to your file location, and double-click it. What happens next depends on the file type you chose:

   - **Text and delimited files (.txt, .csv, and .prn)** open the Text Import Wizard, shown in Figure 8-11. Select how the data is organized in Step 1 of the wizard, preview your data and make any necessary adjustments in Step 2, and then apply data formats to the columns in Step 3. Click **Finish** when done.

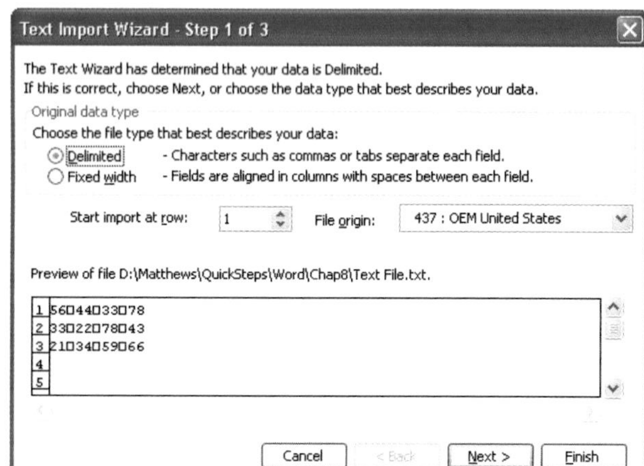

Figure 8-11: The Text Import Wizard lets you tell Graph how text is separated and organized before adding the data to a datasheet.

- **Lotus 1-2-3 files (.wks and .wk1)** display data in the datasheet as it appears in the original program file.
- **Microsoft Excel files (.xls and .xlt)** open an Import Data Options dialog box where you select the workbook or enter a range of cells you want to import. Choose whether you want to overwrite data in existing cells. Click **OK** after making your choices.
- **Microsoft Excel files (.xlw and .xlc – Excel 4.0 workbooks, and 4.0 and earlier charts)** display data in the datasheet as it appears in the program file.

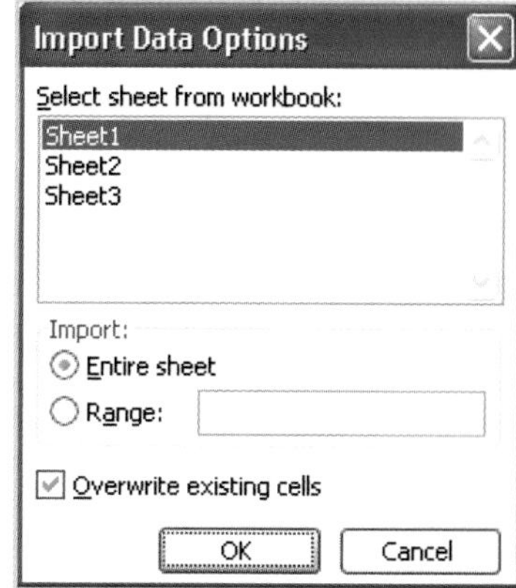

PASTE DATA

You can paste data from another program by either doing a one-time insertion of the data as it exists at the time of the cut or copy, or you can establish the link with the source document so that as the source data is changed, the pasted data is changed as well.

1. Select the data you want to use in a chart, and press **CTRL+C** to copy it.
2. Double-click the chart in Word to display a datasheet, and click the cell where you want the upper-left corner of the data to start (usually the upper-leftmost cell in the datasheet unless you have row and column headings).
3. Press **CTRL+V** to paste the data in the datasheet. The data is inserted and no relationship is maintained to the source document.

   –Or–

   Click the **Edit** menu, click **Paste Link**, and click **Yes** to acknowledge new data will replace all the existing data in the datasheet. The data is inserted and a link is established with the data in the source document. When changes are made to the source data, the linked data in the datasheet is updated.

NOTE

Linking data in a datasheet by using the Paste Link command requires you to update data in only one file. Linking does have the downside of requiring the source file to remain in the same folder location it was in when the link was created. Additionally, documents with linked files are not suitable for sharing outside your local network.

TABLE 8-3: CHART TYPES

CHART TYPE	FUNCTION
Standard Charts:	
Column, Bar, Line, Cylinder, Cone, Pyramid	Compares trends in multiple data series in various configurations, such as vertical and horizontal; and in several shapes, such as bar, cylinder, cone, and pyramid
Pie and Doughnut	Displays one data series (pie) or compares multiple data series (doughnut) as part of a whole, or 100%
XY (Scatter)	Displays pairs of data to establish concentrations
Area	Shows the magnitude of change over time; useful when summing multiple values to see the contribution of each
Radar	Connects changes in a data series from a starting or center point with lines, markers, or a colored fill
Surface	Compares trends in multiple data series in a continuous curve; similar to Line chart with a 3-D visual effect
Bubble	Displays sets of three values; similar to an XY chart with the third value being the size of the bubble
Stock	Displays three sets of values, such as a high, low, and closing stock price
Custom Charts:	
Variations on standard charts, Custom Charts are one of a kind for which there are no sub-types and which are typically used for a specific application. For example, the Logarithmic chart is a line chart with a special scale, while the Column-Area or Line-Column charts are combinations of two standard charts.	
User-Defined Charts:	
Charts that include formatting and unique settings that you might want to save to apply to future charts.	

Use Chart Types

Besides the default column chart you see when first opening Graph, there are 13 other standard chart types available to display your data. Each chart type has two or more sub-types you can choose. Additionally, you can choose from several prebuilt custom charts (variations on the standard chart types) and create a custom chart type from changes you've made to a chart. Table 8-3 describes the chart types.

SELECT AN EXISTING CHART TYPE

1. Double-click the chart in Word, click the **Chart** menu, and click **Chart Type**. In the Chart Type dialog box, click the **Standard Types** tab (see Figure 8-12).

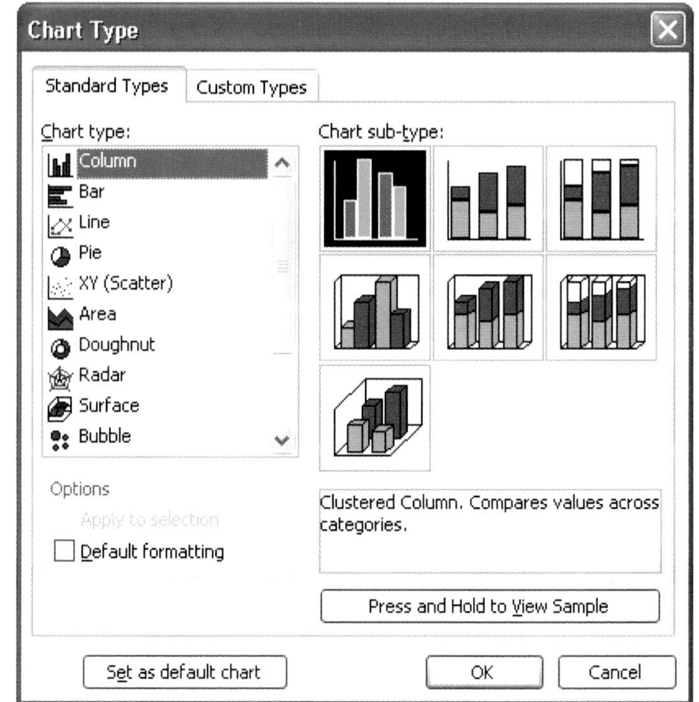

Figure 8-12: Each standard chart type has at least two sub-chart types and often a custom chart associated with it.

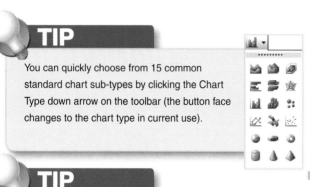

1 2 3 4 5 6 7 8 9 10

TIP

You can quickly choose from 15 common standard chart sub-types by clicking the Chart Type down arrow on the toolbar (the button face changes to the chart type in current use).

TIP

You can change the chart type that is displayed when you first create a chart. Double-click a chart in Word, or create a new chart (see "Create a Chart"). Click the **Chart** menu, click **Chart Type**, select the standard or custom (built-in or user-defined) chart you want, and click **Set As Default Chart**. The next time you create a chart it will start out as your selected chart type.

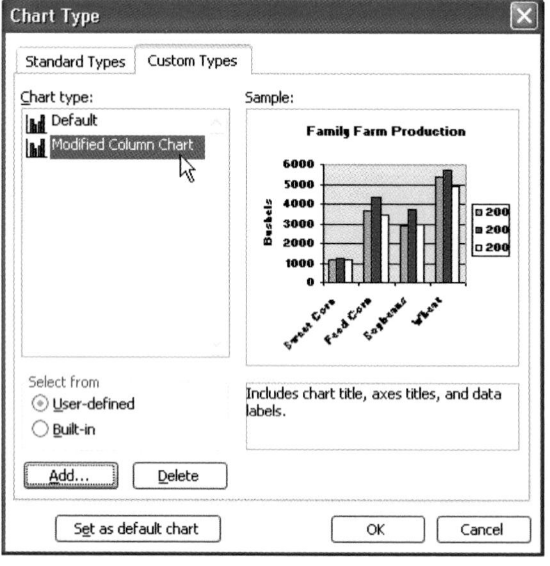

Figure 8-13: Your user-defined chart appears in the Chart Type dialog box just like the standard and custom charts Graph provides.

2. To view samples of standard chart types, click the type from the Chart Type list, click the sub-type from the Chart Sub-Type list, and click **Press And Hold To View Sample**, which shows the chart type with your data.

   –Or–

   To view a custom or user-defined chart, click the **Custom Types** tab. In the Select From area, click the chart type category you want, and click the chart type in the Chart Type list.

3. Click **OK** to change the appearance of the current chart to your selected chart type.

DEFINE YOUR OWN CHART TYPE

After you have applied formatting and added or removed chart items, your chart may not resemble any of the standard or even custom chart types provided by Graph. To save your work so you can build a similar chart at another time:

1. Double-click the chart in Word, and modify the chart using the Graph toolbars and menus.
2. Click the **Chart** menu, click **Chart Type**, and click the **Custom Types** tab.
3. In the Select From area, click **User-Defined**, then click **Add**. The Add Custom Chart Type dialog box opens.
4. Type a name and description for the chart, and click **OK**. The chart appears as a user-defined chart type that you can choose in the future, as shown in Figure 8-13. Click **OK** to close the Chart Type dialog box.

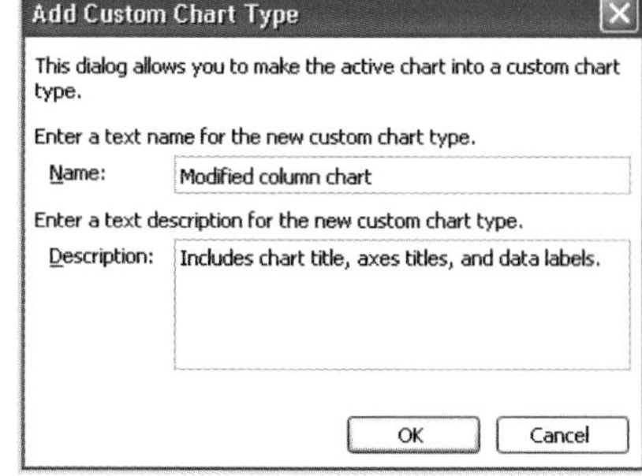

QUICKSTEPS

SELECTING CHART ITEMS

You can select items on a chart using a toolbar, keyboard, or by clicking the item with the mouse. When selected, items will display small, rectangular handles (for some items these are sizing handles; for others, they just show selection).

SELECT CHART ITEMS FROM THE CHART TOOLBAR

1. Click the chart you are working on.
2. Click the **Chart Objects** down arrow to open its drop-down list, and click the item you want to select.

SELECT CHART ITEMS USING THE KEYBOARD

1. Click the chart.
2. Use the arrow keys on your keyboard to cycle through the chart items. The name of the selected item is shown in the Chart Objects drop-down list on the toolbar.

SELECT CHART ITEMS BY CLICKING

Place the mouse pointer over the item you want selected, and click. The name of the selected item is shown in the Chart Objects drop-down list on the toolbar.

TIP

You can add a second category and/or value axis that can have its own title. A second axis is typically used when the values in one data series is proportionately a lot different from the others and needs a different scale of values. Right-click the chart in Graph, click **Chart Type**, and click the **Custom Types** tab. Select the **Line-Column On 2 Axes** (or another 2-axes chart type), and click **OK**.

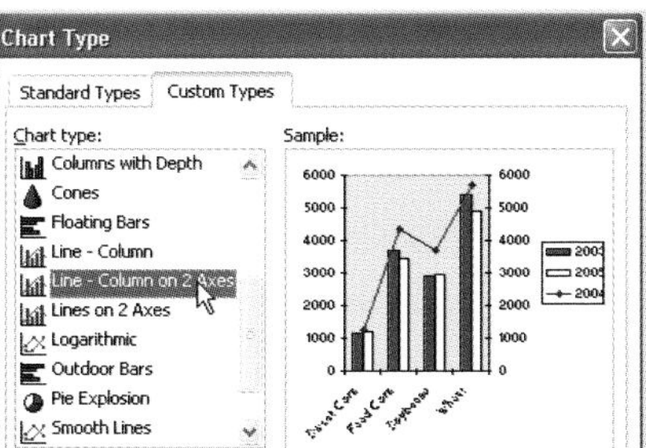

Work with Chart Items

You can add or modify several items on a chart to help clarify and emphasize the data it represents. Right-click a blank area of the chart area, and click **Chart Options;** or click the **Chart** menu, and click **Chart Options**. The Chart Options dialog box, shown in Figure 8-14, displays several tabs that contain options and features for the chart items.

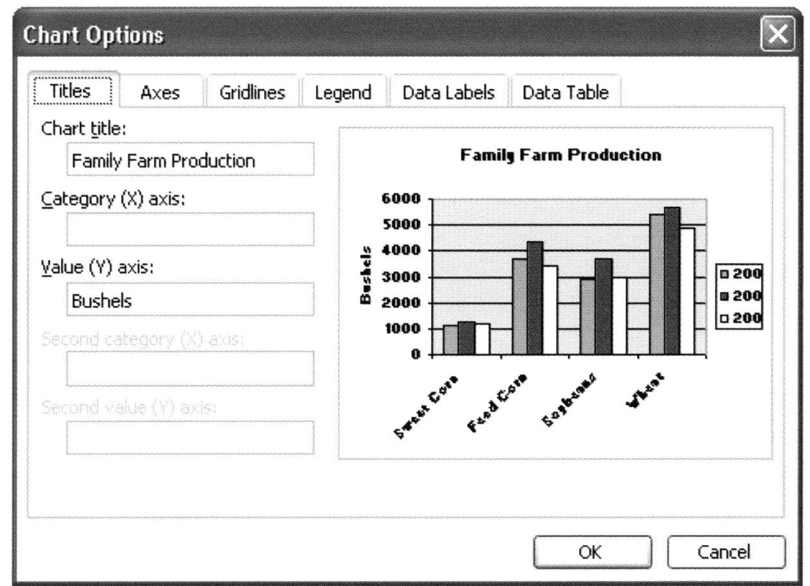

Figure 8-14: The Chart Options dialog box lets you customize chart items.

1
2
3
4
5
6
7
8
9
10

UNDERSTANDING DATA SERIES AND AXES

There are a few guidelines for setting up data for charting, as well as some assumptions Microsoft Graph uses:

- Text, which is used solely to create labels, should only be in the topmost row and/or the leftmost column. Text encountered in the datasheet outside these two areas is charted as zero.
- Each cell must contain a *value* (or data point). Values in the same row or column are considered to be related and are called a *data series*. The first data series starts with the first cell in the upper-left of the selected data that is not text or formatted as a date. Subsequent data series are determined by Graph, continuing across the rows or down the columns.
- As Graph determines whether there are more rows or columns selected, it will assume the lesser number to be the data series and the greater number to be categories that are plotted on the category *X* axis. In Figure 8-9, there are three columns and four rows of data in the datasheet; therefore, Graph plots the three years' of values each as a data series and considers the rows to be categories.
- The value *Y* or *Z* axis displays a scale for the values in the data series.

Format Chart Items

Each chart item has an associated Format dialog box with one or more tabs that provide formatting options. Table 8-4 shows the formatting options that are available.

TABLE 8-4: FORMATTING OPTIONS AVAILABLE TO CHART ITEMS

FORMATTING OPTIONS *(by tab)*	DESCRIPTION	APPLY TO:
Patterns	Adds borders and backgrounds, tick mark styles and labels, and table layout options	Titles, Legends, Chart Area, Axes, Gridlines, Data Series, Data Labels, Plot Area, Data Table
Font	Changes the font, font style, font size, color, and other effects of characters	Titles, Legends, Chart Area, Axes, Data Labels, Data Table
Alignment	Rotates text and controls text direction (for several Middle Eastern and East Asian languages)	Titles, Legends, Axes, Data Labels
Scale	Provides scaling parameters, such as start and end values, interval between minor and major units, and where the axes cross	Axes, Gridlines
Number	Provides the same number formats as the Format Cells Number tab, such as currency, accounting, date, and time	Axes, Data Labels
Placement	Provides location options on the chart	Legend
Axis	Plots the series on a secondary axis	Data Series
Y Error Bars	Graphically displays error notations (plus, minus, or both) from a plotted value and sets the error amount	Data Series
Data Labels	Allows you to set the label to series name, category name, value, and other criteria	Data Series
Series Order	Sets the order that the series are plotted (example: if you plotted three consecutive years, you could plot them in reverse order)	Data Series
Options	Provides the gap spacing between categories, overlap of data series columns or bars, and color variation	Data Series

To format a chart item:

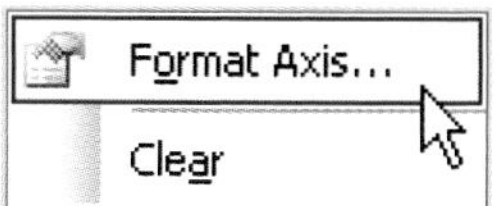

1. Right-click the item and click **Format *chart item*** on the context menu, or double-click the item. A Format dialog box tailored to that item opens, as shown in Figure 8-15.
2. Find the formatting option category you want from Table 8-4.
3. Click the tab that contains the formatting option you want to apply.
4. Select and/or adjust the formatting option, and click **OK**.

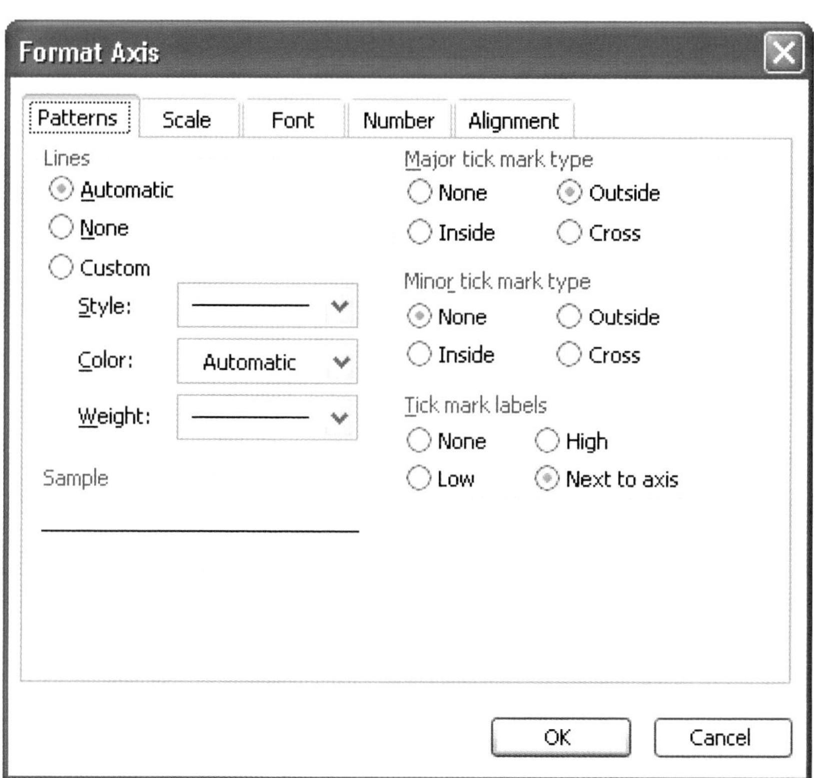

Figure 8-15: A typical Format dialog box, tailored to a chart item.

1 2 3 4 5 6 7 8 9 10

QUICKSTEPS

WORKING WITH THE DATASHEET

Datasheets have properties similar to tables and spreadsheets. Figure 8-16 displays elements of a datasheet. (See Chapter 6 for information on working with tables, which share many characteristics with datasheets.)

DISPLAY THE DATASHEET IN WORD

Double-click the chart in Word, click **Data Table** on the toolbar, and click a blank area outside the chart. The chart and data display together in Word.

ADD AND REMOVE ROWS AND COLUMNS

- To remove a row or column, right-click the row (numbered cells on left edge) or column (lettered cells on top) heading, and click **Delete**.
- To add a row, right-click the row heading below where you want the blank row, and click **Insert**.
- To add a column, right-click the column heading to the right of where you want a blank column, and click **Insert**.

FORMAT CELLS

1. Select the cells you want to apply number or font formatting by clicking the upper-leftmost cell in the range and dragging to the lower-rightmost cell.
2. Right-click the selection and click:
   - **Number** to open the Format Number dialog box. Click the number category you want, and set any options that display on the right side of the dialog box.
   - **Font** to open the Font dialog box. Set the font characteristics and effects you want to apply.
3. Click **OK**.

SELECT ALL CELLS

Click the cell in the upper-left corner of the datasheet (at the intersection of the row and column headings).

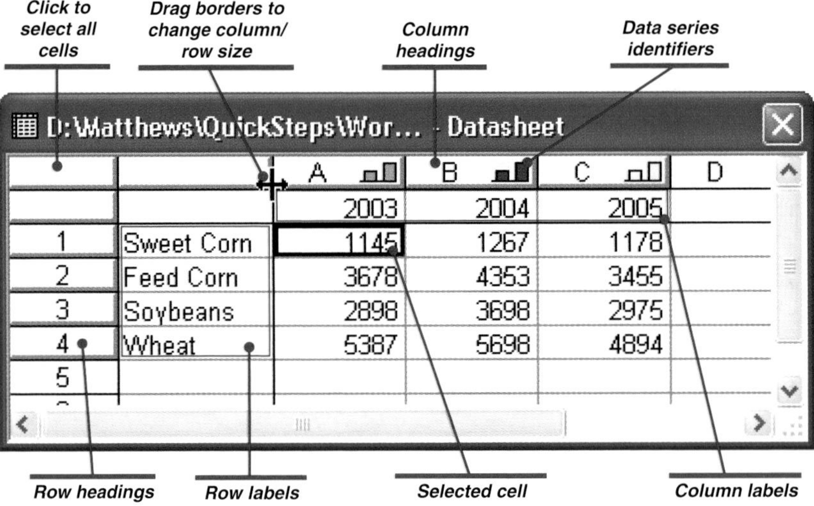

Figure 8-16: Datasheets are similar to tables and spreadsheets.

How to...

- *Create a Web Page*
- *Save Word Documents as Web Pages*
- *Choosing Suitable Web File Formats*
- *Configure Web Options in Word*
- *Understanding HTML and How Word Uses It*
- *Insert a Hyperlink*
- *Understanding Hyperlinks*
- *Using Word to Create HTML Elements*
- *Check How a Page Will Look*

Chapter 9
Creating Web Pages

You can use Word 2003 to create and save documents as web pages. These features enable you to put Word documents onto a web site or an intranet site (a web site internal to an organization) in a format in which they can be viewed using a web browser, such as Internet Explorer. Word also allows you to work with existing web pages and provides a number of settings to control them.

Create and Save a Web Page in Word

Word offers many tools to help you produce a moderate quantity of web pages. These include a web page template, the ability to save documents as web pages, as well as a number of web page-oriented tools.

> **TIP**
>
> If you have a modest number of web pages to produce, then Word offers a reasonable tool to do that. If you have a more extensive job, then dedicated web tools, such as Microsoft Office FrontPage 2003, are more appropriate. See *Microsoft Office FrontPage 2003 QuickSteps*, published by McGraw-Hill/Osborne.

Create a Web Page

Word gives you two ways to create a web page: using the Web Page Template and creating a web page from scratch. Both end up giving you the very same starting place. The Web Page Template that is installed with Word gives you a new blank page in Web Layout view, as does starting it from scratch.

1. If Word is not already open, start it. Click the **File** menu and click **New**. The New Document task pane will open.
2. Under Templates in the task pane, click **On My Computer**. In the General tab, double-click **Web Page**, as shown in Figure 9-1. Word opens a new, blank web page.

   –Or–

   In the New area, click **Web Page**. Word opens a new, blank web page.
3. Create content on the page by using standard Word techniques as described in the early chapters of this book. For example:
   - To enter text, type it as usual.
   - To apply a style, click the **Style** drop-down list on the Formatting toolbar, and then click the desired style name.
   - To apply direct formatting (for example, bold or italic), select the text to which you want to apply it, and then click the appropriate button on the Formatting toolbar.
   - To create tables and add pictures and other graphic elements, use Word's extensive table creation and graphics tools.
4. Save the document as described in the section "Save Word Documents as Web Pages," later in this chapter.

New Document
New
Blank document
XML document
Web page
E-mail message
From existing document...
Templates
Search online for:
Go
Templates on Office Online
On my computer...
On my Web sites...
Recently used templates
Professional Letter
QuickSteps6.dot
Normal.dot
Calendar Wizard

Figure 9-1: Word provides a template for creating a web page that sets up the view and file type.

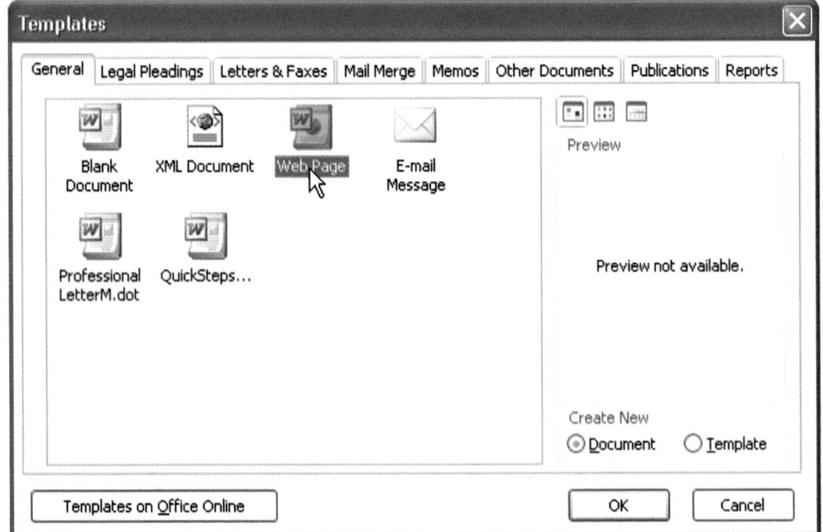

NOTE

Instead of starting a new web page from scratch, you can create one by opening an existing Word document and then using the Save As Web Page command on the File menu to save it in a web format. See "Save Word Documents as Web Pages" for details.

TIP

Both the Web Page Template and the New Document Web Page open a document in Web Layout view. You can change to this view on your own either by clicking the **View** menu and clicking **Web Layout**, or by clicking **Web Layout View** in the view bar in the lower left of the Word window.

Save Word Documents as Web Pages

To save an existing Word document as a web page:

1. Start Word if it is not already running, or switch to it.
2. Click the **File** menu, click **Open**, select the existing document you want to save as a web page, and then click **Open**. The document opens.
3. Click the **File** menu, expand the menu if needed, and then click **Save As Web Page**. The Save As dialog box appears (see Figure 9-2).
4. Use the Save In drop-down list and the main list box to specify the folder in which to save the web page.
5. In the Save As Type drop-down list, select the file format you want to use (see the "Choosing Suitable Web File Formats" QuickFacts in this chapter for a discussion of the available formats).
6. In the File Name text box, type the file name. If you want to use the .html extension instead of the .htm extension (for a file in either the Web Page format or the Web Page, Filtered format), or the .mhtml extension instead of the .mht extension (for a file in the Single File Web Page Format), type the extension as well.

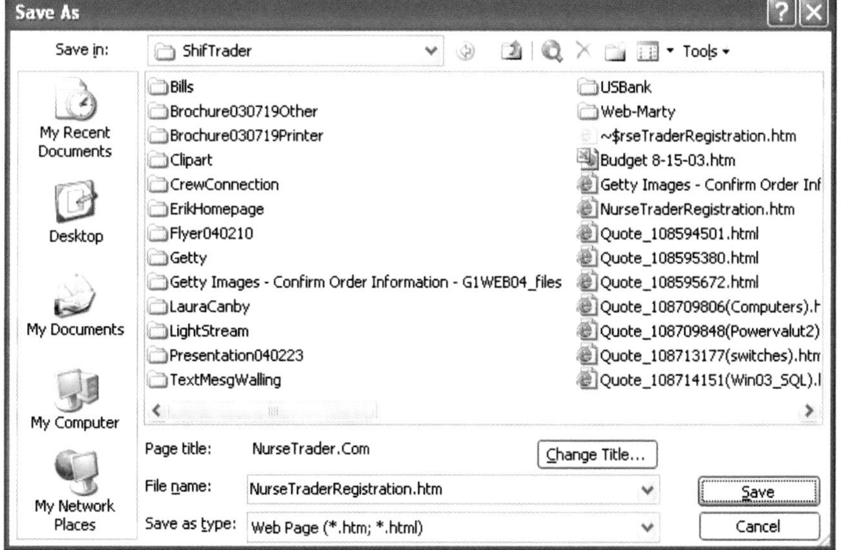

Figure 9-2: Word's Save As dialog box for saving web pages includes the Page Title area and the Change Title button.

CHOOSING SUITABLE WEB FILE FORMATS

Word offers three HTML formats to choose from; before you save a file in HTML, you should understand how the formats differ from each other and which format is suitable for which purposes.

Word offers the Single File Web Page format and the Web Page format. Word also offers the Web Page, Filtered format.

WEB PAGE FORMAT

The Web Page format creates an HTML file that contains the text contents of the document, together with a separate folder that contains the graphics for the document. This makes the web page's HTML file itself smaller, but the page as a whole is a little clumsy to distribute because you need to distribute the graphics folder as well. The folder is created automatically and assigned the web page's name followed by _files. For example, a web page named Products.htm has a folder named Products_files.

Files in the Web Page format use the .htm and .html file extensions. These files also use Office-specific tags to preserve all of the information the file contains in an HTML format.

SINGLE FILE WEB PAGE FORMAT

The Single File Web Page format creates a web archive file that contains all the information required for the web page—all the text contents and all the graphics. Use the Single File Web Page format to create files that you can easily distribute.

Continued...

7. Check the title displayed in the Page Title area. (The page title is what appears in the title bar of the browser.) To change it, click **Change Title**, type the new title in the Set Page Title dialog box, and then click **OK**.

Set Page Title
Page title:
NurseTrader.Com
The title of the page is displayed in the titlebar of the browser.
OK Cancel

8. Click **Save**. Word saves the document as a web page.
9. If you've finished working with the document, click the **File** menu, and then click **Close**. If you've finished working with Word, click the **File** menu, and then click **Exit**.

Work with Web Pages in Word

Word provides a number of tools and settings that allow you to work with web pages to give you the features you want on a web site.

Configure Web Options in Word

Before you start using Word to create web pages, you must configure the web options in Word. These options control how Word creates web pages. Once you've specified the options you want for web pages, you probably won't need to change them. If you do need to change them for a particular file, you can do so when you're saving the file as a web page.

DISPLAY THE WEB OPTIONS DIALOG BOX

To configure web options, first display the Web Options dialog box:

1. If Word is not already running, start it now.
2. Click the **Tools** menu, and then click **Options**. The Options dialog box appears. Click the **General** tab if it is not automatically displayed, and then click **Web Options**. The Web Options dialog box for the application appears, as shown in Figure 9-3.
3. Choose options as discussed in the following subsections, click **OK** to close the Web Options dialog box, and then click **OK** to close the Options dialog box.

CHOOSING SUITABLE WEB FILE FORMATS (Continued)

Files in the Single File Web Page format use the .mht and .mhtml file extensions. These files use Office-specific tags to preserve all of the information the file contains in an HTML format.

WEB PAGE, FILTERED FORMAT

The Web Page, Filtered format creates an HTML file that contains the text contents of the document, together with a separate, automatically named folder that contains the graphics for the document. However, this format removes Office-specific tags from the document. Removing these features reduces the size of the file, but the file uses items such as document properties and VBA code, so this format is not useful for "round-tripping" (being brought back into and edited with Word) complex documents.

Files in the Web Page, Filtered format use the .htm and .html file extensions.

CHOOSE BROWSERS TAB OPTIONS

Figure 9-3 shows the Browsers tab of the Web Options dialog box for Word. Table 9-1 explains the options and shows for which browsers they're turned on (with the check box selected) or off (with the check box deselected).

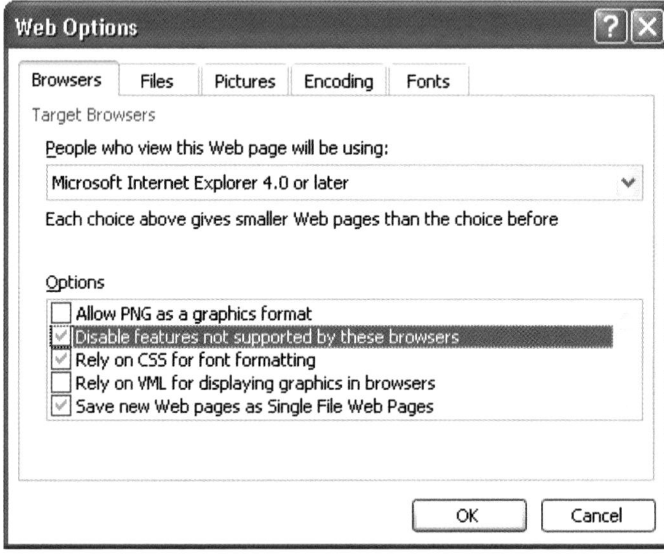

Figure 9-3: You can create web pages for specific browser versions.

TABLE 9-1: OPTIONS ON THE BROWSERS TAB OF THE WEB OPTIONS DIALOG BOX

OPTION	EXPLANATION	IE 3, NAVIGATOR 3	IE 4, NAVIGATOR 4	IE 4 OR LATER	IE 5 OR LATER	IE 6 OR LATER
Allow PNG As A Graphics Format	Enables web pages to contain graphics in the PNG format. All current browsers can display PNG graphics.	Off	Off	Off	Off	On
Rely On CSS For Font Formatting	Uses Cascading Style Sheets for font formatting	Off	On	On	On	On
Rely On VML For Displaying Graphics In Browsers	Uses Vector Markup Language for displaying graphics	Off	Off	Off	On	On
Save New Web Pages As Single File Web Pages	Uses the Single File Web Page format for saving new files	Off	Off	On	On	On
Disable Features Not Supported By These Browsers	(Word only.) Turns off HTML features the browsers don't support.	On	On	On	On	On

UNDERSTANDING HTML AND HOW WORD USES IT

Many web pages, including those created with Word, use HTML to specify how the page will look and behave in a web browser.

UNDERSTAND HTML

HTML (Hypertext Markup Language) is responsible for many of the wonders of the Web. HTML enables you to specify the contents of a web page and control how it looks and behaves in a web browser. All modern computer operating systems have browsers, so pages created using HTML can be displayed on almost any computer. An HTML file consists of plain text and pictures with *tags*, or formatting codes, which specify how the text or pictures will look on the page.

For more information on HTML, see *HTML QuickSteps*, published by McGraw-Hill/Osborne.

UNDERSTAND HOW WORD USES HTML

Word uses HTML for creating web content, automatically applying all necessary tags when you save a file in one of the web formats. Word uses standard HTML tags for creating standard HTML elements (such as headings, paragraphs, and tables) that will be displayed by a web browser, and custom, Word-specific tags for saving Word–specific data in a web-compatible format.

This combination of standard and custom tags enables Word to save an entire Word document. Saving all the information like this is called *round-tripping*: saving a file with all its contents and formatting so that the application that created the file can reopen the file with exactly the same information and formatting as when it saved the file.

Continued...

The best way to select the options is to click the **People Who View This Web Page Will Be Using** drop-down list and select the earliest browser version that you want to support. The choice you make in this drop-down list automatically selects the appropriate check boxes in the Options group box. You can then select or clear check boxes manually to fine-tune the choices you've made.

- Choosing Microsoft **Internet Explorer 4.0, Netscape Navigator 4.0, Or Later** provides a reasonable baseline for most web sites.
- If you need maximum browser compatibility, choose **Microsoft Internet Explorer 3.0, Netscape Navigator 3.0, Or Later**.
- If your pages don't need support for Netscape Navigator, choose **Microsoft Internet Explorer 4.0 Or Later**.
- If your pages don't need support for Netscape Navigator but need to use features available only in a later version of Internet Explorer, choose **Microsoft Internet Explorer 5.0 Or Later** or **Microsoft Internet Explorer 6.0 Or Later**.

Figure 9-4: The Files tab of the Web Options dialog box determines where web files are stored and how the files are edited.

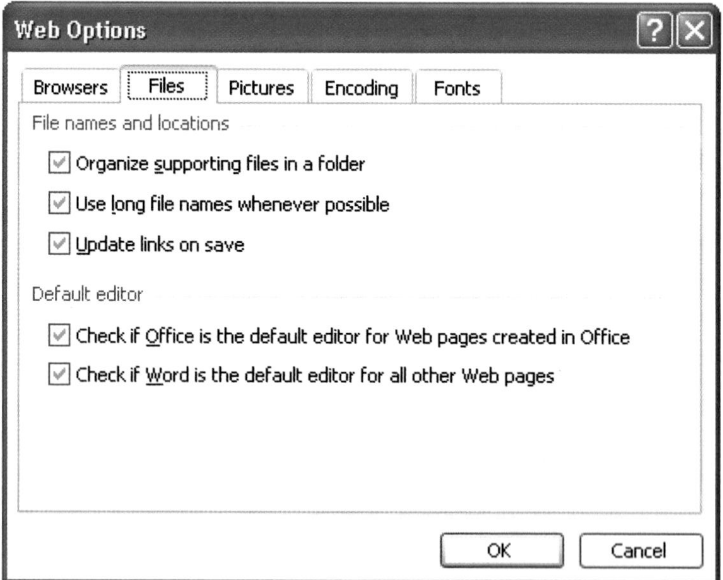

UNDERSTANDING HTML AND HOW WORD USES IT *(Continued)*

Round-tripping enables you to create HTML documents instead of Word Document format (.doc) files. However, you must always remember that the Word-specific data is saved along with the HTML data. Any visitor to your web site can view the entire source code for a web page, including any Word-specific data, by using a View Source command in a browser.

Word enables you to remove the Word-specific tags from a web page you save. You may also choose to use Word to create specific HTML elements that you then paste into another HTML editor (such as Windows NotePad), where you can integrate them with the code you directly enter. (See the "Using Word to Create HTML Elements" QuickSteps later in this chapter.)

NOTE

Word also offers one other web-related file format, .xml, which uses the Extensible Markup Language (XML) to organize and work with data. XML is beyond the scope of this book.

NOTE

You must set the web options separately for each Office application. The settings you make in Word don't affect the settings in Excel, PowerPoint, or the other applications.

CHOOSE FILES TAB OPTIONS

On the Files tab of the Web Options dialog box, choose options for controlling how Word handles file names and file locations in the web pages you create, and specify whether to use Office as the default editor for web pages created by Word. Figure 9-4 shows the Files tab of the Web Options dialog box.

The following options are included in the Files tab:

- Select **Organize Supporting Files In A Folder** if you want the application to save graphics and other separate elements in a folder that has the same name as the web page plus "_files"—for example, the web page named "products.html" receives a folder named "products_files". The application automatically creates a file named "filelist.xml" that contains a list of the files required for the web page.
- Deselect the **Use Long File Names Whenever Possible** check box to prevent the application from creating long file names that include spaces, which may not be compatible with the web server you're using. It's best to keep file names short and to use underscores instead of spaces when you need to separate parts of the file name.
- Select the **Update Links On Save** check box if you want the application to automatically check each link and update any information that has changed each time you save the file. In most cases, this automatic updating is helpful.
- Select the **Check If Office Is The Default Editor For Web Pages Created In Office** check box if you want Internet Explorer to check if Word is your default HTML editor for web pages created by Word when you click the Edit button in Internet Explorer. Clear this check box if you want to use another application to edit the web pages you've created with Word.
- Select the **Check If Word Is The Default Editor For All Other Web Pages** check box if you want Internet Explorer to open Word for the editing of all non-Office-created web pages. Clear this check box if you want to use another application for this function.

CHOOSE PICTURES TAB OPTIONS

On the Pictures tab of the Web Options dialog box, choose options for the pictures you include in your web pages:

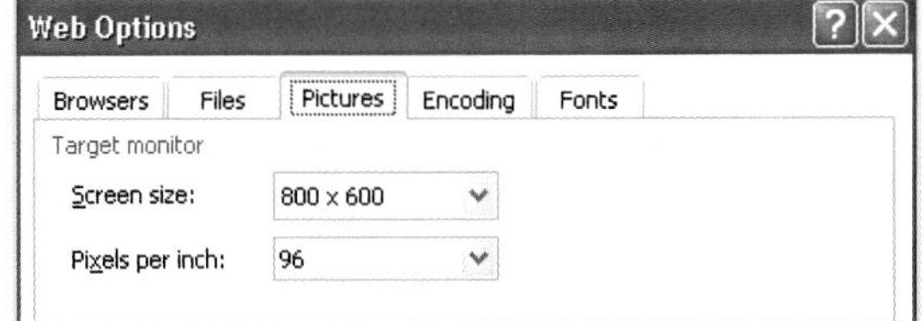

TIP

In Fall 2004, Internet Explorer had approximately 93.5 percent of the browser market. Internet Explorer 6 had 66.3 percent, Internet Explorer 5.5 had 14.5 percent, and Internet Explorer 5.0 had 12.7 percent. Mozilla and Mozilla Firefox had 4.1 percent together. Other browsers had 2.4 percent altogether. Netscape Navigator, once the dominate browser, is now under 2 percent and Mozilla is growing rapidly. These figures show that choosing **Microsoft Internet Explorer 5.0 Or Later** on the Browsers tab of the Web Options dialog box, and then checking that your web pages work with Mozilla and Mozilla Firefox, will ensure that your pages are viewable by the vast majority of people online.

NOTE

Word web documents keep all their text and all embedded elements (such as graphics) in the same file. Linked items, such as graphics or Automation objects from other applications, are kept in separate files.

NOTE

Unicode is a scheme for representing characters on computers. For example, a capital *A* is represented by 0041 in Unicode, and a capital *B* is represented by 0042. *UTF-8* is the abbreviation for Universal Character Set Transformation Format 8-Bit. *ISO* is the short term used to denote the International Organization for Standardization.

- In the Screen Size drop-down list, select the minimum resolution that you expect most visitors to your web site to be using. For most web sites, the best choice is 800 × 600, a resolution that almost all monitors manufactured since 2000 support. If you're creating an intranet site whose visitors will all use monitors with a higher resolution than 800 × 600, you can choose a higher resolution.
- In the Pixels Per Inch drop-down list, select the number of pixels per inch (ppi) to use for pictures in your web pages. The default setting is 96ppi, which works well for most pages. You can also choose 72 ppi or 120 ppi.

CHOOSE ENCODING TAB OPTIONS

The Encoding tab of the Web Options dialog box lets you specify which character-encoding scheme to use for the characters in your web pages. Word in North America and Western Europe uses the Western European (Windows) encoding by default. This works well for most purposes, but you may prefer to choose Western European (ISO) for compliance with the ISO-8859-1 standard, or Unicode (UTF-8) for compliance with the Unicode standard.

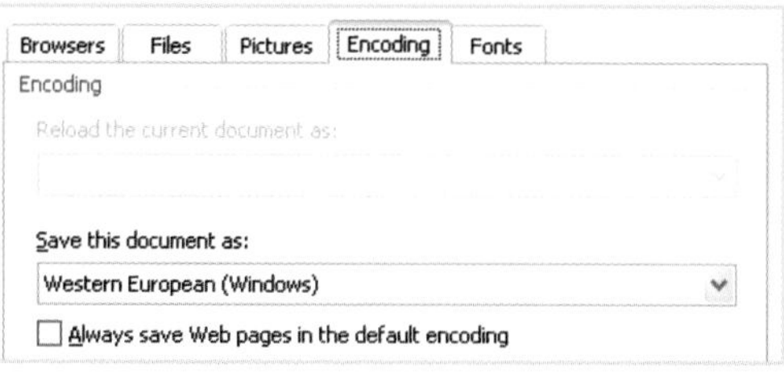

Select the encoding you want in the Save This Document As drop-down list. Then, if you always want to use this encoding, select the **Always Save Web Pages In The Default Encoding** check box. Selecting this check box disables the Save This Document As drop-down list.

CHOOSE FONTS TAB OPTIONS

The Fonts tab of the Web Options dialog box (see Figure 9-5) offers the following options:

- Use the Character Set list box to specify the character set you want to use for your pages. Use the English/Western European/Other Latin Script item unless you need to create pages in another character set, such as Hebrew or Arabic.

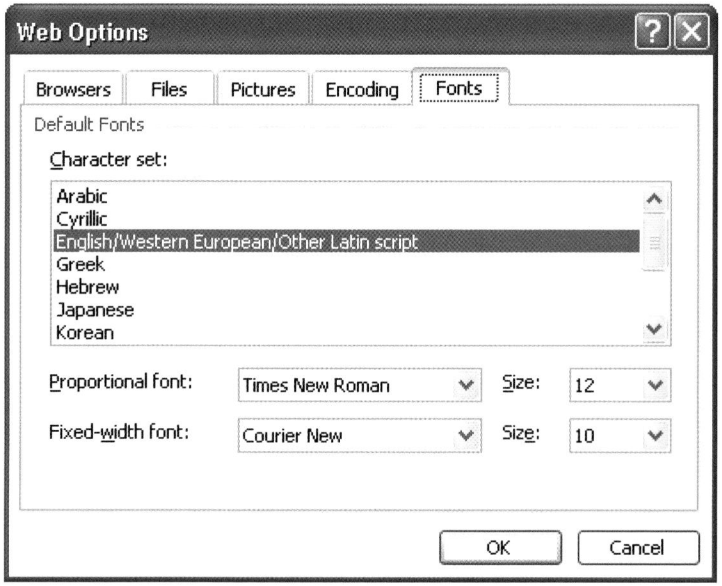

Figure 9-5: Word gives you the capability of choosing a number of different character sets to use on web pages.

NOTE

Keeping the supporting files together in a folder is usually helpful, because you can move the web page and its supporting files easily to another folder. If you clear the **Organize Supporting Files In A Folder** check box, Word saves the graphics and other separate elements in the same folder as the web page. This behavior tends to make your folders harder to manage, as you cannot see at a glance which supporting files belong to which web page. However, if you do not have permission to create new folders in the folder in which you are saving your web pages, you may need to clear the **Organize Supporting Files In A Folder** check box so that Word does not attempt to create new folders for your web pages.

- Use the Proportional Font drop-down list and its Size drop-down list to specify the proportional font and font size to use for your pages.
- Use the Fixed-Width Font and its Size drop-down list to specify the monospaced font and font size.

After you finish choosing settings in the Web Options dialog box, click **OK** to close the dialog box, and then click **OK** to close the Options dialog box.

Insert a Hyperlink

There are several different types of hyperlinks. In Word, all of them are inserted on a page by first displaying the Insert Hyperlink dialog box, as described here. You then need to follow the steps in the subsequent sections for the particular type of hyperlink you want to create.

1. Start Word and open the file in which you want to insert the hyperlink, as described in "Create a Web Page."
2. Select the text or graphic where you want the hyperlink to appear.
3. Click the **Insert** menu, expand the menu if necessary, and then click **Hyperlink**. The Insert Hyperlink dialog box appears (see Figure 9-6).
4. Complete the hyperlink with one of the following sections depending on whether you want to create a hyperlink to an existing file or web page, a place in the current document, a new document, or an e-mail address.

QUICKFACTS

UNDERSTANDING HYPERLINKS

Hyperlinks provide the means to switch, or "jump," from one web page to another or from one location on a web page to another location on the same page. Hyperlinks can also be used to open files such as pictures and programs. The hundreds of millions of hyperlinks on all the web pages on the Internet are what give the Web its name. A hyperlink requires the address of the page or file to which it will switch or open. A web page address is called a *URL,* or Uniform Resource Locator. A URL is used by a browser to locate and open a web page or file. An example of a URL is http://www.mcgraw-hill.com/about/northamerica.html#california.

- "http://" identifies the site as using Hypertext Transfer Protocol, a set of standards for communication and identification.
- "www" identifies the site as being on the Internet or World Wide Web, although today the space used by "www" in a URL can contain other information used to segment a web site and still be on the Internet.
- "mcgraw-hill.com" is a *domain name* that is the principal identifier of a web site.
- "/about/" is a folder name identifying a subarea within a site.
- "northamerica.html" is a web page in the About folder in the web site.
- "#california" is a particular location on the web page and is called a *bookmark.*

A hyperlink is a word(s), a graphic, or a picture which, when clicked, tells the browser to open a new page at another site whose URL is stored in the hyperlink.

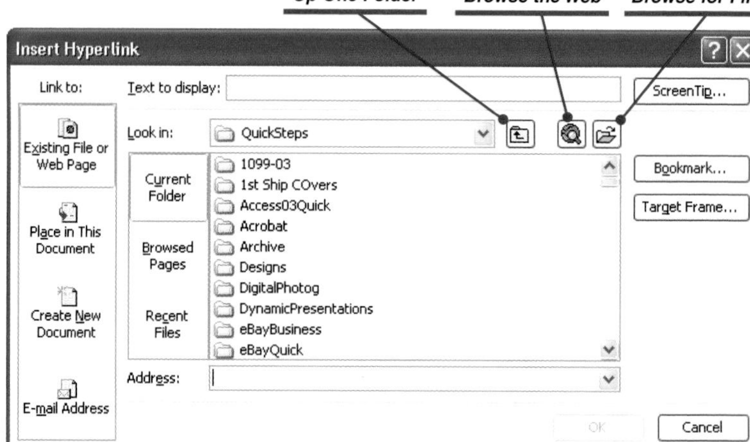

Figure 9-6: The Insert Hyperlink dialog box enables you to create hyperlinks to web pages, places within the same file, files, or e-mail addresses.

CREATE A HYPERLINK TO AN EXISTING FILE OR WEB PAGE

To create a hyperlink to an existing file or web page:

1. In the Link To column on the left side of the screen, click the **Existing File Or Web Page** button if it is not already selected.
2. Navigate to the file or web page in one of these ways:
   - Use the Look In drop-down list (and, if necessary, the Up One Folder button) to browse to the folder.

     –Or–
   - Click the **Browse The Web** button to make Windows launch or activate an Internet Explorer window, browse to the page to which you want to link, and then switch back to the Insert Hyperlink dialog box. Word automatically enters the URL in the Address text box (see Figure 9-7).

     –Or–
   - Click the **Current Folder** button to display the current folder. Click the **Browsed Pages** button to display a list of web pages you've browsed recently. Click the **Recent Files** button to display a list of local files you've worked with recently.

     –Or–
   - Select the address from the Address drop-down list.

CAUTION

If Internet Explorer is not your default browser, the Browse The Web button will not work correctly. Clicking the button opens your default browser, but when you return to the Insert Hyperlink dialog box, Word tries to get the URL from Internet Explorer rather than from your default browser. Instead, browse to the web page in your default browser, copy the address from the Address bar, and then paste it into the Address box in the Insert Hyperlink dialog box.

NOTE

Bookmark addresses cannot have spaces, hyphens, or any other special characters except an underscore (_).

3. Change the default text in the Text To Display text box to the text you want displayed for the hyperlink. (This is the text that the user clicks to access the linked page. If you have selected text on your web page, it will appear here.)
4. To add a ScreenTip to the hyperlink, click **ScreenTip**, type the text in the Set Hyperlink ScreenTip dialog box, and then click **OK**.

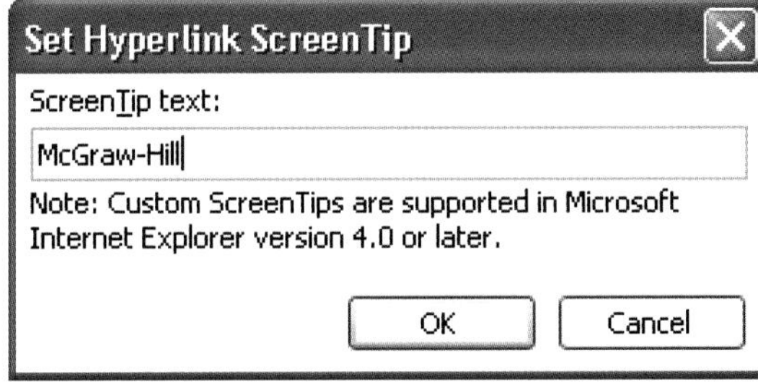

5. To make the hyperlink connect to a particular location in the page rather than simply to the beginning of the page, click **Bookmark**, choose the location in the Select Place In Document dialog box (see "Create a Hyperlink to a Place in the Current Document").
6. Click **OK**. Word inserts the hyperlink.

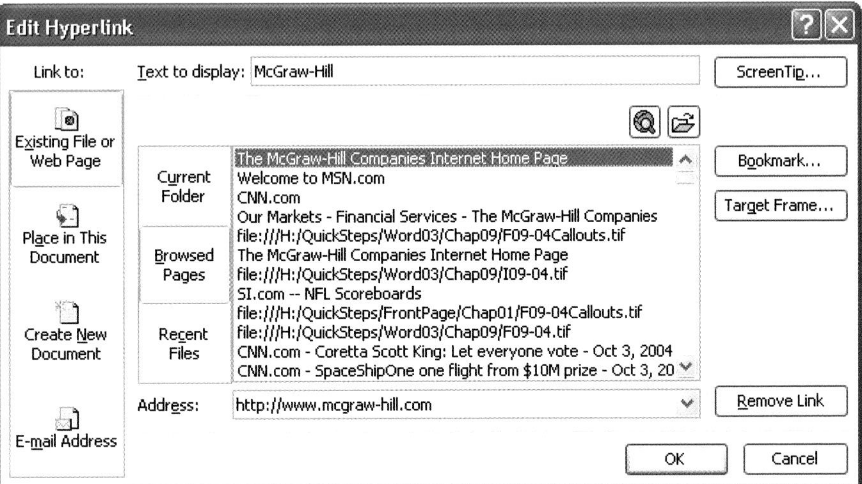

Figure 9-7: Browsed Pages will give you a list of the web pages and files that you have viewed so you can select one of them for a hyperlink.

1 2 3 4 5 6 7 8 9 10

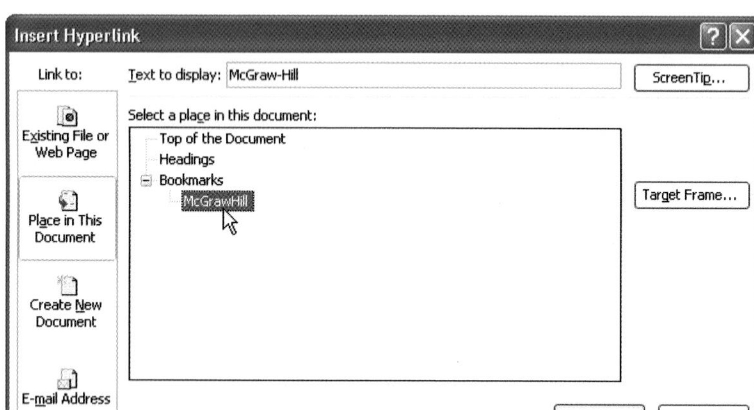

Figure 9-8: Word enables you to link to a particular place in either the current or a destination document—for example, to a heading or bookmark in a Word document.

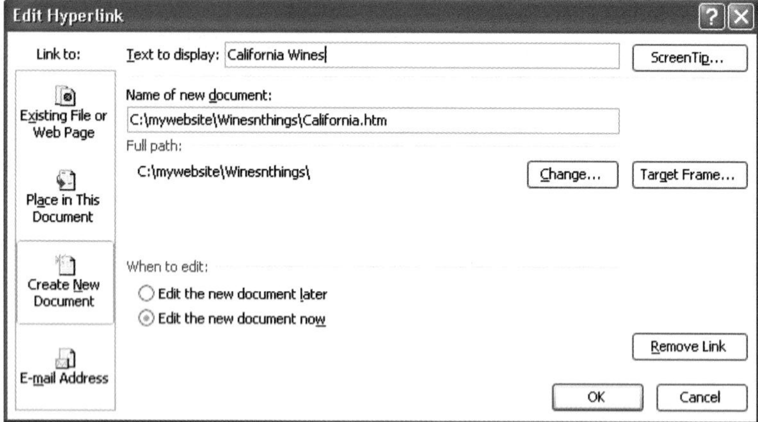

Figure 9-9: When you need to link to a new document, Word lets you create the new document immediately to ensure that it is saved with the correct name and location.

CREATE A HYPERLINK TO A PLACE IN THE CURRENT DOCUMENT

To create a hyperlink to a place in the current document:

1. In the Link To column, click the **Place In This Document** button. Under Select A Place In This Document, click a heading or a bookmark that is displayed (see Figure 9-8).
2. Change the default text in the Text To Display text box to the text you want displayed for the hyperlink. (This is the text that the user clicks to access the linked page and is the text you first selected, if you did so.)
3. To add a ScreenTip to the hyperlink, click **ScreenTip**, type the text in the Set Hyperlink ScreenTip dialog box, and then click **OK**.
4. Click **OK**. Word inserts the hyperlink.

CREATE A HYPERLINK TO A NEW DOCUMENT

To create a hyperlink to a new document:

1. In the Link To Column, click the **Create New Document** button (see Figure 9-9).
2. Type the file name and extension in the Name Of New Document text box. Check the path in the Full Path area. If necessary, click **Change**. Use the Create New Document dialog box to specify the folder, file name, and extension; then click **OK**.
3. Change the default text in the Text To Display text box to the text you want displayed for the hyperlink. (This is the text that the user clicks to access the linked page and is the text you first selected, if you did so.)
4. To add a ScreenTip to the hyperlink, click **ScreenTip**, type the text in the Set Hyperlink ScreenTip dialog box, and then click **OK**.
5. By default, Word selects the **Edit The New Document Now** option button. If you prefer not to immediately open the new document for editing, select the **Edit The New Document Later** option button.
6. Click **OK**. Word inserts the hyperlink.

NOTE

Word automatically creates a hyperlink when you type a URL, an e-mail address, or a network path in a document and then press **SPACEBAR**, **TAB**, **ENTER**, or a punctuation key. If you find this behavior awkward, you can turn it off: Click the **Tools** menu, expand the menu if needed, click **AutoCorrect Options**, click the **AutoFormat As You Type** tab, clear the **Internet And Network Paths With Hyperlinks** check box, and then click **OK**.

NOTE

In Figure 9-11, in the original Word document, the bulleted paragraphs are single spaced, but in a web browser they are doubled space because browsers add a blank line after a paragraph end, but not after a new line. If you were to use a new line here, though, you would lose the bullets.

CREATE A HYPERLINK TO AN E-MAIL ADDRESS

To create a mailto hyperlink that starts a message to an e-mail address:

1. In the Link To column, click the **E-mail Address** button (see Figure 9-10).
2. Type the e-mail address in the E-mail Address text box (or click it in the Recently Used E-mail Addresses list box) and the subject for the message in the Subject text box.
3. Change the default text in the Text To Display text box to the text you want displayed for the hyperlink. (This is the text that the user clicks to access the linked page and is the text you first selected, if you did so.)
4. To add a ScreenTip to the hyperlink, click **ScreenTip**, type the text in the Set Hyperlink ScreenTip dialog box, and then click **OK**.
5. Click **OK**. Word inserts the hyperlink.

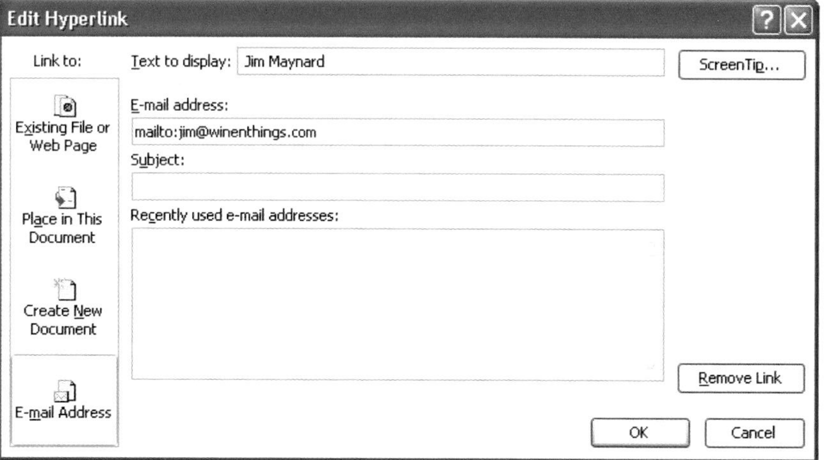

Figure 9-10: The Edit Hyperlink dialog box lets you quickly create a mailto hyperlink to a recently used e-mail address.

QUICKSTEPS

USING WORD TO CREATE HTML ELEMENTS

If you choose not to use Word as your main HTML editor, you may still want to use Word to create some HTML elements so that you can include them in your web pages. To do so, follow these general steps:

1. Start Word if it is not already running.
2. Open an existing document, or create a new document that contains the desired content.
3. Save the Word document in one of the HTML formats.
4. View the resulting page in your browser.
5. View the source code of the web page. For example, in Internet Explorer, click the **View** menu, and then click **Source**.
6. Select the code for the element you want to copy, and then issue a Copy command (for example, press CTRL+C).
7. Switch to your HTML editor, position the insertion point, and then issue a Paste command (for example, press CTRL+V).
8. Close Word and your browser if you are finished working with them.

NOTE

There are two web-related toolbars in Word: Web and Web Tools. The Web toolbar is the basic toolbar for viewing web pages in a browser in Word. The Web Tools toolbar has several controls for creating web forms, such as check boxes, as well as controls for adding movies, sounds, and pictures. Web Tools is beyond the scope of this book; see *Microsoft Office FrontPage 2003 QuickSteps* for more information.

Check How a Page Will Look

Before you save an Office document as a web page, you may want to use Web Page Preview to check how it looks:

1. If needed, start Word and open the web document.
2. Click the **File** menu, expand the menu if needed, and then click **Web Page Preview**. The application creates a temporary file containing the page in a web format, and then displays the page in Internet Explorer. Figure 9-11 shows an example file in Word on the left and the file being previewed in the Internet Explorer on the right.
3. After viewing the web page, click the **File** menu, and then click **Close** to close the Internet Explorer window.

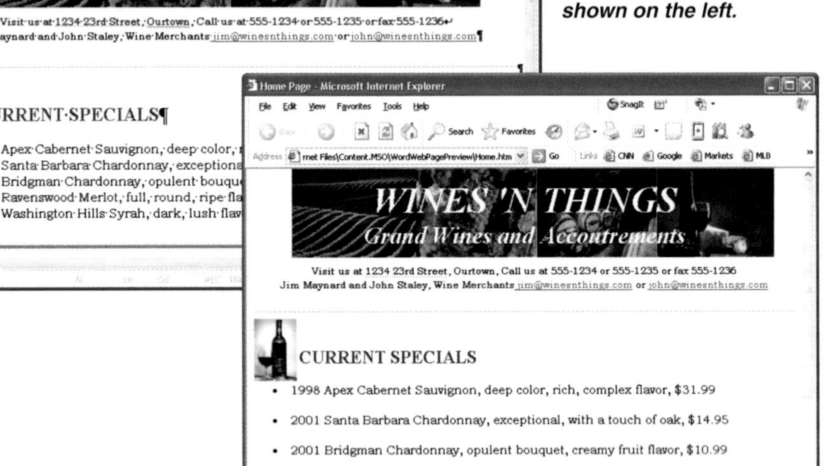

Figure 9-11: Web Page Preview enables you to identify problems with your web pages while you are still working on them in Word. Here the original document in Word is shown on the left.

How to...

- *Track Changes*
- *Review Changes*
- *Creating Reviewing Shortcuts*
- *Add Comments*
- *Highlight Objects*
- *Use Versions*
- *Compare Documents*
- *Compare Side by Side*

Chapter 10

Using Word with Other People

In the first nine chapters of this book, we've talked about the many ways you can use Word on your own. In this chapter we'll address how you can use Word with other people. Word has a number of features that allow multiple people to work on the same document and see what each other has done. These features include marking changes, both additions and deletions that multiple people make to a document; adding comments to a document; highlighting words, lines, and paragraphs of a document; having multiple versions of a document; and comparing documents.

TIP

By moving the insertion point over a change, you can see who made the change and the date and time it was made.

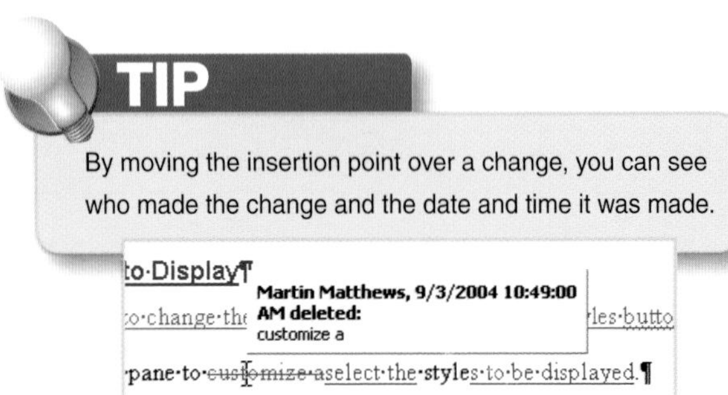

Mark Changes

When two or more people work on a document, it is helpful to see what the other people did without having to read every word and accurately remember what the text was before it was changed. You can view other people's work in Word by using the Track Changes features. *Track Changes* identifies the changes (additions or deletions) made to a document by everyone who works on it. Each person is automatically assigned a color, and the changes they enter are noted in that color. For example, Figure 10-1 shows a section of Chapter 2 in a hypothetical editing process. After all the changes are made, they can be accepted or rejected, one at a time or all together.

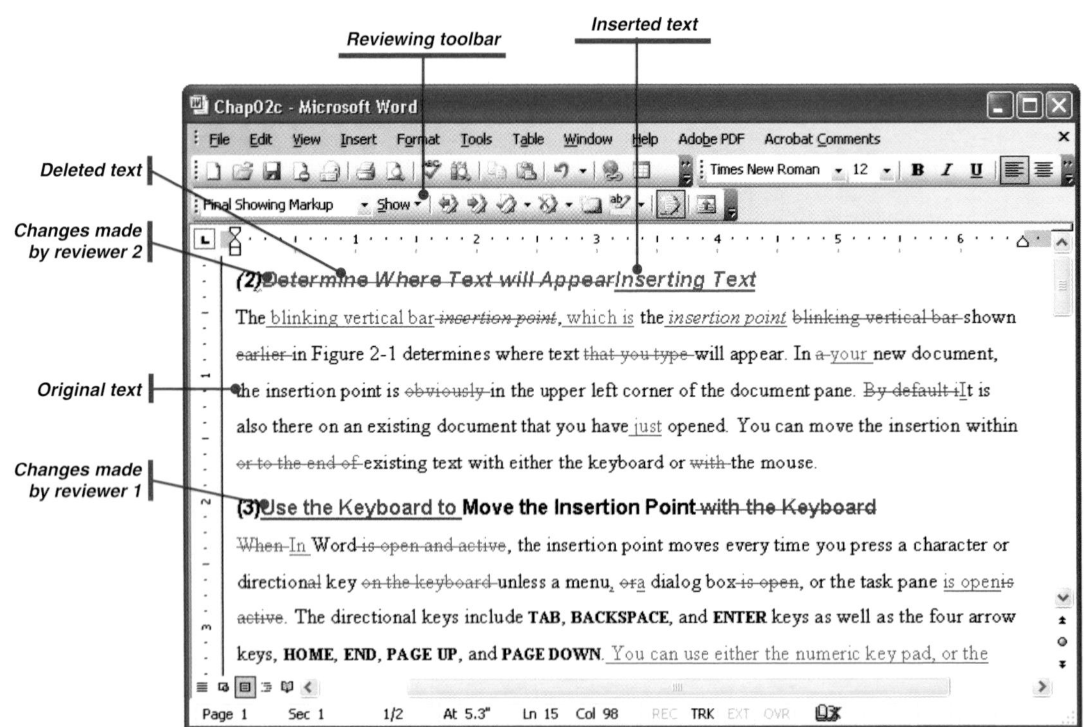

Figure 10-1: By using Track Changes, multiple people can make changes to a document and you can see what each reviewer has done.

NOTE

In Figure 10-2 you see a Reply With Changes button on the Reviewing toolbar. This only appears if the document you are reviewing was e-mailed to you for review. See "E-Mail a Document for Review" later in this chapter.

TIP

The Reviewing toolbar can be dragged away from the other toolbars to become a floating toolbar, as it is in Figure 10-2.

Track Changes

To use Track Changes, you must turn it on. Before turning it on, anything anyone types looks like ordinary text, and there is no way of telling the difference between the new text and what was on the page before the change was made. Once Track Changes is turned on, anything anyone types or does to the document will be shown in the color automatically assigned to that person; keep in mind that these changes are fully reversible if desired. To turn on Track Changes:

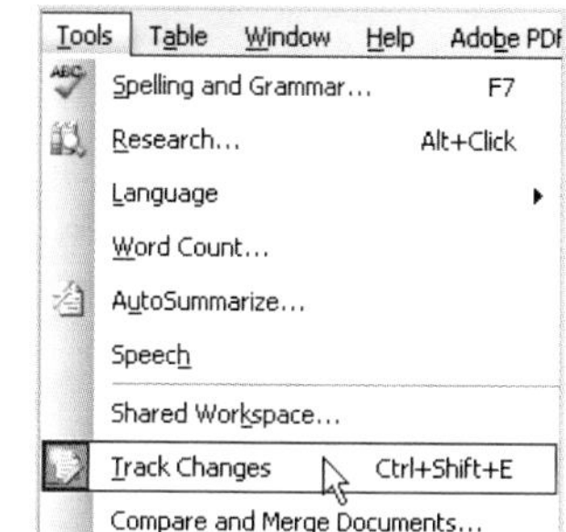

1. Start Word and open the document in which you want to track changes.
2. Click the **Tools** menu and click **Track Changes**.

   –Or–

   Press **CTRL+SHIFT+E**.

USE THE REVIEWING TOOLBAR

The Reviewing toolbar provides a number of features that you can use as you and others edit a document, as shown in Figure 10-2. Depending on the type of computer you have and the features on that computer, you may have one, two, or three more buttons on the Reviewing toolbar than shown in Figure 10-2. If you have audio capability with a microphone on your computer, next to Insert Comment you will have an Insert Voice button, which will let you record a comment and attach it to the Word document. If you have a Tablet PC, you will have Insert Ink Annotations which will allow you to draw and write by hand on the document, and Ink Comment which will insert a handwritten comment.

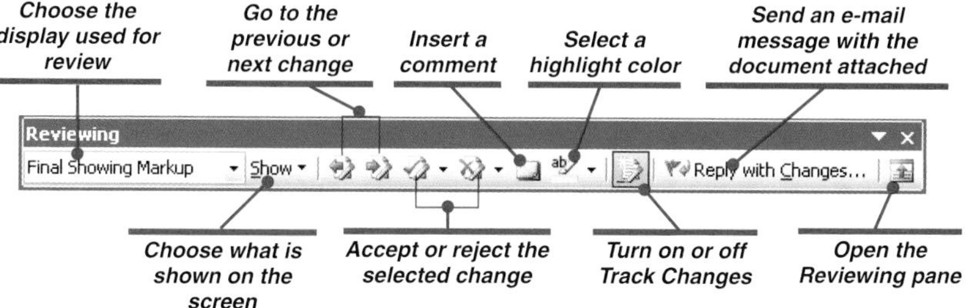

Figure 10-2: The Reviewing toolbar can be used to examine an edited document and accept or reject changes.

To turn on the Reviewing bar:

Click the **View** menu, click **Toolbars**, and click **Reviewing**.

SET THE OPTIONS FOR TRACK CHANGES

Word gives you a number of options for how changes are displayed with Track Changes. These options are set in the Track Changes tab of both the Options dialog box and the Track Changes dialog box, shown in Figure 10-3. To Open and set these changes:

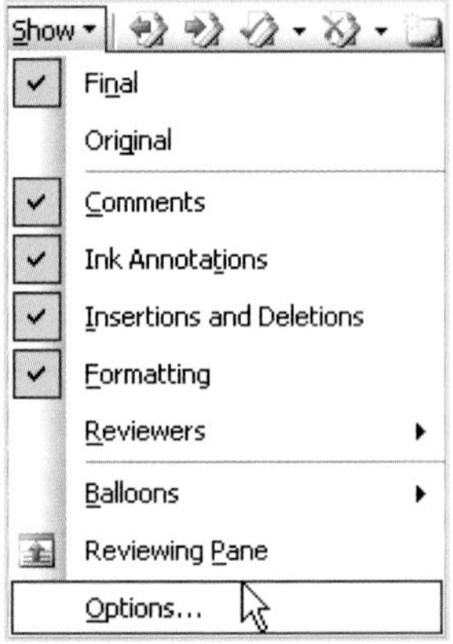

1. Click the **Tools** menu, click **Options**, and click the **Track Changes** tab.

   –Or–

   On the Reviewing toolbar, click **Show** and click **Options**.
2. Open the drop-down list next to Insertions, Deletions, Formatting, Changed Lines, and Comments Color to review and change the options for displaying each of these items. Also, you can change the color used for each of these.
3. When you are ready, click **OK**. (Balloons are discussed in the following section.)

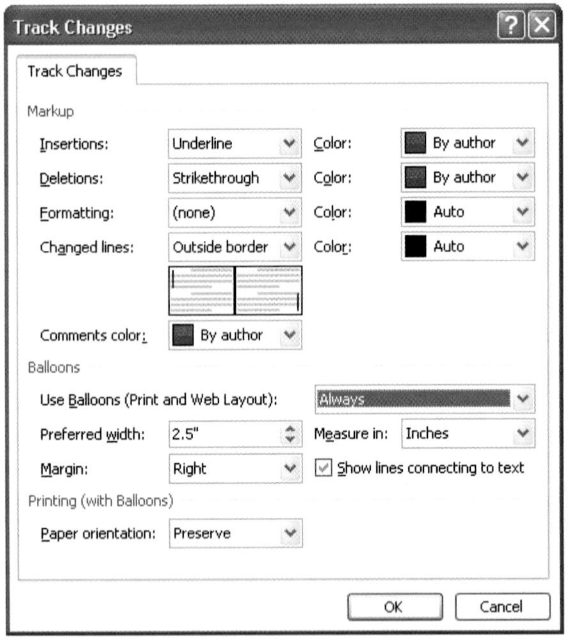

Figure 10-3: While you can select colors for each type of change, the best practice is to let Word automatically select the color for each reviewer (By Author).

PUT CHANGES IN BALLOONS

Word gives you two ways of viewing changes, both on the screen and when you print the document. One option is an inline method in which the changes are made within the original text, as shown in Figure 10-1. The other way is to put changes in balloons on the right of the text, as shown in Figure 10-4. What is in the balloon and what is in the text depends on your choice of the Display For Review. The default, shown in Figure 10-4, is Final Showing Markup, which shows the text with the final wording, and the balloons show primarily deletions. The options available for the Display For Review are described in Table 10-1.

You can turn off the balloon changes (it is on by default when you install Word), or you can turn it back on and set other balloon-related options:

1. Click the **Tools** menu, click **Options**, and click the **Track Changes** tab.

   –Or–

   Click **Show** on the Reviewing toolbar, and click **Options**.

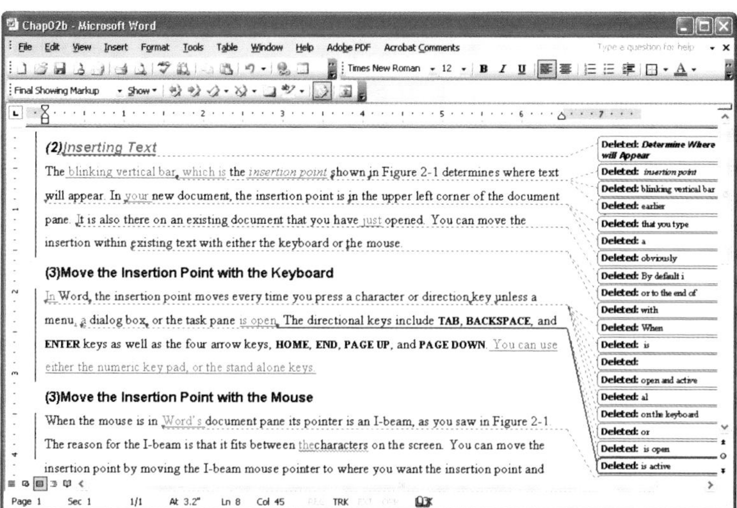

Figure 10-4: Using balloons for changes can provide for easier reading of the final text and can show changes in formatting, but it is harder to see what has been changed.

TABLE 10-1: DISPLAY FOR REVIEW OPTIONS

DISPLAY OPTION	WHAT IS IN THE TEXT	WHAT IS IN THE BALLOON
Final Showing Markup	Final text with insertions	Deletions and format changes
Final	Final text without markings	Nothing
Original Showing Markup	Original text with deletions	Insertions and format changes
Original	Original text without markings	Nothing

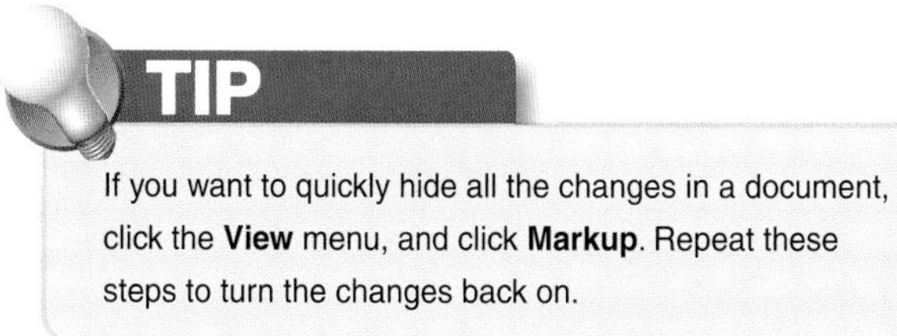

TIP

If you want to quickly hide all the changes in a document, click the **View** menu, and click **Markup**. Repeat these steps to turn the changes back on.

2. Under Balloons, opposite Use Balloons (Print And Web Layout), select **Never** to turn off Balloons, select **Always** to turn on Balloons, or select **Only For Comments/ Formatting** to use balloons in that way.

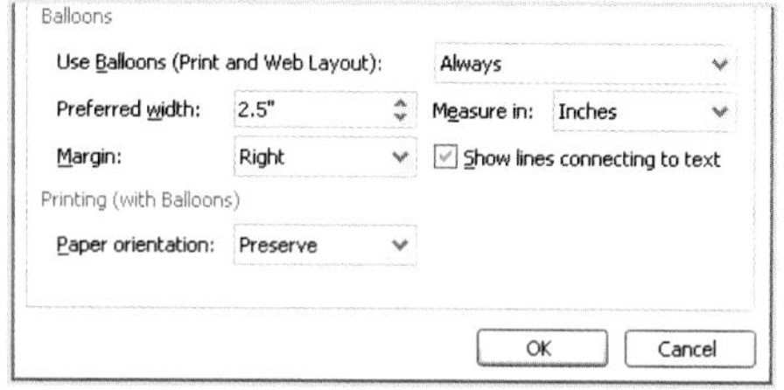

3. If you choose to turn balloons on, you can:
   - Set how wide you want the balloons to be, along with the unit of measure to use.
   - Determine which margin the balloons should be in.
   - Decide whether there are connecting lines between the balloon and the text.
   - Choose whether to print a document with balloon changes in its normal portrait orientation, or force it to be printed in landscape orientation to better keep the original text size.
4. When you are done with the balloon settings, click **OK**.

TIP

If there are multiple reviewers on a single document, you can easily see who is represented by what color by clicking **Show** on the Reviewing toolbar and then clicking **Reviewers**.

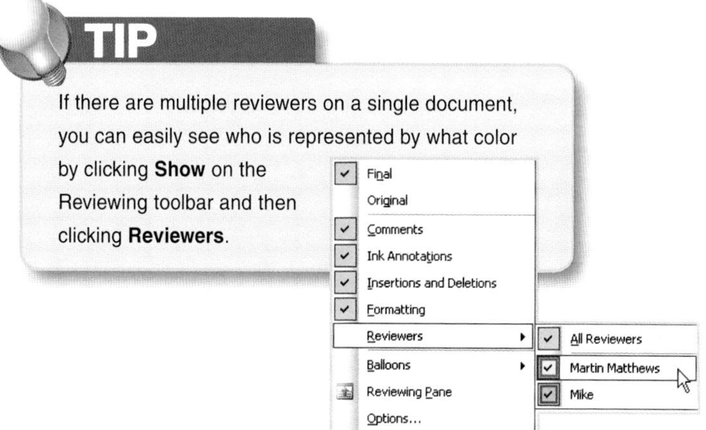

1 2 3 4 5 6 7 8 9 10

TIP

If you want to accept or reject all changes in a document, click the down arrow next to Accept Change or Reject Change, and click **Accept All Changes In Document** or **Reject All Changes In Document**.

Figure 10-5: For many, keyboard shortcuts are faster than clicking the mouse, especially if you use two hands to type.

Review Changes

Changes are made to a document by simply adding, deleting, and reformatting the text. If Track Changes is turned on, the changes appear either in the text or in balloons in the margins. Once all changes have been made to a document, you will want to go through the document, look at the changes, and decide to accept or reject each one.

1. With the document you want to review and the Reviewing toolbar open in Word (see "Use the Reviewing Toolbar" earlier in this chapter), click **Track Changes**, if it is turned on, to turn it off.

2. Press **CTRL+HOME** to position the insertion point at the beginning of the document, and click **Next** on the Reviewing toolbar to select the first change.

3. Click **Accept Change** on the Reviewing toolbar if you want to make the change permanent.

   –Or–

   Click **Reject Change** on the Reviewing toolbar if you want to remove the change and leave the text as it was originally.

4. Click **Next** on the Reviewing toolbar, and repeat Step 3 for each of the changes in the document. (See "Creating Reviewing Shortcuts" for creating keyboard shortcuts for these reviewing tasks.)

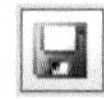

5. When you are finished, click **Save** on the Standard toolbar to save the reviewed document.

USE THE REVIEWING PANE

Word's Reviewing pane provides another way to look at changes, as shown in Figure 10-6. This pane opens at the bottom of the Word window and lists each individual change with its type, the author, and the date and time the change was made.

QUICKSTEPS

CREATING REVIEWING SHORTCUTS

If you are reviewing proposed changes in a large document, it can be tedious to look at each change and accept or reject it by clicking the mouse first on **Next** and then on **Accept** or **Reject**. A partial solution for this is to make keyboard shortcuts.

To assign shortcut keys to each of the three functions Next, Accept Change, and Reject Change:

1. Click the **Tools** menu and click **Customize**. The Customize dialog box opens.
2. Click **Keyboard** to open the Customize Keyboard dialog box.
3. Click **All Commands** in the Categories list, click **AcceptChangesSelected** in the Commands list, click in the **Press New Shortcut Key** text box, and press the key(s) you want to use. For example **ALT+A** for Accept Changes Selected (see Figure 10-5). Click **Assign**.
4. Repeat Step 3, first for Next by clicking **NextChangeOrComment** in the Command List and assigning, for example, **ALT+N**; then for Reject by clicking **RejectChangesSelected** and assigning, for example, **ALT+R**; and clicking **Assign** for each.
5. When you are done, click **Close** twice.
6. Open a document for which you want to review changes.
7. Press **ALT+N** to go to the first change. Then press either **ALT+A** to accept the change or **ALT+R** to reject the change. Repeat this for the remainder of the changes.

1. With the document you want to review and the Reviewing toolbar open in Word, click **Reviewing Pane** to open it.
2. Scroll through the changes in the Reviewing pane. Then use the Next and Previous buttons on the Reviewing toolbar to display each change in the Reviewing pane as well as highlight them in the document pane.
3. When you are finished making changes, click **Save** on the toolbar.

E-MAIL A DOCUMENT FOR REVIEW

Word makes using e-mail with the reviewing process easy. You can easily send out a document for review, and you can also easily return a document with your changes.

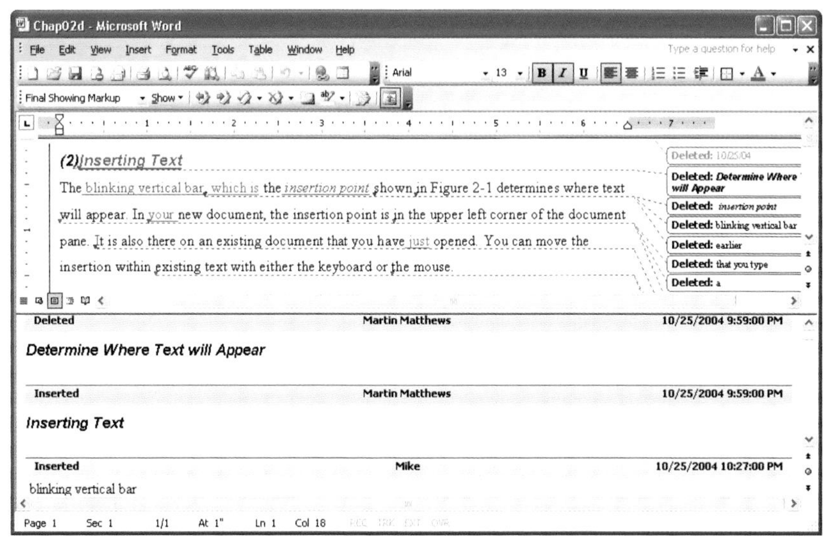

Figure 10-6: The Reviewing pane provides a detailed way of looking at each individual change.

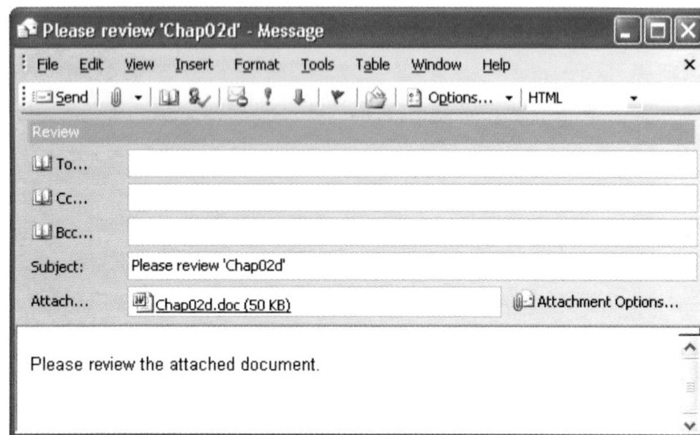

Figure 10-7: When you use the Send To Mail Recipient (For Review), the Subject, Attachment, and a brief message body are all filled in for you.

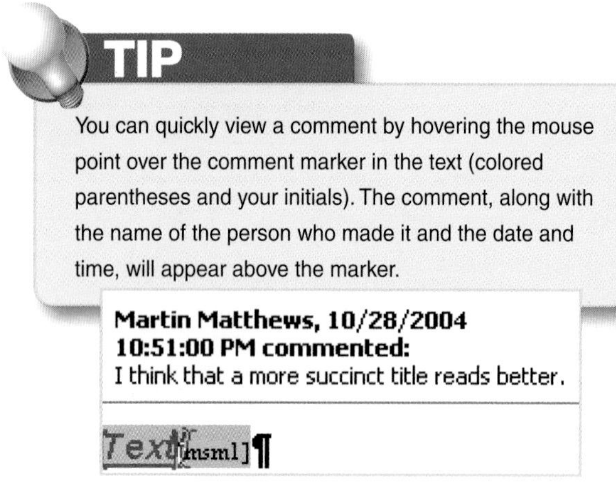

TIP

You can quickly view a comment by hovering the mouse point over the comment marker in the text (colored parentheses and your initials). The comment, along with the name of the person who made it and the date and time, will appear above the marker.

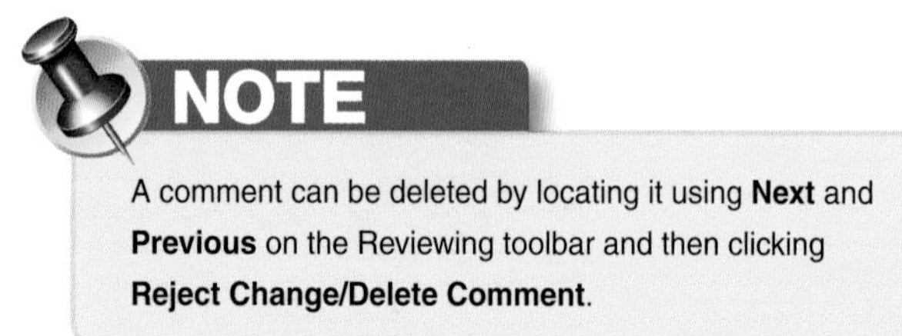

NOTE

A comment can be deleted by locating it using **Next** and **Previous** on the Reviewing toolbar and then clicking **Reject Change/Delete Comment**.

To send out a document for review:

1. Click the **File** menu, click **Send To**, and click **Mail Recipient (For Review)**. The Please Review message window opens (see Figure 10-7).
2. Fill in the name of the addressee plus those who are to get copies, make any desired changes to the Subject and the body of the message, and when you are ready, click **Send**. You then get an End Review button on the Reviewing toolbar. Clicking the button opens a message box asking if you want to the end the review of the document for all reviewers (see the Reviewing toolbar in Figure 10-8).

E-MAIL A REVIEWED DOCUMENT

Reply with Changes...

When a document has been e-mailed to you for review and you have completed making changes, a new button appears on the Reviewing toolbar: Reply With Changes.

1. On the Reviewing toolbar, click **Reply With Changes**. The message window will open.
2. Add any addresses for those who are to get copies, and make any desired changes to the Subject and the body of the message. When you are ready, click **Send**.

Add Comments

When you review or edit a document, you may want to make a comment instead of or in addition to making a change. To add a comment:

1. With the document to which you want to add a comment and the Reviewing toolbar open in Word, position the insertion point at the location you want a reference to your comment to appear.
2. Click **Insert Comment** on the Reviewing toolbar. An annotation with your initials will appear where the insertion point was in the text, and the Reviewing pane will open (if it isn't already open) with a new comment area, as you can see in Figure 10-8.
3. Type a comment of any length, and then click back in the document pane to continue reviewing the document.
4. If you wish, you can close the Reviewing pane by clicking **Reviewing Pane** on the Reviewing toolbar.

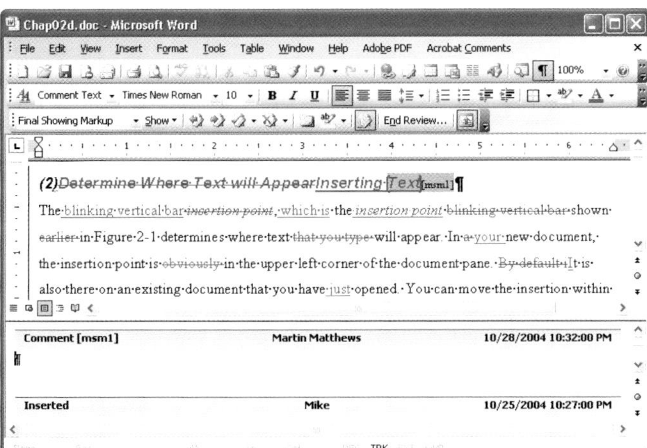

Figure 10-8: Comments allow you to explain why you make a change.

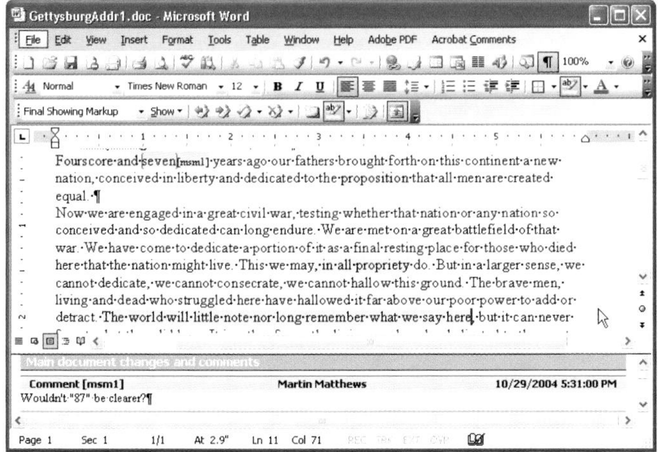

Figure 10-9: Even though the Comment tool provides its own highlight, oftentimes reviewers use highlighting to identify the text to which their comment refers.

Highlight Objects

As you review and change a document, you may want to highlight some text so you can discuss it in a comment or otherwise call attention to it. You can do this using the Highlight tool in either the Formatting or Reviewing toolbar.

The highlighting that is placed on a page can be any of 15 different colors, so you first need to select the color:

1. Click the **Highlight** tool down arrow to open the color palette.
2. Click the color you want to use. Remember you want whatever color text you are using to show up well with the highlighting color.

When you set out to highlight, you can select the Highlight tool first, or you can select the text to be highlighted first.

SELECT THE HIGHLIGHT TOOL FIRST

To highlight several sections of text, it is easiest to first select the Highlight tool:

1. With the document you want to highlight open in Word, click **Highlight** in either the Formatting or the Reviewing toolbar. The mouse pointer becomes a highlighter superimposed on the I-beam.
2. Drag over as much and as many separate pieces of text as you want to highlight, also entering comments as needed (after entering a comment, simply click back in the document pane to restore the Highlight tool). See Figure 10-9.
3. When you are done with the Highlight tool, you can either press ESC or click the **Highlight** tool on the Reviewing or Formatting toolbar to return to the normal I-beam insertion point.

SELECT THE TEXT FIRST

To highlight a single piece of text, it is easiest to first select the text:

1. Drag across the text you want highlighted.
2. Click the Highlight tool in either the Reviewing or Formatting toolbar.

NOTE

You can remove highlighting by selecting the highlighted text, clicking the down arrow next to the Highlight tool, and clicking **None**.

CAUTION

Highlighting shows when you print a document with it. This is fine with a color printer, but if you print on a black and white printer, the highlight is gray, which will make black text under the highlighting hard to read.

Work with Multiple Documents

As you are going through the reviewing process with several people, it is likely that you will end up with multiple copies of a document. Word offers two good strategies for handling this: using versions and comparing documents.

Use Versions

Word provides the ability to save several versions of a document. This allows you to return to a different or earlier version at any time. Word also has the ability to compare two versions of a document as explained in the next section.

SAVE A NEW VERSION

1. With the document for which you want to create versions open in Word, click the **File** menu, extend the menu if needed, and click **Versions**. The Versions dialog box, which is shown containing several versions in Figure 10-10, opens.
2. Click **Save Now**. The Save Version dialog box opens. Enter any comment you wish, such as who worked on this version or what makes it unique, and click **OK**.

OPEN A DIFFERENT VERSION

1. With a multiple-version document open in Word, click the **File** menu, extend the menu if needed, and click **Versions**. The Versions dialog box opens.
2. Double-click the version you want to open. A second window will open and be tiled with the first version that was already opened, as shown in Figure 10-11. Here you can visually compare the two documents and copy, cut, and paste between them.

Figure 10-10: You can store several versions of a document in a single file.

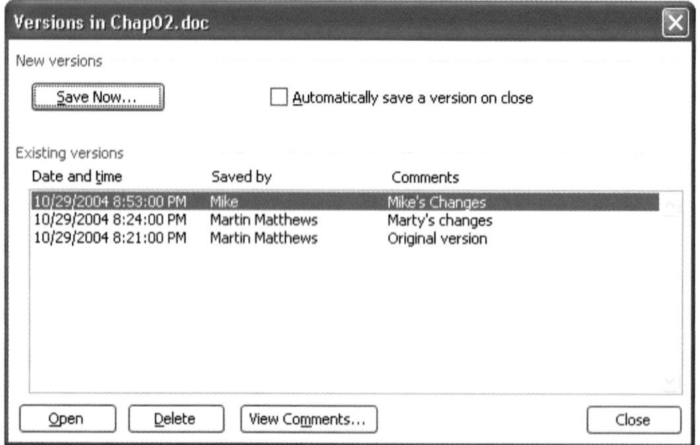

CAUTION

Word's Version feature does not save a separate file for each version of a document. Rather, Word saves a separate instance of the document within the original file. If the document is substantial, this will make for a very large file, and therefore Word requires that you use the Version feature to remove unwanted versions.

TIP

You can automatically create a new version every time you close a document by clicking **Automatically Save A Version On Close** in the Versions dialog box.

Compare Documents

If changes have been made to a version or copy of a document without using Track Changes, Word has the ability to compare the two and merge them into a single document with the differences shown as they would be with Track Changes.

1. In Word open the document into which you want the changes merged. In other words, the differences in the second document will show up as changes to the first document.
2. Click the **Tools** menu and click **Compare And Merge Documents**. The Compare And Merge Documents dialog box will open.
3. Select the document you want to compare and merge into the first document, and click **Merge**. The second document will open and display the changes it makes to the first document.
4. If you want to save the merged document under a new name, click the **Merge** button down arrow, and click **Merge Into New Document**.

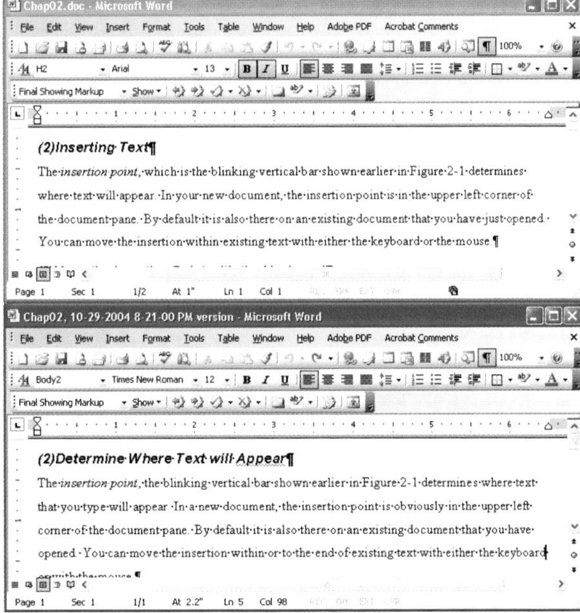

Figure 10-11: When you open a second version of a multiversion document, Word automatically tiles the two windows so you can see them both at the same time.

NOTE

To have the merged document look most like Track Changes, first open the original document that was sent out for review. Then use Compare and Merge Documents to load the copy returned by the reviewer.

NOTE

You can remove unwanted versions by opening the Versions dialog box, selecting the version you want to delete, clicking **Delete**, and then clicking **Yes** when asked if you are sure.

Compare Side by Side

You can also compare two documents side by side on the screen by opening both documents in two separate copies of Word (simply open a second document).

Click the **Window** menu, and click **Compare Side By Side**. The two Word windows will be tiled vertically, and a Compare Side By Side toolbar will open, as shown in Figure 10-12.

The Compare Side By Side toolbar provides three tools: Synchronous Scrolling, which turns on and off the simultaneous scrolling of the two windows; Reset Windows Position, which retiles the two windows vertically; and Close Side By Side, which returns the two windows to the position they were in before Compare Side By Side was clicked.

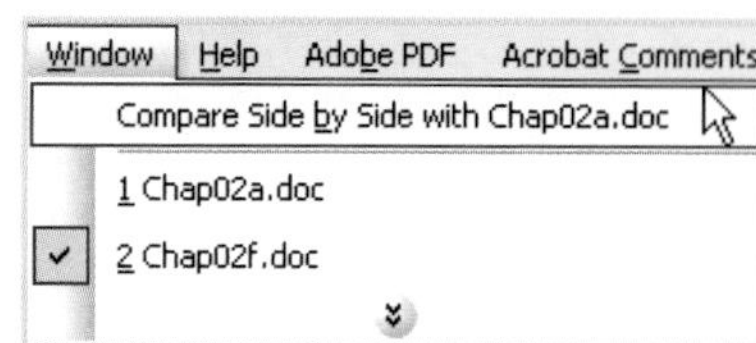

Figure 10-12: Compare Side By Side allows you to look at two documents and compare them visually while scrolling them simultaneously.

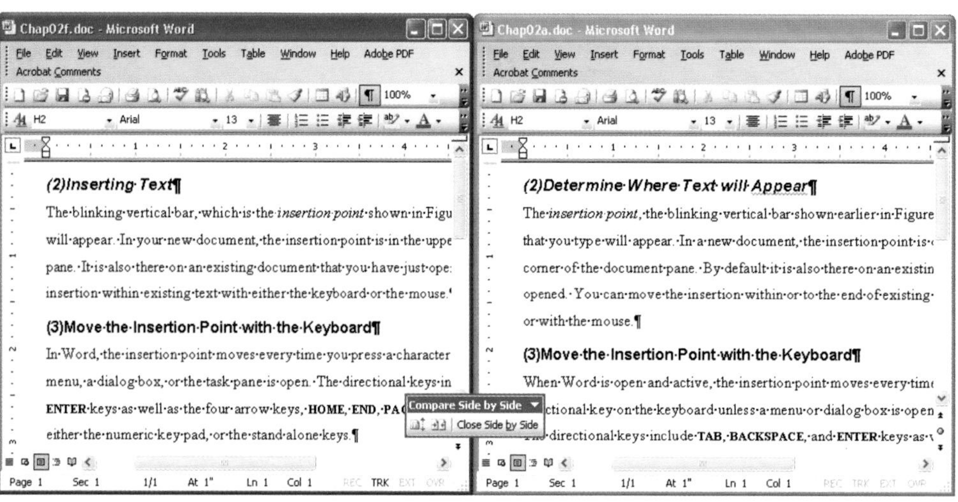

Index

Note: Italicized page numbers indicate definitions of terms.

U

V

W

X

Y

International Contact Information

AUSTRALIA
McGraw-Hill Book Company Australia Pty. Ltd.
TEL +61-2-9900-1800
FAX +61-2-9878-8881
http://www.mcgraw-hill.com.au
books-it_sydney@mcgraw-hill.com

CANADA
McGraw-Hill Ryerson Ltd.
TEL +905-430-5000
FAX +905-430-5020
http://www.mcgraw-hill.ca

GREECE, MIDDLE EAST, & AFRICA
(Excluding South Africa)
McGraw-Hill Hellas
TEL +30-210-6560-990
TEL +30-210-6560-993
TEL +30-210-6560-994
FAX +30-210-6545-525

MEXICO (Also serving Latin America)
McGraw-Hill Interamericana Editores S.A. de C.V.
TEL +525-1500-5108
FAX +525-117-1589
http://www.mcgraw-hill.com.mx
carlos_ruiz@mcgraw-hill.com

SINGAPORE (Serving Asia)
McGraw-Hill Book Company
TEL +65-6863-1580
FAX +65-6862-3354
http://www.mcgraw-hill.com.sg
mghasia@mcgraw-hill.com

SOUTH AFRICA
McGraw-Hill South Africa
TEL +27-11-622-7512
FAX +27-11-622-9045
robyn_swanepoel@mcgraw-hill.com

SPAIN
McGraw-Hill/Interamericana de España, S.A.U.
TEL +34-91-180-3000
FAX +34-91-372-8513
http://www.mcgraw-hill.es
professional@mcgraw-hill.es

UNITED KINGDOM, NORTHERN,
EASTERN, & CENTRAL EUROPE
McGraw-Hill Education Europe
TEL +44-1-628-502500
FAX +44-1-628-770224
http://www.mcgraw-hill.co.uk
emea_queries@mcgraw-hill.com

ALL OTHER INQUIRIES Contact:
McGraw-Hill/Osborne
TEL +1-510-420-7700
FAX +1-510-420-7703
http://www.osborne.com
omg_international@mcgraw-hill.com